# Gernika, 1937

THE BASQUE SERIES

# Gernika, 1937

## THE MARKET DAY MASSACRE

Xabier Irujo

UNIVERSITY OF NEVADA PRESS / *Reno & Las Vegas*

THE BASQUE SERIES

University of Nevada Press, Reno, Nevada 89557 USA

Manufactured in the United States of America

Library of Congress Cataloging-in-Publication Data
Irujo Ametzaga, Xabier.
Gernika, 1937 : the market day massacre / Xabier Irujo Ametzaga.
pages cm. — (The basque series)
Includes bibliographical references and index.
ISBN 978-0-87417-978-1 (cloth : alk. paper) — ISBN 978-0-87417-979-8 (e-book)
1. Guernica (Spain)—History—Bombardment, 1937. 2. Spain—History—Civil War, 1936–1939—Aerial operations, German. I. Title.
DP269.27.G8178 2015
946.081'48—dc23 2015002785

The paper used in this book meets the requirements of American National Standard for Information Sciences—Permanence of Paper for Printed Library Materials, ANSI/NISO Z39.48-1992 (R2002). Binding materials were selected for strength and durability.

FIRST PRINTING
23 22 21 20 19 18 17 16 15
5 4 3 2 1

# Contents



*Illustrations follow page 82.*

# Preface

This book is a description of the events that took place in Gernika, a small city in the Basque Country, on April 26, 1937, and their international diplomatic and political impact. For the first time in Europe, an entire city was reduced to rubble by an aerial attack. For the first time, an attack on an undefended civilian population was conceived as a war experiment intended to measure the impact of the raid on the morale of the enemy by inflicting the maximum number of casualties and the greatest material damage.

This book analyzes the bombardment strategy developed by the commanders of the Spanish, German, and Italian air forces during the course of the war in the Basque Country between March and June 1937. The bombing of Gernika was a turning point in the history of terror bombing and also a prologue to the saturation bombing that occurred during World War II. In Gernika the German air command tested what was later called "carpet bombing" and "shuttle bombing." Flying three abreast in close formation through an aerial corridor, successive waves of bombers dropped their cargoes over the urban area, using a carefully calculated mixture of incendiary and high-explosive shells, while fighter planes kept the surviving civilians on the ground under constant machine-gun fire.

In this sense, it is revealing to study the bombardment techniques developed by the German and Italian air commands during these crucial months of the war. Overall, both German colonel Wolfram von Richthofen and leading Italian commanders such as General Vincenzo Velardi and Captain Stefano Castellani emphasized the value of airpower as a psychological weapon, while acknowledging the limited effect of an air force as tactical support for infantry units at the front. The logical conclusion of this analysis was a preference for terror-bombing attacks rather than tactical or strategic bombing. The bombing of Gernika was from this perspective a practical experiment and, according to Richthofen, the factotum of the attack, a complete technical success.

But the bombing of Gernika was not only the product of tactical or strategic planning but also a consequence of the personal aspirations of Hermann Göring, the commander in chief of the German Luftwaffe, in the power struggles within the Nazi government. In this sense, I have analyzed the bombing in the context of the differences and hostilities between Göring and Werner F. von Blomberg, minister of war and commander in chief of the German armed forces. The attack helped Göring to convince Hitler that terror bombing was the most perfect National Socialist way to engage in a war and that the air force would be decisive in achieving a German victory in "the next war." The bombing of Gernika therefore constituted, from this perspective, one of the steps that Göring took between 1936 and the end of the war in Spain in April 1939 to win the coveted second place in the German Reich by forcing the resignation of the ministers of war, economy, and foreign relations.

This first massive destruction of an open city during an aerial attack had a significant international effect. This book also traces the roots of international diplomacy regarding the Gernika attack in Europe as well as in the United States. It offers some fresh perspectives on the bombing of Gernika through the use of new documents and considers, for first time, the role played by the Roosevelt administration at the diplomatic level and the debate in the US Congress about the bombing of Gernika in the context of current policies of noninterventionism and isolationism.

As the documents reveal, the US government showed a strong interest in the war at the Basque front, and the Roosevelt administration was in contact with the British Foreign Office regarding the specific case of the bombing of Gernika. US ambassador to the Spanish Republic Claude G. Bowers and US consul William E. Chapman had no doubt about the nature of the bombing of Gernika, and they informed the State Department in unambiguous terms that the Luftwaffe was responsible for it. In light of documents found in the Bowers files at the National Archives, we know that the US Embassy and consequently the US State Department knew in full detail the nature and scope of German and Italian involvement at the Basque front.

Moreover, the reports and correspondence that I have found indicate that President Roosevelt and his wife, Eleanor, were personally involved and wanted to take diplomatic action regarding the bombardment of open cities after the bombing of Gernika. An important point that the documents reveal is Roosevelt's intention to make an international appeal on the bombing of open cities only five days after the *Appeal to the Conscience of the World* was made public on May 15. However, the British Embassy in Washington asked the US government to avoid any public statement on the bombing of open cities that was not in line with the British proposal to the Non-Intervention

Committee. The United States acted accordingly, but a year later the White House did not remain silent, and two years later President Roosevelt issued the *Appeal on Aerial Bombardment of Civilian Populations*.

The circumstances leading up to the bombardment of Gernika refer to international adherence to the principle of nonintervention. As stated by Ambassador Bowers in his memoirs, the Non-Intervention Agreement proved to be a dishonest farce.[1] While the Germans, Italians, and Portuguese openly participated in the Spanish war in support of the rebel leader, Generalissimo Francisco Franco, most of the democratic governments fought just as effectively—if unconsciously—as collaborationists of the totalitarian regimes under the pretense of honoring the principle of nonintervention. This book examines previously unstudied reports and debates in the US Congress about the bombing. New documentation provided by this book helps to elucidate certain controversial topics about the undeclared war in the Basque Country and the people involved in it and makes a significant contribution to the study of twentieth-century warfare in Western Europe.

Rather than looking at the bombing of Gernika as a local and isolated war incident, approaching it from the international perspective helps us recognize the events that led to World War II. Although members of the democratic parliaments assumed that Italy, Germany, and even Portugal were observing the Non-Intervention Agreement, tons of war matériel consigned to Generalissimo Franco poured into Portuguese ports from Italy and Germany. Although it was still officially a secret, by September 1936 the active intervention of Germany and Italy in the Spanish war was common knowledge to most European administrations and also to the US government, and it led finally to open international conflict.

The story of the bombing of Gernika did not end in April 1937. This book deals with the philosophy behind the attack and the conception of war developed by the German air command, and it documents the extent to which the planning of the Spanish Nationalists contributed to the terror-bombing campaign conceived by German colonel Wolfram von Richthofen.

The destruction of Gernika has been considered an atrocity of enduring universal significance, so Gernika is also a symbol of the defiance of international covenants, such as the Charter of the League of Nations and the Non-Intervention Agreement, which was drawn up by twenty-seven countries, including the principal transgressors, Germany and Italy. However, despite overwhelming evidence against them, none of the main perpetrators were ever taken to court, convicted, or sentenced for their role in the massacre or, in general, for provoking a war. Gernika in 1937 remains an open case, and the Basque town has become today the World Capital for Peace and a symbol of redemption and human understanding. And this is the enduring legacy of the bombing. Also, the discussion of attempts made by the Basque government in exile during the Nuremberg trials to link the bombing of Gernika to other atrocities committed by the Axis powers during World War II is particularly illuminating in revealing how the Basques viewed the role played by Germans and Italians in the war in the Basque Country.

Three key books in English describe the event from different perspectives: George L. Steer's *The Tree of Gernika: A Field Study of Modern War*, Gordon Thomas and Max Morgan-Witts's *Guernica: The Crucible of World War II*, and Herbert R. Southworth's *Guernica, Guernica: A Study of Journalism, Diplomacy, Propaganda and History*. There is also Ian Patterson's skillful book about the symbolic use of the massacre in twentieth-century fiction. Steer focuses on the central role that the bombing of Gernika had in the context of the war in the Basque Country and gives a firsthand description of the attack as an example of terror bombing. Southworth focuses his remarkable work on the impact of the bombing on the international press. My book provides a revisionist description of the bombing based on new documents found in the National Archives and various European archives and offers the reader a new dimension of the international diplomatic impact of the bombing while filling a major gap in the existing literature about the politics and diplomacy surrounding the bombing of Gernika.

The present book is based primarily upon printed collections of documents, unpublished archival documentation, and interviews, including information about US involvement and eyewitnesses' descriptions of the attack. I have compiled and cataloged more than twelve thousand documents from the archives mentioned in the "Notes on Sources." Readers should understand that if a cited document is available in printed form, I have used the edited version from the US Government Printing Office to allow future researchers easier access to the source.

This book is the result of a long process. The number of people to thank is exhaustive, and any list may exclude someone, so my apologies in advance. First, I wish to thank the eyewitnesses whose testimonies provided a great deal of the primary research for this book, among them Mari Carmen Egurrola, Joxe Iturria, Kontxi Martija, Iñaki Murua, Miren Begoña Urrutikoetxea, Kontxi Zorrozua, and Luis Iriondo. In addition, I wish to thank Ana Teresa Núñez, Iñaki Goiogana, Mark Lucas, and the personnel of the National Archives at College Park, Maryland, for providing me thousands of documents relevant to the study of the bombing. I would also like to express my debt to Pello Irujo and Arantzazu Ametzaga, who gave me the first insights into this story and brought Joseba Elosegi to me. I owe a debt of gratitude to the people who have helped me in the preparation and critical examination of the present book—Pete Cenarrusa, Hilari Raguer, and Ángel Viñas, among many others.

My thanks also to my editors, Margaret Dalrymple and Annette Wenda; their excellent work has made this book possible. Thanks to the Editorial Board of the Center for Basque Studies, which supported my research from the outset. Finally, to my wife and five children, *anitz esker.*

# Gernika, 1937

# Introduction

## Gernika, the Holy City of the Basques

Gernika lies in the Oka River valley, surrounded by the gentle hills of Goikoburu, Urkonaga, Nabarniz, and Artibiri, none of them higher than 1,500 feet. The town is also encircled by several small villages: Forua and Kortezubi to the north, Axangiz to the east, Muxika to the south, and Errigoiti to the west. Gernika's highest point is 472 feet, where the San Pedro Chapel stands. From there, the land slopes down a mile to the city center, which is no more than 33 feet above sea level. Bilbao is only 19 miles away; Bermeo, on the coast, 8.5 miles; Lekeitio, 14 miles; and Ondarroa, 22 miles.

The site of the town has been inhabited for at least twenty thousand years. The first inhabitants survived the long glacial winters and protected their families in caverns. The Cave of Santimamiñe in Kortezubi shelters some of their paintings of horses, bison, boars, and other animals. Millennia later, the Romans occupied the town and nearby areas, looking for a fluvial port to the northern sea.

The inhabitants of Gernika received their first engraved legal code on April 28, 1366. The town adopted a plan with four parallel streets—Goienkale (High Street), Azokekale (Market Street), Artekale (Middle Street), and Barrenkale (Inner Street)—crossed by a single thoroughfare, Andra Mari. The latter takes its name from the Roman church erected sometime before the eleventh century, later rebuilt in the Gothic style between the fifteenth and seventeenth centuries and dedicated to the Virgin Mary.

From the fourteenth century on, Gernika was one of the compulsory stops for every king who wanted to be recognized lord of Bizkaia through his affirmation of the *foruak,* or ancient laws of Bizkaia. But Gernika was not considered the capital of the Basques, since the ancient laws, strongly confederationist, denied the title of capital to any town within the old Basque republics. However, the Oak of Gernika sheltered open assemblies of the people, which by tradition were announced by the blowing of five horns. There, for at least six hundred years, the lord had to kneel before the assembly and recognize the ancient laws, which preceded and prevailed over his rule. During the ceremony, the king had to take an oath to recognize and validate the Bizkaians' privileges, customs, exemptions, freedoms, and laws.[1]

Gernika became a battlefield in a succession of nineteenth-century wars meant to end the secular independence of the Basque republics.[2] One after the other, the French Revolution (1789–99), the Convention War (1793–95), the Napoleonic Wars (1808–15), the First Carlist War (1833–39), and the Second Carlist War (1872–76) were fought in the Basque Country. The Napoleonic invasion of the Iberian Peninsula brought with it the idea of a centralized unitary state. The French (in 1789) and the Spanish (in 1876) established central governments, and Gernika, with its hundreds of trees that had sheltered open assemblies from the seven Basque states (Araba, Bizkaia, Gipuzkoa, Lapurdi, the two Navarres, and Zuberoa), would remain only a symbol of unfulfilled Basque democracy.

The termination of the Basque states' political independence ultimately ignited the nationalism that brought forth the first Statute of Autonomy within the Spanish state on October 1, 1936—only seven months before the bombing of Gernika. The world today mainly knows Gernika for the events that took place there during that Market Day Massacre. That may be because the events of that day represent not just a brief episode in the life of the town, or even of the Basque countries, but a paradigmatic experience in the history of terror bombing.

# 1

## The Coup d'État of July 18, 1936

On July 17, 1936, a group of Spanish army officers launched a revolt in Spanish Morocco against the government of the Republic. Thus began the international "civil" war.[1] The coup was devised and initially directed by Generals Emilio Mola, José Sanjurjo, and Francisco Franco, but the latter soon became the sole leader of the so-called National Movement. On September 29, General Miguel Cabanellas, president of the Consejo Nacional de Defensa (Board of National Defense), the chief branch of the Spanish military government, approved Decree 138, which appointed Franco "head of the government," giving him unchecked powers over the new state.[2] Franco, acting as head of state, established the Technical Board (military government) in Burgos on October 3, 1936, to replace the previous National Defense Council. General Fidel Dávila presided over the new board under the direct and sole command of Generalissimo Franco.

The National Movement was a complex political coalition that incorporated a number of ultraconservative totalitarian doctrines, among them Fascism, Nazism, Carlism,[3] monarchism, and National Catholicism. Under the motto "For the Empire Toward God," National Catholicism was the dominant and unifying ideology of the National Movement. The foundation of the National Movement was the conviction that the military uprising was a crusade against separatism (including Basque and Catalan nationalism), Communism, and atheism. The political unity of the Spanish state was a central tenet and founding principle of National Catholicism. Indeed, along with the army, the Spanish Catholic Church would become the main champion of the coup. The cardinal and prime archbishop of Toledo, Isidro

Gomá, a major ecclesiastical authority in Spain, considered General Franco the "instrument of the plans of God on Earth."[4]

According to the cardinal, there were two main reasons to support the National Movement: to safeguard the unity of the Spanish state in the face of Galician, Catalan, and Basque nationalism and to organize an autocratic Catholic state. Gomá believed that democracy, parliamentarianism, universal suffrage, and freedom of thought and creed were some of the greatest absurdities of the Republican government and among the greatest threats to Western civilization.[5] He justified the war as necessary to restore a hierarchic, strongly centralized, and Catholic Spanish state. In the words of Miguel de los Santos Díaz Gómara, bishop of Cartagena, "Blessed are the cannons if in the breaches they open the Gospel blooms."[6]

The bishop of Salamanca, Enrique Pla y Deniel, also openly declared his support for the military uprising. In a pastoral letter entitled "The Two Cities," signed on September 30, 1936, Pla y Deniel defended the military coup d'état as a necessary uprising against the tyranny of the Republican order.[7] The archbishop of Santiago de Compostela, Tomás Muniz de Pablos, and Eustaquio Cardinal Ilundain, archbishop of Seville, also demonstrated support for the ideas of the military regime.[8]

Cardinal Gomá was the author, along with Monsignor Leopoldo Eijo Garay, the bishop of Madrid-Alcala (who was in 1946 named patriarch of the West Indies), of a joint message to the Pope entitled *Collective Letter of the Spanish Episcopacy on the Civil War,* which called for the Vatican to publicly support the military regime.[9] Nearly 90 percent of the Spanish episcopacy endorsed the letter, dated July 1, 1937, including forty-eight prelates—eight archbishops, thirty-five bishops, and five vicars. The letter denounced the Spanish Republican government as anti-Christian and anti-Spanish and held it responsible for the death of innocent members of the clergy.

Only two prelates refused to sign the document—the Catalan cardinal of Tarragona, Francesc Vidal i Barraquer, who was exiled to Rome, and the Basque bishop of Gasteiz, Monsignor Mateo Mugica. Their objections were based on moral grounds. Mugica later declared that he believed the Catholic Church could not share the doctrines or strategies of any Fascist, Nazi, or totalitarian movement.[10]

At the international level, the apostolic nuncio Ildebrando Antoniutti and the German cardinal Michael von Faulhaber openly supported the coup d'état. Faulhaber exhorted his parishioners to pray for those who "defend the sacrosanct rights of God, so that He grants the victory of those who are fighting a sacred war."[11] Even Pope Pius XI provided assistance to the rebels, and on September 14, 1936, he received an audience of five hundred Spanish citizens who had fled the Republican zone. He named them the "first martyrs." Over all worldly and political consideration, declared Pius XI, "our blessing goes in a special way to those who have assumed the difficult and dangerous task of defending the rights and the honor of God and Religion."[12]

In 1937 William F. Montavon, director of the legal department at the National Catholic Welfare Conference in Washington, DC, published a pamphlet entitled *Insurrection in Spain,* in which he referred to Pius's encyclical and called for collaboration with the rebel government against the Republic.[13] Eugenio Cardinal Pacelli, too, did not hide his affection for the new authoritarian regime. Pacelli, who became Pope Pius XII in March 1939 after Pius XI died, sent a telegram to Franco in April 1939 congratulating him on his victorious conclusion to the civil war.[14]

Despite the intervention of the Catholic Church, a policy of exterminating political opponents, civilians or not, inexorably followed the advance of the rebel troops. On August 11, 1936, Colonel Juan Yagüe initiated an offensive in Badajoz that ended on August 14. Two days later about four thousand people, both civilians and soldiers, were machine-gunned inside the bullring of the city. When American journalist John T. Whitaker of the *New York Herald Tribune* interviewed Yagüe about the incident, the colonel declared, "Of course we shot them. What do you want? Do you suppose that I was going to take 4,000 Reds with me while my column advanced against the clock? Do you suppose that I was going to leave them free at my back so they could build a new Red Badajoz?"[15] Along the same lines, during his first interview with the international press on July 29, 1936, Generalissimo Franco told journalist Jay Allen of the *Chicago Tribune* that he would continue the war, even if he had to kill 50 percent of the Spanish people.[16]

## The Bombing of Otxandio and the Construction of Antiaircraft Shelters

The first terror bombings in the Basque Country took place only four days after the coup, even before the first German or Italian planes arrived in the Basque Country to support the rebel troops. On July 22, 1936, Otxandio was bombed for the first time on orders from General Emilio Mola. Three days earlier he had stated that "we must spread terror. . . . It is imperative to show that we are the ones in control by eliminating unscrupulously and without hesitation all those who do not think like us."[17] Mola later added that if he saw his father fighting with the enemy, he would shoot him.[18]

One of the pilots who took part in the bombing of Otxandio was Ángel Salas Larrazabal. As his brother, Jesús Salas Larrazabal, later wrote,[19] Ángel took off from Logroño on July 22 and, with two other aircraft, bombed Otxandio. Salas mentioned only seven people killed: a woman, two girls, and four soldiers. Actually, the three aircraft caused more than sixty-one casualties, mostly civilians gathering at Andikona Square to celebrate a town festival.[20] This was the first aerial bombing of a Basque town, the first mass bombing of the war, and one of the first aerial assaults of the whole conflict. Ángel's Breguet 19 had an open cockpit, and the pilots were flying low enough to see where they were dropping their grenades. Moreover, as several witnesses noted, the pilots passed over the town several times before dropping their cargoes while children in the square waved to them.[21]

People in Otxandio knew nothing about war, and some probably did not even know the country was at war. As Carmelo Bernaola, one of the witnesses to the attack, reported later, the town's main square was filled with children who had watched a plane drop leaflets only two days earlier; when they saw the same plane again, they started shouting "Leaflets, leaflets!" and instead of running for shelter, they ran to catch the falling papers. They died greeting the aircraft that came to kill them.[22]

Jose Antonio Marulagoitia, a doctor in Otxandio, recounted the massacre to a reporter for the Basque nationalist newspaper *Euzkadi:*

> It was about nine o'clock in the morning. . . . I saw two aircraft flying rather low. Their approach aroused curiosity but no fear. Nobody expected an attack, especially when in Otxandio there were only about two hundred armed men, soldiers and civilians, who in no way could think of attacking Gasteiz. I noticed that one of the planes threw out something. I thought that there would be leaflets, since the truth is that I could not think otherwise. However, I was pulled from my belief by the horrendous noise of several explosions, truly barbaric. . . . Then I came into the street and went toward Andikona Square. Despite having attended, due to my profession, very harmful episodes, none was as terrible as the sight of Andikona Square. . . . People shattered, children mutilated, decapitated women. It was the cries of the villagers, in Basque, imploring for help; it was the torrent of blood that ran into the water from the little fountain that stands in the middle of the square.

> I required help, and I was promptly and diligently helped. . . . I proceeded to attend the most urgent cases. There were some, many, who unfortunately did not need anything. They had perished, killed by the barbaric shrapnel from the many bombs that had been dropped. . . . Others, boys and girls, with hanging limbs, turned to me with phrases in Basque that I still have riveted in my heart.[23]

One of the main effects of the attacks against Otxandio and Bilbao—which was bombed by German planes two months later, on September 25 and 26—was the construction of antiaircraft shelters in every town and city within the region controlled by the Basque government. Before the attack against Otxandio and the first raids on Bilbao, people had no idea what to do during an air attack. On August 16, 1936, two weeks after the first air strike, the Basque authorities distributed leaflets with instructions on what to do in the event of a raid—basically, as soon as planes were observed flying over a town, all citizens had to take refuge in the basement or lowest floor of the buildings, not forming crowds in the streets. Automobiles were to be parked far from the center of town.[24]

The construction of shelters began in the fall of 1936, and the Commission of Defense Works of the Basque government recruited workers to build shelters all over Bizkaia.[25] Jose Labauria, mayor of Gernika, commissioned Castor Uriarte, the municipal architect, to build antiaircraft shelters according to provisions set forth by the Basque government. Uriarte wrote that the shelters in Gernika were built with pillars made from pine logs that measured 8 feet long and 14 inches in diameter.[26] Similar logs were used as ceiling beams, and the roofs were assembled from 1.4-inch-wide steel sheets with two layers of sandbags on top.[27] The walls consisted of reinforced concrete. Naturally, smoking was prohibited in the shelters in order to preserve the purity of the air, and occupants were advised to sit or lie on the floor. However, the shelters were generally too crowded to allow everyone to sit, so it was common for adults to stand and have children sit quietly on their shoulders, since during the bombings smoke and dust filtered into the shelters and the air was purer close to the roof than down on the floor.

In some cases—for example, the shelters at the city hall and in the villa of Count Arana, which were solidly built of stone—this construction was done on the first floor or in the basement. Shelters were also built elsewhere. The narrow street of Santa Maria (Andra Mari) in the center of the town, between Barrenkale and Artekale Streets, was completely covered, and this space was used as a shelter. This refuge was 40 meters long and 3.5 meters wide and had two entrances. According to Uriarte, this was the only shelter still uncompleted on April 26: "That morning I informed the managers of the factory near Bilbao that the steel plates had not yet arrived, although we had placed sandbags over the beams."[28] That shelter collapsed during the bombing, killing most of the people inside, about 450, according to Labauria.[29] Uriarte stated that "the safest shelters were the ones located on the west side of Plaza de la Unión. The wall on this side of the square rested against a hillside. We simply excavated four caves that served as shelters at the base of the hill. They were about 10 meters deep."[30] These shelters were designed for people who would be in the area of the market and fair.

According to Uriarte, there were five municipal shelters in Gernika by April 1937: the basement of the city hall building; the basement of the Loizaga house on San Juan Street, on the opposite end of the town hall; an underground shelter in the yard between the provincial headquarters and the Uribe family home in Asilo Calzada Street (today Juan Calzada Street); four shelters at the Plaza de la Unión, which consisted of four barrel-vaulted chambers excavated underground, with the entrance covered by the arcades of the square (these four shelters were built by Gamboa & Domingo, a company that specialized in reinforced concrete construction); and a covered stretch of Andra Mari Street, which was not finished.[31]

However, Labauria reported that six municipal shelters were completed in Gernika by April 1937 and that another six were under construction when the bombing occurred, not only one, as Uriarte claimed. The completed shelters were the two on Asilo Calzada Street, two at the Talleres de Guernica factory, one at the city hall, and one in the Loizaga house on San Juan Street. If we add to these the four shelters in the Plaza de la Unión, there was a total of nine or ten shelters, depending on whether we consider the two shelters on Asilo Calzada Street as one or two. According to Labauria, the shelters still unfinished on April 26, 1937, were the one on Andra Mari Street, one in the Plaza de la República (at the old pelota court), one in the sacristy of the San Juan Church, and one at the railroad station. There were also some smaller shelters, such as the one in the basement of Count Arana's villa on old Puerto Street near San Juan Square and one in the house of the widow Ezenarro.[32]

As confirmed by Labauria, two large shelters were also built in the backyards of the weapons factories for their staff and, in general, for all the workers in the industrial area who were considered to be at risk. One of these shelters is today part of the Astra culture house and may be visited. The back of the choir in Andra Mari Church served as a shelter for many people. Also, another small shelter was built in the garden of a villa owned by Castor Uriarte and his in-laws on Iparragirre Street.[33] This makes a total of between ten and sixteen antiaircraft shelters of various sizes, both municipal and private, with capacity for three thousand to thirty-five hundred people. All of them were located in strategic areas of town, so that anyone who was in Gernika during an air raid would have access to one of them. All this should have been more than adequate for a town such as Gernika, where no bombing was expected.

Church bells were generally used as an alarm. After the first aerial attacks, some people decided to keep their children far outside the towns and cities during the day, since the Germans and Italians did not fly at night. For the same reason, people soon learned that when the weather was rainy, windy, or cloudy, they were safe. With no antiaircraft batteries to protect small towns, bad weather was about all they could hope for.

## Italian Intervention

After the proclamation of the Second Spanish Republic on April 12–14, 1931, Benito Mussolini, the Fascist prime minister of Italy, openly opposed what he considered a revolutionary government in Spain. Il Duce condemned all political parties and governments that he viewed as leftist, whether Social Democrat, Socialist, Marxist, or anarchist, under the catchall term *communism*. Most of the democratic forces that supported the new Spanish Republic were strongly antifascist after having endured seven long years (1923–31) of the monarchist military dictatorship headed by King Alfonso XIII. Mussolini, fearing that a weak liberal democracy could easily open the gates to "communism," opposed all democratic forces in the Spanish state, even conservatives such as the moderate Republicans and Christian Democrats.

Documents recently brought to light by Professor Angel Viñas indicate that negotiations between the rebels and the Italian government concerning the shipment of Italian war matériel to Spain actually began many months before the coup. In March 1934 Pedro Sainz Rodríguez, Luis María

Zunzunegui, and Antonio Goicoechea traveled to Rome to seek aid for a military uprising against Spain's civilian government.[34] The nature and price of the requested Italian war matériel were established just after the Popular Front won elections in February 1936.[35] Talks took place in Rome, and on July 1, 1936, sixteen days before the uprising in the Spanish colonies of Morocco, the first four contracts for the shipment of military equipment were signed in Rome by Pedro Sainz Rodríguez.[36] Under the first contract, the Italian regime arranged to send twelve Savoia-Marchetti SM.81 aircraft (worth 14.4 million lire), pumps, aircraft fuel, and other war matériel. The total price of the shipment amounted to 16,246,750.55 lire.[37] The delivery was to be made before the end of the month. The other three contracts included airplanes (twenty-four Fiat CR.32s, three Macchi M.41 seaplanes, and three Savoia-Marchetti SM.81s), explosives, ammunition, and military equipment, all of which were to be delivered before the end of August. The amount of the four contracts (which specified the shipment of a total of forty-two airplanes) amounted to 39.3 million lire.[38] It happened, however, that nobody had advised Rome of the exact date of the uprising, so when the rebel envoys went to Rome to request military assistance, via the military intelligence service of Tangier, Mussolini was greatly surprised, because the earlier negotiations were with other individuals. His intelligence services had informed him that the initial rebel blow from Tangier was done under the direction of an unknown general named Francisco Franco, but no one in Rome had negotiated with or even heard of Franco before.

On July 20, 1936, General Franco personally met with Major Giuseppe Luccardi, military attaché at the Italian Consulate in Tangier, to discuss the shipment of Italian planes to transport at least twenty thousand of the nearly forty-seven thousand rebel troops under General Franco's command from Spanish Morocco to the Iberian Peninsula. Because of the Republican government's naval superiority during those first days after the uprising, the rebels were unable to transport enough troops by sea from Africa to attempt a quick strike against Madrid.

On July 22 Franco met with Italian consul Pier Filippo De Rossi del Lion Nero. Both Luccardi and De Rossi strongly supported the idea of assisting General Franco and communicated that sentiment to Italian foreign minister Galeazzo Ciano, who also seemed to favor recognizing Franco as the leader of the Spanish military uprising.[39] Unlike the Spanish delegations sent to Rome in 1932, 1933, and 1934 to negotiate with Mussolini, Franco now commanded a national uprising supported by the Spanish Catholic Church, most of the military, about half of the Guardia Civil, and the Fascist political force Falange Española. However, Mussolini still rejected the proposed sale of aircraft to the Spanish rebels.

The same day Franco ordered Juan Ignacio Luca de Tena, director of the rightist newspaper ABC, and Luis Bolín, the rebel military government's press director, to meet with Count Ciano in Rome to negotiate the shipment of war matériel and troops.[40] Ciano expressed his support for sending planes to the rebels, but he apparently realized the challenge of convincing Mussolini to agree and did not attend a meeting scheduled for the following day. Instead, Ciano sent his secretary Filippo Anfuso, who informed the rebel delegation that the promised assistance could not be ensured. In fact, Mussolini again refused to provide any support. However, he agreed to meet with former Spanish king Alfonso XIII,[41] a devoted Fascist who was trying to solicit military aid for the rebels to prevent the establishment of a Communist regime in the western Mediterranean.

On July 24 Pedro Sainz Rodríguez, Luis María Zunzunegui, and Antonio Goicoechea traveled to Rome to clarify the situation.[42] Ciano met with them and promised to send twelve airplanes if they would pay cash before delivery. Following their positive response, Mussolini ordered that the first of the four contracts, which was the most urgent, be executed. On July 27 Ciano told De Rossi that the planes were in Sardinia, ready to fly to Spanish Morocco. Spanish financier Juan March provided the funds, and Goicoechea deposited one million lire on July 28.

Mussolini had three sound reasons to back the insurrection. First, there was ideological compatibility. Both the Italian regime and the Spanish rebel movement were totalitarian in nature, although the Spanish regime was not purely Fascist or Nazi. However, there were doubts in Italy about the sincerity of the Spanish rebels' ideology. As noted by Roberto Cantalupo, the first Italian ambassador to the Spanish Nationalist government, helping to form a conservative, reactionary, clerical, and military regime in Spain was not the responsibility of Fascist Italy.[43]

There were also geopolitical factors. Ending British naval hegemony in the Mediterranean was one of the main geopolitical aims of the Italian regime. By collaborating with Franco, Italy could secure military bases in the Balearic and the Canary Islands (a natural gate to the Atlantic), and in the event of hostilities between Great Britain and Italy, Italian forces could carry out a combined sea and land attack on Gibraltar, depriving the British Empire of one of its most vital naval bases in the western Mediterranean.

Economic incentives also played a part. From 1931 on, the Italian government's spending significantly outpaced its income, particularly after the 1935 Abyssinian campaign left a deficit of more than forty billion lire. To diminish the deficit, the government needed to export large quantities of war matériel and to import raw materials at bargain prices. This was another reason to sell planes to the rebels.[44]

However, beyond the geopolitical or economic motivations, two factors finally convinced Mussolini to adopt a firm resolution on the Spanish issue. A report by the Servizio di Informazione Militare (the Italian military intelligence agency from 1925 to 1945) on July 27, 1936, informed the Ministero degli Esteri (Foreign Office) that the French government had decided to adopt an attitude of strict neutrality toward the Spanish insurrection, similar to the policy embraced by the British. The same day Il Duce received the Berardi report, which said that the Soviet government would also adopt a position of nonintervention with regard to the war.[45] Mussolini rightly expected from both the British and the French governments the same passivity they had shown after the Italian invasion of Abyssinia in 1935. Indeed, the assistance that the Portuguese regime was already providing to the rebels could be explained only by assuming the tacit acquiescence of the British.[46]

If De Rossi, Luccardi, and Ciano had tried to convince Il Duce that Franco's victory was guaranteed, international negotiations leading to the Non-Intervention Agreement of August 1936 solidified that presumption. The rebels could reasonably assume that they were going to receive strong military and political support from abroad, while the Spanish Republican government could expect only a weak political response from the League of Nations. Five days after Goicoechea's delegation visited Rome, on July 30, 1936, the Italian regime sent the first shipment of airplanes, including twelve Savoia-Marchetti SM.81 bombers drawn from the 55, 57, and 58 Squadriglie under General Giuseppe Valle, chief of staff of the Regia Aeronautica (Italian air force) since 1929 and undersecretary of the Ministry of Aviation.[47]

On October 24 Ciano met with Hitler at Berchtesgaden, his mountain retreat in the Bavarian Alps. They discussed the British rearmament policy as well as the foundation of a German-Italian alliance to confront the

Western European democracies. The countries of concern included Great Britain and France, Europe's two main political and economic powers, and what they called the "small democracies," namely, the Spanish Republic, Holland, Belgium, Denmark, and the Baltic states. Hitler and Ciano agreed that anti-Communism should be used as a diplomatic justification but also as a political masquerade to hide the true aims of their coalition.[48] The meeting ended the following day with a friendship accord based on four conclusions: Italy would recognize Germany's claims over Austria, Germany would recognize Italy's authority in Abyssinia, both governments would work toward a broader and more comprehensive agreement, and both governments would reinforce their military and political presence in Spain and officially recognize the new Spanish regime once the rebels took over Madrid.[49] Indeed, in a meeting with the German ambassador to Italy, Ulrich von Hassell, early in October, Mussolini had already decided not to recognize the Francoist regime until Madrid was captured by the rebels.[50]

In a brief communiqué from Berlin following the meeting, German officials expressed their optimism over the possibility of peace in Europe and, to the satisfaction of both parties, what they called "a concurrence of views and the intention of the two Governments to devote their joint activities to the promotion of general peace and reconstruction."[51] Count Ciano stated that both governments recognized that the government of General Franco had succeeded in establishing order and civil discipline in Spain, "in contrast to the anarchy existing previously," and they proclaimed—with utter insincerity—their adherence to the principle of nonintervention. Germany and Italy also agreed not to recognize an independent Catalan state.[52]

Mussolini named the October agreement that outlined the two countries' "parallel interests" the Rome-Berlin Axis. In less than a month, the agreement led to three more resolutions: official recognition of Franco's regime on November 18 (even if the Francoist forces had failed to capture Madrid), the Anti-Comintern Pact between the Japanese Empire and the German Reich on November 25, and a protocol of mutual assistance between the Spanish and Italian regimes on November 28.

The meeting at Obersalzberg was important because the Italian regime had not yet engaged with Nazi Germany and was still seeking agreements with Great Britain to maintain the status quo in Western Europe. The ensuing diplomatic agreements between Germany, Italy, Spain, and Japan changed the system of alliances between the European powers and ultimately set the stage for World War II. The October agreement between Italy and Germany also hastened official recognition of the Franco regime and allowed the shipment of additional troops and war matériel.

Approval of the mutual assistance protocol between Italy and Franco's rebel regime in November prompted a sharp increase in the shipment of war matériel and troops between December 15, 1936, and February 1, 1937. According to data provided by the British Foreign Office,[53] between December 20 and January 11, 1937, fourteen deliveries under escort of Italian warships were recorded, including the ports and dates of departure and arrival and the quantity and nature of the cargoes. In addition, at least four hundred motor vehicles and planes were sent to Spain. Many of the soldiers were armed only with carbines, which confirmed the fact that most of them were troops in tank or artillery units.

As the Fisher Memorandum delivered to Secretary of State for Foreign Affairs Anthony Eden outlined, during the first three weeks of January 1937, 15,000 Italian troops arrived in areas controlled by the rebels, which brought the total to approximately 51,000 Italian troops in Spain at the beginning of February 1937.[54] According to Foreign Minister Yvon Delbos of France, on February 20, 1937, six ships left Naples and Gaeta carrying more troops and munitions, and by the last week of February there would be more than 60,000 Italian troops engaged in the Spanish war.[55]

On February 23, 1937, Horace H. Fuller, military attaché at the US Embassy in Paris, reported that the military attaché at the German Embassy had told him that there were between 40,000 and 50,000 Italian troops and about 30,000 German troops fighting beside Franco's armies at that time.[56] US ambassador Claude G. Bowers recorded the arrival of about 31,000 Italian troops through January 1937.[57] Bowers's number is perhaps the most accurate, since, according to the final report prepared by the Ufficio Spagna on troop shipments to the war, 3,692 troops had been transported in November, 4,711 in December, 31,926 in January, and 6,847 in February. As Bowers stated repeatedly, the presence and numbers of Italian troops in Spain were common knowledge.[58]

It is important to note that the British, French, and US governments all had access to these data, despite the fact that Eden, Delbos, and US secretary of state Cordell Hull all repeatedly asserted before their respective legislative bodies that there was as yet no evidence of German or Italian participation in the war.[59] This explains why the Spanish Republic's foreign minister, Julio Álvarez del Vayo, was forced to go before the League of

Nations on September 27 and November 27, 1936, and again on March 13, 1937, to prove and condemn Italy's involvement in the war.

At the beginning of March 1937, the Italian Corpo di Truppe Volontarie consisted of a complete regular army on foreign soil under the command of General Mario Roatta, who was using the pseudonym "General Mancini."[60] The CTV was organized into four main divisions plus an autonomous branch, the Littorio Division (a regular Italian army division consisting of two regular infantry regiments and an artillery regiment).[61] The CTV regiments were equipped with tanks and armored cars under Colonel Carlo Rivolta and antitank and antiaircraft artillery under General Ugo Zanotti.

The air force unit sent to the Spanish rebels was called the Aviazione Legionaria (Legionary Air Force). In January 1937, it consisted of approximately 523 men[62] under the command of General Vittorio Velani (who was actually Vincenzo Velardi, using a pseudonym).[63] According to the US Department of State, by the end of March 1937 close to half the Spanish rebel air force was Italian.[64] This estimate was very accurate. According to data provided by General Pietro Pinna, deputy chief of the general staff of the Royal Italian Air Force, in April 1937 the Italian Aviazione Legionaria in Spain consisted of 5 Savoia-Marchetti SM.79 Sparviero medium bombers and torpedo bombers, 23 Savoia-Marchetti SM.81 bombers, 4 Breda Ba.65 dive-bombers,[65] 77 Fiat CR.32 fighters,[66] 28 IMAN Romeo Ro.37[67] and 3 Ro.41 reconnaissance aircraft, 4 CANT Z.501 strategic reconnaissance seaplanes, and 3 Macchi M.41 flying boats.[68] According to the data provided by General Pietro Pinna, the Italian Air Command had 133 of the 147 mentioned planes operating directly under it in April 1937: 28 bombers, 79 fighters, 23 reconnaissance aircraft, and 3 seaplanes.[69] The rest—that is, 14 planes—were operating under Spanish command, in Spanish units. This makes a total of 147 planes, 43 percent of the planes at the disposal of the Spanish Aviación Nacional in April 1937, two weeks before the bombing of Gernika.

In March 1937, after the disastrous defeat of Italian forces at Guadalajara, Mussolini told Ambassador Ulrich von Hassell of Germany that no more troops would be sent to Spain. Henceforth, only commanders, subordinate commanders, and equipment would be replaced. Indeed, Il Duce "had informed the Italian command at war that none of them should return home alive unless they achieved victory."[70] Mussolini saw the humiliating defeat of Italian troops at the Battle of Guadalajara as an affront to Italian honor and was convinced that it was the poor leadership that was affecting his troops and not the number of soldiers. He needed a victory for the Italian troops to enhance Italy's image as an important military power. Moreover, he could not openly send more troops to Spain because of the control system of the Non-Intervention Committee. At this time, Italy was not officially engaged in a war in Spain.

The CTV was reorganized after the defeat at Guadalajara to begin a spring offensive in the Basque Country. Lieutenant General Mario Berti was sent as assistant commander to help restructure the Italian units, and General Ettore Bastico, a former corps commander in Abyssinia—where he was nicknamed "Bombastico" for his extensive use of bombers—replaced General Mario Roatta at the end of March. He arrived in Salamanca on April 16.[71] General Gastone Gambara replaced Lieutenant General Emilio Faldella as chief of staff of the CTV. According to the report by General Pietro Pinna of January 15, 1937, there were now 107 officers of the Italian air force engaged in the war.[72]

After the debacle at Guadalajara, the Aviazione Legionaria began to act under the command of the German Condor Legion in the Basque Country, led by its chief of staff, Colonel Wolfram von Richthofen. The general headquarters of the Aviazione Legionaria were in Seville, but the mission command headquarters were in Salamanca. Gasteiz was chosen as the headquarters of the combined Italo-German air command against Bilbao, the major city of the Basque Country. The air base for the Italian bombers was in Soria, and the Italian fighters were located in the airfields of Gasteiz (together with the German bombers) and Logroño.[73] The headquarters of the infantry unit, the so-called Brigada Mixta Italiana-Spagnola, was in Deba. This unit was in charge of the attack against the northeast front in the Basque Country.

By January 1937 the Aviazione Legionaria had 523 men and 158 planes in the war.[74] After hearing that the Russians were sending 113 additional Soviet aircraft to the Republicans, Mussolini agreed to send more fighters to the rebels.[75] Thus, the last major shipment of Italian war matériel before the bombing of Gernika arrived at the end of March to provide heavy aircraft cover for the Italian infantry during the spring offensive on the Basque front. After these deliveries for the Basque campaign, the rebels achieved absolute air superiority on the northern front.

## German Intervention

Unlike the Italian regime, the German government had no official contacts with Spanish Fascist or ultraconservative political forces before 1936. There were some contacts between Spanish Fascist elements and German politicians in the 1920s, when Spain was a totalitarian monarchy headed by King Alfonso XIII. Between 1915 and 1930, Admiral Wilhelm Franz Canaris,[76] who had served as a German secret agent in Spain during World War I and became head of the Abwehr, the German military intelligence service, in 1935, traveled several times to Cádiz to supervise the construction of twelve U-boats and torpedoes for the navy of the Weimar Republic, which was beginning a tentative process of rearmament. Although such activity was forbidden to Germany under the postwar international covenants, the Spanish government welcomed the revenues from Berlin. After the Republic was declared in 1931, the construction of U-boats in Cádiz was stopped.

After the start of the war in Spain in July 1936, the German government agreed to the international declaration of nonintervention on August 17. But Hitler had already decided to send war matériel and troops to the rebels. George L. Steer reported that when Karl Gustav Schmidt, a young German radio-telegraphist, was captured after his plane was shot down in January 1937, his Basque captors found that his silk parachute had been issued by a German factory only twenty-four hours before Germany adopted the Non-Intervention Agreement.[77]

On July 21, three days after the military uprising, Franco tried to contact the German government to seek military assistance, but his petition was not positively received by German foreign minister Konstantin von Neurath. However, Ortsgruppenleiter Adolph P. Langenheim and Johannes Bernhardt, two members of the Auslands-Organisation (an umbrella organization of the Nazi Party outside of Germany) in Morocco, offered to represent Franco in negotiations with their government concerning the shipment of ammunition and war matériel. The offer came only a few days after a National Socialist German Workers Party rally in Nuremberg that had focused on the Bolshevik threat to Western Europe, including that perceived to be posed by the Republican government of Spain, which both the Germans and the Italians regarded as communist. Franco accepted, and an incident the following day favored the German decision to help the Spanish rebels. A Junker Ju52 plane of the Lufthansa postal service was detained by Republican authorities in Las Palmas, accused of transporting rebel general Luis Orgaz.

Langenheim and Bernhardt contacted their superior, Ernst W. Bohle, chief of the Auslands-Organisation, who, ignoring orders from the Foreign Ministry, contacted Rudolf Hess, the Nazi Party deputy führer. Hess scheduled a meeting for Franco's emissaries with Hitler at Bayreuth. The führer, who had just attended a performance of Wagner's opera *Siegfried* led by Wilhelm Furtwängler in the Fuehrer Haus Wahnfried, excitedly agreed to help the coup, even against the advice of a number of staff officers and the minister of foreign affairs. The operation would be known as Operation Feuerzauber (Magic Fire) because the third act of *Siegfried* represents the heroine Brunhilda enclosed within a magic circle of fire from which only the hero can rescue her. Adolf Hitler, Joachim von Ribbentrop, Hermann W. Göring, and Joseph Goebbels were present, among others, at that meeting, and on July 26 it was decided to send twenty Junker Ju52s for the transportation of troops directly from Dessau to Seville, along with six Heinkel He51 fighter escorts and eighty-six pilots and mechanics.[78]

German officials saw several reasons to involve Germany in the Spanish conflict. First, the main geopolitical reason was to gain control of the gate to the Mediterranean and to separate Spain from the influence of Soviet Communism. With the rebels victorious, the new Spanish dictatorship would not be expected to remain neutral in a European conflict but would actively participate on the side of the Reich by providing, for instance, safe ports for German U-boats.

Also, the Spanish uprising facilitated a rapprochement between the Italian, Portuguese, Spanish, and German regimes, while providing substance to anti-Communist propaganda campaigns within the Reich and across Europe. Indeed, anti-Communism became one of the most powerful diplomatic weapons against leftist governments in the French Republic and other states in Western Europe. Anti-Communism was a more powerful cause than anti-Semitism in the international arena, and Franco and Mussolini were more anti-Communist than anti-Semitic. Within Spain the radio and press were strongly centralized and controlled for propaganda purposes. From October 1936 to January 1937, Radio Salamanca, under the directorship of Vicente Gay, head of the State Delegation for Press and Propaganda (Delegación del Estado para Prensa y Propaganda), became the primary national broadcaster of the Spanish regime. Its chief mission was to associate the Republicans with Communism and the Nationalists with anti-Communism.

There was also a tactical reason to enter the war. As mentioned, the British and French strategy of nonintervention was the best guarantee of a rebel victory. While the Republic was forced to rely solely on Soviet military aid, the Italian, Portuguese, and German regimes were helping Franco build a strong military force. Indeed, foreign intervention became the biggest factor in the failure of the Republic.

In the event of a rebel victory, the Third Reich would gain access to raw materials and become a key trading partner with Spain. Moreover, that trading relationship would negatively affect Britain's rearmament program, which partly relied on Biscayan iron ore.

Finally, by participating in the Spanish war, the German armed forces would gain significant combat experience. Almost all European powers had tested their air forces in combat during the years immediately preceding 1936, and the decisions of the military commands in the course of these wars between 1919 and 1936 reveal trends that were to characterize their conduct during World War II.[79] In the course of combat in Libya prior to 1935 and during the Abyssinian War (1935–36), Italian pilots gained experience in the use of various types of bombs, including toxic gas shells and incendiary bombs, and in aerial strafing techniques. The Ethiopian conflict also gave Italian flight commanders the opportunity to experiment with new techniques, such as the supply of ammunition and food from the air, allowing ground troops to undertake long marches. Because Germany had lost all its colonies as part of the peace settlement after World War I, it had no opportunity to intervene in conflicts after 1919, and according to the Treaty of Versailles, signed on June 28, 1919, which came into effect on January 10, 1920, Germany was allowed to have only a small standing army without modern weapons such as tanks or airplanes. Specifically, Article 198 determined that Germany should have no air force, and Article 201 provided that during the six months following the treaty's entry into force, the manufacture and importation of aircraft, parts of aircraft, aircraft engines, and parts of aircraft engines would be strictly forbidden throughout Germany. Therefore, the Spanish war would give the German air force an opportunity to test an "unused" army.[80]

Neither Ribbentrop nor Werner E. F. von Blomberg, the minister of war and commander in chief of the German armed forces—both present at the meeting on July 25 with the Spanish representatives—was enthusiastic about participating in the coup. As already noted, Foreign Minister von Neurath had rejected the initial request for aid. Only Joseph Goebbels, the Reichsminister of public enlightenment and propaganda, welcomed the Reich's involvement in the conflict. Despite his initial reservations, Göring enthusiastically seconded Hitler's decision, and the referred first shipment of twenty Junker Ju52 transports, six Heinkel He51 fighter planes, and eighty-six troops was launched soon after. This was actually double what Franco had requested.[81]

It is also relevant to study the reasons behind Göring's interest in the Spanish war. Andre Geraud, "Pertinax," editor of *L'Echo de Paris*, wrote an article on April 30, which was reproduced by the American press, in which he stated that Göring was eager to show Hitler what the air force was capable of with the purpose of advancing his own political career and that consequently the bombing of Gernika was due largely to the need to demonstrate empirically, on the ground, that the Luftwaffe could wipe out entire populations, a capability not available to ground forces (artillery) or the German navy.[82] Seventy-five years later, we have documentation that helps to confirm this thesis.

Regardless of Hitler's and Goebbels's ideological, geopolitical, and commercial reasoning,[83] Göring had personal reasons to launch the German regime on a military adventure in the Iberian Peninsula and to start a bombing campaign of terror. Werner von Blomberg was then minister of war and general commander of the Wehrmacht, a position that Göring desired. A war scenario such as the one happening in Spain provided a suitable framework for Göring to convince Hitler that the Luftwaffe was the most powerful weapon of the Reich "in the future war" and, as a consequence, to allow him to take over the Ministry of War and climb over Blomberg within the Reich's administration. Furthermore, the conflict offered him the chance to take control of trade between the German and Spanish regimes and consequently to assume responsibility for the economic planning of the Reich and, by extension, for the German Ministry of Economy. Finally, the war would permit Göring to acquire extensive powers with regard to international relations with the Spanish regime. These circumstances would make available to him more funding and more power within the military command. In sum, Franco's war was going to provide Göring with the opportunity and the means to eliminate three of the ministers of the German state and to become the second in command of the German Reich, after only Hitler.

With respect to the control of economic affairs of the Reich, the development of the Luftwaffe was particularly costly because it required a prodigal use of raw materials, huge production facilities, large training centers, and vast, complex, and very expensive technological plants. The constant criticism and administrative restrictions from both the staff of the Wehrmacht and the Ministry of Economy regarding the financial resources absorbed by the Luftwaffe hovered over Göring and convinced him to take control of the Reich's economic affairs. Like Hitler, Göring opposed any measure of disarmament or reduction of military spending, and he defended large-scale rearmament and autarkic economic policies to free Germany from its dependence on foreign raw materials. In line with General Ludendorff's theory of total war, the German government promoted full state control of arms factories in order to direct and coordinate the network of industries in the armament sector. The result of these autarkic economic policies was the absorption of companies such as the one owned by Hugo Junkers, which Göring planned, conducted, and completed by early 1933. This was the company that produced the planes that bombed Gernika four years later.[84] The German government also promoted the creation of state-owned industrial plants processing raw materials in order to ensure the supply of these necessary resources.

The uprising led by General Franco and the subsequent German intervention in the conflict gave Göring a unique opportunity to convince Hitler that his administration of the Reich's economy would place in German hands control of Spain's exports of raw materials, taking them from those who had previously enjoyed them, the British. As a consequence, in August 1936, when the Reich's Ministry of Economy recommended the reduction of military spending, Hitler issued a plan to increase expenditures for the Wehrmacht, the embryo of the Four-Year Plan that would be released only one month later, in September 1936.[85] The main goal of the Four-Year Plan was to prop up the military-industrial sector and prepare Germany to face a war within four years. Göring quickly grasped that taking the lead of the plan would place him over the Reich's Ministry of Economy. Blomberg rejected the plan, not primarily because he was opposed to rearmament and the militarization of German industry, but because he was opposed to Göring. But he was at a disadvantage. Göring's strong support of the Four-Year Plan turned him in Hitler's eyes into the champion of two of the pillars of National Socialism—autarky and rearmament. Hitler deliberately chose the Nazi Party rally in Nuremberg (September 8–14, 1936) to announce the Reich's new economic policy and, for the first time in public, the German regime's intent to intervene in what Hitler regarded as a war against Bolshevism.[86]

Hitler appointed Göring director of the Four-Year Plan on October 18, 1936, with extraordinary powers. One of the first consequences of Göring's appointment was an increase in the Luftwaffe's budget, which had already increased significantly between 1933 and 1936. Obviously, this new policy stoked the debate about the disproportionate allocation of financial resources to the arms industry in relation to the total expenditure of the government.[87]

At the time three treaties governed economic relations between Germany and Spain: the Commercial Treaty of May 7, 1926; the Commodity Agreement of March 9, 1936; and the Payments Agreement of December 31, 1934. The Commodity Agreement expired on December 31, 1936, but was extended until March 31, 1937, with the agreement of Franco's Nationalist government. To regulate trade with the rebels, the German Ministry of Economy sent Reichsbank mediators to Burgos and Seville. However, after Göring was appointed commissioner of foreign exchange and raw materials in April 1936, he wanted to assume total control over all German operations in Spain. Acting without consulting the Ministry of Economy but ensuring Hitler's approval, Göring ordered the creation of two new corporations, the Rohstoff-Waren-Kompensation Handelsgesellschaft in Berlin and the Sociedad Hispano-Marroqui de Transportes in Seville[88] "as a temporary measure" to regulate trade between the two regimes.[89] The two companies, HISMA in Seville and ROWAK in Berlin, established a monopoly on imports and exports to and from Spain. This ploy was part of the struggle within the Nazi regime between Göring and Reichsminister of the Economy Hjalmar Schacht for control of the Ministry of Economy. As a result, Germany became the first country to import raw materials from Franco's new Spanish state, mostly minerals such as iron ore, iron sulfide, cinnabar, and tungsten. Having been appointed head of the Four-Year Plan and having taken control of the commodity trade with Franco's regime, Göring had won the war for control of the German Ministry of Economy. In November 1937 Schacht was forced to resign and was replaced by Göring.

With respect to international relations, until the fall of 1936 Göring was subordinate to Blomberg in the field of foreign policy with regard to all military matters. Göring's role in this area was thus limited to serving as Hitler's confidant in informal contacts with foreign agents in Italy, Austria, Poland, and the Balkans. Germany's participation in the Spanish war allowed Göring to operate outside the Foreign Ministry and its diplomatic outreach to the Spanish rebels, a campaign led by Lieutenant General Wilhelm Faupel, who was appointed by Hitler as *encargado de negocios* (delegate for business affairs) of the Reich to the Franco regime in October 1936. In February 1937, after Germany officially recognized the Franco regime,

Faupel was appointed German ambassador to Spain. However, in practice Faupel was undermined by the direct intervention in diplomatic affairs of General Hugo Sperrle and Richthofen of the Luftwaffe. Obstructed by Göring and Sperrle, and by Franco himself, Faupel was forced to resign in September 1937, almost one year after being appointed chargé d'affaires in November 1936 and only seven months after being appointed ambassador to Spain. His resignation was followed by the dismissal on February 4, 1938, of German foreign minister Konstantin von Neurath, in the context of the Blomberg-Fritsch scandal that, as we shall see, was planned and led by Göring and Himmler, with Heydrich's help. Faupel's and Neurath's dismissals left Göring's hands free to control the international relations of the Reich in all matters related to Spain. However, Hitler appointed Ribbentrop as Neurath's successor on February 4, 1938, and soon strong animosity developed between Ribbentrop and Göring, who never stopped pursuing greater control of the Reich's foreign affairs.

The Spanish war also allowed Göring to gain control of the War Ministry and overthrow Werner von Blomberg, Göring's immediate superior as head of the Wehrmacht and Ministry of War. To depose Blomberg, Göring had to gain Hitler's confidence and convince him that the Luftwaffe was unquestionably the Wehrmacht's best weapon. Göring had to prove that the air force would be of more value in any future war than the navy and that the performance of ground forces would be determined by whichever side controlled the air above them. It was not hard to convince Hitler that terror bombing was the most genuinely National Socialist way to win a war and that it was obvious that terror bombing was a monopoly of the air force. As Göring later testified at Nuremberg, he urged Hitler to give support under all circumstances, in order to "test my young Luftwaffe at this opportunity in this or that technical respect and in order that the personnel, too, might gather a certain amount of experience."[90]

Göring's testimony was substantiated by documents discovered much earlier. On August 31, 1936, Wilhelm Henckels had been arrested in Barcelona on suspicion of being a German secret agent (working in collaboration with another agent, Bernhard Funk, who fled before being arrested). When the police searched his house, they found several documents containing information on Spanish airports, including details on four airfields in Morocco and four in Catalonia. Among other things, the reports summarized the number of officers and men on duty at the airfields, specifying the number of pilots, observers, wireless operators, and others. There were also details about antiaircraft defenses, artillery, machine guns, illumination available for night flights, and the personnel employed in defense. Finally, the reports had information about the number of aircraft and the speed, radius, condition, age, bomb-carrying capacity, armament, and position of each airplane. The information gathered by the agent showed that by the end of August 1936, Göring was already working to convince Hitler to restrict Germany's military assistance to Franco to the Luftwaffe.[91]

It was not a coincidence that the initially modest Operation Feuerzauber of July was replaced by the much more ambitious Operation Rügen and the subsequent creation of the Condor Legion in late October 1936, coinciding with Göring's appointment as head of the Four-Year Plan.[92] Indeed, when Göring had to decide what kind of assistance to send to Franco in October 1936, he decided to send a contingent formed almost exclusively of units of the Luftwaffe, keeping the navy and the infantry outside the war. He saw this as the only way to demonstrate the benefits of the independent management of the air force in combat. By going to war, the German air force would gain significant experience in air-to-air and air-to-ground attack and in high- and low-altitude bombing.

Göring reported in February 1937 to Seidl Hellmuth, the Italian Regia Aeronautica major who was assigned to him as a flight attendant during his stay in Italy,[93] that in "the next war," the air force would play a decisive role as a weapon against naval forces, while admitting that it was difficult with the means then available to destroy from the air a ship two thousand to twenty-five hundred meters long.[94] He added that by the spring of 1939, the Luftwaffe would be "the most powerful of three branches of the Wehrmacht" and that "it would occupy the first place." He maintained that during World War I and until 1937, the army had been the main branch of the Wehrmacht.[95] Göring estimated that by 1940–41, the Luftwaffe would have built 14,000 aircraft organized into 1,000 squadrons (Staffeln), each of them with 9 first-line planes, 3 in reserve, and 2 for training new pilots. That goal would be achieved in several stages: by April 1, 1937, the Luftwaffe was going to consist of 250 squadrons, or a total of 3,500 units; by the spring of 1938, it would be doubled to a total of 7,000 aircraft organized in 500 squadrons; and, by 1940, the Luftwaffe would be ready for war with 14,000 aircraft organized into 1,000 squadrons, with an expected budget of forty million marks (equivalent to three hundred billion lire) in 1939.[96]

Göring was obsessed with convincing Hitler that his land-attack planes could sink heavy ships and that therefore it was wiser to invest in airplanes than in vessels. From this it follows that the head of the air force had to become the head of the Wehrmacht. However, by early 1937 Göring had not yet had the opportunity to demonstrate the effectiveness of airpower against naval units. During a meeting between Göring and Mussolini at the Palazzo Venezia in Rome on January 23, 1937, the marshal explained to Il Duce that following the launch of several 250-kilogram bombs on the Republican 15,452-ton battleship *Jaime I* (built in 1914) while it was docked in Málaga, it was found that the damage planes could do to a battleship was still very small, but that the attempt was promising.[97] Indeed it was, because between July 1936 and March 1939, the Republican fleet lost 554 ships, with 141 of those losses credited to German and Italian action in the form of U-boat and air attacks. In addition, 106 foreign ships carrying supplies to the Republicans were sunk, many by aircraft in open violation of the Nyon Agreement that came into force on September 14, 1937, to the protection of all merchant ships not belonging to either of the conflicting Spanish parties.[98]

It is particularly relevant with regard to the bombing of Gernika to note that Göring was firmly convinced that the Luftwaffe had to acquire a distinctly offensive character and that, as a consequence, it was essential to promote the design and mass production of bombers. Specifically, according to Göring, the strategy of the whole army in a future war would revolve around decisive offensive action by the air force, rather than around defensive action ("Defense would be attained by preventive and tempestive offensive actions").[99] In Göring's opinion, between 75 and 78 percent of the air units should be bombardment units.[100] In short, he had to show Hitler that the air force would play a central role in a blitzkrieg operation and that with sufficient bombardment units, the Luftwaffe could not only jeopardize an enemy navy but also substitute for artillery by paving the way for the infantry through an overwhelming initial bombardment campaign. This theory would be tested only two months later, in Gernika.

Indeed, the war in general allowed Göring to take full control of the Ministries of War and Economy and partially of the Ministry of Foreign Affairs. The bombing of Gernika in particular also played a crucial role in this regard. As we shall see in detail, the data available to us indicate that the bombing was originally planned for Monday, April 19, the day before Hitler's birthday. However, the bombing could not take place that day because some of the units that were to take part had not yet arrived at the air base in Burgos. This delay was used by Göring's enemies in the German Foreign Ministry, specifically by Faupel, who sent a telegram to Berlin stating that Bilbao would never be taken by the rebels and that the action of the Condor Legion was not encouraging a rapid advance of Franco's troops into Bilbao. It was true that the rebel troops were advancing only an average of a half mile per day. The bombing took place a week later, on Monday, April 26, and the parade commemorating Hitler's birthday was also delayed one week, making it coincide with the bombing itself. This was not the only time Göring gave importance to the führer's birthday celebration. When at the end of the Spanish war in April 1939 Göring organized victory parades in Hamburg (the port of arrival for the returning troops of the Condor Legion) and Berlin, Hitler's birthday celebration was also delayed until June, to make it coincide with the victory parades.

As for Blomberg, Göring played several cards against him. First, Göring made clear to Hitler whenever he had opportunity that he was the one who represented the true spirit of National Socialism in debates about the policies of rearmament and autarky. For example, during a meeting in November 1937, in which Hitler defended the ideas expressed in the Hossbach Memorandum on rearmament and preparation for a future war, the führer was visibly upset with the negative point of view of certain army leaders, including the minister of war, while Göring seconded Hitler's views.[101]

Both Göring and Himmler, knowing that Blomberg lacked Hitler's support, conspired to oust him. The opportunity came in October 1937 when Blomberg sought Göring's support in a matter in which he had embarked with a "lady with a past."[102] Blomberg, who was then sixty years old, wanted to marry Erna Gruhn, a twenty-six-year-old typist.[103] Heydrich's security services discovered that Gruhn had posed as a pornographic model in 1932 and had a criminal record for prostitution. However, at this point Göring told Blomberg that he was willing to help him and even offered to organize the extradition of Gruhn's former lover, who was immediately sent to Argentina. Göring agreed to support Blomberg's marriage and promised not to say anything about the bride's background. He even agreed to be a witness of the bond and persuaded Hitler also to serve as a witness. The wedding was held hurriedly on January 12. Then, less than two weeks after the wedding, Göring, claiming that the police had uncovered evidence that Blomberg's new wife was a former prostitute, informed Hitler. Hitler was furious, but he did not discharge Blomberg. Göring then proposed that he would go to Blomberg and tell him that the marriage should be annulled or else he should resign in order to avoid scandal (something that does not seem to have been decided by Hitler). At the same time, Göring spread the news among the general staff of the Wehrmacht. Blomberg resigned on January 27, 1938.[104] The same day that Blomberg's resignation was made public, Göring was promoted to field marshal. A few days later Blomberg's successor, General Werner von Fritsch, followed the same fate after being falsely accused of homosexuality by Himmler and Göring. After Fritsch's fall, Hitler appointed Walther von Brauchitsch to replace him, but he also took direct command of the Wehrmacht to avoid further scandals.

In sum, by 1938 Göring had achieved most of what he had planned in the summer of 1936. The war in general and the bombing of Gernika in particular turned him into the second man of the German Reich by the beginning of World War II.[105] He, who had managed to depose and kill Ernst Röhm during the struggle for control of the SA (Sturmabteilung, the Storm Detachment or Assault Division) in 1934, managed to topple Werner von Blomberg and Werner von Fritsch in the context of their confrontation with the staff of the Wehrmacht and the struggle for control of the Ministry of War, and at the same time he managed to purge the Luftwaffe of elements related to the general staff of the Wehrmacht. Göring also managed to topple Hjalmar Schacht during the struggle for control of the Ministry of the Economy, and then he managed to depose Foreign Minister Neurath and Ambassador Faupel and to corner Joachim von Ribbentrop for control of the Reich's Ministry of Foreign Affairs. Even though Hitler refused to appoint Göring minister of war, reserving for himself the title of commander in chief of the Wehrmacht, by January 1938 Göring had become the highest-ranked officer in the German armed forces after Hitler. On the first day of World War II, Hitler confirmed Göring as second in command in the Reich and his successor.[106]

On August 6, 1936, the *Manchester Journal* reported the shipment of German troops to Spanish Morocco on the German destroyer *Leopard*. The reporter wrote that German Blueshirts had even marched in the open, singing Nazi songs and shouting "Heil Hitler!" A day later, First Lieutenant Rudolf von Moreau led a Junker Ju52 squad from Africa to the Iberian Peninsula, transporting the first Moorish and Spanish troops to the conflict. Moreau would be one of the bomber squad leaders in the attack on Gernika on April 26, 1937. By August 28 the German regime had shipped twenty-six bombers, fifteen fighters, twenty antiaircraft guns, fifty machine guns, and eight thousand rifles to the rebels.[107] Without that help Franco could not have tried to invade Andalusia. Between late July and mid-October

1936, the Luftwaffe transported approximately thirteen thousand Spanish and Moorish soldiers and three hundred tons of war matériel from North Africa to the Iberian Peninsula. Hitler would later remind Franco that he owed Germany a monument to the Junker Ju52.[108]

In late October the German regime decided to expand the Feuerzauber operation under the name Operation Rügen. It deployed the air unit known as the Condor Legion, which was composed of approximately five thousand men, mostly from the air force. The Condor Legion was led between November 6, 1936, and October 31, 1937, by General Hugo Sperrle, commanded by Helmuth Volkmann between November 1, 1937, and October 1, 1938. The chief of staff was Alexander Holle until January 20, 1937, and Wolfram von Richthofen until January 1938, when, because of differences with Volkmann, he requested a transfer to Berlin. When Volkmann was deposed in October 1938, Richthofen, now ranked general, briefly took the leadership of the legion from November 1, 1938, until the end of the war in April 1939. Basically, his job was to dismantle the unit. According to information provided at the end of October 1936 by Major General Hugo Sperrle to Admiral Canaris, the Condor Legion was divided into various groups: one bomber group, one fighter group, one long-range reconnaissance squadron, one flight of short-range reconnaissance planes, two signal companies, three heavy antiaircraft batteries, and two searchlight platoons.[109]

The Condor Legion was rapidly built by November 1936 and organized according to the following: Group Führungsstab S/88, the general staff; Group Kampfgruppe K/88, bombers; Group Jagdgruppe J/88, fighters; Group Aufklärungsstaffell A/88, reconnaissance; Group Gemischte Aufklälungs und Bombenstaffel AS/88, sea fliers; Group Flak-Abteilung F/88, antiaircraft batteries; Group Luftnachrichten-Abteilung LN/88, aerial information; Group Luftzeuggruppe und Luftpark P/88, maintenance; Group Sanitäts-Abteilung San/88, medical service; Group Lazarett Laz/88, campaign hospital; Group Wetterstelle W/88, meteorology services; and Group Verbindungsstab VS/88, communication with the Spanish and Italian air forces.[110]

Many of the military prototypes sent to war were experimental. By January 1937 two additional groups were created to test new models and their capabilities: Group Versuchsbomberstaffel VB/88, an experimental bomber squad, and Group Versuchsjagdstaffel VJ/88, an experimental fighter squad.

According to data provided by General Pietro Pinna, deputy chief of the general staff of the Royal Italian Air Force, in April 1937 the Condor Legion had a total of 157 aircraft on the Iberian Peninsula: 38 Junker Ju52 bombers, 3 Junker Ju86 bombers, 3 Heinkel He111 medium bombers, 3 Dornier Do17 light bombers, 4 Henschel HS123 dive-bombers, 50 Heinkel He51 fighters, 7 Messerschmitt Bf.109 fighters, 7 Heinkel He45 reconnaissance planes (also used as light bombers), 16 Heinkel He46 close reconnaissance planes, 16 Heinkel He70 fast reconnaissance aircraft, 3 Heinkel He59 and 2 Heinkel He60 reconnaissance seaplanes, 4 Dornier Do J Wal (Whale) flying boats, and 1 Messerschmitt Bf.108 personnel transport and liaison aircraft. This was a total of 51 bombers, 57 seven pursuit planes, 39 reconnaissance aircraft, 5 reconnaissance seaplanes, 4 flying boats, and 1 personnel transportation plane.[111] In mid-April 30 out of 36 (83.3 percent) bombers under German command were based at airfields in Burgos or Gasteiz, destined for the Basque front.

The Italian Aviazione Legionaria had approximately 83 modern planes (18 of them bombers) in the Basque Country.[112] According to data collected by the American intelligence services by April 19, 1937, four days before the attack against Gernika, the rebels had received approximately 200 planes from Italy and Germany: 40 bombers of the Junker and Savoya types arrived in Morocco in July and August 1936; 40 pursuit planes, both German and Italian, arrived in August; 50 German pursuit planes reached the front at the end of November; 50 Italian pursuit planes arrived at the end of November; and 40 miscellaneous types (observation, commercial, transport, and the like) arrived from August to November 1936.[113]

This figure is supported by data provided by General Pinna, who estimated that on April 17, 1937, out of a total of 340 planes at the disposal of the rebels, 157 (46 percent) were German, 147 were Italian (43 percent), and only 37 were under direct Spanish command (11 percent).[114] In sum, out of a total estimate of 340 planes at the disposal of the Spanish Aviación Nacional on April 17, 1937, ten days before the bombing of Gernika, 304 were of German or Italian origin (89 percent), among them 79 bombers and 137 fighters. These figures were known to the British and French intelligence services and also to the US Department of State, which in a report at the end of March 1937, just before the beginning of aerial attacks against Basque cities and towns, stated that close to half the Spanish rebel air force was Italian.[115] However, political cynicism was on the rise in Italy, and the

Italian government passed Royal Decree no. 562 on April 10, 1937, prohibiting the transport of troops or ammunition to the Iberian Peninsula on Italian vessels. The decree even specified the control systems required for these vessels to depart from Italian ports.[116]

The Condor Legion also included the Imker-Gruppe infantry units (mainly cavalry and artillery) and a group of instructors called Imker-Ausbilder, under the command of Wilhelm Ritter von Thoma. Panzer crews mostly operated Panzerkampfwagen I light tanks and 88-mm heavy antiaircraft artillery units. Also, the German naval unit Gruppe Nordsee under the command of Rear Admiral Rolf Carls took part in operations coordinated under the code name Operation Ursula. An estimated eight German and fifty-eight Italian U-boats took part in the war. US agents spotted several German U-boats in Pasaia (Gipuzkoa) at the Basque front.

In April 1937 the Condor Legion was under the command of Major General Hugo Sperrle (war name "Sander"), and Colonel Wolfram von Richthofen was the chief of the general staff (from January 20, 1937, until November 1, 1938). Initially, the commanders of the different groups of the Condor Legion were as follows: Group Kampfgruppe K/88, Major Robert Fuchs; Group Jagdgruppe J/88, Major Hubertus M. von Bernegg; Group Aufklärungsstaffell A/88, Commandant Heinz Heinsius; Group Gemischte Aufklälungs und Bombenstaffel AS/88, Lieutenant Colonel Karl Heinz Wolff; and Group Flak-Abteilung F/88, Lieutenant Colonel Hermann Lichtenberg. Colonel Erwin Jaenecke and General Adolph Galland of the general staff supervised operations.

The first unit of the Condor Legion, composed of 697 men, arrived in Seville on November 16, 1936, on board the vessel *Fulda*, but the first bombings by the German air force had taken place in Bilbao three months earlier. According to newspaper reports, on the morning of September 25, 1936, seven airplanes "rained death on the city" for more than an hour and a half. In the afternoon four aircraft carried out a second bombing that lasted almost an hour. The next day the rebels again bombed Bilbao. According to data provided by the District Court of Bilbao and Getxo, the Department of Statistics of the City Council of Bilbao, and the Department of Health of the Basque Government, 96 people were killed and 650 wounded during these two days of bombing in Bilbao and Areeta.[117] On October 21 Bilbao was bombed again, which resulted in 8 casualties.[118]

With the arrival of the Italian Blackshirt (in Italian Camicie Nere, or CCNN) armored divisions and the Luftwaffe air units in the middle of March

1937, the numerical and technical superiority of the rebel forces at the Basque front became absolute. Ambassador Bowers was accurate when he told Secretary of State Hull in October 1937 that Mussolini might accept the withdrawal of his troops, but only after Franco's victory was ensured. By the end of 1937, it seemed clear to the American ambassador that after the French and the British governments had banned the shipment of arms and ammunition to the Republican government while the Italian and the German regimes continued to deliver war matériel and troops to the rebels, the Fascists' victory was ensured. Bowers claimed that this flagrant violation of the nonintervention system was possible only with the implicit approval of the British and the French governments. He claimed that Sir Henry G. Chilton, British ambassador to the Spanish Republic, was prorebel:

> I have no hesitancy in expressing the conviction that the British Government is entirely partial to this plan of Mussolini. I base this conviction on the fact that, (1) from the first week of the war the British ambassador here has been an open and bitter partisan of the rebels, (2) the misrepresentations and suppressions of Mr. Eden in the Commons can leave no doubt of the profound dislike of the present British Government for the Government of Spain, and (3) the British chargé d'affaires in Valencia, Ogilvie-Forbes, who was really neutral, has been displaced by Mr. Leach who, according to information from everyone from Valencia I have seen, is very nasty toward the Government.[119]

Bowers was not wrong. As the Division of European Affairs of the US Department of State viewed it, London businessmen predominantly favored an agreement with Franco, who seemed to have the winning side by mid-1937, in order to protect British investments and with a view to being "in early" on any favors Franco might be in a position to grant. For instance, Juan March, one of Franco's principal financial backers, was a frequent visitor to London and had very wide contacts in the leading British financial houses. The author of the report of July 7, 1937, for the Division of European Affairs was informed by Georges Martelli, foreign editor of the *Morning Post*, that on account of March's activities in London, "Franco's stock was going up" in 1937 and that "the sooner the British government came to a discreet understanding with the Insurgents, the sooner there would be an end to the Spanish mess."[120] In other words, London businessmen wanted Franco, but not a Franco controlled exclusively by the Germans and the Italians. London entrepreneurs had knowledge of the Italo-German consortium formed in 1934 and of the creation of ROWAK and HISMA to exploit Spain's mineral wealth, and they were initially sympathetic with a policy of aloofness until it was made clear that Franco's bargain with the Fascist states was not exclusive of British interests. At the end of May 1937, sentiment in London began to veer. Since victory was within Franco's grasp, British businessmen felt that their country should come to terms with him before it was too late.

## The System of Nonintervention

André Léon Blum, prime minister of France, was concerned about the international implications of the Iberian conflict, which as early as July 1936 was widely viewed as a prologue to another world war. However, maintaining French neutrality was not an easy diplomatic undertaking. The Parti Socialiste Français had announced at the outbreak of the rebellion its "solidarité total avec les Républicains espagnols."[121] Moreover, one of José Giral's first official acts after being appointed prime minister of the Spanish Republic (July 19–September 4, 1936) by President Manuel Azaña was to ask the French government for military assistance and war supplies. Prorebel Juan Francisco Cárdenas, Spanish ambassador to the Quai d'Orsay until July 23, 1936 (assisted by Antonio Barroso and Cristóbal Castillo, military attaché and chargé d'affaires of the Spanish Embassy, respectively), leaked the request to the French press, where it was discussed in great detail.

Blum was the leader of the left-wing Front Populaire, a political coalition closely aligned with the Spanish Frente Popular under Manuel Azaña. Both leaders were elected in the spring of 1936. The French Front Populaire was a union of the Socialist Party (Parti Socialiste Français), the Communist Party (Parti Communiste Français), the French Section of the International Worker's Union (Section Française de l'Internationale Ouvrière), and the Radical Socialist Party (Parti Radical-Socialiste). Likewise, the Frente Popular was created in January 1936 in the image of the French coalition and included the Spanish Worker's Socialist Party (Partido Socialista Obrero Español), the Workers' General Union (Unión General de Trabajadores), the Spanish Communist Party (Partido Comunista de España), the Workers' Party of Marxist Unification (Partido Obrero de Unificación Marxista), the Republican Left (Izquierda Republicana), and the Republican Union (Union Republicana). The only possible excuse for the left-leaning French government not to involve itself politically in the war in which its Spanish counterpart was engaged was under the pretext of the

Non-Intervention Agreement. As Johannes Welczeck,[122] German ambassador to the Quai d'Orsay, noted, this was not the first time a war in Spain had given rise to a war between Germany and France.[123] Realizing the danger of inspiring a new war between France and its belligerent neighbor to the east, the French government opted for the peaceful diplomatic maneuver of adhering to the Non-Intervention Agreement.

The British government did not have the same political and diplomatic bonds with the Spanish Republic that the French did. However, one of Britain's key goals between July 1936 and April 1939 was to prevent international interference in Spanish politics. This was part of Stanley Baldwin's strategy as prime minister between June 7, 1935, and May 28, 1937, and then that of his successor, Neville Chamberlain. The United Kingdom was not prepared for a general war, and the Chamberlain government "without any doubt" was going to do everything in its power—even "swallow their pride and, seek compromise"—in order to avoid a drift toward overt hostilities. Chamberlain was determined to "exercise caution, patience and restraint" in the Spanish question in order to save the peace of Europe. The two cardinal points of British policy toward Spain were to ensure that the Spanish settle their own fate and to prevent other states from embroiling themselves any deeper than they already had in the Spanish quarrel.[124]

The British and French governments did not realize that Hitler and Mussolini also felt they were not ready in 1937 to address "the next war." In fact, the goal of the Four-Year Plan headed by Göring was to prepare Germany to face a war by 1940, because most high-ranking German officers thought Germany was not yet prepared for a general confrontation. During the meeting between Mussolini and Göring at the Palazzo Venezia in Rome on January 23, 1937, both dealt with the "political falsity of the democratic governments." Göring told the Italian leader that the German administration understood that Italy had decided not to abandon the League of Nations during the Abyssinian War but that Germany did not understand why they remained members of the league in 1937. Mussolini replied that the issue of Abyssinia was not yet closed, but that Italy would soon abandon the league, for which he had no sympathy. Göring said that Germany would agree to reenter the league only on condition of a revision of the Locarno Agreement, and both understood that the League of Nations was "a kind of invisible alliance against Italy and Germany." With respect to the Spanish war, they agreed that it was necessary to maintain uniform standards in what they both understood was a fight against Bolshevism.

Göring made clear his fear that the constant shipments of war matériel and troops would generate "a general war." Mussolini replied that there were about forty-four thousand Italian volunteers at war and that he was willing to send more, but that he wanted to avoid the danger of a large-scale conflagration.[125]

In Britain Stanley Baldwin had started a rearmament program in the early 1930s, and Chamberlain continued it, quietly preparing Great Britain for what they believed was an eventual war with Germany and Italy.[126] Sir Eric C. E. Phipps, British secretary to the Paris Peace Conference in 1919 and ambassador of Great Britain in Berlin from 1933 to 1937, noted in a letter to British secretary of state for foreign affairs Anthony Eden that in spite of British efforts to gain peace, neither Göring nor Goebbels inspired confidence in Germany's good faith.[127]

Ambassador Bowers never understood France's reasons for promoting the nonintervention system, which seemed in many ways contrary to French interests. In a report to Secretary of State Hull, Bowers stated that "the almost pathetic anxiety of the French to hold on to their understanding with England has been taken advantage of in London to force France into policies clearly dangerous to France."[128]

However, just fifteen days after the insurrection started in Morocco, the French government appealed to the British and Italians to create an agreement of nonintervention concerning the Spanish coup d'état. By August 4 the French had received the assent of both governments. Then French ambassador André François-Poncet called on German foreign minister Konstantin von Neurath,[129] asking whether the Reich would take part in a joint declaration regarding nonintervention in the internal affairs of the Spanish Republic.

On August 6, 1936, the French dispatched a note to the British government, proposing a ban on the exportation and transit of arms and munitions to both parties at war on the Iberian Peninsula. On August 8 the Council of Ministers of the French Republic passed a unilateral embargo on arms to the Spanish Republic, and seven days later Yvon Delbos, French minister for foreign affairs, informed Sir George R. Clerk, Britain's ambassador in Paris, that the embargo had been adopted. The same day Clerk responded that the British government had also prohibited the direct or indirect exportation, reexportation, or transit, to any destination in Spain or the Spanish possessions, of all arms, munitions, and materials of war, as well as all aircraft, assembled or dismantled, and all vessels of war.[130]

The British government was ready to put the nonintervention scheme into effect as soon as France, Germany, Italy, the Soviet Union, and Portugal should likewise agree to it.

By early September twenty-seven European governments had made similar declarations, all providing that war materials would be prohibited from being sent to the Spanish state and its colonies, that the contracting governments would keep each other informed of measures taken to stop the arms trade with the parties at war, and that the prohibition could not be unilateral. The application of measures would take effect only after all three European political blocs and their satellites adhered to it: the British and French democracies; the German, Italian, and Portuguese totalitarian governments; and the Soviet Union.

There was no single written document to be signed by all the parties. The agreement was, rather, a vague and informal international moratorium. Its implementation depended solely on the goodwill of each government, and breaches of the agreement would not be penalized. For instance, Germany and Italy (as well as Hungary, Latvia, Luxembourg, Poland, and Turkey) did not explicitly endorse the preamble of the British declaration and consequently did not unambiguously vow to abstain from direct or indirect interference in Spain's internal affairs. The parties had different reasons for adopting the declaration, even if the wording they settled on was similar. This is especially clear from the immediate German and Italian involvement in the war. By August 1936 both Germany and Italy had already sent troops and munitions to the rebels, and arrangements were being made to send more. Unlike the British and French, the German and Italian regimes were interested in training their armies for the impending world war, and they appear to have signed nonintervention declarations primarily to prevent the transport of arms and ammunitions to the Republican forces. The German ambassador to Great Britain, Joachim von Ribbentrop, was delighted with the accord, which eliminated the Spanish Republic's right to receive international assistance while allowing the rebels to obtain ample weaponry (including airplanes) and regular troops from Germany and Italy—that is, the Non-Intervention Agreement denied the Spanish Republican government arms and ammunition while turning a blind eye on glaring violations by Germany and Italy.

The committee's tacit decision not to set up a system of punishments for any countries that broke the accord prevented sanctions against violators or even discussion at the League of Nations. In fact, several charges were raised before the committee (mainly against Italy and the Soviet Union), but all were dropped after being judged "unverified." In most of the many cases of violation of the Non-Intervention Agreement, the action of the British and French governments was limited to sending notes to the foreign ministers of the German and Italian regimes, such as, for example, the note that the British Embassy in Rome sent to the Italian government regarding the continuing shipment of "volunteers" to the war, contrary to the Non-Intervention Agreement.[131] In this case, as in the rest, no further action was taken. On September 27, 1936, Spanish Republican foreign minister Julio Álvarez del Vayo forwarded to the secretary-general of the League of Nations documents containing detailed information on violations of the nonintervention accord by the Italian, German, and Portuguese regimes.[132] But no action was ever taken in this case either.

In the early 1800s Secretary of the Foreign Office Henry John Temple, Viscount Palmerston, had stated that the United Kingdom "professes non-intervention, but only when this principle does not oblige us to violate treaties or to sacrifice our national interests."[133] This principle was observed by the Non-Intervention Committee under the presidency of Lord Plymouth. The committee was charged with preventing the active participation of regular foreign troops in the war. In reality, Lord Plymouth's major responsibility was to avert at all costs the onset of another world war. German and Italian troops and war matériel had been present at the front since July 1936, always under the label of "forces of volunteers" or "free troops." By the end of October, the German and Spanish governments had agreed on the command of the Condor Legion, which was already bombing unprotected cities in the Basque Country. On October 19, 1937, the Italian Foreign Office finally dared to announce that there were Italian troops at war in Spain.[134]

As stated by Bowers, "The Non-intervention Pact was proving itself a dishonest farce. The Fascist powers fought openly, defiantly, with arms; most of the democracies fought just as effectively, if unconsciously, as collaborationists of the Fascists under the mocking cloak of 'non-intervention.'"[135] The pact had become a mockery by October 1936. It was common knowledge that arms and ammunition consigned to Franco poured into Portuguese ports and were hurried through to Franco's forces without inspection at customs. Later deliveries were made openly through Cádiz, Vigo, Pasaia, and Málaga. Bowers informed his government that in September 1936, some war correspondents had reported to him that rebel aviation consisted largely of German bombers and Italian pursuit planes and that in Seville they had seen German officers in the cafés. He added that all this was happening while British ministers were assuring the House of Commons that they had "no information" that any Italians were involved in the war when Bowers knew that the British Embassy in Hendaia was informing London to the contrary.[136]

Some of the documents I have found at the National Archives show beyond a reasonable doubt that the British, French, and US governments had certain knowledge and accurate data regarding the shipment of military supplies to the rebels by the German and Italian regimes. The memorandum of Charles W. Yost of the Office of Arms and Munitions Control to Secretary of State Hull is an extensive and very precise report on the presence of Italian troops and weapons in Spain.[137] The May 1937 report of Colonel Stephen O. Fuqua on British, French, and American civilians fighting in the ranks of the Spanish Republican army,[138] with a comprehensive report on the participation of German and Italian troops with Franco's forces, is also very accurate and admits no doubt.[139] Also, Colonel Fuqua's July 1937 report to Secretary of State Hull on German naval support for the rebel cause is precise and informative.[140] Although the Italian command ordered that officers and troops use war names or pseudonyms, the report submitted by Samuel Reber, second secretary at the US Embassy in Rome, indicates that US intelligence services had perfect knowledge of the identity of the Italian officers involved in the war. The document shows that it was known that the supreme command of the CTV was held by General Bastico, command of the Littorio Division by General Terussi, command of the Fiame Nere (Black Flame) Division by General Frusci, command of the March 23 Division by General Bergonzoli, and command of the Frecce Nere (Black Arrows) Division by General Piazzoni.[141] In this same sense, Ambassador Bowers's report on Italian participation in the war after the fall of Santander indicates that at least ten Italian generals were involved directly in the Basque front: Bastico, Perti, Roatta, Frusci, Piazzoni, Bergonzoli, Francisci, Biscaccianti, Velardi, and Manca. The report also notes that General Teruzzi, inspector of the Blackshirt units, and General Favagrossa, superintendent of supplies, participated actively at the front.[142]

Elmer Isaak accused *New York Times* journalist William P. Carney of "maddening insolence" in reporting that the loyalist cause was simply Soviet agitation, while the open and effective intervention of the Italian and German troops remained unreported.[143] According to the "reliable estimate" of the Foreign Office regarding the number of foreign volunteers and regulars of various nationalities in Spain at the beginning of 1937, there were approximately 100,000 foreign volunteers at war.[144]

The Republican forces also received foreign assistance, although much less than the rebels had. Colonel Fuqua, military attaché at the US Embassy in Madrid, informed the State Department in May 1937 that 1,700 US volunteers had engaged in the war, out of which 500 had been killed or wounded and 6 had deserted. A thousand British citizens had also volunteered; 600 of them were killed or wounded, and 35 deserted. Finally, 15,000 French volunteers fought for the Republican government; 3,000 of them were killed or wounded, and there were about 1,000 desertions. Fuqua indicated that the numbers were estimates, though they had been checked personally by the US, British, and French consuls in Madrid and were based upon the best data then available.[145]

But the war went on. Only twenty-three days after the Non-Intervention Committee's adoption of the observation and control measures, Italian planes bombed Otxandio, Elorrio, and Durango, killing more than 350 people in a single day. In April 1937 Gernika and thirty-one other towns and cities in the Basque Country were bombed by German, Italian, and Spanish planes. After news of the bombing of Gernika had covered the first pages of most newspapers in Europe and the Americas, Wolfram von Richthofen, executor of the bombing of Gernika, sardonically expressed in a letter signed on May 25, 1937: "The irritation caused by the bombing [of Gernika] is naturally absolutely unjustified, as here there are exclusively Spanish armies! In Gernika nevertheless, I behaved in a very rude way, of course!"[146]

We may conclude that the main purpose of the nonintervention system was to prevent the war on the Iberian Peninsula from becoming a world war. But preventing the dictatorships from assisting Generalissimo Franco was not feasible because their first troops had already embarked for Spain before the nonintervention system was approved in August. Furthermore, it was not possible to accuse the dictatorships of violations or to impede the shipment of war matériel without creating a crisis that risked leading to a broader international conflict. Consequently, the Western democracies had no practical control over German and Italian assistance. British and French officials obstructed, blocked, and covered up investigations into German and Italian participation in the war to avoid an international crisis, and they always denied or raised doubts about evidence presented to the Non-

Intervention Committee and at the League of Nations. They also lied to their own parliaments. German and Italian leaders identified this as a sign of weakness or fear, which encouraged both regimes to move toward war.

At the end of January 1939, two months before the end of the Spanish war, André Léon Blum, one of the main promoters of the nonintervention system, proclaimed before the French Assembly that the nonintervention policy had been an international farce and that the best proof of this was that the French had allowed the Fascists to take Irun, in the Basque Country, when only a few thousand rifles could have prevented them. However, Blum's complaints came too late.

# 2

## Terror Bombing at the Basque Front

Immediately after the outbreak of the revolt in July, leaders of the Basque Nationalist Party (EAJ-PNV)[1] and the Popular Front promoted the idea of an autonomous Basque government to stop the quick advance from Navarre of rebel troops led by Colonel José Solchaga against Gipuzkoa and Bizkaia. After five years of delays, the Republican government decided to hasten the administrative process that was blocking Basque autonomy, and the Spanish Congress passed the Statute of Autonomy on October 1, 1936. On October 5, the Basque government called for elections in the Basque territories. Because wartime conditions made general elections impossible, city councilors were given authority to elect the first president, or *lehendakari*, of the Basque government. José Antonio Agirre, a member of the Basque Nationalist Party, was elected by 291,471 votes, representing 99.96 percent of the total. One week later, on October 7, Agirre took the presidential oath beneath the Tree of Gernika, and the autonomous Basque state was created. One day later, the first Basque government was formed.[2]

In some respects, the statute was approved too late. The rebels had quickly won control of Navarre, and large parts of Araba had already been captured in the absence of any opposing forces. However, the rebels were unable to advance toward Bilbao as fast as the military and diplomatic situation required. In August 1936, the German ambassador to the French Republic, Johannes Welczeck, informed Admiral Canaris that supplies for the Nationalists' Northern Army were urgently needed, since only the Southern Army engaged in the siege of Madrid had thus far been supplied. The Northern Army required planes, bombs, rifle and machine-gun ammunition, hand grenades, and sidearms. In Welczeck's opinion, Germany's liaison with Franco was still not satisfactory, so it was extremely urgent to dispatch an expert to appraise the question of supplies for both the Northern and the Southern Armies. This appraiser should report to the northern group in Iruñea-Pamplona, where Colonel José Solchaga was in charge of the general command at the Noain airport.[3]

In September Colonel Solchaga's troops launched an assault on Gipuzkoa, on September 4 the rebels took over Irun, and Donostia (San Sebastián), capital of Gipuzkoa, fell on September 13. On September 25, General Mola issued one of the first ultimatums for the unconditional surrender of the Basque forces: "General Mola's troops have continued their advance westward toward Bilbao and they are 25 miles thereof. His ultimatum for the unconditional surrender of the city before midnight tonight, with the alternative of its attack from land, sea, and air, was not answered."[4] In early October, Mola pledged that the rebels would take over Bilbao within a week.

However, approval of the Statute of Autonomy on October 1 and the creation of the Basque government did allow the Basques to organize a civil militia to stop the quick advance of Solchaga's forces. The rebels' attack on Madrid, which began on October 18, diverted some of their energies; the strong defense of that city made its conquest impossible, but it also prevented the National Movement from sending reinforcements to the Basque front. By the end of October, Agirre's government had raised a force of about forty thousand volunteers, organized into forty-seven battalions representing specific ideological and political factions. The Basque government also undertook the construction of defensive fortifications in Bizkaia.

On November 7, General Francisco Llano de la Encomienda was named commander in chief of the Basque army. Llano ordered a coordinated attack on all fronts to take pressure off besieged Republican forces defending Madrid. The offensive would begin in the north, starting in Asturias, then proceed into Santander and the Basque Country. The objective was to push the rebels south by occupying Arbalan, Gasteiz-Vitoria, and Miranda de Ebro. The offensive, led by Commander Modesto Aranbarri, would also prevent the advance on Gipuzkoa of rebel troops from the east. Aranbarri's volunteers had to confront a professional contingent inferior in number but superior in training and equipment, and they had to do it without air support. The assault prevailed initially, and Aranbarri's preliminary military objectives were achieved, softening the siege on Madrid and checking the advance of rebel troops in Gipuzkoa. Basque troops then advanced south to Villarreal de Araba, where the arrival of rebel reinforcements and the National Movement's aerial superiority stopped them. The Euzko Gudarostea, the Basque army, suffered serious losses, estimated at one thousand casualties. The attack stabilized the front until the end of winter in March 1937.

After the defeat at Guadalajara and before the impasse in Madrid, Franco signed an order to start the spring offensive in the Basque Country on March 21, 1937. General Emilio Mola was designated commander in chief of the Northern Army, a multinational coalition of troops of diverse origin (Navarrese, Moroccan, Spanish, Italian, and German). Apart from military strategy, there were economic factors that convinced Franco to undertake an offensive against the Basque Country. As Ambassador Bowers reported to the US secretary of state, Franco had been paying Germany and Italy for their assistance with products from mines in rebel-controlled territory, but Germany was complaining about not getting the minerals it expected, such as iron ore from the Basque mines.

However, Bowers claimed that the assault on Bilbao had more to do with propaganda than anything else. The insurgents had continually tried to create the impression that the rebel government was fighting against atheists and Communists and that they were taking a stand against "the burners of churches and killers of priests." However, the Basque government, headed by staunchly Catholic Basque nationalists, was notably respectful of the church. The fact that there had been no interference with worship in the Basque Country and that the Basque church had remained decidedly loyal to the Basque government contradicted the insurgents' propaganda. And when fifteen Basque priests went to Ireland to combat the rebels' propaganda there, the Spanish Nationalist leaders began to focus their animosity on their fellow Catholics in the Basque Country.[5]

This was also the focus of the Italian command. According to General Ettore Bastico, commander in chief of Italian troops in Spain, the capture of Bilbao was of particular importance to the Spanish military command in general and in particular to the Italian government. The capture of Bilbao would allow a strong armed contingent of rebel forces to move easily from there to other fronts, and from a strategic standpoint, capturing Bilbao would give the rebels control of the Cantabrian coast. Bilbao, the industrial and mining center of Bizkaia, was also an important economic objective. Taking Bilbao would also resolve an important political challenge, the defeat of the Basque government, the only Catholic group fighting the rebel forces, and it would mean the defeat on the battlefield of strongly pro-independence Basque political nationalism. Moreover, the capture of Bilbao would lift the morale of the Italian troops after their failure at Guadalajara, and the surrender of Basque troops to Italian commanders would be widely used by Italian Fascist propaganda in Italy.[6]

As the spring offensive of 1937 began on March 31, the Nationalist attack on the Basque Country was led by four Navarrese units, the Brigadas Navarras, each consisting of thirty-five hundred to five thousand privates. The brigades were commanded by Colonel Camilo Alonso Vega, Colonel Rafael García Valiño, Colonel Pablo Cayuela, and Colonel Latorre. All of them were under the direct command of Colonel Solchaga and Colonel Juan Vigón, chief of the general staff of the brigades. Apart from the Navarrese units, the army consisted of Moroccan, Spanish, Italian, and German infantry and artillery units, each of them under the direct command of a unit officer. The Italian units (Corpo Truppe Volontarie) were initially divided into two groups, the Camicie Nere, or Blackshirts, and Group March 23, but they were ultimately combined as the Penne Nere, or Black Feathers, under the command of General Ettore Bastico.[7] Lieutenant General Alessandro Piazzoni commanded the Italian units at the Basque front, and Wilhelm Ritter von Thoma was in charge of all German ground troops.[8] The army was supported by a Spanish fleet and also a German fleet under Rear Admiral Carls Rolf.[9] The Spanish rebel air force was under the command of General Alfredo Kindelán, the Italian Aviazione Legionaria was under General Vincenzo Velardi,[10] and, as already mentioned, the German Condor Legion was commanded at this time by Major General Hugo Sperrle.

On March 20, Sperrle received plans for the capture of Bilbao crafted by the Spanish general staff. Two days later, he met with Colonel Vigón, General Mola, and the chief of staff of the Condor Legion, Wolfram von Richthofen, to discuss the plans. As Richthofen noted in his war diary on March 26, 1937, operations would take place according to conditions determined by him and Colonel Vigón: (1) Spanish and German military officials would plan maneuvers by common agreement; (2) German officers would oversee operations conducted by the combined Spanish, Italian, and German air forces; (3) execution of the plans regarding the air support would be in the hands of German authorities of the Condor Legion; (4) each morning, the Spanish and German officers in charge would determine the exact time for air force assaults depending on weather conditions; and

(5) the combined air forces would attack prior to the infantry, so that air raids would begin only when the artillery and infantry units were ready to move. These provisions clearly indicate that German officers could not choose a target without the prior consultation and agreement of the Spanish authorities. Finally, on March 27, Generals Mola and Kindelán met in Gasteiz-Vitoria to outline the last details regarding the campaign on the Basque front.[11]

Because the Euzko Gudarostea lacked an air force that had to be neutralized, the German war effort focused heavily on coordinating ground and air forces. One of Germany's main objectives in the Basque Country was to experiment with the development of a highly efficient strategy for cooperation between land and air forces. Richthofen was particularly interested in coordinating the Condor Legion's air strikes with the attacks of ground troops, devoting several pages of his diary to the matter of communication between planes and infantry units. On the Basque front, the diverse nationalities of the rebel forces created additional difficulties that required further coordination. The Condor Legion's information section, the Group LN/88 aerial information battalion, played an essential role on the battlefield by managing radio communications with the Spanish command.

However, German officers believed that the key mission of the Luftwaffe on the battlefield was not, as often espoused by Mola, bombarding the front lines. Many of Germany's primary war objectives focused on the rear guard. The basic strategic purpose of raids was, according to Richthofen, to destroy the enemy's sources of ammunition and food supply, to destroy its means of communication and interrupt the transportation of troops and war matériel, and to destroy the enemy's morale by terrorizing the civilian population. Consequently, the German air force not only attacked the enemy's frontline positions (tactical bombing) but also struck "local reserves" far behind the lines (strategic bombing), with no concern about contingent damage to the civilian population (terror bombing).[12] Thus, civilians would suffer the effects of bombings as much as enemy troops, especially when air attacks were focused on the principal villages, towns, and cities of the Basque lands.

As outlined in 1933 by Alsatian nobleman Karl Ludwig von Oertzen in his essay "Principles of Military Policy," "If the cities are destroyed by flames, if women and children are victims of poison gases, if the population of open cities, located far from the front, falls victim to bombs and torpedoes dropped by airplanes, an immediate end of hostilities is then possible, and even a government whose nerves resist all will not be able to resist this for a long time."[13] Only ten days after the massacre at Gernika, a similar idea was sketched in the May 1937 issue of *Militär-Wochenblatt:* "No state today can decline to bomb open cities. Until now, such bombings were contrary to human rights. If we deny ourselves these bombings, we put victory at risk. Until now, the enemy's rear guard was left in peace. It could be done without disadvantages, since this territory was practically untouchable. But technology has given us aviation, with which the enemy's economy in its rear can be attacked during the war."[14]

The terror-bombing campaign against Basque villages and towns starting on the last day of March 1937 was meticulously planned. Using their observations of the results of German bombing campaigns in other parts of the peninsula, the Luftwaffe ordered large amounts of explosive and incendiary bombs. As reported by Luis Jimenez de Asua of the Spanish Information Bureau in Prague on May 19, 1937, between March 16 and April 10, 182 railcars transported five thousand incendiary and fifteen thousand explosive bombs (one-third of which were high-powered shells) from their production sites in Germany to the towns of Grossenhain, Röderaue, and Zeithain, about 130 kilometers from the Polish border. A special ammunition dump, serving as a depot, was constructed at Zeithain, and the bombs were placed there. An airfield was built nearby for planes adapted to carrying explosives and gasoline tanks. The work crews and guards at these facilities were rigorously supervised and recruited from the elite of the regular air corps. The personnel of the flying corps were very carefully chosen, and the soldiers and workers recruited to serve at Zeithain were subjected to a rigorous examination of their political convictions. They were extremely well trained and able to load nine planes in only twenty-five minutes. Beginning on March 18, large German planes capable of flying long distances landed at the airfield. Once they were loaded and filled with gas for an eight-hour flight, they left. The crews of the transport planes were not permitted to leave the cabin or show themselves to the personnel on the ground. Planes came every night, and transport was not interrupted except for bad weather. Usually, the planes left Zeithain at 11 P.M., and at 2:00 A.M. they landed at the Freibourg-im-Breisgau airfield. Then, flying over Switzerland and France under the cover of night, at high altitude, they went directly to Spain, reaching their destination at the break of dawn, about 7:00 A.M. However, after April 6 this system of transportation was abandoned because the shorter night hours no longer made it certain that the German planes would not be seen. Instead, they left Zeithain at 7:00 P.M. and landed in Munich-Oberwiesenfeld and then made their night flight in the direction of Italy. "The result has been the destruction of the open (undefended) cities, Durango, Eibar, and Guernica, the death of thousands of women and old people whose savage slaughter has horrified the conscience of the civilized world."[15]

Mussolini and Ciano wanted a rapid military advance to restore the credibility that the Italian military had lost in Guadalajara, and Mussolini demanded a victory to feed the Italian propaganda mills. During a meeting with German ambassador Ulrich von Hassell, Mussolini showed ill-concealed dissatisfaction with Italian achievements in the war. Both Italian leaders felt that the shame of the debacle at Guadalajara would readily be dissipated by a new victory.[16] However, Franco's plans did not call for a fast victory. During a meeting with Italian ambassador Roberto Cantalupo on April 18, 1937, in the first days of the offensive at the Basque front, the generalissimo stated that "the work of pacification and moral redemption must necessarily be undertaken slowly and methodically, otherwise military occupation will serve no purpose."[17] As underlined by Paul Preston, Franco's determination to move slowly derived from his belief that there would be no turning back, not only from the physical extermination of political opposition but also from terrorizing the rest of the population into political support or apathy. Franco and, by extension, the rest of the leaders of the National Movement were conscious of the extent to which repression not only terrified the enemy but also inextricably tied those involved in its implementation to the movement. Massacres followed the capture of a multitude of cities, including Badajoz, Toledo, Málaga, Bilbao, Teruel, and Barcelona.[18]

General Mola ordered his troops to drop leaflets bearing his personal message onto Basque cities and towns: "I have decided to quickly finish the war in the north of Spain. The lives and properties of those who surrender and are not guilty of murders will be respected. But if the surrender is not immediate, I will devastate Bizkaia to the ground, beginning with the industries of war. I have the means to do it."[19] Mola also expressed his plan to raze the city to a British newspaper: "We shall raze Bilbao to the ground and its bare, desolate site will remove the British desire to support the Basque Bolsheviks against our will. We must destroy the perverted people who dare to defy the irresistible cause of the national idea."[20] The idea of razing Bizkaia generated more than one discussion between General Mola and Richthofen. The German officer felt that Mola's plans for devastating Bizkaia were "too stupid" because it made no sense to bomb industry in the Basque Country just days or weeks before those resources would be captured by the attacking rebel troops. But Mola's plans went far beyond military strategy. According to Richthofen, Mola was convinced that the Basque and Catalan economies were too strong and well developed, and thus constituted a real danger for the unity of the Spanish state.[21] Therefore, razing Bizkaia was not only a tactical or a strategic measure but a political goal: a unified Spanish state was possible only by completely devastating the Basque Country and Catalonia.

From a political point of view, the bombing of Durango, Elorrio, Gernika, and other Basque towns was the logical consequence of this policy of managing terror that Franco and Mola had embraced. From a strategic point of view, the bombing of Gernika and other Basque places reflected Richthofen's, Pinna's, Bastico's, and other air commanders' theory of *guerra integrale*.

## The Spring Offensive of 1937: The Durango Blitz

According to *Times* reporter George L. Steer, by March 31, the day on which the spring offensive against the Basques was to begin, the rebel air command had gathered at the airfields of Burgos and Gasteiz more than sixty bombing and pursuit planes, among them five or six of the new cruiser-bomber type, the two-engine medium bomber Heinkel He111, and some new light-bomber Dornier Do17s. There were two squadrons of German Heinkel He51 pursuit planes and a third of Italian Fiat CR.32s. Each squadron consisted of twelve planes, formed into four flights, of which one flight was always kept in reserve, so there were thirty-six fighting planes ready at the airfield in formation. Heavy bombers at Gasteiz added ten more planes to the total.[22] In light of the archival documentation we have today, the data provided by Steer were extremely accurate, since by mid-April there were seventy-four bombing and pursuit planes stationed at Burgos and Gasteiz, plus sixteen more Italian bombers at the air base in Soria, and twenty-five more fighters and two bombers in Logroño.[23] We also know now that sometime between April 12 and 17, at least five bombers, all of which took part in the bombing of Gernika (two Junker Ju52s, one Dornier Do17, and two Heinkel He111s), and at least thirteen fighters (seven Heinkel He51 fighters and at least six Messerschmitt Bf.109s) were transferred from the airfield in Seville to the Basque Country.[24]

German aircraft stationed at air bases in Burgos and Gasteiz could reach their targets (Bilbao, for instance) in approximately twenty minutes. Apart from the Group LN/88 aerial information battalion, the German air force was composed mainly of bombers: Group K/88, bomber planes—Junker Ju52, Junker Ju86, Heinkel He111, Henschel Hs123, and Dornier Do17 Fliegender Bleistift (Flying Pencil); Group J/88, fighter planes—Heinkel He51 and Messerschmitt Bf.109; and Group A/88, reconnaissance planes—Heinkel He46 and Heinkel He70.

The Italian Aviazione Legionaria in the Basque Country was under German command and stationed at air bases in Donostia, Gasteiz, Lasarte, Logroño, and Soria. It was composed primarily of Savoia-Marchetti SM.79 Sparviero (Sparrowhawk) and Savoia-Marchetti SM.81 bombers as well as Fiat CR.32 fighters. The Italian bombers stationed at Soria were not intended for service at the Basque front. However, on March 2 Vigón asked General Kindelán for the use of aircraft stationed in Soria to provide support for the spring offensive against the Basques.

On October 12, 1936, General Mola had predicted that he would capture Bilbao in a week. Eight months later, the Basque militia was still defending the city's frontline positions. Now, in March 1937, with a powerful army under his command and absolute control of the air and the seas, Mola's new goal was to capture Bilbao in three weeks.

By March 26, the generals had settled on the broad outlines of the attack, and on March 27, Generals Mola and Kindelán arrived in Gasteiz-Vitoria.[25] Their basic plan was to attack from the east (Bergara) and from the south (Gasteiz) toward Bilbao. After the first attack, the Basque forces would be forced to retreat through the Durango-Otxandio border. The generals anticipated that Otxandio, the Basque base in this sector, would be taken in two or three days. Durango, hub of communications for the whole Basque front, would be occupied in a fortnight, and the rebels in Durango would cut off most of the Basques to the east, in Udala and Elgeta on the Gipuzkoan border. Thus, the rebels planned to make a hole thirty-one miles wide in the Basque lines within a fortnight and then push on quickly against Bilbao's "Iron Belt." Pressed by the sea blockade and attacked from all sides on land, this main Basque city was expected to surrender by the end of the third week of April. The rebels would then control the industrial port of Bizkaia and its iron ore.

According to data collected by Steer, the offensive began with twelve to twenty thousand infantrymen (Navarrese, Spanish, Italian, and Moroccan), but the total rebel military would reach about thirty-five thousand men, since ten to fifteen thousand Italian Blackshirts would provide support. Along with the infantry, the attacking army would have a force of about eighty tanks, most of them Italian Fiat-Ansaldos, and some German vehicles, plus artillery.[26] A marine blockade of the Gulf of Bizkaia would be led by the cruiser *Canarias* and two German U-boats.

At the beginning of the war, the Basques had twenty battalions of their seventy-nine total (forty-five thousand men) spread over a huge front 120 kilometers long. The Basque artillery was only half the strength of the enemy, and, at the beginning of the offensive, the Basque army had only six fighting planes—Russian Polikarpov I.16s led by Felipe Del Río.[27] William E. Chapman, the US consul at Bilbao, recognized that the aerial inferiority of the Basque forces would be a key issue in the campaign. He believed that the Basques could not win unless they received a good number of airplanes to resist the enemy's formidable air fleet, which had been attacking every day that the weather permitted.[28] Indeed, strategy at the Basque front would depend to an extent on the success of the air raids. As Steer pointed out, so rapid an advance across mountainous country depended on the use of airpower on a scale not yet seen in the Basque Country—or in the world at large. A new airfield was constructed at Gasteiz-Vitoria under German supervision, and fresh orders for German pilots and planes—Dornier Do17 light bombers and Heinkel He111 cruiser bombers—were placed in Berlin. Hundreds of packing cases arrived at Gasteiz-Vitoria, containing bombs, machine-gun ammunition, and new Heinkel He51 fighting planes shipped in parts.[29]

The schedule for operations on the morning of March 31 was to bomb Durango with four SM.81 aircraft dropping eighty 50-kg bombs and Elorrio with five planes dropping eighty-eight 50-kg bombs.[30] In the afternoon, three aircraft carrying twelve 100-kg bombs, twenty 50-kg bombs, and fifty-six 15-kg bombs would attack Durango again. Then five planes carrying twenty-two 100-kg and fifty-four 50-kg bombs would attack the city a third time.[31] Finally, three aircraft would drop ten 100-kg bombs and thirty-six 50-kg bombs on Elorrio. Thirty-three fighters would provide protective cover throughout the day.[32] On March 31, the Spanish general staff placed the Italian Aviazione Legionaria, under Richthofen's command, in charge of bombing Durango.[33]

As planned, the spring offensive started on March 31, at 8:00 A.M., preceded by an air raid over the unprotected towns of Elgeta, Otxandio,

Elorrio, and Durango. The attack was carried out in four steps. First, the Basques' frontline positions were bombed prior to an attack by the infantry. Then the air force attacked the roads until all traffic was completely stopped. Finally, Otxandio and Elorrio, two towns where the headquarters of the Basque army were established, were bombed indiscriminately, as was Durango, an open town and a communication center between Bilbao and the Basque front.

Approximately sixty-seven tons of bombs were dropped on these four towns and the surrounding areas that day. The bombing of Durango was the most intense. At about 8:30 A.M., five Italian Savoia-Marchetti SM.81 bombers departing from the air base in Soria bombed Durango for the first time, escorted by nine CR.32 fighters from the Logroño airfield. In the afternoon, at 5:45 P.M., eight Italian bombers from Soria bombed Durango for the second time, escorted by fifteen CR.32 fighters departing from Logroño. The Spanish command decided to bomb Durango on Wednesday because it was a market day, and consequently a greater number of people were expected to be on the streets. Since the market was held in front of the entrance to the Andra Mari Church, this building was very seriously damaged by the bombs. About 256 people died during this first bombing of Durango,[34] most of them civilians, among them 14 nuns at the Santa Susana Convent.[35] As George Steer wrote, this was the first time an unprotected city had been attacked as a military target in such a way in Europe. Modern warfare had begun. In his own words, "It was a new method of war, more terrible than any practiced against Madrid."[36]

Three witnesses to the attack on Durango recorded their impressions—British journalist George Steer,[37] Canon Alberto Onaindia, and Joseba Elosegi, a Basque soldier. Elosegi wrote:

> I stared at a horrifying spectacle. The town was hidden behind a thick and dirty ball of smoke. It was like a dense gray fungus continually emitting fire roses from its base, widening the circle of the great ball. The planes seemed to be quiet in the air. They were like huge birds of prey and seemed to contemplate from the air the hell they had caused. . . . I had never before contemplated such a spectacle. . . . [T]he bombardment of a defenseless population was horrible, and it is inconceivable that there could be a man capable of committing such a monstrosity. Those poor people, who were not prepared and believed themselves to be far from the calamities of war, were now suffering much more than the combatants. War had no limits anymore, war did

> not respect anything any longer. The entire population should suffer equally the same burden. But how could the killing of women and children be profitable for the proper conduct of war?[38]

Richthofen, the architect of the bombing, laconically described the effects of the blitz in his diary: "Durango. Small and beautiful city, with beautiful noble palaces. Following a double bombing by the Italians, it looks horrible. It is as if the bombs had precisely sought out the churches. The great church, which at that time was just celebrating High Mass, received a minimum of six bombs, a church convent (the convent in true was a barrack for the Reds), at least four. Only the outside walls remain standing. It increased significantly the number of casualties in the church (it is said to be more than one hundred and fifty)."[39]

In Steer's opinion, the main objective of the bombing of Durango was to terrify the population and break the morale of the Basque army, which consisted of nonprofessional volunteers. Steer wrote what he saw:

> So terrible was the panic, so rigid the moral paralysis that seized the people of Durango: children, loved in Spain, unrecognised dead in Durango. Slowly the bodies were lugged out of the masonry and laid on slabs in the cemetery of Durango and ticketed 1 to 127. All blue in the face, dried blood streaking in thin lines from their nostrils and their eyes and the corners of their mouths to their necks. Mouths sagging open in the senility of death. Their hair and torn, dusty clothes matted with blood, and bones showing jagged from their crushed hands. They looked a fashionable congregation. They were buried in two common graves, and in the tombs of their families. Lorries took the wounded back over a bumpy road to Bilbao, where 121 more died in the hospitals.[40]

Durango suffered further attacks with still more casualties.[41] On April 2, at 5:00 P.M., three Savoia-Marchetti SM.81 bombers bombed Durango for the second time, and on April 4 Durango was again bombed by rebel aviation. But by then the town was deserted. The population had fled to either other towns or suburban buildings. Following Richthofen's idea of modern war, the bombers left the city's small industry untouched. Moreover, during subsequent bombings of Durango, the weapons factories and roads connecting the city were almost untouched. But the material damage was considerable: overall, between March 31 and April 4, Italian planes dropped about 281 bombs, or 14.84 tons of explosives, on Durango, which caused about 336 deaths, mostly civilians; 71 buildings were completely destroyed and 321 others damaged.[42]

The April 7 report of Captain Griffiss and Colonel Fuqua, compiled from rebel and governmental dispatches and interviews with witnesses, stated:

> In the Northern Sector rebel aviation bombed Durango about 6:00 A.M. Several trimotor planes escorted by pursuit planes took part in the raid. Many casualties resulted. In the Basque Provinces rebel planes flew over unprotected towns in our rearguard, dropping bombs and causing victims among the civil population. . . . [On April 2] Durango was again bombed by rebel planes. Shortly after 2:30 P.M. three trimotors dropped a number of bombs in several streets and on some buildings, causing great damage. Many of the buildings were completely destroyed. A short time after, more planes appeared and chose as their main objective the railway station, where many bombs were dropped. [There are nine lines here deleted by the censor.] The town of Durango endured a truly tragic afternoon as the enemy planes carried out several attacks, the last of which occurred at 6:10 P.M.[43]

In another report, Fuqua added that several rearguard towns, particularly Durango, "were subjected to terrible bombing which, in addition to the damage inflicted on military objectives, caused many victims among the civilian population."[44]

However, both Sperrle and Richthofen considered the opening of the offensive a complete failure because the rebel ground troops did not advance and the quantity of bombs dropped was considered small. Richthofen had a heated discussion with Mola—the first of many to come—in which he accused the Spanish commander of lacking "fighting spirit" and adequate leadership. Mola argued that Richthofen was unaware of the nature and composition of his troops (many of them volunteers) and was more concerned with the speed of the advance rather than the quality and strategic relevance of the positions captured. Mola also insisted that at least half of Bizkaia's industry had to be completely razed before Durango was captured.

The Basque government denounced the bombing of Durango in the press and on the radio. Lehendakari José Antonio Agirre also sent telegrams to the government of the Republic on March 31 and April 2. Accordingly, on April 1, the major Basque and Spanish newspapers reported the attack. Shortly after the bombing, the Basque government published a booklet entitled *Durango, 1937* in English, French, and Spanish, denouncing the bombing and its aftermath. There was also a wave of international outrage. The French-Spanish Committee of Paris issued a brochure entitled *Durango, Martyred City: The Bombing of the City of Durango by German Planes.*[45] In Stockholm R. Erikson published a leaflet entitled *Durango martyrstaden.* In London the Farleigh Press published *Spain: Durango, a Martyred City* by Isabel Brown. A pamphlet, *Durango,* written by Louis Martin-Chauffier, was published in Prague. Peruvian poet César Vallejo wrote *Redoble fúnebre a los escombros de Durango* (Funeral drum-roll for the ruins of Durango).

The bombardment was also extensively covered by the international press.[46] Steer's reports had a huge impact on the US and British press. On April 2, the newspapers *Asahi Osaka* in Osaka and *Yomiuri* in Tokyo reported on the event. On April 6, the Paris newspaper *Ce Soir* published an article on the front page entitled "A Sensational Document: The First Report on the Bombing of Durango." The article reported 300 deaths and 2,500 wounded and included a chronicle and photos of the bombing.

On April 2, an international commission of British and French observers traveled to Durango to check the status of the town after initial reports of bombing. However, while the commission was there, Durango suffered another attack. The commission drafted a press release that circulated at the international level, signed among others by Hewlett Johnson, the "Red" dean of Canterbury; John MacMurray, a Scottish professor of moral philosophy at the University of London; David R. Davies, chairman of the Labour Party's National Executive Committee; Margarita Biers, writer and speaker for the London Committee of Propaganda; and Monica Whately, a Catholic activist for women's rights and civil liberties and a member of the London Country Council.[47] Ralph C. Stevenson,[48] the British consul at Bilbao, also went to Durango to see the effect of the bombings. George L. Steer was in Durango on April 8 and described the scene for the *Times* (London).

Information about the bombing quickly made its way to the highest levels of government. Jean Casteran, French consul in Bilbao, sent a confidential report to the French minister for foreign affairs on the bombing, estimating the number of casualties at 130. The British government also received timely information from Ralph Stevenson, its consul in Bilbao. Ambassador Bowers sent a report on April 12, 1937, to Secretary of State Hull, stating that insurgent planes, flying low, had deliberately and with full knowledge bombed the church crowded with worshippers.[49] The US consul at Bilbao also sent a detailed report on the incident, stating that the insurgent planes had caused all the major damage done to Durango and commenting that he had received no evidence that the Basques or the "Reds" had destroyed property in Durango. According to Chapman, the destruction of Durango involved a plain-enough case of the ruthless bombing of an open town without any previous warning.[50]

Even Sperrle and Richthofen recorded their military achievements. On May 30, 1939, an article about the bombing of Durango appeared in *Die Wehrmacht*, the official magazine of the Ministry of War, for a special issue on German participation in the Spanish conflict entitled *Wir kämpften für Spanien* (We fought for Spain).[51]

However, the Spanish rebel government and its supporters firmly denied that Durango had been bombed, or at least emphasized that only military targets were attacked. On April 1, the rebel newspaper *Norte* claimed that the Basque government had invented the bombing of Durango to justify the high number of Basque casualties on the battlefield. On April 2, Radio Valladolid flatly denied the shelling of the city and even reported that the churches had been set afire by the Basque militia with people worshipping inside. Radio Club of Portugal denied that civilians had been bombed and repeated Radio Valladolid's claim that the Basque militia had burned the churches. General Queipo de Llano, from Radio Sevilla, asserted that the priests and nuns who were victims of the bombardment had died at the hands of the "socialist and communist" Basques.[52] More than a year and a half later, on December 4, 1938, Alfonso Merry del Val, one of Franco's attachés in London, published a letter in the *Sunday Times* acknowledging that Durango was indeed a military target and that the churches had been bombed because they were being used for military purposes. Years later, Ambassador Bowers wrote in his memoirs that the martyrdom of the little town of Durango was the most terrible bombardment of a white civilian population in the history of the world up to March 31, 1937.[53]

William E. Chapman, US consul, testified that many other small towns on the path to Bilbao were also destroyed, such as Amorebieta, which was heavily bombed. After the town's destruction, the rebel propaganda service immediately broadcast that the "Reds" had burned the town.[54] Meanwhile, Richthofen wrote in his diary on April 5, "Killed and shattered people everywhere, heavy trucks, carrying part of the ammunition, were destroyed by the explosions."[55]

By 1937 the people of Otxandio were well aware of what terror bombing meant, after the bombings of Otxandio and Bilbao in July and September 1936. However, none expected the brutality and intensity of the bombings that would come. The Otxandio region, including the town itself, suffered the first terrible air raids of the battle. It is believed that about a hundred tons of bombs and forty-five thousand machine-gun rounds were fired over the Otxandio area during the first days of the offensive. After the first bombing on March 31, Mola ordered his troops to advance toward Otxandio, but the Basque militia stopped them on April 3. After further intense artillery fire and shelling from the air, Mola's troops took what remained of the town on April 4, 1937. Steer estimated that from April 1 through April 4, there were as many as forty bombers over Otxandio nonstop every day between noon and nightfall. The Saseta Battalion, which was in charge of the defense of the village, lost two-thirds of its forces in the battle.

## Swooping Low Like Winged Monsters

Despite the initial advance, the results of the first attacks of the spring 1937 offensive ordered by Mola were not what he expected. A week after the first bombings, it was clear that it would take much longer than three weeks to reach Bilbao. On April 11, Basque troops even managed to counterattack and recover some positions around Mount Seibigain, which they held until April 15. The battles that took place from April 20 to April 24 at Mount Intxorta, near Elgeta, were especially brutal. For three days, the defenders repelled heavy artillery, air raids, and an onslaught from the infantry, even though they occupied a line of four peaks, 690 to 737 meters high, with no antiaircraft batteries and a remarkably light line of artillery.[56] From March 31 to April 26, the rebel forces advanced only 9.5 miles, an average of about 0.5 miles a day.

After their debacle at Guadalajara, the Italians feared another humiliating defeat on the Basque front during the 1937 campaign. The recruitment of troops for the Northern Army became a priority for Count Ciano, who informed the German ambassador to Italy, Ulrich von Hassell, that the rebels were handicapped by a lack of matériel and appalling aerial inferiority. This was explicitly false, but nonetheless Italy was sending seventy-two fighter planes, of which the first squadron of twenty-four arrived at the beginning of April. Ciano also wanted an estimated fifty German bombers to supplement them.[57]

According to Richthofen, a lack of matériel was not the real cause of the impasse at Bilbao. In his opinion, the Italians were unreliable and erratic, and Mola was incapable of leading the offensive. On April 2, during the advance toward Otxandio, Mola and Richthofen engaged in heated discussions about the conduct of the attack, and their relationship would grow even more strained as the weeks passed without a significant advance by rebel troops. On April 11, 1937, Richthofen sent Franco a report on the situation at the Basque front in which he underlined his disapproval of Mola's conduct. German ambassador Wilhelm Faupel declared to Franco that the stalemate at the front was due to a "wholly insufficient training of the troops and mistakes of the commanders."[58]

The Italians were becoming discouraged about their efforts to take Bilbao, and thus the Germans were as well.[59] As Faupel wrote after a meeting with General Mario Roatta (who acted under the pseudonym Mancini), the offensive had bogged down, and unless something quite unforeseen occurred, the rebels could no longer count on the capture of Bilbao. Roatta also reported that Franco had asked the Italians to give him the Littoria Division for the attack on Bilbao, in addition of the fourteen battalions and seven artillery sections already at his disposal. However, the Italian Supreme Command judged that even if the Littoria Division were committed, Bilbao could not be taken.[60]

What Faupel understood by "something quite unforeseen" would turn out to be the first instance of massive carpet bombing in pre–World War II Europe. The more unsuccessful the combined infantry was, the more aggressive and destructive the raids of the German and Italian air forces became. Steer reported seeing the first aerial incendiary bombardments on Sunday, April 25. Bombed to pieces in Eibar, assailed frontally from the east and southwest at Santa Marina Zahar, the Basques fell back toward Markina. Only the coastal corner of the original line was left, near Ondarroa, and orders were sent to the Basque battalions here to retreat at once before the road was cut. "It looked like the finish," wrote Steer. "Certainly the Staff did nothing to save the situation. It was only the natural discipline, the astonishing power of recrystallisation of the Basques that enabled them to defend Bilbao for nearly two months more. I do not think that any other force, led and equipped as they were, would have done it. Particularly after the morrow, when the attack was aimed at the village which was the centre of their national feeling, and destroyed it utterly."[61]

## The Purpose of the Attack Against Gernika

I have already mentioned the political and strategic reasons for launching a terror-bombing campaign in the Basque Country. However, these reasons do not explain why Gernika was chosen as the primary target or why a Basque town that would be captured by the rebels only sixty-five hours later was completely destroyed. Apart from the "logic of war," there were other reasons to choose a small town like Gernika rather than, say, Bilbao.

Göring needed to demonstrate the deadly capability of the German air force, an idea first posited by André "Pertinax" Géraud, foreign editor of *L'Echo de Paris*. On April 30, he published an article, later reproduced by the American press, stating that the orders for the massacre at Gernika came directly from Göring, who was "anxious to show the unconvinced German General Staff what his air force could do."[62] Germany was using the war as a training school for military airmen, and, according to Pertinax, Göring took the initiative in ordering that a town be destroyed in order to give a practical demonstration of what air warfare could achieve and to vindicate some of his strategic and tactical theories, which had been challenged by the army's general staff. But he gave no source for this interesting theory.

Today we have fresh evidence that reinforces Pertinax's hypothesis. According to an April 12 report on the Condor Legion air units, the legion provided thirty-five bombers ready for use on the Basque front: twenty-three Junker Ju52s (two in Seville), three Junker Ju86s, two Dornier Do17s (one in Seville), three Heinkel He111s, and four Henschel Hs123s. There were also twenty-six fighters—twenty Heinkel He51s and six Messerschmitt Bf.109s (five in Seville)—and twelve Heinkel He70 reconnaissance aircraft.[63] In light of the data provided by General Pietro Pinna on German air units on April 17,[64] we conclude that in the five days between April 12 and 17, at least five bombers were transferred to the Basque front (two Junker Ju52s, one Dornier Do17, and two Heinkel He111s) and at least thirteen fighters (seven Heinkel He51s and at least six Messerschmitt Bf.109s). Given that there were only ten Heinkel He70 reconnaissance planes in Burgos, we must conclude that perhaps two of these were transferred from Burgos to Seville and that seven Heinkel He45 reconnaissance aircraft arrived in Gasteiz from Seville or perhaps directly from Germany. All of these planes, especially the experimental squadron led by Rudolf von Moreau, came to take part in the bombing of Gernika, which was intended as a war experiment. Some pilots, such as Hans J. Wandel (who flew a Heinkel He51 over Gernika with Kramay on April 26),[65] arrived several days later, which suggests that some units that were supposed to take part in the bombing did not arrive in time to bomb Gernika on April 19, one day before Hitler's birthday.[66]

The operations of the Condor Legion during the war were being meticulously monitored in Berlin for any failure that could be utilized against the commanders of the Luftwaffe. The offensive that had begun on March 31 with the bombing of Durango had not yielded the expected results. Durango, a city that the rebels expected to capture just a few days after the bombing on March 31, was not captured until almost a month after the start of the offensive. Indeed, after three weeks of fighting on the Basque front, the ground troops had hardly advanced, and the Italian commander expressed concern about the mere possibility of taking Bilbao. Indeed, the Italian command was in dire need of a victory in the Basque Country after the disgraceful failure at Guadalajara. During a meeting in Berlin on April 2 between Italian ambassador to Berlin Bernardo Attolico and Göring, the latter expressed his concern about the failure at Guadalajara and showed Attolico a report from the German command on the causes of the failure, among which he emphasized the massive use of inexperienced volunteers.[67]

The German minister of the exterior, still struggling with Göring for control of the Reich's foreign relations with Franco's regime, saw in the slow advance of the rebel units a chance to undermine Göring's credibility in Berlin. In this context, General Bastico, new commander in chief of Italian troops in Spain, asked General Mario Roatta to meet with Faupel to discuss the political and military situation on the peninsula. Faupel briefed German foreign minister Neurath in Berlin on April 21—that is, a day after Göring met with Hitler to celebrate the führer's birthday, as he had duly recorded on his agenda. As Faupel wrote after the meeting with Roatta, the offensive had come to a dead end, and, in his opinion, "unless something quite unforeseen occurred," he did not count on the capture of Bilbao. Faupel's message to Berlin was loud and clear: the air units of the Condor Legion alone could not win a war, and, unless new infantry units supported the legion, the German air-control strategy would not give the results so vividly announced by Göring. In the same vein, Faupel mentioned that Roatta reported that Franco had requested from the Italian command the motorized Division Littoria for the attack on Bilbao, to be added to the fourteen infantry battalions and the seven artillery sections that the Italian command had already made available to him. However, the Italian command felt that even sending the Littoria Division to the Basque front did not guarantee the capture of Bilbao because the Basques had had several weeks to concentrate their forces on the northern front and reinforce new positions.[68] Faupel finished his report by saying that the Italian supreme command, therefore, was considering whether Franco's request should be addressed.[69]

This report forced the Luftwaffe commanders to act with greater determination. It is particularly relevant to point out that, in the context of the discussion on the morale of the Republican troops that had taken place on April 2, Göring put great emphasis on the effectiveness of bombing the Basque population with high explosives. Moreover, Göring stressed the fact that because the siege of Bilbao would be decided "by an optimal use of bomber units," he favored mobilizing two hundred additional aircraft.[70] Even more suggestive is the fact that Göring had scheduled a meeting with Hitler and other members of the German command on April 11, during which he had to face the criticism of certain members of the army, who were reluctant to increase the participation of German air units in the conflict—participation that everyone knew logically redounded to Göring's benefit.[71] Therefore, according to the April 24 report of the commander of the Italian Aviazione Legionaria, Vincenzo Velardi, on April 20 the German command set in motion "tutta la massa di Aviazione Italiana, Tedesca e Spagnola."[72] It was not a coincidence that the bombing of Gernika occurred only five days after Faupel's report was unveiled in Berlin.

After celebrating Hitler's birthday in Berlin on April 20, Göring stopped for a few hours in Rome on his way to Naples, where he remained for two weeks while his wife went to a health cure on the island of Ischia. The April 23 telegram of the US ambassador to Italy on the meeting that Göring had held in Rome emphasized the need of German and Italian commanders for a quick victory on the Basque front and the impossibility of returning volunteer troops to Rome and Berlin without a victory.[73]

It is in this context that the bombing of Gernika took place on Monday, April 26. We will not review in this chapter the strategic doctrines and tactics that German and Italian commanders discussed and agreed on during the campaign in the Basque Country, but we can say that in mid-April 1937, Sperrle, Richthofen, Bastico, and Pinna thought that the war on the Basque front was being conducted in an "overly humanitarian way" and advocated ending the war with a blow, a "colpo decisive," or "un successo rápido e decisivo" (a quick and decisive incident).[74] What Faupel understood as "something quite unforeseen" was going to become the first case of massive saturation bombing in prewar Europe. As said, the less successful the combined infantry advance against Bilbao was, the more aggressive and destructive the raids against Basque cities, towns, and villages were becoming.

Presumably, aerial photographs of the bombing and those taken in Gernika itself after the town was captured by the rebels pleasantly impressed Hitler, although they would have been more helpful if the bombing had taken place a week earlier, before his birthday. In any event, the parade for the celebration of the führer's birthday was delayed a week and took place in Berlin on April 26, the same day Gernika was bombed.[75] In 1939 Göring orchestrated the delay of Hitler's birthday celebration from April to June, to make it coincide with victory parades in Hamburg and Berlin in honor of the Condor Legion, when Richthofen and the rest of the commanders of the legion were received with honors by Hitler.

It is important to note that Blomberg was not informed of the bombing, which placed him in a difficult position with Hitler, because as commanding general of the armed forces he was not aware of an attack of such magnitude, which demonstrated his marked lack of control over the course of the war. The Foreign Ministry retaliated by emphasizing in Berlin the difficult diplomatic maneuvers that the bombing of Gernika had forced them to perform with the Non-Intervention Committee in London, which further distanced Neurath, Faupel, and Ribbentrop from Göring.

Nevertheless, we have to point out that Göring probably knew nothing about Gernika itself. He only wanted to be able to show the picture of a town completely destroyed by the action of the air force as proof that this deadly capability was exclusive to the Luftwaffe, not the artillery or navy. Therefore, Gernika must have been selected as a target by someone at the front, someone who knew about the location of the town and the symbolic relevance of the "sacred city of the Basques."

There has been much debate about the origin of the attack in order to establish responsibility for the bombing of Gernika. Jesús Salas, Vicente Talón, and Ricardo de la Cierva have defended the idea that the bombing of Gernika was an action taken unilaterally by the Germans, without the assistance of General Franco and Emilio Mola. De la Cierva claimed that none of the Spanish commanders "had prior knowledge of the German action on the city."[76] But documents indicate that all decisions of the commanders of the Condor Legion had to be made in agreement with the Spanish command.

As indicated, Sperrle received the plans for the capture of Bilbao prepared by the Spanish command on March 20, 1937. For administrative and logistical support, commanders of the legion depended on the command center of the Luftwaffe in Berlin. However, as part of the legion's partnership agreement with the rebels, it was agreed that for all matters relating to the operation of the war, the legion commander and chief of staff had direct access to General Franco, his general staff, and adjuncts.[77] On March 26, it was agreed with Colonel Juan Vigón that every morning the Spanish and German commanders would determine, by agreement, the schedule and nature of the day's raids, depending on weather conditions. The air attacks would take place only after receiving news from artillery commanders indicating that the artillery fire was ready and only after the infantry commanders indicated that ground units were in position and ready to attack. Rebel troops were required to wear white marks on their backs and to march waving the Spanish national flag, in order to prevent casualties among them.[78] In sum, as Richthofen underscored in his war diary on March 26, 1937, operations should always take place according to the conditions agreed between him and Colonel Vigón, chief of staff of the Navarrese brigades led by General José Solchaga.

It is clear, therefore, that the German command could not choose to attack a target without prior consultation with and the agreement of the Spanish general command. The errors that occurred at the beginning of the offensive on the Basque Country, as recorded by Richthofen in his diary, indicate that this modus operandi was not only a chain-of-command requirement but also a strategic necessity, because air operations were under the control of General Mola.

Richthofen was in constant contact with the commanders of the Spanish units (Emilio Mola and Juan Vigón), the commander of the Spanish air force (Alfredo Kindelán), and the Italian air command (Vincenzo Velardi). Velardi himself was very explicit in his report of May 6 that in relation to the bombings and use of fighters, from March 30 until almost the end of April the Italian command used its air units in close agreement with and under the direct command of the Spanish Northern Army and the command of the German Condor Legion.[79] A telegram signed on June 24, 1937, by General Bastico, commander of the CTV, stated that the Italian air force continued bombing cities and industrial centers "following the orders of the Spanish command."[80]

A report dated February 10, 1937, from the military attaché at the Italian Embassy in Berlin, Colonel E. L. Marras, states that the Italian-German air command was not independent and required the coordination of General

Franco and Sperrle. Sperrle, as commander in chief of the German forces on the peninsula, was to be considered "il consigliere militare responsabile di Franco" (Franco's military adviser) and not "uno stato maggiore independente da detto comandante" (an independent chief of staff). The document reveals that any action required General Franco's approval because, "in order to ensure the unity of criteria of the German and Italian General Staff, the two staffs have to deal strictly in accordance" with Franco's orders.[81]

In sum, the German command depended upon Franco. The liaison between the German command and Franco was chief of the general staff Richthofen or Sperrle himself. Colonel Funk was in charge of "staff liaison" with the Italian units. As a consequence, the decision to bomb towns such as Durango and Gernika had to be made by the Spanish command (Franco and Mola) with the mutual agreement of the Spanish and German commanders (Kindelán, Sperrle, and Richthofen) and with the acquiescence of the Italian air command (Bastico and Velardi). An example of this procedure is the order of March 29, 1937, indicating that on March 31, the German air force had to act in close collaboration with the Spanish ground forces. Richthofen wrote in his diary that Mola himself ordered the bombing of Galdakao on April 9. The same can be said about the actions that took place on the morning of April 26, when German and Italian planes bombed and strafed Munitibar and other nearby areas. This is particularly evident in the case of Gernika, which focused on a single target most of the rebel air units for the whole northern front and 20 percent of the planes in the entire Iberian Peninsula in April 1937. Richthofen recorded that he went to Bergara on the night of April 25 but could not find Vigón, and they agreed to meet the next morning at 7:00 A.M. Vigón spoke by phone with Richthofen at 6:00 the next morning and met with him in Bergara one hour later to work out the details of the operations that would take place that day, among them the bombing of Gernika. Nothing in this proceeding indicates that the Spanish or the German command followed an unusual modus operandi or that Richthofen or Vigón decided not to report to their superiors about the operations, schedules, and number of aircraft and bombs to be used and the designation of the units to be mobilized.

It has been argued as evidence that Franco did not give the order to bomb Gernika that there is no written order signed by Franco. This implies that all orders were passed in writing, which is far from certain, but it should also be noted that there is no written order signed by any of the German or Italian commanders, either. With respect to the chain of command, the order for the attack on Gernika or any other military action went through several echelons. Franco was at the top of the pyramid of command, so orders were transmitted directly by him or were agreed between Franco and Mola. Mola, acting commander of the Spanish Northern Army, transmitted orders to Colonel Vigón, who coordinated air actions with Richthofen and, if necessary, also with General Kindelán. Vigón in turn transmitted the information to the commanders of the ground units. Richthofen in turn informed Sperrle and ordered his men at the airfields in Burgos and Gasteiz and the Italian air control (General Velardi) how and where to attack. From this point, the Italian command communicated orders directly to their field officers at the airfields in Soria and Gasteiz. And the respective field officers transmitted the orders to the heads of the air squadrons. From all of this chain of command, we have documentary evidence of only the last step—that is, the order of the Italian air command to their pilots in Soria (we do not have the order to the Italian fighter pilots stationed in Gasteiz).

Moreover, as stated in the letter that Richthofen wrote to Kindelán on August 9, 1937, the order to attack Gernika was given to the various units by teletype on April 26 at 14:45. We do not have these teletypes or the order sent to the command of the Italian air force. However, Ferdinando Pedriali, pilot of the Aviazione Legionaria, stated that "the Spanish commanders requested the Italian intervention. The air units of the air base in Soria were alerted and, since the aircraft were ready for action, they intervened before the aircraft of the Condor Legion did."[82] Furthermore, the telegram from the headquarters in Salamanca to General Sperrle of May 7, 1937, indicates that the order to bomb Gernika came from the commander of the Spanish ground units: "Frontline units directly asked cross road to be bombed, [and the bombing was] carried out by German and Italian air units and, owing to the lack of visibility due to fumes and dust clouds, planes bombed the village."[83] There is a telegram from General Carlo Bossi, former consul general of Italy in Barcelona, dated April 27, in which he states that Franco had ordered that statements by Basque president José Antonio Agirre regarding the aerial bombardment of the "sacred place of the Basques" be denied. According to Bossi, Franco also ordered a fierce denunciation of the "Reds'" systematic burning of all urban centers before their retreat.[84] This document shows that Franco knew of the bombardment only hours after it happened, on April 27, at least by 7:00 A.M., the time the telegram was sent. Moreover, he had already decided to deny the bombing.

Consequently, although there is no written order indicating the direct involvement of Generals Franco and Mola (or of Göring and Sperrle) in the bombing, it is hard to believe that they had no certain and detailed knowledge of the operation, which would entail accepting that both Richthofen and Vigón had decided not to inform their superiors, as was required, of which, again, there is no evidence. Moreover, there is no reason to suppose that Franco and Mola expressed objections to such actions. Mola had no strategic or ideological reason for refusing a full-scale bombing, which he never did before or after the attack on Gernika. Mola and Richthofen had repeatedly discussed the destruction of cities, towns, and industrial plants in Bizkaia. The bombings of Elorrio, Otxandio, and Durango, as well as the sixty tons of bombs dropped in a single day on Mount Sebigain, constitute a precedent in this regard. And it was Mola who threatened before and after the bombing of Gernika in unambiguous terms that he would "sweep Bizkaia to the ground" if the Basque government did not surrender its troops.[85] As Natividad Apraiz and Juan Zabala recalled after the bombing of Durango, General Queipo de Llano had announced on the radio that the Spanish national aviation would render Gernika "flatter than my last name."[86]

The lack of a written order to bomb Gernika is no indication that something happened out of the ordinary on April 26. In fact, there are few direct orders involving Franco in this or other bombings on the Basque front between March 31 and June 19, 1937. Under this criterion, we would have to conclude that Franco had barely any knowledge of the bombings that took place throughout the war. Moreover, this was not the only time that the press or the diplomatic and military representatives exonerated General Franco of ordering bombings. Such is the case of the bombing of Barcelona on March 16–20, 1938. On that occasion, Eberhard von Stohrer, the German ambassador in Salamanca, declared that these bombings, which had mobilized dozens of planes for five days, were an operation organized and executed by the Italians on their own, acting in disregard of Franco. This claim was false, since we have documentary evidence that shows the participation of German air units during such attacks.[87]

Gernika was selected as a target for six main reasons. First, the town was the appropriate size, large enough to be a suitable target and small enough to be destroyed by the number of planes available at the time. The destruction of a city the size of Bilbao was not possible with the bombers at Richthofen's disposal on the Basque front at the end of April 1937 (roughly fifty, including Italian and Spanish units). In addition, it would have been diplomatically inappropriate to destroy Bilbao, taking into account that the Germans were part of the nonintervention system. By April 1937, it was predictable that a large-scale terror attack against a major city like Bilbao would have generated a highly negative public reaction at the international level. Consequently, the target had to be relatively small in size.

Second, Monday was the weekly market day in Gernika, so the streets were bound to be crowded, which would allow the Germans to test the effectiveness of air-ground strafing. According to the census of July 1936, Gernika was a town of 5,630 residents.[88] Gonzalo Cardenas estimated 6,000 residents in Gernika,[89] and the Memory for the Reconstruction of Gernika of the General Department of Devastated Regions estimated that Gernika had 5,075 inhabitants in 1930 and 6,234 in 1936,[90] not including approximately 3,000 refugees who had come there from towns near the front line. Jose Labauria, mayor of Gernika, calculated a total population of 10,000 to 12,000 people in Gernika on April 26, 1937,[91] because it was considered a safe area, well away from the front and the seat of the weekly market of the area, which ensured a good source of food for refugees, wounded soldiers, and reserves. Also, Gernika was on one of the secondary roads used by refugees fleeing to Bilbao from the Markina or Lekeitio areas. Labauria added that "we installed a welfare service at the Sociedad Gernikesa. There we fed over 400 people daily. Many others . . . were staying in rooms requisitioned by the Councils of Defense at first, and by me as the Mayor of Gernika after the Councils of Defense were disbanded. Many people were taken in by families and charitable patriots at their homes: there were families who welcomed in their homes three and up to four people coming from Gipuzkoa."[92]

The data provided by Labauria are corroborated by numerous witnesses. President Agirre told the Agence Espagne special correspondent that Gernika had 10,000 people on April 26.[93] George Steer estimated that there were about that number of people in the town that day, and Noel Monks and Christopher Holme agreed with this figure.[94] The special envoy of the Havas Agency calculated the same number.[95] British consul at Bilbao Ralph C. Stevenson also estimated that this was the actual population of Gernika that day.[96] Alberto Onaindia estimated that about 7,000 people were living in Gernika and that 5,000 more people came to town that day, including refugees from towns in the frontline sector and people attending the weekly market, or a total of about 12,000 people.[97] Four of the nurses at the hospital of Karmele Deuna also thought the number of people in Gernika on April 26 was around 12,000.[98] Maria Goitia estimated that the population of the town was about 13,000.[99]

Mayor Jose Labauria forbade the customary evening handball matches, but according to the testimony of several eyewitnesses, the market was held and handball matches were played throughout the morning. Many people in Gernika owed their lives to Labauria's orders. The *pilota* court was one of the targets for the German planes. If the court had been crowded, as it normally would have been, probably many more people would have died. Moreover, the Basque government, mindful of the rebel air force attacks during the last days of April, ordered Francisco Lazkano to visit Gernika and prohibit the market assembly. Vicente Talón and Jesús Salas have deduced from this order that the market was not held in Gernika on the twenty-sixth or that very few people attended it.[100] There are at least thirty-three direct testimonies independently recorded in 1937—among them the testimonies of seven foreign reporters who went to Gernika on April 26 and in the days following the bombing—that confirm that there was a market in Gernika on Monday, April 26, and that thousands of people attended it.[101] If we add to these testimonies those registered after 1937, we have at least one hundred confirmations that the Gernika market met on April 26. No direct witness has ever denied that the market took place. Moreover, President Agirre's order that the market be canceled was signed on April 27, the day after the bombing.[102] Indeed, holding the market was not an option but a legal requirement. On January 30, 1937, the Department of Trade and Supply issued an order requiring municipalities to "facilitate and recommend the biggest concurrence of farmers and consumers" to markets in their area.[103] The order stated that city councils should overcome any difficulties in supplying the people living in their districts.[104] The mayors of the district met on February 9 in Gernika and agreed to establish a Permanent Committee of Councils of the Gernika District on February 15, 1937. The purpose of the committee was to coordinate the interests of farmers, ranchers, and producers in order to prevent abuses and to ensure the flow of food in the markets and flea markets and encourage the celebration of these markets, seeking to favor the concurrency of producers and consumers in all towns of the district.

Even if the war had made some difference to Gernika's farmers, there was still good business at the markets.[105] In fact, one of the main reasons the rebels chose Gernika as a target was because the town was the seat of the weekly market that fed the population of a large geographical area comprising thirty-three city councils. Without this source of provisions, refugees would be forced to move to Bilbao, increasing the food shortages that were already battering the city. Also, Gernika was the seat of the main hospitals of the district. By destroying the hospitals, this area of the front was left without infirmary services and thus unable to help the hundreds of wounded soldiers resulting from the battles for Markina, Eibar, Durango, and Mount Oiz. That explains why nine-year-old Imanol Agirre reported after the attack that factories were the safest places to be during a bombing of the Condor Legion, far safer than hospitals.[106]

Another reason for choosing Gernika was that the town was completely undefended (no antiaircraft batteries protected the town), and the weather was perfect for the attack. It was a tranquil spring day, with the kind of conditions that German pilots called *Flugwetter*, or "flying weather."[107] The only defensive weapon in town was an old Czech Skoda machine gun that belonged to the *gudari*[108] Faustino Pastor, an antique from the Great War. That very morning, Commander Roke Amunarriz had ordered the placement of the machine gun on a hill. However, it was not designed for firing upward, and it easily jammed in this position.[109] The rest of the troops resting in Gernika, including Commander Joseba Elosegi, had only guns or rifles.

Most of the buildings in Gernika were attached to each other in closed blocks, separated by narrow streets, and constructed with stone walls and wooden internal structures, which would put to the test the destructiveness of the new German incendiary bombs. According to the Memory for the Reconstruction of Gernika of the Division of Devastated Regions, houses in Gernika were "mostly built on pieces of land 10 or 13 feet wide by 49 or 52 deep. The main façade [faced] the street and the back faced a 2.9-feet-wide sanitation alley called a 'carcaba.' All rooms were distributed between these two façades; the one facing the main street was the living room, most bedrooms lacked any light and ventilation, and the rear part was the kitchen, with no natural light but that coming from the narrow alley. The façades were made of local ashlar stone and the interior structure was made of wood."[110] According to the report, sandstone came mostly from quarries in the area (from Forua, Busturia, and Ereño), while the oak timbers came from the mountains of Jata and Sollube, also nearby. The day before the attack on Gernika, Richthofen had noticed the old wooden-structured buildings in Elgeta, all in close proximity—an attractive target for testing the new German incendiary bombs.[111] In the morning of the day Gernika was bombed, he visited Eibar to study the effects of the bombs on the wooden structure of the buildings.

Another advantage that Gernika offered was that it was only 14 miles from the front lines—specifically, 14 miles from Lekeitio, 12.5 miles from Bolibar, and 17.5 miles from Markina—so it could be occupied immediately after the raid, before the Red Cross or other international agencies could arrive to report on the massacre. In fact, the town was captured only sixty-five hours after the attack, on Thursday, April 29, at about 12:30 P.M. This rapid occupation and the presence of rebel troops interfering with the recovery of corpses and clearing the town of any evidence of the bombing are some of the reasons the number of victims remains uncertain.

The guiding principle of terror bombing is that the morale of the enemy population may be severely affected by air strikes, causing neurological disorders and dissatisfaction among military or civilian authorities, and consequently defeatism. The enemy's sense of powerlessness before air actions increases in proportion to the number of attacks, all of which amplifies the desire for submission among military authorities.[112] Gernika was one of the traditional capital cities of the Basques, where deputies of the independent republic of Bizkaia met biennially under the "Holy Tree" to legislate: Gernika was a symbol of democracy. As Steer pointed out, it was an excellent target to demoralize the population and the troops: "The object of the bombardment was seemingly the demoralization of the civil population and the destruction of the cradle of the Basque race. Every fact bears out this appreciation, beginning with the day when the deed was done."[113] The attack would demonstrate the impact of annihilating an entire town on the morale of the Basque army, a nonprofessional militia composed mostly of voluntary corps.

It is important to stress that, combined with the bombings, terror campaigns were nourished by propaganda leaflets and radio messages that—while making no direct reference to the atrocities that were being committed—emphasized the destructiveness of the air units and the impotence of enemy cities to resist them. Following this logic, on April 27 all three allied commands, Spanish, German, and Italian, requested the complete surrender of the Basque troops under the threat of bombing Bilbao in the same manner.

# 3

## The Market Day Massacre

According to Richthofen's diary, on Saturday, April 24, 1937, he held a "paper war" until noon, most probably to discuss the situation at the Basque front and to plan future actions. Although we do not know who was present at that meeting, it is unlikely that Generals Mola and Franco were unaware of what was discussed. Furthermore, it would defy credulity to think that in an operation involving at least twenty-seven bombers and thirty-two pursuit planes for three and a half hours against a single target—roughly 20 percent of the aircraft at the rebels' disposal and more than 80 percent of the German bombers available—the chief generals of the campaign, Mola and Franco, were not informed.[1]

Richthofen wrote in his diary that on April 26, he spoke with Colonel Vigón by telephone at 6:00 A.M. and that an hour later he met with him. It is highly unlikely that Vigón did not inform his immediate superiors of the meeting. Moreover, the Italian order of attack shows that it was issued by the Spanish command, and, as already mentioned, the Germans had agreed with the Spanish command at the beginning of the campaign, on March 24 and 26, that the Germans would not attack without the express orders of the Spanish command and that all operations would be coordinated and carried out by common agreement.[2]

The first air raids organized by the Condor Legion according to the new theories of terror bombing took place in March 1937. Good weather on Sunday, April 25, permitted the bombardment of several towns, including Erandio, Elorrio, Zaratamo, and Zuzazo, and "the Junkers drop very beautifully big bombs on Ermua [next to Eibar]." Also, Richthofen's diary entry for the day commented that "the Italians missed the target again and mistakenly bombed Eibar [a nearby conurbation of about fourteen thousand inhabitants]. It is a bit in flames."[3] This is an example of Richthofen's irony, common in his diary. The German commander visited the blazing ruins of Eibar, and what he expressed as a city "a bit in flames" meant in real numbers that 140 buildings had been completely destroyed, more than half of the total, including almost all buildings in the city center.[4] Despite what Richthofen recorded in his diary for April 25, it seems that it was under his direct orders that Eibar was heavily bombed on April 24 and 25; seventy-four deaths were recorded and ninety-seven people wounded, mostly civilians. However, because the Basque authorities did not have time to recover, register, and identify the corpses before the rebels captured the city on April 26, just one day after the second bombardment, the bombing probably caused more victims. Eibar was not completely rebuilt until 1949.

Basque soldiers at the front said that a "blue sky meant three motors." That was the case on Monday, April 26, 1937. At approximately 6:00 A.M., Richthofen ordered several Heinkel He70s to fly over Gernika and photograph the area to be bombed later that day. A few minutes later, he ordered three more reconnaissance planes to depart from Gasteiz—a Heinkel He46 and two other aircraft—to confirm the information provided by the first aircraft. Alfons Kössinger, one of the photographers of the expedition, later claimed that the reconnaissance groups did not know the purpose of their mission because information about the planned attack was severely restricted.[5] For the planners, however, it was important to have reliable information about weather conditions and the location of possible anti-aircraft batteries before almost every Ju52 at the disposal of the Condor Legion was committed to the attack against Gernika.

Only after examining the photographs from the early-morning observation flights, and after Richthofen had contacted Colonel Vigón by telephone, did the general staff decide to proceed according to the plan: to bomb and machine-gun the Basque rearguard. As indicated, no German aerial operations could take place without the Spanish chief of staff's acquiescence, in order to avoid bombing their own troops, as had happened during the battle for Otxandio in early April when the general staff of the IV Navarrese Brigade was attacked by mistake. The commanders needed to know when and where ground troops were operating and when and where air units were striking.

Munitibar and its outlying areas, among other locations, were selected as strategic hubs and circled on the map to be attacked on the morning of April 26.[6] The official aim of this attack was to stop the retreat of the Basque troops at Gerrikaitz. Also, the road connecting Elorrio to Bilbao, which links Eibar, Ermua, and Durango from east to west, would be shelled extensively because the rebel forces expected to capture Eibar and Ermua that very day. The decision was communicated to the chief of operations. Most probably his assistants Lieutenant Heinz Raunce and Second Lieutenant Hans W. Asmus passed the orders directly to the pilots who were assigned to fly the raids.

Because of the presence of German, Italian, and Spanish bombers near Gernika, the bells of Andra Mari and other churches and convents in the area rang out continual alarms, starting with the observation of planes swooping over Markina at 8:00 A.M. More planes were seen about 10:30 A.M. to the south and east, and starting at approximately 1:45 P.M., bombers were sighted over Munitibar.[7] Markina and Bolibar were also bombed. Gerrikaitz was attacked for about a half hour, a preamble to the forthcoming raid. These attacks caused heavy casualties. According to the report of the Basque government, during the bombing of Arbatzegi (Munitibar) thirty people were killed and twelve others injured, four of whom were seen by Steer as he passed through the town. Canon Alberto Onaindia saw several corpses in Munitibar and requested a battalion of *gudaris* to take them to Bilbao.[8] In Markina the bombers caused seven deaths and twelve injuries, and one person was killed in Arratzu and two others injured.[9]

George Steer was an eyewitness to the attack against Arbazegi after 4:00 P.M., when Gernika was about to be bombed for the first time. According to his statement, the raid left four dead near the church and two cottages in smoking ruins across the road. The bomb craters were the largest he had ever seen, "warm and stinking of metal still. They were over twenty feet deep and forty feet wide. They were moon craters."[10] While Steer was studying the holes, six fighter planes flew in echelon from the direction of Gernika and in a few seconds were over the village. They were so low that the pilots and every detail of the Heinkel 51s could be seen with the naked eye.

> Then they circled and spotted us. For between fifteen and twenty minutes they dived over our hole at full throttle, loosing off their double guns at us from anything down to two hundred feet. The only thing was to pretend to be dead already, and sometimes we wondered whether we were. Old Cor-

> man was spinning a long story about the ineffectiveness of aerial machine-gunning on entrenched positions, but somehow to-day he sounded much less impressive, and I asked him to be silent and to wait and see. It struck me, too, as very undignified for an Englishman to eat earth before the German aviation.[11]

By this time, Eibar, Ermua, and the Republican positions near Mount Oiz were about to be captured, and the Basque troops were retreating to the west, toward Gernika from the northern lines and toward Amorebieta from the southern lines. As planned, the air group of about fifty-nine German and Italian planes[12] commenced the attack on Gernika at about 4:20 P.M.

One of the most controversial issues concerning the bombing of Gernika is the calculation of the exact number of German planes that took part in the attack, mainly because we do not have the flight diaries of the German bomber and fighter crews. Most scholars consider the figures given by Steer, Monks, and Stevenson, among others, quite accurate—between fifty and sixty aircraft.[13]

The German K/88 bombers were organized into several squadrons:[14] a squadron of experimental bombers composed of two Heinkel He111s and one Dornier Do17 *Fliegender Bleistift*, led by First Lieutenant Rudolf von Moreau;[15] the First Junker Ju52 bomber squadron, under the command of Lieutenant Colonel Karl von Knauer;[16] the Second Junker Ju52 bomber squadron, under the command of Colonel Hans Henning von Beust;[17] and the Third Junker Ju52 bomber squadron, under the command of Captain Ehrhart Krafft von Dellmensingen.[18] The J/88 fighter squadrons were organized into two groups: the Heinkel He51 first fighter squadron, led by Oberleutnant Harro Harder; and the Messerschmitt Bf.109 fighter second squadron, led by Lieutenant Colonel Günther Lützow.[19] Major Robert Fuchs from Burgos[20] flew that day over Gernika with Knauer, and Hans Joachim Wandel, a Heinkel He51 pilot with the pursuit-plane squadron stationed in Gasteiz, also testified to having participated in the bombing.[21] Colonel Erwin Jaenecke was at the air base monitoring the attack and the effectiveness of the methods developed by the German air force.[22]

Sperrle and Richthofen had limited "auxiliary" Italian air force support to a minimum (three bombers, according to the Italian flight orders). In addition to the Germans' conviction that the Italian bomber units were inaccurate and unreliable, the German general staff felt that the Italians were not needed to carry out the attack. Moreover, the participation of the

Italian air force would generate additional coordination problems, even if they were under German command at the northern front. Finally, since the main purpose of the bombing was to measure the Condor Legion's destructive capacity, Italian participation was redundant and unwanted.

However, General Francesco Biondi later wrote that at least two Italian air units flying from Soria and Gasteiz took part in the bombings on April 26,[23] namely, a group of bombers from the air base in Soria under the command of Colonel Ferdinando Raffaelli and his assistant Guido Simini[24] and two more pursuit-plane units departing from Gasteiz under Captain Mario Viola and Lieutenant Corrado Ricci.[25] Thus, there were three Savoia-Marchetti SM.79 Sparviero[26] bombers from Squad 280 in Soria, piloted by Captain Stefano Castellani, Lieutenant Porro, and Lieutenant Roberto Fracaso,[27] engaged in the attack on Gernika. Three Italian Fiat CR.32 fighter squads from Gasteiz under Captain Viola and Lieutenant Ricci also took part in the attack, mainly patrolling the front, searching for enemy planes and machine-gunning from the air.[28]

In sum, while at the moment there is no documentary evidence to establish with certainty the exact number of aircraft involved in the attack, the available data indicate that at least twenty-four German bombers and nineteen German pursuit planes, three Italian bombers, and thirteen Italian fighters took part in the attack.[29] That is, there was a total of about fifty-nine aircraft (about twenty-seven bombers and at least thirty-two fighters, some of which made more than one flight that day over Gernika).[30] This represents a force of 127 bomber and pursuit-plane crewmen, a minimum of 31 Italians[31] and about 96 Germans.[32] To these, we have to add the reconnaissance planes that flew that day over the area (at least three Italian IMAM Romeo Ro.37s from the air base in Logroño and an indefinite number of German and Spanish planes from the bases in Burgos, Gasteiz, and Lasarte).[33]

The bombers and the pursuit planes came from three air bases: the German planes from Burgos (bombers) and Gasteiz (fighters) and the Italians from airfields in Soria (bombers) and Gasteiz (fighters). Gernika is about thirty miles northeast of Gasteiz, seventy miles northeast of Burgos, and eighty-seven miles north of Soria.[34] This means that fighter planes departing from Gasteiz could reach Gernika in less than fifteen minutes, attack their targets, return to their base to refuel and rearm, and attack again. Bombers coming from Soria and Burgos also had a relatively short flight to the target.

It required complex organization to attack in perfect order and successive waves. Air commanders had to take into account departing schedules (takeoffs), navigation routes, the meeting points of the bombers and fighters coming from different air bases, altitude of flight and bombing, timing over the target for the bombers and fighters, flight and bombing speeds, direction and speed of the wind in Gernika, return routes, and general communications. The chief of operations in Gasteiz and his team of navigation, intelligence, and meteorological officers coordinated all such analysis.

The route to be flown was similarly complex. Fighters and bombers coming from Burgos and Gasteiz met somewhere southwest of Gernika. From there, they flew northward over Munitibar to Elantxobe on the coast, then veered south to follow the Mundaka estuary and the Oka River to Gernika. The Ju52 bombers broke into the Oka Valley from the north, pushed by the northeastern wind, and swooped down over Gernika following a north–south path along the river and the railroad (except for the squadron of experimental bombers led by Moreau, which attacked from the east). Attacking from the direction of the sea meant that the planes could fly unobserved for longer, so there would be no time for the air-raid alarm bells in Gernika to ring.

Because there were no antiaircraft batteries in Gernika, the bombers could fly much lower than the usual 3,900 to 5,900 feet,[35] bombing without difficulty from less than 3,300 feet. Richthofen himself said that the bombers dropped their bombs on Gernika from an altitude of 1,968 to 2,264 feet (600 to 800 meters).[36] Today we know that the German and Italian bombers dropped their bombs from that altitude because, according to the meteorological reports of April 26, there were clouds at 600–900 meters, and therefore the bombers could not have bombed from a higher altitude.[37] The fighters flew even lower, well under 600 feet.[38] The strike was conducted in four carefully planned stages: a first bombing raid, an attack by the fighters, a second heavy bombing, and a final raid by fighters with a final light bombing.[39]

Everything started at noon when a Heinkel He51 fighter squadron composed of seven to twelve planes departed from Gasteiz to machine-gun the nearby areas of Munitibar and Gerrikaitz, where soldiers in retreat were supposed to be found.[40] This fighter squad was reported to be flying and machine-gunning for at least two hours (most probably from about 1:00 to 3:00 P.M.).[41]

As Steer reported, when the market was full and farmers were still arriving, the church bells rang the alarm for approaching airplanes, and the population sought refuge in shelters, cellars, and dugouts. A biplane Heinkel He51 pursuit plane dropped the first bombs on Gernika at about 4:20 P.M., near the train station, as witnessed by the *gudari* Jose Ramon Urtiaga, who was standing with *gudari* Antxon Zabalia on Burgogana, a 623-foot-high mountain above Ajangiz, a mile east of Gernika.[42] The *gudaris* Xabier Alkorta, Iñaki Rezabal, and Faustino Pastor (who shot at the biplane with a Skoda machine gun) also noted that the first bombs were dropped from a biplane that flew very low and released its bombs somewhere between the train station and Don Tello Street.[43]

A few minutes later, three planes from the experimental flight squadron VB/88, including two Heinkel He111s and a Dornier Do17, departed from Burgos at about 3:35 P.M., led by Rudolf Moreau.[44] Moreau, approaching from the east (Mount Oiz), reached Gernika some minutes after 4:20 P.M. and dropped nearly twenty 50-kilo bombs on San Juan Church.[45] Then two Heinkel 111s[46] passed (east to west) over Gernika and bombed Geltoki Plaza, the square in front of the train station.[47] They returned around 5:00 P.M. to the air base in Burgos, landing at about 5:45 P.M.[48] Also at 3:30 P.M., three Savoia-Marchetti SM.79s of Squadron 280 departed from Soria under Captain Stefano Castellani, probably escorted by the Fiat CR.32 fighters from Gasteiz.[49] They reached Gernika at approximately 4:30 P.M., minutes after von Moreau had bombed the town for the first time,[50] and dropped a second load of bombs (approximately thirty-six bombs of 50 kilos each) on the train station and nearby areas of the town. They then returned to Soria and landed at 5:05 P.M.[51] According to most eyewitnesses, these first bombers were escorted by fighters, and five Fiat CR.32 pursuit planes under Corrado Ricci flew over Gernika and the surrounding area for about one and a half hours (from 4:20 to about 6:00 P.M.).[52]

This first small-scale attack from west to east alerted the town's inhabitants, who ran into the shelters and stayed in them for about forty minutes. Indeed, the purpose of these first attacks was to send people under cover, to cut off communications (the railroad, the main road between the towns, and the telephone lines), and to destroy the water-supply pumps. The fact that the bombers did not approach, as later, from the sea, from north to south, reveals that the German command did not intend to take people by surprise with this first attack, since they were warned by the ringing of bells in the towns over which the planes passed on their way to Gernika.

In fact, as Captain Joseba Elosegi pointed out, the objective of the first attack was to drive the population into the city center.[53] This first bombing was of the magnitude of previous bombings carried out by rebel aviation elsewhere in the Basque Country, so after the first attack no one expected a second attack by a wave of bombers of the magnitude of what arrived an hour and a half later. Those who sought refuge in the shelters came out of them after the first attack to try to extinguish the fires and rescue the injured—that is, instead of fleeing the town, the natural reaction of most people was to rush into the city center. Most of the witnesses reported that the main targets of this first attack were the downtown area, where most of the people were concentrated, and the water-supply facilities northwest of the town, to impede the work of firefighters after the massive release of incendiary bombs during the second attack. Even if this first attack was not as lethal as the ones to come, several eyewitnesses described seeing pieces of bodies everywhere, mainly among the people concentrated in the middle of the square who did not have time to run to the nearby shelters. Fathers Eusebio Arronategi, Juan Jose Goikoetxea, Andres Untzain, and Alberto Onaindia took action, helping the wounded while bombs fell around them and pursuit planes nose-dived, machine-gunning women and children.[54] Thanks to the efforts of these priests and the *gudaris*, good order was maintained and more lives were saved.[55]

After a short interval of about fifteen minutes, at about 5:15 P.M., the second phase of bombing started. The Heinkel He51 fighter squadron in charge of this attack, which was composed of seven to twelve planes led by Harro Harder, departed from Gasteiz at about 5:00 P.M.[56] The Messerschmitt Bf.109 fighter squadron, led by Lützow, probably left Gasteiz a little later, at about 5:45, to escort the first waves of Junker Ju52s.[57] During this second phase of the attack, the population was intensely machine-gunned by Heinkel He51s for approximately one hour. The strafing took place between the raids, after one wave of bombers had returned to base but before the next wave arrived in town.

This second fighter assault surprised the survivors, who, believing they were safe, had come out from under cover. According to most of the eyewitnesses, the fighters flew extremely low and machine-gunned civilians from 5:15 to about 6:15 P.M.[58] However, as witnesses have said, during this time the fighters did not strafe downtown, since they were not interested in scaring people away from the city center. Indeed, pursuit planes began to fly around the outskirts of Gernika, circling the city center to hold the majority of the population within the "perimeter of fire" and cause the highest number of casualties among them. As Steer reported, "In the intervals people moved out of the town, but the fear of the fighting plane and separation from their families persuaded many to remain in Gernika. And then the planes returned with their tinsel tubes to shower over Gernika, and another part was destroyed, and more were buried in the refugios."[59] As numerous survivors reported, the fighters also dropped light grenades. Indeed, each of the He51 and CR.32 pursuit planes had six 22-pound bombs. Sheep gathered in the market were also targeted, as were their shepherds.[60]

Steer described this phase of the attack in detail:

> As the terrified population streamed out of the town they [the planes] dived low to drill them with their guns. Women were killed here whose bodies I afterwards saw. . . . The little fighting planes came down in a line, like flashing dancing waves on shingle. They burst in spray on the countryside as they merrily dived. Twenty machine guns working together in line, and the roar of breakers behind them from ten engines. . . . Always they flew nose towards Gernika. For the pilots it must have been like surfing. The terrified people lay face down in ditches, pressed their backs against tree trunks, coiled themselves in holes, shut their eyes and ran across sweet green open meadow. Many were foolish, and fled back before the aerial tide into the village.[61]

At approximately 6:15 P.M., the third phase of the attack started: a second bombing, on a much larger scale, in successive waves. Departing from Burgos, the first K/88 bomber squadron, which consisted of at least seven Junker Ju52s under Karl von Knauer, was given the green light at about 5:15 P.M. Immediately after, the second and third bomber squadrons led by Hans Henning von Beust and Ehrhart Krafft von Dellmensingen took off, also composed of a minimum of seven bombers each. The last bomber group took off at about 5:38 P.M. This time the bombers approached from the north, from the sea, so they would not be spotted until the last minute and would take the survivors packed in the center of the town by surprise.

Flying three abreast and covering an air corridor about five hundred feet wide, with a distance between them of four thousand feet, the twenty-one Ju52s grouped in seven waves[62] bombed downtown Gernika in successive waves, basically following the axis made by Portu and Asilo Calzada Streets. As reported by many witnesses, the Junker Ju52s made several passes over Gernika. Aurelio Artetxe noted that "the first wave of bombers turned and came over for another pass. At the same time we saw the pursuit planes flew at high altitude while the bombers were once again upon us. The gudaris kept on shooting at them. Then the second wave came back to make a second pass. Soon I lost count. The bombers were making repeated passes over the town while new waves were coming from the south. The sky seemed to be filled with planes."[63]

Steer stated:

> Fifteen minutes passed, and the people were coming out of their shelters. A heavy drumming of engines was heard to the east. It was what we called in lighter moments the tranvias—the trams—the Junkers Ju52, who were so clumsy that they seemed to clang rather than to fly. These were the heaviest bombers that Germany had sent. . . . Besides many fifty- and hundred-pound bombs, they dropped great torpedoes weighing a thousand. Gernika is a compact little town, and most of these hit buildings, tearing them to pieces vertically from top to bottom and below the bottom. They penetrated refuges. The spirit of the people had been good, but now they panicked.[64]

This second wave of bombers dropped heavy bombs as well as the first incendiary bombs over a period of about fifteen minutes (from 6:15 to 6:30 P.M.). The town then started to burn heavily. The incendiary fluid easily entered the cracks in buildings caused by the 551-pound bombs that had been dropped earlier,[65] so people in basements or underground shelters would burn or be asphyxiated. Indeed, nearly 450 people were buried in the shelter on Andra Mari Street, and 33 people died at the Calzada Asylum hospital when a heavy bomb crushed part of the roof of the building, which had a big red cross painted on it.

After the first wave of bombing, the damage was so widespread that the pilots could hardly see because of the smoke. As Beust wrote, the pilots could only estimate where the bombs were going to fall because of the dense smoke and dust generated by the flames, so they randomly dropped their bombs on the city center.[66] The German pilots called this strategy "shuttle bombing" and "carpet bombing,"[67] because the objective was to completely devastate an area by dropping as many bombs as possible within an aerial corridor in successive waves of planes. Adolf Galland, a member of the Condor Legion staff, described this new system of bombardment (although omitting any mention of Gernika) in his memoirs.[68]

One of the effects of dropping all those bombs over the many tightly enclosed spaces of the city center is that the fire within those structures began to absorb oxygen from the surrounding area and emit hot air, creating a deadly whirlwind that impeded breathing. Many of the survivors of the attack described "waves of heat." The high temperatures created by the fire generated a great lack of oxygen, and the destruction of the water-supply facilities prevented the intense fire from being controlled. Dozens of corpses were found in different points of downtown Gernika; those people had all been asphyxiated. According to Steer:

> All the windows were blown in by the divine efflatus, the wounded militiamen were thrown out of their beds, the inner fabric of the building shook and broke. On the shattered houses, whose carpets and curtains, splintered beams and floors and furniture were knocked into angles and ready for the burning, the planes threw silver flakes. Tubes of two pounds, long as your forearm, glistening silver from their aluminum and elektron casing; inside them, as in the beginning of the world in Prometheus' reed, slept fire. Fire in a silver powder, sixty-five grammes in weight, ready to slip through six holes at the base of the glittering tube. So, as the houses were broken to pieces over the people, sheathed fire descended from heaven to burn them up. Every twenty minutes fresh raiders came.[69]

After a brief interval, at approximately 6:40 P.M., the fourth phase of the attack started. After more than two hours of attack, once the smoke of the two first raids had started to clear, the last wave of Fiat CR.32s led by Mario Viola and Heinkel He51 pursuit planes led by Harder flew over Gernika from about 6:15 to probably 7:30 P.M., machine-gunning the survivors and dropping their last 22-pound bombs.[70] Because of the total absence of antiaircraft batteries, the fighters could fly very low, descending down to two hundred feet, strafing survivors who were trying to escape from the urban area.[71]

The task of the pursuit planes was to ensure that people stayed within the perimeter of the fire to be burned or killed by suffocation. Indeed, the purpose of this final phase of the attack was to prevent the reorganization of ground defenses after an air raid. We must remember that the bombing was a war experiment. Had the town been a military target and the civilians, the wounded in the hospitals, and the refugees been soldiers, by machine-gunning them the fighters would have managed to keep them within the limits of the city, which would have made it possible for the infantry to advance safely and quickly take the ruins of the city by assault.[72]

At approximately 7:40 P.M., with the approach of dusk, the attack concluded, and the last fighters left Gernika. Most of the eyewitnesses said they left the shelters at 8:00 P.M., about twenty minutes after the last attack.

The results of the attack were overwhelming.[73] Canon Alberto Onaindia, who witnessed the attack, wrote:

> I arrived at Gernika on April 26 (1937), at 4:40 P.M. I had hardly left the car when the bombardment began. The people were terrified. They fled, abandoning their livestock in the market-place. The bombardment lasted until 7:45 P.M. During that time five minutes did not elapse without the sky being black with German aeroplanes. The method of attack was always the same. First there was machine-gun fire, then ordinary bombs, and finally incendiary. The planes descended very low, the machine-gun fire tearing up the woods and roads, in whose gutters, huddled together, lay old men, women, and children. Before long it was impossible to see as far as 500 yards owing to the heavy smoke. Fire enveloped the whole city. Screams of lamentation were heard everywhere, and the people, filled with terror, knelt lifting their hands to Heaven, as if to implore Divine protection. The aeroplanes descended to 600 ft., letting loose a terrible machine-gun fire. I reached my car and just had time to take refuge in a small group of oaks. I have not heard of any inhabitants who survived after entering the shelters, neither of any survivors among the ill and wounded in the hospitals. The first hours of the night presented a terrible spectacle of men and women in the woods outside the town searching for their families and friends. Most of the corpses were riddled with bullets.[74]

The Republican Army's war report of April 27 was succinct: "Army of the North. Basque Front. The struggle continues on the Guipuzcoa fronts; our forces fighting with great aggressiveness. The criminal insurgents' artillery[75] bombarded some towns in the rear acting especially upon Guernica."[76] Much more eloquent and affecting is the account of Imanol Agirre, who survived the bombing as a young boy:

> The bells always rang . . . when planes passed over on their way to bomb Bilbao. We got used to it. That day, too, when the town was full of peasants and cattle for the market the bells rang, but nobody took much notice. Suddenly there were crashes. I saw spurts of flame and smoke coming from the far side of the town. To the shelters! To the shelters! People began to run in all directions in a wild panic. I ran with a friend and my uncle toward a small

> factory where shell-parts were made. There was a high wall we could get behind. Bombs were dropping without a stop; we were almost choked with smoke and dust. But no bomb hit the factory. Factories are the safest places to be, far safer than hospitals. My uncle called out: "Let's run to the fields," and he started off across the street. A plane swooped down and he fell on his side with blood spurting from his head. There was nothing to do and we were frightened, so we left him. Later we both ran out through the orchards and up to the hills where we sheltered under a tree. It wasn't much protection, but it saved our lives. The planes, five of them, circled round us for about twenty minutes on and off. We heard the machine guns rattle, but they didn't hit us. We saw terrible things. One man near us had been hunting. He ran across to take shelter in a hut and we saw the planes kill both him and his dog. We saw a family of people we knew from our street run into a wood. There was the mother with two children and the old grandmother. The planes circled about the wood for a long time and at last frightened them out of it. They took shelter in a ditch. We saw the old granny cover up the little boy with her apron. The planes came low and killed them all in the ditch, except the little boy. He soon got up and began to wander across a field, crying. They got him too. It was terrible; we were both crying so much we could not speak. Everybody was being killed, there were bodies all over the fields. We had to pick them up in baskets afterwards. A lot of them. After an age the planes went away and we went back into Guernica. It was all smoking ruins. I went to what had been our house and nothing was left, not even a piece you could preserve to remind you of your home. There was a doctor driving about in his car helping to pick up the wounded. I don't know how he escaped death. Sixty people had been killed in a half-built refuge. The airmen had played jokes, too, and dropped spanners and hammers. One dropped a wicker basket with food in it which hit a friend of mine. Then they dropped some leaflets. They promised us bread and a warm hearth if we surrendered. The warm hearth will be like Guernica, I expect.[77]

Richthofen described the macabre scene left behind by his planes as a complete success:

> Guernica, city of 5,000 inhabitants, literally leveled. Attack was launched with 250 kg bombs and firebombs, these about 1/3 of the total. When the first Junkers arrived, there was already smoke everywhere (from the experimental bomber squadron, which attacked first with three planes). Nobody could see roads, bridges, or suburban targets anymore, so they just dumped

> their bombs in the midst of it all. The 250s knocked down a number of houses and destroyed the municipal water system. The firebombs now had time to do their work. The type of construction of the houses—tile roofs, wooden floors, and half-timbered walls—facilitated their total destruction. Inhabitants were generally out of the town because of a festival;[78] most of those fled at the outset of the attack. A small number died in wrecked shelters. Bomb craters in the streets are still to be seen. Absolutely fabulous![79] City was completely closed off for at least 24 hours; that would have guaranteed immediate conquest if troops had attacked right away. But at least it has been a complete technical success[80] with our 250s and EC.BS.[81]

Mola, whose aim after the attack was to continue bombing, had a different take on the event.[82] "Bilbao next," proclaimed the general on April 29. The bombing campaign was a constant subject of subsequent Republican army war reports: "The insurgent's aviation force has continued its criminal bombardments with considerable intensity without pursuing in its incursions any military objectives."[83] But this idea had already been noted by Richthofen days earlier, on April 23, and carefully written down in his war diary.

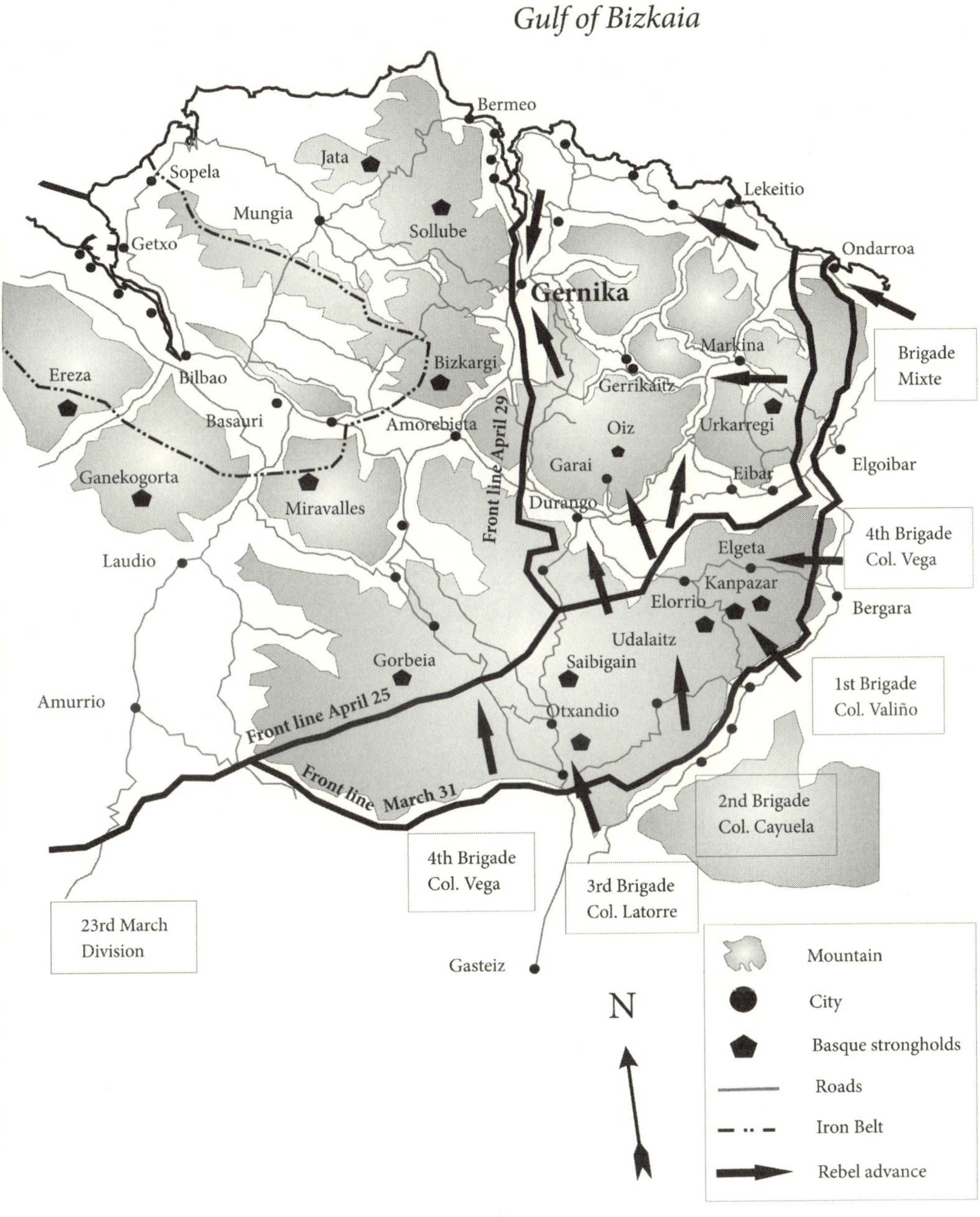


The Basque front from March 31 to April 29, 1937

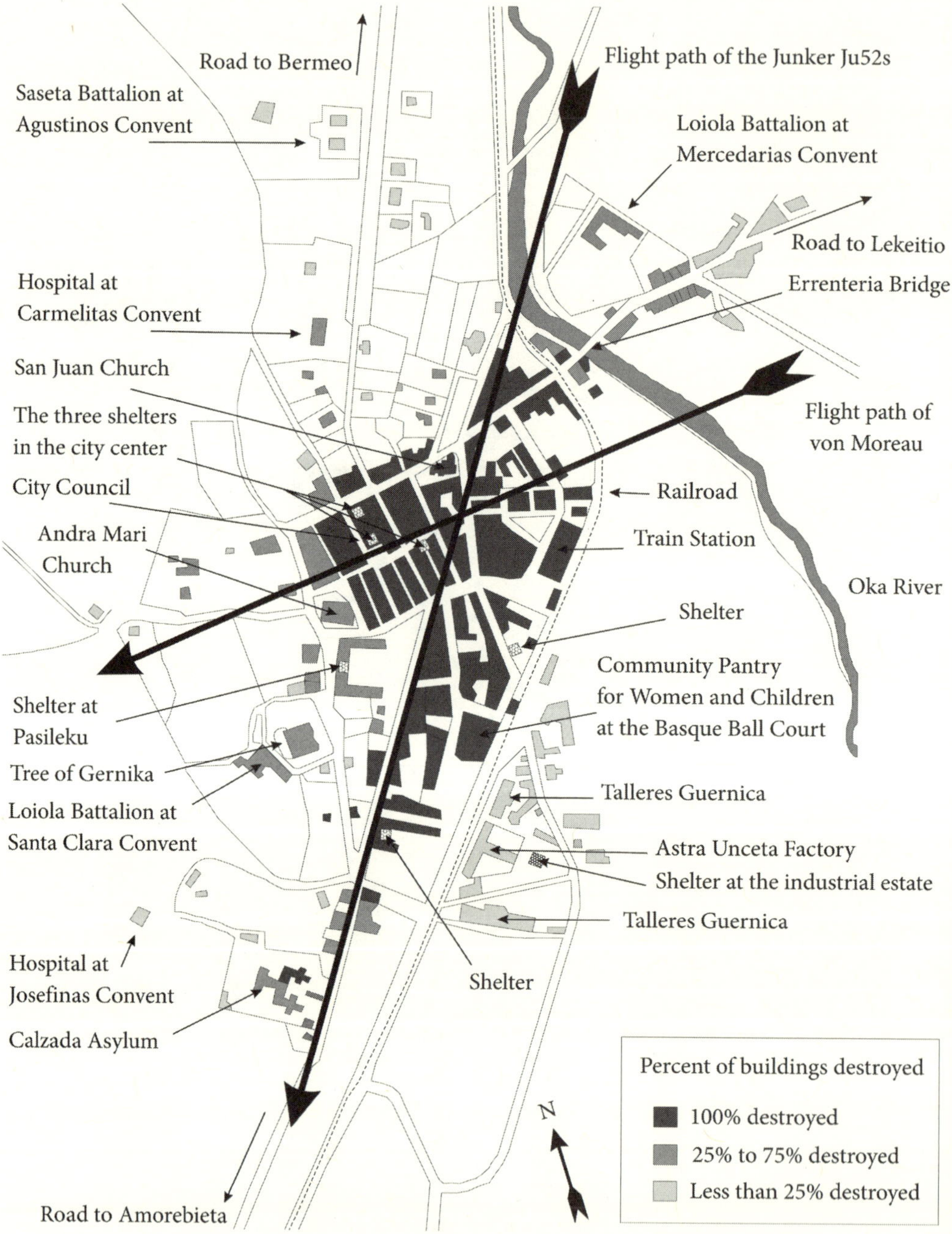


Map of downtown Gernika. Magnitude of the material destruction.

Basque children marching in Bilbao to raise money to buy an airplane for the Basque government. The main strategic reason for the military defeat of the Basque forces was their lack of airpower. Courtesy of the Documentation Center on the Bombing of Gernika, Gernika Peace Museum Foundation.

Air attack. People running to the bomb shelters after the alarm bells rang in Bilbao, spring 1937. Courtesy of the Documentation Center on the Bombing of Gernika, Gernika Peace Museum Foundation.

Panoramic view of Gernika before the attack on April 26, 1937. Courtesy of the Documentation Center on the Bombing of Gernika, Gernika Peace Museum Foundation.

Gernika burning during the night after the bombing. Courtesy of the Documentation Center on the Bombing of Gernika, Gernika Peace Museum Foundation.

Aerial view of Gernika the morning after the attack. Courtesy of the Documentation Center on the Bombing of Gernika, Gernika Peace Museum Foundation.

FACING PAGE:

*Top:* Ruins of downtown Gernika the morning after the bombing. Courtesy of William Smallwood.

*Bottom:* Street scene in downtown Gernika. Courtesy of William Smallwood.

View of San Juan Church and adjoining plaza where the first bombs were dropped. Courtesy of the Documentation Center on the Bombing of Gernika, Gernika Peace Museum Foundation.

Ruins of Azokaleku, the marketplace of Gernika. Courtesy of the Documentation Center on the Bombing of Gernika, Gernika Peace Museum Foundation.

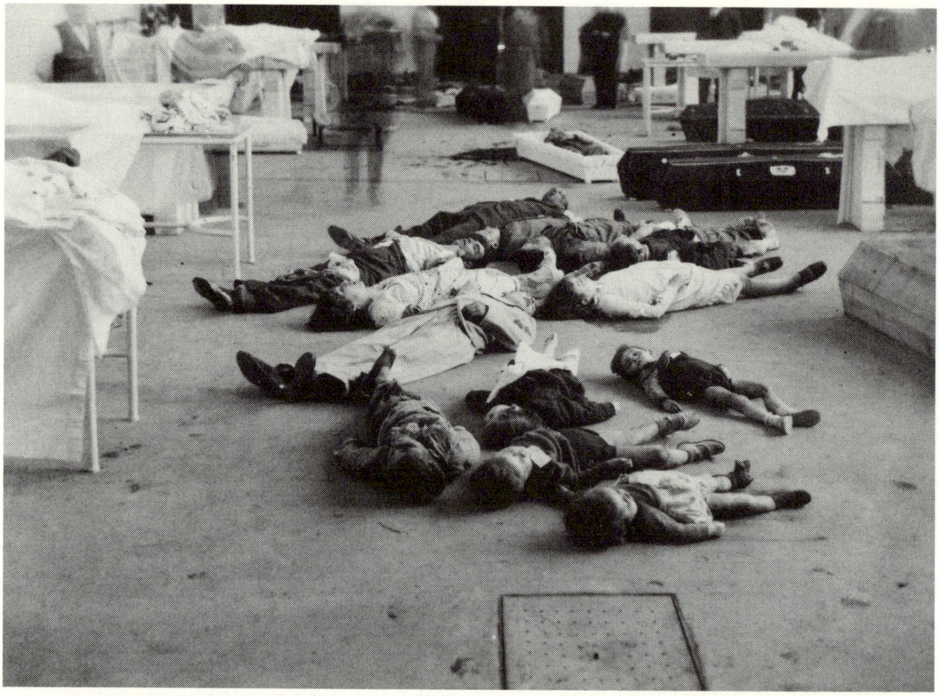

Civilians were often the victims of air raids. Here, the bodies of children and adults are laid out on the floor of a military hospital after an air raid. Courtesy of the Irujo-Ametzaga Archive.

Four eyewitnesses of the bombing of Gernika giving their testimonies on Radio Euzkadi in Bilbao on May 4, 1937. *Left to right:* Father Eusebio Arronategi; Bonifacio Etxegarai; the mayor of Gernika, Jose Labauria; and George Steer. Courtesy of William Smallwood.

The Tree of Gernika today. Courtesy of the Irujo-Ametzaga Archive.

# 4

## An Analysis of the Attack

It is interesting to study the bombing in relative terms in order to specify, with the tangible data at our disposal, the true extent of the bombing regarding the number of aircraft and the amount of bombs dropped. From this analysis, we can deduce the true dimension of what happened in Gernika on April 26, 1937.

Based on the April 10, 1937, report by the Italian air command and information provided by the American and British secret services, we know that the entire Nationalist air force in April 1937 consisted of the following units:[1]

Number of rebel planes by type and nationality in April 1937

| Aircraft | Italian | German | Spanish | Total |
|---|---|---|---|---|
| Bombers | 28 | 36 | 15 | 79 |
| Reconnaissance | 23[a] | 18 | 46 | 87 |
| Fighters | 79[b] | 30 | 25 | 134 |
| Hydroplanes | 3[c] | 5 | 8 | 16 |
| Total | 133 | 89 | 94 | 316[d] |

[a] Twenty-eight in total, 23 of them operative.
[b] There were 80 Fiat CR.32s, of which 20 were being assembled and 1 was out of service.
[c] Seven in total, 4 out of service.
[d] As noted, we should add to these 316 operating units 20 Fiat CR.32s and 4 Breda Ba.65s that were being assembled in Seville, which makes a general total of 340 units.

These data match the figures in General Pinna's report of January 15, 1937, in which he stated that at the beginning of 1937, there were 30 SM.81 bombers, 92 Fiat CR.32 fighters, and 28 Ro.37 and Ro.41 reconnaissance planes on the Iberian Peninsula.[2] Pinna's report of April 17, 1937, is also consistent with these data[3] and also with figures provided by US military attachés Captain Townsend Griffiss and Colonel Stephen O. Fuqua on March 16, 1937,[4] a memorandum from the Office of Arms and Munitions Control of the US State Department entitled *Italian Troops and Supplies in Spain*,[5] and finally data provided by the Fisher Memorandum of February 1937.[6] From these reports, we can establish with reasonable accuracy the number and type of aircraft in each of the airfields of the Aviación Nacional.

From the data provided by these reports, we can conclude that in mid-April 1937 30 of the 36 bombers at the disposal of the German command were stationed in Burgos and in Gasteiz and were therefore operating in the Basque Country. We also know that at least 2 Heinkel He111s and 1 Dornier Do17 were transferred to the Basque Country to take part in the attack against Gernika. That is, more than 80 percent of the German bombers in Spain were operating over the Basque front in April 1937.

The Italian Aviazione Legionaria had approximately 73 aircraft (18 of them bombers) acting in the Basque Country (approximately 50 percent of the Italian air force).[7] This represents 64 percent of the Italian SM.79 and SM.81 bombers under Italian command in the entire war theater.

From the data regarding the total number of planes involved in the bombing of Gernika, we may deduce facts of undoubted interest for the study of the bombing. Taking into consideration that at least 27 bombers and 32 fighters[8] participated in the bombing—that is, a total of at least 59 aircraft between fighters and bombers—and that the rebel command had 93 aircraft (49 bombers[9] and 44 fighters)[10] at the airfields of Burgos, Gasteiz, and Soria, we conclude that 54 percent of the bombers at the bases in Burgos, Soria, and Gasteiz[11] took part in the bombing of Gernika. Seventy-two percent of the German bombers at the air bases in Burgos and Gasteiz[12] and 18 percent of the Italian bombers at the air base in Soria participated in the bombing of Gernika.[13] At least 72.7 percent of the 44 fighters[14] stationed at the air bases of Burgos and Gasteiz[15] and at least 55.88 percent of the German fighters at the air bases in Gasteiz and Burgos took part in the bombing of Gernika. One hundred percent of the Italian fighters in Gasteiz took part in the attack. In addition, 63.4 percent of the total attack force (bombers and fighters) at Burgos, Soria, and Gasteiz took part in the bombing of Gernika.

If we consider the general war theater, the data are even more meaningful. Considering that the rebel air force had a total of 73 bombers and 105 fighters of Italian or German origin in the whole Iberian Peninsula in April 1937—that is, 178 attack aircraft—we conclude that 42.1 percent of the total

German attack force and 47 percent of the German bombers in the Iberian Peninsula took part in the bombing of Gernika. This means that 33.14 percent of the rebel air attack units of Italian or German origin in the entire Iberian Peninsula took part in the bombing of Gernika—that is, 36.98 percent of the bombers and at least 30.47 percent of the fighters.

If we consider only the units under German command—that is, the planes of the Condor Legion—the proportions are even higher: 66.7 percent of the bombers and 63.3 percent of the fighters of the legion participated in the bombing of Gernika. As regards the Aviazione Legionaria, 10.7 percent of the bombers and 21.7 percent of the fighters available to the Italian air force participated in the bombing. If we consider all the 79 bombers and 114 fighters under German, Italian, or Spanish command in the entire war theater, we may conclude that 34.2 percent of the rebel bombers and 28 percent of the rebel fighters in the entire war participated in the bombing of Gernika. If we take the total number of fighters and bombers—193 units—we conclude that 30.6 percent participated in the bombing of Gernika. Almost 1 in 3 planes available to General Franco in April 1937 participated in the bombing of Gernika. Finally, if we consider every plane available to the rebels, including the seaplanes, we conclude that 20 percent participated in the bombing of Gernika.

It should be noted that not all aircraft were operative, but all of them have been included in the calculations. In this sense, the appendix to General Pinna's report of January 14, 1937, states that out of a total of 24 SM.81 bombers, only 15 (62.5 percent) were operational, and of a total of 86 Fiat CR.32 fighters, only 65 (75.6 percent) were functioning. Of the total of 139 aircraft at the disposal of the Aviazione Legionaria in January 1937, only 103 were operational—that is, 74 percent.[16]

The extant German dispatches do not mention the exact number of bombs dropped over Gernika. The only way to estimate an approximate number of bombs is to calculate the bomb load that each of the 27 bombers could drop in normal circumstances. Based on different reports, approximately 31,000 to 41,000 kilos (68,343 to 90,389 pounds) of explosive and incendiary projectiles were dropped on the small center of Gernika.[17]

We also have evidence that the Germans loaded boxes of incendiary bombs in the Junker Ju52s, to be dropped through the doors of the planes. And these have to be added to the bombs that the planes carried in the ESAC-250 bomb carriers. Moreover, as Adolf Galland wrote in the original manuscript of his memoirs—and was later censored when the memoirs were published—the Condor Legion dropped barrels of gasoline through the doors of the planes together with incendiary bombs when it attacked Asturias in the summer of 1937.

Also, Richthofen mentioned in his diary entry of April 30, 1937, that the 2.2-pound incendiary bombs constituted only about one-third of the total shelling, which is hard to believe.[18] From the analysis of the data on the tons of explosives launched by the Aviazione Legionaria in the Basque Country in April 1937, we can estimate the scope of the bombing of Gernika in relative terms. The report entitled *Bomb Load Dropped During the Month of April in the Basque Country* shows that Italian bombers released 285,027 pounds of bombs, according to the following proportions:[19]

| Type of bombs by load | Total number | Proportion | (%) Total kilos |
|---|---|---|---|
| Bombs of 100 kg | 370 | 4.46 | 37,000 |
| Bombs of 50 kg | 1,543 | 18.60 | 77,150 |
| Bombs of 20 kg | 36 | 0.43 | 720 |
| Bombs of 15 kg | 56 | 0.67 | 840 |
| Bombs of 12 kg | 100 | 1.20 | 1,200 |
| Bombs of 2 kg incendiaries | 6,188 | 74.61 | 12,376 |
| Total | 8,293 | 100 | 129,286 |

The data provided in this report are quite revealing for several reasons. First, Richthofen stated that only one-third of the bombs dropped on Gernika were incendiary, but this figure does not correspond to the proportion of incendiary bombs dropped by the Italian air force in April 1937—75 percent. There is no reason to believe that the Italians used twice as many incendiaries as the Condor Legion during the month of April, especially if we consider that all the rebel aircraft operated under German command. Moreover, this figure matches the proportion of incendiary bombs launched on European cities during World War II, ranging from 60 to 75 percent.

The data for the month of May prepared by Colonel Porreta match the data from the previous month, showing that 88.53 percent of the bombs dropped were incendiaries.[20] Data for the first fifteen days of June 1937 indicate that 49.73 percent of the bombs dropped in the Basque Country were incendiaries.[21] We may conclude that the Italian air command ordered the release of a total of 984,254 pounds of bombs in the Basque Country between April and mid-June 1937. This represents a total of 40,543 explosive bombs, 33,550 of them incendiary, or 82.75 percent. The release of about 80 percent of incendiaries is a litmus test of the nature of the rebel attacks at the Basque front if we consider the main use of these bombs—the destruction of buildings.

In view of these data, as well as data on the quantity of explosives dropped by the Luftwaffe in the Basque Country, we may deduce that Richthofen was likely lying when he wrote that only a third of the bombs dropped on Gernika were incendiary. Such heavy use of incendiaries is difficult to explain when arguing—as the rebels later did—that the purpose of the bombing of Gernika was the destruction of a bridge. Accepting that about 75 to 80 percent of the bombs released were incendiary would be conclusive proof that the goal of the bombing was the destruction of the entire city.[22]

This disproportionate use of means was logically followed by an astounding level of material destruction. According to the Herrán Report, the village had 300 houses, of which 71 percent were completely destroyed (which the report estimated at some 213 buildings), 7 percent (about 21 houses) seriously damaged, and the remaining 22 percent (about 66 houses) damaged to varying degrees.[23] Many authors have based their calculations of the material destruction of Gernika on this propaganda booklet, which lacks credibility and does not match the data provided by the Dirección General de Regiones Devastadas y Reparaciones (General Division of Devastated Regions and Preservation), the agency in charge of the reconstruction of the town.[24]

According to the last report on the material damage caused by the bombing, which was made between 1940 and 1941 by the architect of the Division of Devastated Regions, Gonzalo Cárdenas, the number of houses destroyed in Gernika amounted to 271, since some of the buildings that in 1938 and 1939 had been described as "seriously damaged" had to be reclassified and registered as "completely destroyed" after a closer examination conducted before undertaking the reconstruction of the town.[25] The project for the reconstruction of Gernika, dated February 7, 1941, that was drafted by the technical office of the Bizkaia Commission of Devastated Regions, stated that 271 buildings were completely destroyed during the bombing.[26] It should be noted that this project was made based on cadastral information in order to carry out the necessary expropriations and subsequent auction of the houses and that therefore the authors could neither manipulate nor hide data. Moreover, unlike the Herrán Report, this project was not an instrument of propaganda but an internal project that, although public, was not subject to censorship. In sum, because of the abundance of data and the amount of documentation attached to it (reports, records, plans, and several annexes), the 1941 project for the reconstruction of Gernika constitutes the main and most reliable source of information about the physical destruction caused by the bombing.

According to the plans of the reconstruction project, Gernika had 318 buildings in April 1937.[27] Considering that 271 buildings were completely destroyed, it follows that the bombing completely destroyed 85.22 percent of the buildings in Gernika. In addition, most of the rest of the houses, 14.78 percent, were severely damaged. Less than 1 percent of the houses in Gernika were not affected by the bombing. This figure matches that given by British consul Ralph Stevenson, who after visiting the town reported that "nine out of ten homes were completely destroyed."[28] In any case, this figure—85.22 percent of the buildings in Gernika completely destroyed—represents a substantially higher figure than the one that is usually repeated without any material evidence of 71 percent.[29]

Moreover, according to Gonzalo Cárdenas, the 271 houses completely destroyed represent 67.58 percent of the 401 houses listed as completely destroyed in Bizkaia during the war, excluding Bilbao.[30] The Division of Devastated Regions estimated the value of the buildings completely destroyed in Gernika at 11,940,791 pesetas.[31] This represents 34.1 percent of all costs incurred by the damage in Bizkaia (which amounted to 35 million pesetas), excluding the capital, Bilbao.

## The Bridge Hypothesis

While following Franco's direct orders, the Spanish, Italian, and German governments officially denied that Gernika had been bombed, members of the military leaked news of the attack, presenting it as strategic bombing aimed at destroying the Errenteria Bridge. These reports were written in response to the intense international diplomatic appeal and the worldwide impact of the bombing, which was expressed in editorials and columns and on the front pages of hundreds of newspapers in Europe and the Americas.

This is the case of Richthofen's report to General Alfredo Kindelán, signed at Burgos on August 9, 1937. Written three months after the attack, when the bombing had already become an event of international scope, Richthofen cynically stated that incendiary bombs were dropped as a signal to indicate the completion of the bombing and to reveal to the infantry when and where to advance. He also stated that three bombers were launched against Gernika (in reference to the experimental squadron led by von Moreau during the first phase of the bombing), flying at medium altitudes, to "warn the population," and that only after the residents had been alerted and people had time to escape did the planes drop their bombs on the target "with pretty good precision." According to Richthofen, observers on these aircraft reported that Gernika had been set afire at different points before the first German bombing began, suggesting that Basque nationalists had torched their own town. He added that because of the smoke caused by that fire, by the time the formation of Junker Ju52s reached the town, "it was very difficult to observe targets from above," which would explain why they did not hit the bridge. Finally, Richthofen concluded that, days after the occupation of Gernika by the Nationalists, "the city had been bombed at least four times by the Red aviation and for quite some time also shelled by the Red artillery." And he added that "the insignificant quantity of German bombs dropped on the city cannot in any way have caused the destruction of the city."[32] In conclusion, Richthofen stated that the destruction of Gernika was caused by fires started by the Basques and by the action of Basque aviation and artillery. It is obvious that Richthofen was lying, and he knew that General Kindelán, commander of the Nationalist air force, was well aware that the Basque army had never had bombers. All this indicates that this was a document addressed to governments involved in the Non-Intervention Agreement. Moreover, according to Richthofen's report, the order of attack against Gernika specified that the town was not to be damaged and that the order of attack of the Italian air command, which stated that the target was the Errenteria Bridge, stressed that "the town, for obvious political reasons, should not be bombed."[33] This is difficult to believe if we take into account that the bridge was not touched, but 100 percent of the buildings in the city center were entirely destroyed. Indeed, out of the thirty-two largest bomb craters registered in downtown Gernika, twenty-seven (84.38 percent) were more than 820 feet from the bridge.[34]

Colonel Hans H. von Beust wrote that the town was full of soldiers in retreat and that the bridge and the troops "crowded together" on it were the main military target.[35] But this was not correct either. The few militia troops in town were either in the hospital or on leave, and, as Steer reported, "there were no troops retreating through the town. The armies were beyond Markina, miles to the east, and at Mount Oiz, miles to the south."[36] Moreover, Sabin Apraiz, chief of staff of the Basque army, issued an order forbidding the retreating Basque battalions to pass through Gernika.[37] One of the few army companies in Gernika was the Zarragoitia Fourth Company of the Saseta Battalion, which was sent to rest for four days at the Augustinians' school on the outskirts of town. The Loiola Battalion was also resting at the Santa Clara Convent next to the ancient parliament and the Tree of Gernika,[38] and the Gernikako Arbola Battalion was billeted at the Institute of Secondary Education. The three hospitals in town were located in the convents of the Carmelites[39] and the Josefinas and in the Calzada Asylum on the southern outskirts.[40] Von Beust, like the rest of the squadron leaders, knew all this. They also knew that the town was not a garrison, for they had seen and studied it in detail, which is proven by the photographs taken by the Heinkel He46 and Heinkel He70 observation units on Monday, April 26, and in the days before the attack.

Indeed, different explanations of the bombing were fabricated to cover up its true purpose, among them the contention that the attack was intended to destroy the Errenteria Bridge in order to block most of the Basque troops at the western line, Ondarroa-Markina, by impeding their retreat through Gernika. This plan, revealed by Richthofen in his war diary on April 26, required the combined effort of ground and air forces. The Italian Black Arrows would advance against Ondarroa and Lekeitio from the northeast and occupy Gautegiz and Murueta, putting the roads from Gernika to the north under the fire of the Italian artillery. At the same time, the first and fourth Navarrese brigades would advance northwest, occupying Durango, Ibarruri, and Gorozika successively and cutting off communications from Gernika to the south. Consequently, it was possible to expect the Basque army to retreat toward Gernika. Therefore, if the roads passing through Gernika were bombed and the Errenteria Bridge destroyed, it would be impossible for the Basques to retreat northward, and they would be forced to surrender.

However, there are so many miscalculations in Richthofen's plan that it is difficult to believe that he assumed it was possible to block the retreat of the Basque forces east of Gernika. According to this alleged plan, the First Infantry Brigade was required to advance about 6.5 miles westward from Elorrio to Durango and then, after capturing Durango, advance 7.5 miles more and capture Amorebieta in order to cut one of the possible routes of retreat from Gernika to the south.[41] At the same time, the Brigada Mixta, composed of a third of the Italian units, was to advance about 14 miles to the west, from Ondarroa toward Gernika. The plan also required that the units south of Mount Oiz—the First Brigade—take the summit and advance on

Gernika, reaching this point before the retreating Basque battalions did. This meant that the First Brigade was expected to capture the top of Mount Oiz and from there advance approximately 20 miles from Berriz to Gernika—through Albiz and Elejalde—in a single day.[42]

To have a precise idea of what this meant, between March 31 and April 26 Nationalist forces advanced a total of 15 miles northward (or an average of 0.5 miles a day) and no more than 7.5 miles westward (0.28 miles a day). So Richthofen's expectations far exceeded any goal achieved previously. And, as he himself repeatedly underlined in his war diary, the Italian units were unreliable and the Spanish brigades' advance had often been much slower than expected. Moreover, in regard to April 26, the day of the bombing, Richthofen pointed out in his diary that the pressure on the north was expected to be weak, the Nationalist troops were exhausted, and their right flank was completely exposed, since the Fourth Brigade had stood still the day before.[43] A day earlier, on April 25, the First Brigade could not even capture the Republican positions on Mount Oiz, as established by that day's order of battle. It is hard to believe that Richthofen assumed that General Mola or Colonel Vigón, chief of staff of the Navarrese Brigades, would endorse a lightning advance of such characteristics, as they did not. Indeed, some members of the Condor Legion who participated in the attack claimed that they were not directly informed of these plans or of the true purpose of the attack.[44] Moreover, there is no material evidence of such an order of advance being passed by the Spanish command, and the orders of the Spanish rebel command for April 25 and April 26 do not mention the capture of any of the targets included in Richthofen's alleged plan and do not demand any significant advance. In addition, the Fourth Brigade was ordered to stop and rest on April 26, and, as Richthofen himself wrote in his war diary that day, the order of advance was delayed until April 29, the day Gernika was indeed captured.

Both Richthofen and von Beust, officer in command of one of the squadrons over Gernika, emphasized that destroying the seventy-foot Errenteria Bridge over the Oka River was the principal objective.[45] Also, the order of attack of the Italian air command stated that the target was the bridge and that the city should not be bombed. However, as we may deduce from Richthofen's diary, Gernika had to be reduced to rubble in order to close the roads that passed through the city and block the main route connecting Amorebieta in the south with Bermeo in the north by covering the road with debris. However, this has no logic either. The bridge is located at the end of San Juan Street and connects Gernika with the village of Errenteria in the northeast outskirts of Gernika. From Errenteria, the retreating Basque battalions were forced to take the road that runs northeast to Forua, Sukarrieta, and Bermeo, avoiding the city center of Gernika, so there was no reason to obstruct the roads that passed through Gernika itself, as Richthofen claimed. Indeed, by blocking the roads from the south, Richthofen was destroying the main route of advance for his own forces. But even troops advancing from the south could have easily bypassed Gernika on the roads west or east of the town.

Besides, strategically speaking, it was impossible to cut the retreat of nearly twelve Basque battalions to Bermeo by blowing up a seventy-foot bridge over a stream that in spring was not even five feet deep and no more than ten feet wide. The stream could have been easily crossed by the Basque light infantry units on their way to Bermeo through a dozen other spots north or south of Gernika.

Obviously, nothing worked according to this strategy: the bombing did not prevent the retreat of the Basque battalions, and the rebel troops that captured Gernika on April 29 passed through the town and then pushed toward Bermeo, where they arrived on the thirtieth and were stopped by Basque forces. Moreover, Sukarrieta, six miles north of Gernika, would have been a much more suitable spot to halt the retreat of the Basque battalions on their way to Bermeo, since the road at this site is narrowly confined between the mountains to the west and the tidal inlet to the east. However, Sukarrieta was never bombed.

Pete C. Cenarrusa, who was a dive-bomber and flying instructor during World War II, has examined the Errenteria Bridge. He concluded that if the bridge had been the target, a Henschel 123 or a Junker Ju87 dive-bomber dropping a single 551-pound bomb would have sufficed to destroy it.[46] Richthofen was well aware of the uses of dive-bombers and made extensive use of them during the invasion of Poland and the blitzkrieg against Western Europe. Moreover, the Condor Legion had four Henschel Hs123 dive-bombers stationed at the German air base in Gasteiz, but these were the only operational bombers that the German command decided *not* to use during the attack on Gernika.[47] The Italian command had and made use of Breda Ba.65 dive-bombers in the summer of 1937 on the Santander front, although the air control preferred to use them as reconnaissance planes and even as pursuit planes.[48] Cenarrusa stated that "these planes were designed to destroy static targets such as bridges or defensive positions, and even smaller dynamic targets such as tanks in motion; however, Richthofen would not use them when these devices were specifically designed to blow up targets like the Errenteria Bridge, all of which suggests that the target was not the bridge but the whole city."[49] He concluded:

> As a Curtiss SB2C Helldiver dive-bomber pilot and instructor, I can attest that the destruction of a military static target of the dimensions of the Errenteria Bridge requires a single ground-attack aircraft designed for dive-bombing, such as the Junker Ju87 or Henschel Hs123, models available to the Condor Legion since the summer of 1936. The quantity and quality of the aircraft involved in the bombing of Gernika, their flight formation, the use of a mixing of heavy and incendiary explosives dropped on the town, and the fact that civilians were machine-gunned from the air for hours—coupled with the expense of the mobilization of such an air force—indicate that the target was not the referred Errenteria Bridge and that, therefore, it was not a strategic bombing but a terror-bombing episode aimed at the mass destruction of Gernika.[50]

F. Willard Robinson and Chuck Winder, former pilots, also expressed that "it lacks all logic" to assume that this was a strategic bombing aimed at destroying a bridge.[51] Robinson, a TBM-3E Avenger torpedo bomber pilot during World War II and author of the book *Navy Wings of Gold*, considered it absurd to question the nature of the terror bombing. Cenarrusa added that if one of his men had returned from such a mission, having used such a display of airpower and war matériel without even touching the target, he probably would not have been allowed to fly again for the rest of the war.

There is no example in the course of World War II (either before or after) of an attempt to destroy a bridge like the one at Errenteria using such bombing techniques, massive airpower, and waste of matériel. "It is simply irrational," concur the three war veterans I have interviewed. All three agree:

> The standard procedure for blowing a bridge (about seventy feet long and thirty-two feet wide) from the air, in an open town with no antiaircraft batteries or any other defenses (such as pursuit planes), does not involve twenty-four bombers and twenty-three fighters for a period of time of three and a half hours launching a total of between thirty and forty tons of bombs (a big proportion of them incendiary).
>
> That destroying a bridge of such characteristics is a simple static target that could be achieved with a single dive-bomber or even with a bomber.

> That, at the view of the results (the bridge was not even touched and the city was completely destroyed with a result of 85.2 percent of all buildings demolished), it seems that the real aim of the bombing was not to destroy the bridge but to drive the Basques into surrender by terror bombing.[52]

In other words, the actions of the Heinkel He51 and Messerschmitt Bf.109 fighter squadrons led by Oberleutnant Harro Harder and Lieutenant Colonel Günther Lützow, respectively, do not correspond to such a target; the destruction of a bridge does not require machine-gunning people in the streets for hours. The number of planes involved, the flight formation adopted (waves of bombers flying three abreast within a 500-foot-wide aerial corridor), the time invested in the attack (three and a half hours), such massive use of bombs (31 to 41 tons), and the use of incendiary bombs would have been illogical if the seventy-foot bridge was indeed the target.[53]

Moreover, as Cenarrusa pointed out, the fact that the bridge remained intact after bombarding the city with such technical deployment suggests that the air control "did not want the bridge to be touched or damaged in any way." And he concludes, "To note that after launching 31 to 41 tons of bombs the bridge was not reached is as much as to express that the German pilots who took part in the attack were hopelessly incompetent, too much as to be minimally plausible."[54]

If the attack was in fact intended to blow up a bridge, then we would have to explain why the Spanish government refused for decades to admit that Gernika had been bombed[55] and why members of the Condor Legion stated that they were ordered to make a comprehensive study of the ruins, including aerial photographs.[56] Moreover, as First Lieutenant Karl von Knauer reported later, the Condor Legion's ammunition technicians were ordered to stop bombing the city and to observe and report the results of the attack. One of the photographers sent on that mission was Alfons Kössinger, who arrived in Gernika while the ruins were still burning, probably on April 29. As Kössinger testified, he was ordered to take pictures both during and after the bombing, including photographs taken after the city was captured.[57] The photographers were ordered to remove all material evidence of the attack, including, naturally, the corpses, and to maintain absolute silence and even deny that the bombing had ever happened.[58] Bomb fragments were removed, bomb craters refilled, and records of deceased inhabitants removed from the city registry. This indicates that the results of the raid were carefully studied.

Furthermore, the claim that the bridge was the main target is highly inconsistent with later reports by Sperrle, Jaenecke, and Richthofen. All three agreed that the attack against Gernika was a "complete technical success." However, after dropping between 31,000 and 41,000 kilos (68,343 to 90,389 pounds) of bombs and mobilizing approximately twenty-seven bombers and at least twenty-three fighters for three and a half hours, the German planes did not even touch the bridge. As noted, most of the heavy bombs dropped on Gernika fell more than 820 feet from the bridge,[59] and none of the grenades thrown from fighter planes flying as low as 400 feet touched or inflicted any damage to it. In addition, some survivors and eyewitnesses of the massacre, such as Canon Alberto Onaindia and Francisco Lazkano, reported that they had found shelter under this and other bridges in the area. Trying to provide a viable explanation for these contradictions, Jesús Salas and Ferdinando Pedriali have maintained that although the Errenteria Bridge was the main objective of the rebel aviation, due to technical limitations inherent to the planes of that time the bombers missed the target.[60] It would be pointless to list bridges destroyed by the German air force during World War II, but there are numerous instances of successful pinpoint bombing actions during the German invasion of Poland in 1939, as well as later.[61] To assert that it was difficult to destroy a bridge from the air also contradicts the reports of the Italian command. Velardi stated on April 24, 1937, before the attack, that thanks to measures taken by Colonel Ferdinando Raffaelli, "la perfezione nel puntamento" (perfect accuracy) in precision bombing had already been achieved.[62] If we take into consideration the fact that pursuit planes armed with six 22-pound bombs descended lower than 600 feet and that the Junker Ju52s could bomb from 3,300 feet without the interference of antiaircraft batteries, the claims that technical limitations of the aircraft limited their accuracy seem egregiously false.

Furthermore, there were at least fifteen larger and more strategically important bridges (number of transports and tonnage of ammunition crossing per day) in the Basque Country—for instance, the bridges over the Ibaizabal River[63] and its tributaries in Galdakao, Amorebieta, Durango, Igorre, Elexalde, and Lemoa. In Galdakao there were only four main bridges connecting its neighborhoods, Laminarrieta, Merkadillo, Puentelatorre, and Torrezabal. The rebels needed to use these bridges for a rapid advance toward Bilbao. On the contrary, it was the Basque forces that had damaged some of them (such as Puentelatorre in Galdakao) in order to delay a possible advance of the combined army to the west. Indeed, according to

General Pietro Pinna's report, the Spanish command had decided by April 17, 1937—that is, nine days before the bombing of Gernika—not to destroy bridges, railroads, factories, or electric power stations from the air.[64]

All these data suggest beyond any reasonable doubt that the bombing of Gernika was a war experiment, an episode of terror bombing. As Richthofen himself stated in his diary, in a tone intended to be witty or perhaps ironic, "In Gernika, despite everything, I behaved in a very rude way indeed!"[65]

Most of the German and Italian air commanders agreed that the most effective weapon of the air force was its psychological effect. General Velardi noted in his report to the secretary of state of May 6, 1937, that the objectives of the Italian air force had been the tactical support of ground forces; the bombing of airfields, factories, production centers, and centers for reserve forces; and, finally, objectives of political interest. Among such political targets that the Italian commander mentioned was Caspe, a town the Italians bombed on May 1, believing they would kill politicians and perhaps Republican army commanders celebrating Labor Day.[66]

After the initial air strikes on the Basque front, the rebel air control was very optimistic about the work of the bombers in support of ground troops. General Velardi's report of April 13, 1937—*Actions of the Italian Air Force in the Battle for Bilbao*—emphasizes that the rebel air force was acting "in piena efficienza" against the defensive positions of the Basque troops by using 551-pound projectiles en masse.[67] Additionally, General Pinna stated in the report entitled *Report on the Missions Accomplished in Spain from April 7 to 17, 1937* that regardless of the tactical objective of the actions of the Italo-German air force conducted in coordination with the Spanish ground forces on the Basque front, it was obvious that the German leadership was seeking to achieve a demoralizing psychological effect.[68]

Pinna concluded that, as General Sperrle, Colonel von Richthofen, and General Velardi had informed him personally, the result of the carpet-bombing technique was amazing, especially with regard to the psychological effect on enemy forces. From the analysis of this strategy, the Italo-German air command concluded that during and after an intense air bombing, enemy forces retreated in disorder, allowing the rebel forces to take over their positions without much effort on the part of the infantry.

The information provided by General Pinna is extremely revealing. In fact, the bombing of Gernika was an adaptation of tactical bombardment of defensive positions on the front transferred to urban centers in the rear.

As we have observed, the bombing of Gernika was carried out following the general scheme described by Pinna in his report: the first phase of light bombing, dropping bombs of 22 to 110 pounds; a second phase of heavy bombardment, dropping the whole cargo through a narrow air corridor (carpet bombing) in successive waves (shuttle bombing); and, finally, a third phase, the capture of the target by infantry units without resistance while the pursuit planes machine-gunned and bombed the remaining forces defending the position. It should be stressed that the bombing of Gernika was an experiment undertaken without any intention of taking the city by assault, which explains why Richthofen considered it a "great technical success."

Although air control observed and appreciated the psychological potential of an aerial bombing campaign as a means of terrorizing civilians and disorienting troops, it very soon realized the ineffectiveness of aerial bombardment tactics against frontline mountain trenches. This is, for example, the conclusion of the report to the Ministry of Foreign Affairs of April 13, 1937, written by General Bastico after analyzing the effects of aerial bombing on the Basque army's defensive positions. The report concluded that the capture of Bilbao was going to be "difficult and tough if the morale of the enemy is not broken."[69] Both generals agreed that air attacks against the defenses of Bilbao were "of very scarce material value" and added that the use of artillery was also ineffective because it was not very powerful and was generally misused. However, both generals emphasized in the report that "the main value of aviation lay in the psychological effect that it generated over the enemy troops." Their conclusion was apparently based on the testimony of prisoners of war. Velardi also stated in his report of April 13 that "the psychological effect [of the bombings] has been revealed to be impressive."[70]

These are not the only air-command reports that confirm the commitment of its officers to terror bombing. In response to a questionnaire on bombing techniques, Colonel Ferdinando Raffaelli, commander of the Eleventh Air Company of the Aviazione Legionaria, stated that despite the accuracy of the bombers, the material effect of the bombing against Bilbao's Iron Belt was of little value, while "exceeding all expectations, it had provoked a considerable moral effect."[71] In response to another question, Raffaelli stressed again the psychological impact of the bombings and conveyed that in order to achieve substantial and prolonged effect and thus a considerable moral effect, it was necessary to bomb an area repeatedly.[72]

In response to a question on the effectiveness of night and daytime bombing actions, Major Corrado Corradino, commander of the Twenty-Fourth Air Company, suggested that nocturnal actions produced a greater effect on morale, a fact that was already observed and even quantified during World War I.[73] Corradino concurred with Raffaelli that a more effective psychological effect was obtained if bombing the same area was prolonged in time.[74]

It is particularly relevant that Raffaelli insisted that it was necessary to bomb an area for a long period of time to achieve the greatest psychological effect and that Velardi noted that the psychological effect of bombing was greater when the planes arrived in several waves separated by intervals of a few minutes.[75] According to Velardi, after an initial air strike with bombers, the arrival of a second wave of bombers might provoke a disorderly retreat. Obviously, this retreat could be exploited by the fighters as an opportunity to shoot at disbanded ground units that under these conditions became easy targets. Velardi also stated that bombing actions in the rear, in this case the attacks against Galdakao and Bilbao, had produced a strong psychological effect and caused serious material damage.

As deduced from an analysis of Richthofen's war diary and the reports of the Italian generals Bastico, Velardi, and Pinna, the German and Italian commanders were convinced that the main reason for the advance of rebel troops on the Basque front was the assistance provided by the German and Italian air forces. Moreover, Pinna said that the Spanish rebel troops had made progress "only" because of the assistance of the Italo-German air force.[76] Also, Sperrle, Richthofen, Velardi, and Pinna felt that the manner of conducting the war in the Basque Country was an example of the Spanish military mentality, "unable to conceive a large-scale operations plan and unable to firmly conduct, to the last consequences, a military action."[77] Most probably, Pinna was criticizing General Mola, chief of the Spanish Northern Army, who also came under heavy criticism from Richthofen.

But what is illuminating is not the criticism of Mola's way of conducting the war but the reasons underlying those criticisms. According to the Italian command, the Spanish forces needed a more vigorous commander, because otherwise the war would continue indefinitely. For this reason, the Italo-German air command believed that the Spanish command was unable to understand or conceive of the use of airpower en masse. In this sense, Pinna stated that the Spanish command regarded the air force as a mere tactical force whose strikes raised the morale of the ground troops in their advance toward Bilbao. Indeed, according to Pinna, since this was a civil conflict, the Spanish rebel command was restricted by circumstances and made only "humanitarian use of the air force." Moreover, Pinna pointed out—most probably referring to the bombing of Durango—that when Italian and German bombers attacked urban areas, the Spanish command protested because relatives or friends of persons belonging to the Nationalist side had died.[78]

Pinna stated that Italian and German commanders believed the war in the Basque Country had to be won by a "decisive strike" or "a quick and decisive event" that would cause a reversal of the military situation. Pinna more specifically declared that an intense and fierce intervention of the air force was needed because the main task of the air force should be the heavy bombardment of towns in order to generate a psychological effect on the enemy. Pinna furthermore stressed that bombing was more effective the more intense and prolonged the action of the bombers was, because the moral force of the defenders decreased in proportion to the intensity of the air strikes.[79]

In short, Pinna claimed in his report, written nine days before the bombing of Gernika, that the main reason for the slow progress of the Spanish troops on the Basque front was the "impossibility of conducting a total war" by making indiscriminate and massive use of aerial bombardment.[80] Pinna claimed to have discussed this point with Velardi, Sperrle, and Richthofen and that they were in agreement.

In short, the strategy of bombing the Basques into submission that was performed during the attacks against Elorrio, Otxandio, and Durango at the end of March was the main reason for bombing Gernika. William E. Chapman, US consul in Bilbao, stated in a report of March 31, 1937, that the aim of the rebel bombing of Santander and Gijon was to revive the morale of the troops and at the same time "to counteract the encouragement endangered in the Government area in North Spain by the recent defeat of the Italians in the Guadalajara sector."[81] He added that, since the defeat of Guadalajara had lit the spirits of the Basque militias, he had expected retaliatory bombings in the Basque Country.[82] In fact, Chapman was reluctant to believe that Bilbao could be taken without significant bloodshed and without carrying out "violent attacks against the Basques."[83]

Following the logic of terror bombing (bombing an enemy into submission), German, Italian, and Spanish commanders demanded the unconditional surrender of the Basque forces immediately after the bombing of

Gernika, threatening further bombardments of the same nature. In fact, General Bastico stated in a telegram signed on April 25 at 10:40 A.M. that General Franco had told him that it was militarily necessary to continue pressing firmly (referring to terror bombings) and, in parallel, to negotiate the surrender of the Basque troops, for which he tacitly had allowed to Bastico the "interference" of the Italian command in peace negotiations with the Basques (in reference to a possible pact like the one that would take place in Santoña months later).[84]

Accordingly, on April 27, a day after the bombing of Gernika, General Bastico sent Count Galeazzo Ciano a report on the negotiations for the surrender of the Basques to the Italian command.[85] The German authorities also attempted to force the surrender of the Basques, as announced by Julio Álvarez del Vayo, foreign minister of the Spanish Republic. As del Vayo stated in Paris on April 28, the German command threatened to bomb Bilbao as they had Gernika, while promising an enduring peace and the beginning of a lucrative raw-materials trade with Germany if the Basques surrendered. Moreover, the German command threatened to launch a campaign of systematic destruction of all towns under the control of the Basque government if the government refused to accept the German terms. Del Vayo added that the destruction of Gernika had been "the first fulfillment of this threat."[86] Spanish military authorities acted in the same way. On the very evening of April 26, the rebel radio broadcast a message in Basque from Donostia, inviting the Basque government to start peace negotiations to prevent the total destruction of Bizkaia.[87] Also, rebel aviation dropped leaflets signed by General Franco demanding the unconditional surrender of the Basque troops, in line with the famous pamphlet signed by General Mola a month earlier.[88]

On April 27, a day after the bombing, Mola again demanded Basque surrender, threatening to leave no stone unturned in Bizkaia: "We will raze Bilbao, and this land, plain and desolate, will make the British abandon their desire of sustaining, against our will, the Basque Bolsheviks."[89] Colonel Fuqua, military attaché at the US Embassy in Donibane Lohitzune, reported on April 28 that the air strikes on the Basque front had intensified and that the morale of the militia might be seriously affected.[90] Cardinal Emilio Gomá urged Canon Onaindia to recommend the unconditional surrender of the Basque government to prevent the destruction of Bilbao, because "whoever the author of the destruction of Gernika is, it is a terrible warning to the big city [Bilbao]."[91]

In conclusion, the attack on Gernika was never conceived either as a precise bombing against the Errenteria Bridge or as strategic bombing intended to block the main roads through Gernika. All the evidence indicates that the bombing was designed, implemented, and executed as terror bombing intended to beat the Basques into submission. Based on information gathered in the combat zone, US military intelligence issued a report in April 1937 indicating that 62 percent of the rebels' bombing actions during the month of April had been carried out against open, undefended cities. In other words, the Condor Legion had set off a terror-bombing campaign.[92]

## The Death Toll

One of the reasons there are differences of opinion about the death toll of the bombing is that the Basque government did not have time to dig out the debris, recover the bodies, and prepare a complete registry of the dead. In addition, when the rebels took Gernika at 12:30 P.M. on April 29, the military authorities ordered that the town be closed and all physical evidence of the bombing be removed. Only a few deaths were recorded. Specifically, the pamphlet entitled *Guernica: The Official Report* (a.k.a. the Herrán Report)[93] registered the recovery of 25 corpses between April 29 and May 29, 1937. As in most cases of atrocities, the perpetrators purged any documentary evidence of the bombing, and, as a consequence, the records of the Basque government disappeared, leaving today no evidence of the bombing in the archives of Bizkaia. That is, the new authorities made no real effort to recover, identify, and record the corpses, but made a big effort to erase any material traces of them. For instance, the work of clearing Gernika did not begin until late February 1939, and by December 1941 the city center of Gernika had not yet been completely dug out. In all that time, the Francoist authorities did not record the discovery of any corpses. If we add to these facts that during forty years of dictatorship, the regime's official version was that Gernika was not bombed but burned by the Basques themselves, and that speaking or writing about the bombing was forbidden and harshly punished (in some cases with up to three years of imprisonment), we can understand why the exact number of deaths caused by the bombing is still unknown. However, we should go through various aspects of relevance to address this issue.

The Basque government reported 800 deaths on April 28. However, six days later, on May 4, after receiving further information from the hospitals, Minister of Justice Jesús María Leizaola reported on Radio Euzkadi that, "one of his duties being to keep record of all deaths in Basque territory and to take testimony of all prisoners of war, he had the records of five hundred and ninety more people who died as a consequence of the air raid."[94] On June 9, the secretary-general of the President's Office (Lehendakaritza) of the Basque government, Anton Irala, presented a new death toll compiled from reports received from local councils and the police, giving a total of 1,654 dead and 889 wounded.[95] Irala added that the final death toll could well be higher because the Basque authorities did not have the time or means to make an exhaustive investigation.

All direct witnesses who were in Gernika during the bombing and in the days immediately after the bombing, and who gave an estimated number of deaths at the time the events took place, reported a death toll of more than 800. Among the witnesses, we must mention 5 members of the Basque government who were responsible for recording the names of victims of air raids in April 1937—Minister of the Interior Telesforo Monzon, Secretary-General of the Presidency Anton Irala, Chief of Security Francisco Arregi, Chief of Motorized Police José María Picaza, and Inspector General of the Police Department Enrique Etxebarria, all of whom went to Gernika shortly after the attack, the first 3 on April 26.[96] The report was made public by Minister of Justice Jesús M. Leizaola. Obviously, this report was made by a larger number of people, including the medical staff of the hospitals in Gernika and the surrounding area, such as Amorebieta, Bermeo, Mundaka, and Bilbao.

Guadalupe and Isabel Urkiola and Angeles and Lucia Atxabal, nurses who worked in Gernika during the bombing, were also consistent with these figures (more than 1,000 deaths) when they reported on the bombing before the World Women's Committee Against War and Fascism during the press conference held in Paris on May 22, 1937.[97] Guadalupe Urkiola testified a second time before Joxe Migel Barandiaran in Jatsu on December 3, 1937, that "Guernica was destroyed on the afternoon of April 26 by German aircraft at the service of General Franco! Just as I testify, so might have testified the thousands of people who witnessed the bombing; proof of what I say are the dead who would be over 1,000, and so many wounded and maimed."[98] Pedro Basaldua, Lehendakari Agirre's personal secretary, set the number of casualties at 3,000.[99] Canon Alberto Onaindia estimated the number of dead bodies of old men, women, and children at more than 1,000: "When I entered the village in flames, the streets were full of dismembered bodies. More than 1,000 people were killed, and the only two military targets in the city, the headquarters and the factory of arms, were untouched. It is obvious that the aircraft aimed to destroy the city."[100] He added that most of the corpses were riddled with bullets.[101] The 3 witnesses who testified on Radio Euzkadi on May 4, 1937, with Minister Leizaola were also consistent with this figure. Jose Labauria,[102] mayor of Gernika, and Eusebio Arronategi, the parish priest who had helped the wounded and assisted the authorities in recovering the bodies, stated that they had all seen "thousands of their countrymen suffocated, dead and wounded, paying tribute to brutality" and agreed with the death toll given by the Basque government.[103] Labauria specifically testified that "the number of casualties caused by the bombing in the town of Gernika was over one thousand."[104] Bonifacio Etxegarai, a member of the Society of Basque Studies, also participated in the May 4 radio broadcast.

The six international reporters who came to Gernika on the night of April 26 and returned to the village the next day gave similar figures. On April 29, after having interviewed 20 residents on April 26,[105] George Steer agreed with the first official number of 800 deaths, mostly women, children, and elderly people.[106] Christopher Holme of the Reuters Agency agreed with Steer's numbers.[107] Mathieu Corman of *Ce Soir* initially mentioned 800 deaths, but on April 29 he increased his first estimate to more than 1,000 victims.[108] The *Ce Soir* photojournalist who was in Gernika on April 27 and 29 also estimated that the bombing had caused more than 1,000 deaths.[109] As Noel Monks reported for *Paris Soir* and the *Daily Express* on April 27, he returned to Gernika, and "I saw 600 bodies. Nurses, children, farmers, old women, girls, old men, babies."[110] These were the bodies of victims laid in front of the Carmelites' hospital (Karmele Deuna) to be identified before taking them to the cemetery. He said that the death toll was 1,000 and added that many bodies remained burned or mutilated. He was overwhelmed because of the smell of scorched human flesh: "Basque soldiers were getting the bodies from the wreckage, many of them weeping. I came to what had been an air raid shelter. In it were the remains of fifty women and children. A bomb had dropped right through the house into the cellar. Does Franco expect the world to believe that fifty women and children fled into an air raid shelter when their house was mined? Or trapped themselves below there while the house above them was set alight? I went back to Bilbao and wrote another story, just what I had seen. Just as I would have written it if it had been a Franco town in ruins."[111] Scott Watson, a correspondent for the *Daily Herald* and the *Star*, also reported seeing 500 lifeless bodies,[112] and the special envoy of the Havas Agency also mentioned 800 corpses.[113]

Twenty priests led by Father Ramon Galbarriatu, vicar general of the Diocese of Gasteiz, and Father Pedro Mentxaka, canon of the diocese, signed a letter on June 11, 1937, entitled *The Basque Clergy Loyal to the Government of the Republic Addresses the Supreme Pontiff to Stress That the Vandal Destruction of Durango and Gernika Was Exclusively Due to the Action of the German Planes*. Following the first figure given by the Basque government and Steer, they mentioned "hundreds of deaths."[114] The letter was addressed to Pope Pius XI and was personally taken to the Vatican by two of the signatory priests, Pedro Mentxaka and Agustín Isusi. The former Basque bishop of Gasteiz Mateo Mugica, who was exiled in Rome, worked to have the delegation received by Cardinal Pacelli.[115] The letter was also signed by ten parish priests in Bilbao, the coadjutor of Santa María de Uribarri of Durango, the parish priest of Abadiano, and the coadjutors of Murelaga, Arbatzegi, Gerrikaitz, Berriatua, Santa Ana, Larrauri, and Markina, ten of them eyewitnesses to the attacks.[116] Another witness, Passionist priest Victoriano Gondra, known as Patxi Aita, who was wounded during the bombing in Gernika, stated in his memoirs that he went to the Karmele Deuna Hospital and saw the bodies of the first victims of the attack. He accepted the figure of "thousands."[117]

British consul Ralph C. Stevenson, who visited the ruins of Gernika while preparing his report to British ambassador Sir Henry Chilton, said that according to the preliminary information available to him, the exact number of deaths would never be known but that he estimated 3,000 casualties.[118] The only international observer in the area, Elizabeth Wilkinson, secretary of the Spanish Women's Committee for Help to Spain, went to Gernika at 1:30 P.M. on the twenty-seventh to see the devastation caused by the bombardment and published an article about it in the *Daily Worker*; she agreed with Steer's figure.[119] Maria Goitia, who sought refuge in one of the houses near the market square, testified that "many dead bodies and injured people were in the streets. One could hear the wounded screaming. Many of the victims perished charred under the rubble."[120] When a reporter of the Havas Agency asked her to give an estimated death toll, Goitia responded, "I do not know exactly. No one will ever know. Thousands and thousands, I am not exaggerating."[121]

Maria Medinabeitia, whose mother died at the Andra Mari Street shelter, calculated the death toll at 2,000 based on information provided to her by the grave digger of Gernika: "In Bilbao [I] saw the gravedigger of Gernika. I asked him if he had seen my mother. He said no. He added that many corpses remained unidentified in Gernika. Furthermore, since there was no space to bury all the corpses in the cemetery, many, especially members like heads, hands, legs, etc. were burned in bonfires lit for that purpose at Ibarra de San Juan Square. The gravedigger estimated that over 2,000 people were killed in the bombing of Gernika by Franco's planes."[122] Ricardo Luzarraga also testified that the death toll of 500 given on April 27 was low, since after a few days many more bodies were found.[123]

Finally, a member of the Condor Legion who flew on a Heinkel He51 over Gernika, Harro Harder, said "surely still thousands dead lie beneath the ruins, superfluous victims. Everywhere there are smoking rubble, bomb craters, empty storefronts."[124] Similarly, the section report from the information service of the German navy high command of April 28 to May 3, 1937, stated that "according to consistent statements, Gernika was heavily attacked by white pilots leading to considerable material damage and serious loss of human lives."[125]

These figures are the initial death tolls produced by eyewitnesses during the days after the bombing and before the recovery of new bodies and the registration of new casualties among the wounded who were transported to hospitals in Amorebieta, Bermeo, Mundaka, and Bilbao. However, apart from these thirty-eight direct testimonies, which represent a perfectly consistent source of historical information, we have the testimony of 6 other people who had access to the information provided by eyewitnesses and also gave a death toll that matches that of the testimonies cited above. President José Antonio Agirre wrote that Gernika had become "a huge bonfire, in which hundreds of innocent victims were burning" and stated that about 2,000 people perished in the tragedy. By virtue of the data provided by the Ministry of Health of the Basque government, after the first day of recovery of corpses in Gernika, Health Minister Alfredo Espinosa estimated 500 deaths.[126]

Leah Manning, secretary of the Spanish Medical Aid Committee, who was in Bilbao at the time of the bombing, estimated 1,654 deaths caused by the bombing, and Katharine Ramsay, Duchess of Atholl, who at the behest of Elizabeth Wilkinson went with her and Eleanor Rathbone to observe the effects of the war on the ground, also estimated that the death toll given by the Basque government was accurate. Finally, Joxe Migel Barandiaran, who met with Father Pedro Mentxaka on June 24 and interviewed at least

7 eyewitnesses to the bombing, estimated 2,000 deaths. Paul Vaillant-Couturier, special envoy for the French newspaper *L'Humanité* who was in Bilbao when the bombing occurred, after interviewing several eyewitnesses concluded that the death toll rose to 1,000.[127] Vaillant-Couturier wrote that "I have seen these children, some dazed, no longer play. And others who are victim of nervous breakdowns at the slightest noise. Suddenly, I saw them running to shelters or the arms of their mothers, when hearing a somewhat strong horn or a truck engine, or the sound of a car that climbs a steep hill, or even because of a door. I interviewed many of them and talked to their parents."[128]

Apart from these reports, we now have the information provided by more than 100 eyewitnesses who were adults when the bombing took place, collected in 1972 by William Smallwood in Gernika. This is the case of the 3 *gudaris* who witnessed the bombing and gave a specific figure of fatalities, and they agreed that the death toll should be more than 1,000. Kaxtor Amunarriz and Xabier Alkorta, who collaborated in the work of collecting and transporting the corpses in Gernika, felt that while it was impossible to know how many people had died because they had no time to start digging out the ruins, the number of deaths "would lie well above 1,000."[129] Jose Ramon Urtiaga, *gudari* of the Lenago-il Battalion, who had come to Gernika retreating from Bolibar, estimated the death toll at around 2,000 people.[130] Besides these, another 4 eyewitnesses of the bombing who were in Gernika on April 26 confirmed the figures given by the *gudaris*. Maria Fe Ormaetxea estimated more than 1,000 deaths. Andoni Perez said that he saw many bodies on the afternoon of April 26 and many more the next day and estimated in "thousands" the number of victims.[131] Txomin Onaindia also estimated the death toll at around 1,000. One of the witnesses interviewed by Smallwood, under the pseudonym of Julio Gorria, stated that "the third day after the bombing (April 29) he went to Bilbao. There was a bombing and I took refuge in the building of La Aurora. There I met a doctor from Gernika and he told me: 'We come now from Gernika and we have counted more than 1,500 corpses so far.'"[132] In general, of the more than one hundred testimonies collected by William Smallwood in Gernika in the spring and summer of 1972, we can conclude a death toll exceeding that given by Steer on April 28 and in line with the official list of the Basque government in June 1937.

The *gudaris* Iñaki Alkain, Faustino Pastor, Pedro Gezuraga, Aurelio Artetxe, Iñaki Rezabal, Sabin Apraiz, and Commander Jon Beiztegi gave no specific figures, but their testimonies indicate a high number of fatalities. Joseba Elosegi, who collaborated in the recovery and removal of bodies, said that Gernika had "a tragic color and the air smelled like burning flesh" and made reference to numerous victims.[133] Jose Arrieta, a *gudari* who lost a finger at the front and was hospitalized in Gernika, saw "two large piles of corpses" in the vicinity of Karmele Deuna Hospital.[134] Other witnesses said that they saw two pits excavated in Gernika and gave other relevant details, but did not give a specific figure, mentioning only that "many people died there."[135] Many other witnesses that I interviewed did not give specific figures.[136]

We can also add to these sixty testimonies the ones recorded in the days after the bombing by Pedro Beitia and Raymond Bossus,[137] as well as the testimony of children such as Imanol Agirre, recorded in July 1937, who despite his young age had to help collect fragments of corpses in baskets after the bombing.[138]

All the eyewitnesses whose testimonies or statements were recorded and published in April or May 1937 agreed with these figures. And it should be noted that, apart from the denial of the bombing by the Spanish, German, and Italian regimes, the thirty-eight direct testimonies cited are the only direct evidence we have of the bombing—that is, they represent 100 percent of the testimonies of adults recorded and registered in the days immediately after the bombing, many among them collaborating in the work of recovering and identifying corpses.

Apart from the eyewitnesses' accounts recorded immediately after the bombing and the more than sixty eyewitness testimonies of the bombing recorded later, we may add a huge number of reports, articles, and communications that offered similar figures in light of the information available. General Jean Armengaud calculated that the rebel bombings in the Basque Country had caused 4,419 casualties in the month of April, following the figure given by the Basque government of 4,046 casualties.[139] A group of 23 French Christian Democrats mentioned hundreds of deaths in Gernika in an article entitled "Pour le peuple basque" (For the Basque people).[140] The examples are endless.

Unlike what happened to the information from press offices controlled by the totalitarian regimes involved in the planning, organization, and execution of the bombing of Gernika, the information provided by foreign journalists was not censored. After the Spanish, German, and Italian regimes denied that Gernika had been bombed, Steer, Monks, and Watson were sent by their newspapers to Gernika on April 27 for the second time in order to corroborate their first reports. When they met with Bruno Mendiguren, head of the press office of the Basque government, he said to them, "Gentlemen, what I can do for you? You really have seen more than I or any other member of my government. Go back to Gernika, talk to anyone you want. There is no censorship today."[141]

Jesuit Father Ramon Arzuaga wrote an article in the *Messenger of the Sacred Heart* that was reproduced by Havas on May 12 and by *La Vanguardia* on May 16. In it Arzuaga wondered why anyone would refuse to accept the testimonies of so many eyewitnesses.[142] The same conclusion was reached by American journalist James M. Minifie, reporter of the *New York Herald Tribune*, who reached the Basque Country when Gernika had already been captured by the rebels. After meeting with several eyewitnesses of the bombing, he concluded that the credibility of the testimonies of Leizaola, Labauria, and Arronategi could not be doubted.[143]

Moreover, there is no indication in the evidence collected from the eyewitnesses that encourages us to conclude that the death toll was any lower than the one provided by Steer. On the contrary, the testimonies show that the removal of the corpses started immediately after the end of the bombing and was interrupted when the town was captured by the rebels on April 29. The bodies recovered during the following days (between April 26 and 28) were found mainly in the streets, forests, and nearby roads, away from the fire and on the top of ruins, uncovered. The bodies were displayed in front of the Karmele Deuna Hospital to be identified and were later transported to the cemetery to be buried there or transported to the cemeteries of their places of origin by their relatives, if possible. The deceased in the Karmele Deuna Hospital who remained unidentified were buried in two mass graves in Gernika.[144] The fragments of bodies that could not be identified were burned on pyres in the Ibarra de San Juan Square in Gernika. The number of corpses lying in the street was so large that, as several eyewitnesses indicated, even after three days of work there were still corpses in the streets: "Three days after the bombing Franco's troops entered Gernika and soon after I came to what our town had been. Arriving at Paseo de los Tilos, in a little road above the cottage of Urdebai [or Urdaibai], in the way up to the Castillo de Perejil, there were still some corpses, but we were so numb, like machines, that we were not even ready to react to them."[145] As Manuela Garai testified, Felipe Bastarretxea's body was not recovered until three days after the bombing: "My brother's mother-in-law went to the cemetery and found his body there and moved it to the cemetery of their town."[146]

After three days, almost no corpses had been recovered from beneath the ruins, because some parts of town were still in flames and inaccessible to the firemen working in the recovery of corpses. The removal of debris did not begin until late February 1939, and by the end of December 1941 the center of Gernika was not yet completely cleared. In other words, after clearing 2,132,582 cubic feet of debris over a period of three years, the Francoist authorities did not record a single death.[147] In fact, today's Gernika is about 5 feet above the Gernika of 1937. Most of the debris was never removed, and the new town was built on top of the ruins of the previous one. As a consequence, the corpses of people buried under the debris were never recovered and registered. Some people around Gernika were forced to remove debris after the town was captured by the rebels, and they continued to find corpses or parts of corpses in such an advanced state of decomposition that some of them refused to keep on working but were forced to continue at gunpoint.

There are only 3 recorded survivors among the 450 people who took refuge in the shelter in Andra Mari Street: Sebastian Uria, who testified that the shelter was packed with people; Jose Monasterio; and an unidentified child. Labauria stated that the shelter held about 450 people and that all of them died under the debris because rescuers could not remove the tons of stone on top of them. Joxe Iturria, a twenty-two-year-old soldier in 1937, has also estimated at 500 the number of people who lost their lives in the Andra Mari refuge and at more than 2,000 the total death toll.[148] Some witnesses reported that on the morning of April 27, the cries of people trapped in that shelter could be heard under the debris, but nothing could be done to help them.

People involved in the events tried to minimize the number and the intensity of the attack. Joachim von Ribbentrop was the first to note that more people had been killed in other places, suggesting that the smaller number of victims somehow diminished the significance of what happened in Gernika. "Less than a hundred people were killed," concluded the committee appointed by the Francoist authorities to investigate the causes of the destruction of Gernika in the Herrán Report, which was published in English to be distributed in the United Kingdom for propaganda purposes. The commission, created ad hoc by the rebel government to promote the idea that the destruction of Gernika was not caused by the bombing, concluded that the town was largely destroyed by fire and subsequent looting by Basque government forces who worked on organizing and implementing such destructive work from April 26 to 28, after a minor bombing by rebel aviation.[149]

Along the same lines, and supported by the conclusions of the Herrán Report, other authors have tried to reduce the magnitude of the attack, the intensity of the bombing, and the number of people killed in Gernika. In 1954 Adolf Galland, a member of the general staff of the Condor Legion, described the bombing as an error and the collateral effect of an attack on the bridge of Gernika.[150] On January 30, 1970, more than thirty years after the bombing, Ricardo de la Cierva stated that the bombing was a "myth" and that "not even a dozen people died."[151] Douglas F. Jerrold wrote that about 100 people were killed in Gernika, but he never provided any data to justify this calculation. Brian R. Crozier simply referred to an air strike and claimed that the destruction of Gernika was mainly due to the fire generated by the "Reds."[152] In 1976 Castor Uriarte, Gernika municipal architect in 1937 and an eyewitness to the attack, stated that the bombing caused 250 deaths,[153] but his data are not consistent with his testimony in 1972. At that time, he told William Smallwood that the number of victims of the bombing was about 200 deaths in the Andra Mari Street shelter and between 50 and 100 fatalities in other parts of the town—that is, a total of between 250 and 300 deaths.[154] It appears that in 1976 Uriarte reduced the estimated number of deaths in the Andra Mari shelter to 45, following testimony included in the Herrán Report.

Jesús Salas said, in line with the data of the Herrán Report, that 120 people were killed during the bombing, because no more corpses were found.[155] Rolf-Dieter Müller also made reference to a "minor attack"[156] and that the number of aircraft involved in the attack and the number of bombs dropped were normal to destroy a bridge of the dimensions of the one at Errenteria—namely, between thirty-one and forty-one tons of bombs to destroy a seventy-foot bridge.[157] James S. Corum wrote in 2008 that the bombings of Gernika and Warsaw were "mythology."[158] He wrote that the figure of 1,654 deaths was "incredibly high" and added, "In reality, the total death toll at Guernica was approximately 300." However, Corum never provided evidence explaining why 1,654 is a high figure or how he came to calculate 300 deaths.

The only reason given by Salas—or by any other author—to calculate the death toll at 120 or a similar figure is that the corpses of only 120 victims of the bombing were ever found. In 1992 Humberto Unzueta recorded for the first time the names of 115 of the victims and added 5 other unidentified persons to this list.[159] He pointed out that it is improbable that rebel authorities made any effort to recover the bodies of the victims of the bombing.

It is not my intention at this point to enter a methodological or historiographical debate, but I must point out that the figure of 120 corpses does not indicate that there were only 120 deaths, neither in the case of Gernika nor in any other atrocity that occurred before or after the bombing. Two main facts explain why we have the records of only 120 corpses. First, the Francoist dictatorship lasted forty years, until 1975, and the regime's enduring official version was that the town had not been bombed but was reduced to ashes by Basque nationalists or, in general, by the "Reds." It was forbidden to speak of the bombing, and those who dared were very harshly punished. William Smallwood reported that after the bombing, a priest brought from outside Gernika and probably from outside the Basque Country repeated every day during the mass, in Spanish, that the people in town should purge their sin for having burned their homes. One of those days, after listening to the sermon, two women went to the sacristy to tell the priest that German aircraft had destroyed Gernika. The priest threw them out. The next morning, they were forced to leave their homes, had their heads shaved in front of their doors, and were marched through the streets with their hands tied to their shoulders. Subsequently, they were convicted in a court-martial and sentenced to thirty-six months in prison. For forty years, the bombing could not be investigated, and many people who had any information about the location of the corpses perished or were officially silenced.[160]

As Francisco M. Vargas pointed out, the documents indicate that the Gernika-Forua Cemetery became the burial place of people who died at the Karmele Deuna Hospital from wounds suffered in the bombing.[161] Andresa Zumeta and Andresa Idoiaga went on the morning of April 27 to the cemetery to help identify corpses that had been moved there to be buried. There were rows of bodies lined up, and although some were easy to identify, others could never be. Most of those identified were people from around Gernika or nearby villages.[162] When identified, these bodies were buried in the various village cemeteries, as shown by the records of the dead. Sabin Apraiz, *gudari* of the Itxarkundia Battalion, reported that "the next morning I went to the cemetery trying to find my girlfriend's sister, but fortunately I knew that she was well. I saw many corpses there. They were lying in rows and had been taken there in cars and trucks. There I saw the Garteiz sisters and Juanita Beotegi who had a wound in the neck but that for the rest seemed to be alive; I also saw the bodies of many other people of both sexes."[163] The bodies of those first unidentified victims of the bombing of Gernika "were buried in a large mass grave, and others in the land annexed to the cemetery which is now part of the cemetery."[164] Apart from these bodies, as Minister of Justice Leizaola said, 590 people died in various hospitals from injuries incurred during the bombing of Gernika. They were buried outside Gernika, in areas adjacent to where they died, mainly in the hospitals of Amorebieta, Bermeo, Mundaka, or Bilbao, where most of the wounded were transferred.[165]

However, none of these sites was ever excavated, and no effort was ever made to list the corpses buried there—just the opposite. As German officers Hans H. von Beust[166] and Alfons Kössinger[167] declared, one of the objectives of the rebel army after the capture of Gernika was to suppress any physical evidence of the bombing. The men involved in the attack were ordered never to mention the bombing.[168] After Gernika was occupied by rebel troops, men from surrounding villages were forced to excavate the town to remove any material evidence that Gernika had been bombed. Pedro Agirre, one of those civilians forced to work in the ruins of Gernika, reported that they found partially decomposed corpses and body parts buried in the rubble. The bodies were simply placed in bullock carts and moved elsewhere.[169] These corpses were not buried in the two mass graves mentioned by Andresa Idoiaga and Andresa Zumeta, because these pits had already been covered by then.[170]

All death registries were erased and the archives purged. One of the few documents relating to the bombing of Gernika that survived the purge in Bizkaia is a fifteen-page file on the repair of irrigation truck BI-2883, which "was burned in Gernika before the entry of the national troops."[171] The records of those 590 people who died days after the bombing in Bilbao and of those who died after being taken to the various war hospitals in Amorebieta, Bermeo, or Mundaka are also missing.[172] There is no official record of deaths caused by the bombing in the books of the court of Gernika, because the pages for the dates between April 26 and May 22 were torn out. The only documentary sources that have survived are the death registries of the parish churches of Gernika, Andra Mari, and San Pedro and of the churches in the towns near Gernika, as well as some of the civil records of the surrounding towns. However, in many of these books, such as in the death registry of Errigoiti, the names of 2 victims of the bombing are crossed out with an X.[173] In the death register of the civil registry of Muxika, 10 records of the bombing were erased, and other names were later written on top of them.[174]

One of the few records that we still have is the census. Gernika had a population of 5,630 inhabitants, according to the census of July 1936.[175] In 1940, three years after the attack, the number of residents recorded in the census was 3,381, a reduction of 40 percent.[176] In sum, Gernika in 1940 had 2,249 fewer residents than in 1936, and we have to add that some of the inhabitants of Gernika in 1940 were new residents (people who were not residents of Gernika in 1936). Of course, among the 2,249 people missing in Gernika in 1940, some were exiles, political prisoners, refugees, migrants, and people living in villages nearby Gernika and elsewhere in the Basque Country after losing their houses in the bombing. But some were also killed in the bombing.[177] Unzueta claimed that the data on population trends indicate that the total population of Gernika (residents or not) actually fell from 9,566 inhabitants in 1930 to 8,082 in 1940—that is, a loss of fewer than 1,484 residents, despite the incorporation into Gernika of the neighborhood of Ajangiz, which had 535 residents in 1940.[178]

There is no official report on the bodies found by rebel authorities after the occupation of Gernika on April 29, 1937, other than the 35 corpses recorded by the Herrán Report and the 18 entries in the civil registry of Gernika.[179] Based on the Herrán Report, several authors have repeated that 45 people were killed in the shelter on Andra Mari Street, which is far from accurate. The report includes the testimony of an eyewitness named Jesús M. Obieta, who stated that "in a certain unnamed shelter were found forty-five dead persons, of whom the corpses had not all been identified, but that they appeared to be those of villagers who had attended the market which had taken place that day in Guernica."[180] This does not mean that 45 people died in the shelter on Andra Mari Street, but shows that 45 bodies were recovered from an unnamed shelter.[181] The information available indicates that many more people were killed in the Andra Mari Street shelter. Basically, this shelter was just the result of putting a roof made of beams in the part of this street between Artekale and Barrenkale Streets. As municipal architect Castor Uriarte said, that shelter was 40 meters long and was as wide as the street itself, which we may estimate at about 3.65 meters,[182] so the shelter had an area of approximately 146 square meters.[183] According to all the evidence we have, people were crowded into all the shelters, to the point that they could barely move, so we can estimate that there were more than 400 people—3 people per square meter—in the Andra Mari Street shelter. And this is a conservative estimate, because 3 people per square meter does not correspond with the extreme overcrowding described by Sebastian Uria, one of the few survivors in this refuge, who later testified that "[the shelter] was jam-packed. We were standing packed like sardines in a bin."[184] Juan Ibai testified that he sought refuge in that shelter but was unable to enter because of the number of people in it, so he had to go to another shelter.[185] Uxua Makazaga could not get into the shelter on Andra Mari Street either, so she had to seek shelter elsewhere.[186] According to the testimony of Mayor Jose Labauria, "Among the debris there were many corpses, but also outside the town, corpses of people machine-gunned by the pursuit planes appeared in the fields. Those in the shelter located between Artekale and Barrenkale streets (that contained about 450 people) were all killed as a result of a bomb that fell on the Ribera butcher's store that demolished the building to which the shelter was attached, collapsing just on top of them."[187]

Furthermore, to state that 45 people lost their lives in the Andra Mari refuge based on the Herrán Report is inconsistent with the report itself because the report registers the recovery of 22 bodies allegedly killed in the Andra Mari Street shelter, of which only 4 could be identified.[188] And we know that Felipe Bastarretxea, who was identified and registered as having died in Andra Mari, did not die there. But regardless of the lack of consistency and credibility of the Herrán Report, to say that a total of 45 people were killed in that shelter implies that the majority of people who sought shelter under the protection of a roof made of beams and sandbags—which was hit by at least two 551-pound bombs, as a consequence of which the roof and facades of the surrounding buildings collapsed on them—survived.[189] This is even less plausible if we consider the testimony of Joseba Elosegi and Sabin Apraiz, confirming that the fire spread before they could dig out the debris and that they could hear the cries of people buried under the ruins in various parts of the town center. Also *gudaris* Jose Ramon Urtiaga and Kaxtor Amunarriz confirmed that they could not save anyone from this shelter.[190] Carmen Zabaljauregi confirmed that even the next day, on April 27, the rescuers were not able to dig out the Andra Mari refuge and rescue anyone from the debris. The heartbreaking testimony of Federico Iraeta also confirms that on April 27, the *gudaris* working on the rescue had not yet been able to dig out an opening to the shelter. Although there were people still alive in ruins, the rescuers could do nothing for them because the building facades had collapsed on the shelter, burying the survivors under tons of rock. Francisca Arriaga also stated that on the morning of April 27, it was possible to hear the cries of people buried under the rubble.[191] Another eyewitness stated:

> The next morning I went to the hospital and, with some other men, I examined the shelters where people still laid buried. We were informed that some people were still alive. I saw the long shelter that had been built in one of the streets [Andra Mari]. I do not know how anyone could have survived in that place. I looked at the two ends and, both were covered by tons of material. I was in town for two days, working in the hospital. I know that we did not receive any corpse from the shelters until then. Mola's troops arrived after that and I do not think they were in a hurry to dig up these people. Given the time factor and the fact that these shelters were in the center of the town, where the fire was most intense, I do not think any of the people who died there were ever identified.[192]

According to the testimony of Maria Medinabeitia, whose mother died in the shelter of Andra Mari and who never recovered her body, everyone in that shelter died except for a single child.[193] We know the names of only 2 survivors, who saved their lives because they were near the entrances, Jose Monasterio and Jose Uria.[194] To these we should add the baby mentioned by Maria Medinabeitia, making a total of 3 survivors.

The data that we can compare with documentary evidence or the testimonies of eyewitnesses allow us to establish with certainty that the Andra Mari Street shelter was full of people; it was unfinished; it had a capacity of 450–500 people; it collapsed due to the direct impact of at least two 551-pound bombs; as a result of the impact, the buildings on both sides of the street collapsed on the refuge, burying the people who sought refuge there; and the next day, the *gudaris* were still trying to remove the debris, but they never got to rescue anyone from there. Moreover, a month after the attack, the refuge had not yet been dug out. Between April 26 and May 29, 22 corpses were recovered, only 5 of which could be identified (and we have evidence that at least 1 of them did not die in the shelter). Apart from the 3 people mentioned, we have no record or information of any other survivor. Finally, there is neither certainty nor any oral testimony confirming that the remaining 21 people who were included on the list of the deaths at the shelter actually lost their lives there. That explains why Humberto

Unzueta included only 10 of the reported 45 deaths in his list of the 120 registered deaths of the bombing, 6 of them identified and 4 of whom could not be identified.[195]

From a historiographical standpoint, it appears that some authors have assumed that 45 people were killed in the Andra Mari shelter on the sole basis of the incorrect translation of information included in a propaganda booklet written under censorship that contradicts the data provided in the report itself (which, as indicated, mentions the recovery of only 22 bodies from the Andra Mari shelter, which is inaccurate). Also, it is difficult to explain why an author would accept one single testimony in the Herrán Report while denying or at least ignoring or discrediting the testimony of Mayor Jose Labauria, Sebastian Uria (only surviving witness in the shelter), Joxe Iturria, or all the testimonies that I have mentioned in the previous paragraphs.

Herbert R. Southworth estimated, like Anton Irala, that there are reasons to believe that the death toll may be higher than 1,645.[196] To assume that there were no deaths other than those bodies that were recovered and recorded is to say that the Basque government was able to find all the corpses while Gernika was still burning, in just two days and without digging out the ruins. Moreover, to assume against all the material evidence we have that the drafters of the Herrán Report recorded all the bodies they found and that after removing 2,132,582 cubic feet of debris in the city center of Gernika, the authorities in charge of the reconstruction of Gernika did not find any additional bodies is intellectually irresponsible. Indeed, this has been precisely one of the major problems that organizations dedicated to the recovery of historical memory have had to face—that in most cases, the perpetrators of atrocities, whoever they are and wherever they have acted, kill witnesses, dig mass graves, burn bodies, hide evidence, destroy documents, and intimidate witnesses. Subsequently, they deny that an atrocity has been committed, and in most cases they blame the victims for what happened. All this behavior can be observed in the case of Gernika.[197]

We must base our calculations on the documents and evidence available. There is no reason to believe that Steer, Corman, Monks, and Watson, or all the eyewitnesses to the attack who were in Gernika during the days following the bombing, lied when stating in unambiguous terms things like "I saw six hundred bodies," not when these figures were first questioned by Joachim von Ribbentrop, who was tried and convicted at Nuremberg for crimes against humanity, or by members of the Franco regime or authors of openly Fascist ideology. This is especially important because there is no factual evidence that leads us to raise doubts about the information provided by the war correspondents or other eyewitnesses, nor is there any material fact that may lead us to establish a lower death toll than that mentioned by all eyewitnesses.

Considering the difficulty of tabulating the number of casualties, there are no compelling reasons to assume that the death toll was anything less than 1,654, the number provided by the people in charge of recovering, counting, identifying, and burying the corpses. We would have to explain why Minister Leizaola was mistaken when he said that 590 people died in Basque hospitals in the days after the attack, why Steer's and Corman's estimates were not correct, why Monks and Watson were wrong when stating that they had counted hundreds of corpses. No such explanations exist. Furthermore, there is no reason to believe that the Basque government or the three war correspondents ever exaggerated or manipulated casualty numbers before or after the attack against Gernika.

As Monks said, all reporters testified under oath that rebel aircraft had bombed Gernika and that 1,000 civilians had been killed. However, Monks added, "When Franco hastened to deny that his German planes have wrecked the ancient Basque capital, he was trying to make liars of the three accredited war correspondents who were on the spot. Another London newspaper correspondent, Reuter's [*sic*] correspondent, and myself. He tried to tell us that we didn't see thirty German Junker bombers flying towards Guernica at four o'clock on the afternoon of April 26, just ten minutes before, according to the stories the survivors told us later, they swooped on the defenceless town. Franco told the world there were none of his planes up that day, because of bad weather."[198] And the three reporters—Monks, Steer, and Holme—went back to Gernika the very next day at the request of their directors in London to verify the information, compare data, and ensure that their stories were accurate. Monks reported:

> Later that day I was to get a bomb addressed to me, personally. So was Steer. So was Holme. It was in the form of a cable from my office: "Berlin denies Guernica bombing. Franco says he had no planes up yesterday owing fog. Queipo de Llano [Franco's foul-mouthed broadcasting general in Seville] says Reds dynamited Guernica during retreat. Please check up soonest."
>
> Please check up!

> Back we went to Guernica, all three of us. We compared notes. We checked each other's experiences the day before. Refugees from Guernica were pouring into Bilbao now. With an interpreter I took one family for a car ride to calm them down, soothe their shattered nerves. Then gently, quietly, I got from them their story. It was the same as the others. We asked [Bruno] Mendiguren to collect the weather reports for us from all fronts. No one had seen fog for a week on our front.
>
> Then came the last straw, for me. We were sitting round a radio at the Presidencia listening to General de Llano make one of his vile broadcasts to the women of Madrid, telling them, in detail, what to expect from the Moors. Suddenly he switched to Guernica. "That Senor Monks," he croaked. "Don't believe what he writes of Guernica. All the time he was with Franco's forces he was drunk."[199]

And, Monks added, "Fact is, I'm a teetotaller. Have been all my life. Ask anyone who knows me. But don't ask me who bombed Guernica. I might take to drink."[200]

It is due to the credibility of the information provided by Monks that when John Carey decided to include a chapter on the destruction of Gernika in his book on historical memory, he chose one of the articles written by Noel Monks.[201] As indicated, based on the eyewitnesses' accounts and the material evidence at his disposal, Herbert R. Southworth estimated that the number of deaths should be higher than 1,654.[202] In the latest edition of his history of the Spanish Civil War, Hugh Thomas noted that while it is very difficult to determine the exact death toll, it might have been up to 1,000.[203] Paul Preston did not provide a figure, but quoted George Steer and Canon Alberto Onaindia and emphasized the credibility of both eyewitnesses.[204] Michael Alpert expressed the same idea.[205] Philip Knightley has argued that the death toll of the bombing of Gernika has not been established with certainty, considering estimates ranging between 1,000 and 2,000 deaths.[206] Recent works on the war, such as those by Helen Graham for Cambridge University Press and Francisco J. Romero for Palgrave Macmillan, rely on the official figures provided by the Basque government.[207] Ian Patterson has also stated that there is no reason to doubt Monks's credibility and has provided the figures given by the Basque government.[208]

As Noel Monks stated, "The full death toll in Guernica may never be known, for although bodies are being unearthed hourly from wrecked homes and buildings, it is believed that many will never be recovered."[209]

Anton Irala has also said that the exact death toll will never be known. Today, the corpses of people killed in the war are constantly being located and exhumed; the body of Basque commander Cándido Saseta was found with other unidentified bodies in March 2008. Most of them lie in the ground with no name and no memories, yet they are being beckoned once again by history. By building evidence for an accurate number of casualties, we will not bring the victims back to life, but when we simply slash the casualty count with no evidence and end the story there, we deny them the right to be remembered after being killed.

# 5

## The Aftermath of the Bombing

"We were not guilty of anything and, being innocent, we are charged with full responsibility for the bombing," said Erwin Jaenecke, a member of the general staff of the Condor Legion. Generalissimo Franco was aware of the possible repercussions of the bombing within the Catholic ecclesiastical hierarchy and in the international political arena, and he instructed Spanish officials to deny that the Nationalists were responsible for the destruction of the city. "Within twenty-four hours, when the grim story was told to the world, Franco was going to brand these shocked, homeless people as liars. So-called British experts were going to come to Guernica, weeks afterwards, when the smell of burnt human flesh had been replaced by petrol dumped here and there among the ruins by Mola's men, and deliver pompous judgments: 'Guernica was set on fire willfully by the Reds.'"[1]

The denial of the bombing began almost immediately after the attack. General Carlo Bossi, in a telegram dated April 27, refers to Franco's order to deny the statements of President José Antonio Agirre relating to air raids and his recommendation that everyone in his government fiercely denounce the Reds' alleged system of burning all urban centers before retreating.[2] This document shows that Franco had news of the bombardment of Gernika only hours after it happened, by 7:00 A.M. on April 27, and that by then he had already decided to deny it and to blame the Basques for having burned their own sacred town.

Following this line of action, Radio Salamanca, one of the National Movement's official broadcasters, sent out the following report a day after the attack:

> It is not the first time that Agirre, "boss" of the Republic of Euzkadi,[3] lies. Agirre has declared today that foreign aviation supporting the nationalist forces in Spain have bombed Gernika and that as a result it has been set afire, in order to inflict the biggest morale impact on the Basques. Agirre lies. He lies and he knows it very well. First, there is not any German or foreign air force in the Nationalist Spain.[4] Secondly, Gernika has not been set afire by us. Franco's Spain does not set fires. The incendiary torch is a monopoly of those people that burned Irun and have burned Eibar. We know that Agirre lies, like what he is, an ordinary delinquent. We have respected Gernika not only for what it symbolizes, but as good Basques, we have respected Gernika as we respect everything Spanish. Franco's army does not set fires. The Basque Country knows that we respect and will respect its traditions. Franco's Spain does not set fires.[5]

On April 29, General Gonzalo Queipo de Llano broadcast a statement via Radio Sevilla claiming that the "Reds" had set Gernika on fire, and his speech was published the next day in ABC. After these claims, the British *Daily Express* interviewed the general, who again insisted that the Basques and Asturian miners had destroyed the city.[6]

Reichsminister of Foreign Affairs Konstantin von Neurath and Joachim von Ribbentrop, Germany's ambassador to Great Britain, were also aware of the possible repercussions of the bombing within the Non-Intervention Committee. As a consequence, Germany adopted the official Spanish version of the massacre. As General Wilhelm Faupel, German envoy to General Franco, reported to Hans Georg von Mackensen, state secretary in Germany's Foreign Ministry, on April 29 and 30 the Nationalist government's press bureau issued an article on the "burning" of Gernika. Faupel subsequently adapted the official version and repeated the same idea, word for word: "Guernica was destroyed with fire and gasoline. It was set afire and reduced to ruins by the Red hordes in the criminal service of Agirre, the President of the Basque Republic. Agirre planned the destruction of Guernica with the devilish intention of laying the blame before the enemy's door and producing a storm of indignation among the already conquered and demoralized Basques."[7] Copies of his statement were given to foreign press representatives.

As a consequence of this policy of denial by the Spanish and German regimes, the press controlled by the four totalitarian governments involved in the war, Spanish and German but also Italian and Portuguese, referred simply to the "burning" of Gernika. But these official fabrications were not consistent. For instance, Joseph Goebbels highlighted the publication of an article on May 6 about the destruction of Gernika in the *Volkischer Beobachter,* based on the French news agency Havas's account of the facts. However, the German newspaper added that the town had been set on fire by Bolsheviks rather than by the less familiar anarchists, as had been stated in the original Havas report.[8] Other newspapers blamed the Basque government, the "Reds," the "anarchists," the "Bolsheviks," the "Jews," or other groups, such as the "Asturian miners," of reducing Gernika to ashes.

Sixty-three hours after the attack, the rebels captured Gernika. The first units of engineers were sent to start clearing the town at 10:30 A.M. on Thursday, April 29, and the first German specialists arrived to analyze the effectiveness of the destruction. Colonel Juan Vigón appointed engineers Vicente Machimbarrena and Joaquín Miláns del Bosch to write a report on the "burning" of Gernika. They arrived in Gernika at about 5:00 P.M., and after two hours of observation they were set to start writing their testimony, which was finished on May 1. The report concluded that Gernika was completely destroyed and that only a few buildings near the ancient Basque parliament, where the Oak of Gernika is located, had survived. The report added that Gernika was not a target from a military viewpoint and that "one could think that someone wanted to punish Basque separatism in the city of the traditional tree, however, apart that such consideration is unfounded, and that this kind of revenge is not consistent with the morale of the armies of Generalissimo Franco, it turns out that the famous tree is precisely among the very little still standing."[9]

The Machimbarrena-Miláns del Bosch report conceded that Gernika had indeed suffered a slight bombing on April 26[10] because they had discovered a few bomb holes and some pieces of explosive shells. However, they asserted that this was not the main cause of the destruction. The authors stated that "as had happened at Eibar and Irun," Gernika was set on fire by the "Red hordes," helped in their retreat by professional Asturian dynamiters, and that the effect of the flames was intensified because of the inactivity of the Basque fire services, which had allowed the fire to spread until it destroyed the entire town. Moreover, according to the report, certain eyewitnesses declared that the fire could have been extinguished "with some few buckets of water."

The Machimbarrena report was written in Spanish to respond to the thousands of press articles on the bombing of Gernika that were published in the democratic countries of Europe and the Americas, but it did not reach its intended audience. A month later, Franco's regime organized a new committee chaired by engineer Estanislao Herrán to prepare another report on "the burning of Gernika." Since the testimonies of international reporters such as Steer or Monks were difficult to deny, this new report also admitted that there was a small bombing by German planes on April 26, but it insisted that the destruction of Gernika was caused not by this bombing but by Basque troops who took advantage of the bombing to burn and loot Gernika. The report was completed by September 1937.[11] It is important to stress that it was published only in English for distribution in the United Kingdom, because to admit that there had been a bombing contradicted most of the articles in the Spanish press and the propaganda pamphlets written in Spanish and distributed in Spain. The Herrán Report was published under the title *Guernica: Being the Official Report of a Commission Appointed by the National Government to Investigate the Causes of the Destruction of Guernica on April 26–28, 1937.* It is important to mention its conclusions because the Herrán Report is still used as a historiographical source, and some authors continue to claim that its conclusions are accurate:

> The Commission, after its work of investigation, and having heard the evidence adduced, has come to the following conclusions:
>
> (1) The destruction of Guernica was caused by fire.
>
> (2) The number of victims in Guernica on the 26th April did not reach one hundred.
>
> (3) No damage was caused to the Tree of Guernica, the Parliament House, the convents converted into military barracks, or to the arms and munitions factories.
>
> (4) At four o'clock on the afternoon of the 26th April the few inhabitants who remained in Guernica observed the appearance of certain aeroplanes. They thereupon took refuge in the shelters and saw nothing of what took place in the town up to half-past seven in the evening, at which hour they ventured forth.
>
> (5) For three hours and a half, and throughout the following night, the inhabitants of Guernica listened to heavy explosions which took place within the town.
>
> (6) Near the network of highways to the east of Guernica several aerial bombs fell. It appeared that the object of these bombs was to cut the communications.

(7) No signs are visible of the explosion of any aerial bombs within the town.

(8) The explosions heard within the town by the inhabitants of Guernica were the result of dynamite detonated in the sewers and in other parts of the town, in accordance with the Basque Government's prearranged plan.

(9) At eight o'clock on the night of the 26th April, when the townsfolk left the shelters, a certain number of houses in Guernica began to burn. It would have been an easy matter to have put out these fires and to repair the damage caused up to that time. After the above-mentioned hour no aeroplanes flew over Guernica, nor in its neighborhood, up to the time our soldiers entered. The destruction of Guernica, therefore, cannot be attributed to German planes.

(10) From this hour onward (eight o'clock in the evening of the 26th April) the inhabitants were able to see what was taking place in the town. The Red militiamen not only took no steps to check the conflagration, but they prevented the townsfolk from taking steps to that end. For three successive days these militiamen continued to set fires alight and to help them to spread; and some of this work was continued later, even after our troops had entered Guernica.

(11) The fire and the explosions caused the total destruction of 71 per cent of the houses in Guernica; 7 per cent were damaged to a less but nevertheless noteworthy extent, and the remaining 22 per cent were damaged slightly.

(12) The destruction of Guernica was the climax of the evacuation order issued by the Basque Government for the 26th of April; this order caused the departure from the town of certain inhabitants who had somehow received notice of it, and who feared the manner in which the evacuation might be carried out.

(13) Apart from the complex political factors involved and its use as world-wide propaganda, the burning of Guernica is similar in its cause and effect to that of Irun, Eibar, and Potes.

(14) The campaign of political propaganda of which Guernica has been made the subject has no basis in fact, but is a clever blend of unrelated events that in no way approximate reality.[12]

As noted by Christopher Holme, during the war the Spanish office of censorship was offering up to one thousand dollars to reporters who would record favorable accounts of rebel activities for Italian radio.[13] It is not a big step from rewarding false news to criminalizing the truth, and at the time of the bombing of Gernika the Nationalist regime had two French reporters in prison or under house arrest "for collaboration with the enemy." Esteban Urkiaga (Lauaxeta), who was apprehended in Gernika with *La Petite Gironde* reporter George Berniard, was shot soon after. The Spanish Nationalist, German, Italian, and Portuguese regimes' press agencies soon gained international notoriety for their methods of censorship, which often resulted in arrests and executions at home.[14] One journalist was expelled from the Republican zone, while more than thirty were expelled from the rebel zone. At least one reporter, Guy de Traversay of the newspaper *L'Intransigeant*, was shot, and nearly a dozen others were interrogated and imprisoned by the rebels.[15] Geoffrey Dawson, editor of the *Times* (London), began receiving German complaints after his newspaper published Steer's reports on Gernika, "but its [Steer's reporting] essential accuracy has never been denied and there has not been any attempt here to rub it in or harp on it."[16]

## The International Impact of the Bombing

The destruction of Gernika, the first massive bombing of an open city in Europe in which civilians were killed as part of a military experiment, had a significant international impact and soon became a symbol of the horrors of war, especially the long-anticipated world war that everyone expected to break out very soon.[17] As US minister to Portugal Robert G. Caldwell reported to the State Department shortly after the bombing, headlines in most papers in Paris, London, and the United States on April 29 and 30 reported the destruction of Gernika from the air and highlighted the outrage expressed in Paris and London.[18]

Before the Fascists disseminated their official version of events, the president of the Basque government, José Antonio Agirre, broadcast the following message on April 29, 1937:

> Before the offensive shamelessness of the rebel elements, affirming that we have set afire our towns, I raise before the world the most energetic and vigorous protest, appealing to the testimony of journalists and consular representatives who, with terror, have contemplated that the instincts of destruction of the mercenaries at the service of the Spanish rebels know no limit.
>
> Before God and History, which will judge us all, I affirm that for three

> hours and a half German airplanes bombed with inconceivable cruelty the defenseless civilian population of the historic town of Gernika, now reduced to ashes, machine-gunning women and children, many of whom perished, while the rest escaped and fled in terror.
>
> I ask the civilized world if it is possible to allow the extermination of a people that has always had as its most valued goal the defense of its liberties and the protection of the secular democracy of Gernika, symbol of which is its millenarian Tree.
>
> I want to believe that the nations will aid the more than three hundred thousand women and children who come to take refuge in Bilbao. We request nothing for the men, because our firm intention to defend the liberties of our nation will compel us to make the greatest sacrifices, with serene spirit and calm conscience.[19]

News of the massacre at Gernika catalyzed worldwide opposition to the bombing of open cities. International public opinion swayed forcefully against the massacre. On April 30, the Spanish Republican representative at the League of Nations, Julio Álvarez del Vayo, denounced the brutality of the German bombing. On May 15, the rebels bombed Valencia, capital city of the Republican government, in retaliation for the bombing of Zaragoza by Republican government forces on May 3 and 6. All of these attacks, plus the shelling of Almería by the German navy on May 31, set off a powerful chain of reactions regarding the bombing of open cities such as Gernika. One of the first protests was organized by the Friends of Spain, which published a booklet entitled *Help Us to Defeat Fascism!* that included texts by Ángel Ossorio y Gallardo, H. G. Wells, Jean Richard, Albert Einstein, Romain Rolland, Pedro Bosch Gimpera, Juan Comorera, Gabriel Alomar, and Heinrich Mann, among others.[20]

Echoes of the bombing soon reached the United States. On April 29, 1937, three days after the attack, Lluis Companys, president of the Catalan government, sent a telegram to President Franklin D. Roosevelt, who received it on May 5.[21] On April 30, after receiving the first reports from his British and French colleagues and his own information services, Ambassador Bowers sent his first report on Gernika to Secretary of State Hull, who received it on May 1.[22] In a subsequent report, Bowers summarized the free world's reaction to the destruction of Gernika and reported that the news had caused some uneasiness in General Franco's camp. The first reaction of the rebels was one of elation, wrote Bowers, but when the thunder of public opinion rolled in, reaching a climax in Lord Cecil's denunciation of the act as the most savage in history, the Nationalists began to issue denials.[23]

The news rapidly reached Basque communities in the Western Hemisphere, from Argentina to the United States, who protested and mobilized their organizations to help the victims. One of the first protests came from Florencio Laucirica, president of the Basque American Benevolent Association in New York, who in the name of Basque Americans strongly protested the destruction of Gernika, "the land of our forefathers," and the inhuman atrocities committed on the civilian population of the democratic Basque Country by Spanish Nationalist forces.[24]

The massacre prompted an immediate process of evacuation that from May to August 1937 would take nearly thirty-two thousand children abroad to remove them from the bombs and starvation in the Basque Country. On April 30, Álvarez del Vayo met with French prime minister André Léon Blum in Paris to discuss the possibility of creating a program to evacuate about a hundred thousand women and children from the Basque Country.[25] Funds to support this evacuation campaign and help other victims were raised in Basque emigrant communities around the world. On December 18, 1937, Dean Driscoll of the Idahoan Basque Sheepherders' Overall Dance Association applied to the State Department to collect money for the relief of Basque refugee children.[26] The request was accepted only two days later. John Archabal[27] was the official promoter, and the group planned to collect money at a dance at the Riverside Pavillion in Boise on December 21. The association raised $1,366, and the funds[28] were sent to the American Red Cross in Boise, to be transferred to the International Red Cross in Bilbao. Another group, the Committee for the Aid of the Basque Refugee Children in France, applied a year later, on November 1, 1938, to be registered with the secretary of state.[29] The committee, led by Florencio Lauzirika and Jerónimo Astoreka of New York, obtained approval a week later.

The bombing prompted widespread press coverage throughout the world.[30] Most American, British, and French newspapers published numerous articles about the bombing between April 27 and the beginning of July, and most newspapers in free Europe, the United States, and the other democracies in the Americas accepted the thesis that the massacre had been ordered and executed by the combined German, Italian, and Spanish rebel armies. Moreover, most of these newspapers expressed their disapproval of the attack. As awareness of the bombing spread, public opinion began to turn against the perpetrators. Also, the position of the

American Catholic Church, which had previously openly opposed the Republican forces, began to turn in sympathy to the innocent victims of the attack.

Several foreign correspondents, among them George L. Steer, Christopher Holme,[31] Noel Monks, and Mathieu Corman, who were in Gernika in the days immediately after the bombing, offered details of the devastation and denounced as completely untrue the statement released by the rebel government in Salamanca claiming that Gernika was destroyed by the "Reds." Steer stated that "I personally talked to over twenty refugees from Guernica in the outskirts of the town on the night of the bombing. Apart from the number of planes involved, all the various accounts match in every detail."[32] The correspondents offered proof that Gernika was destroyed by an aerial attack by citing the countless bullet holes around the town and on roofs that had not burned. "Another journalist with me collected three German bombs dated 1936," Steer reported. He concluded, "I was in Guernica until 1.30 in the morning [on the night of April 26 to 27], and there was no smell of petrol anywhere."[33] He was thus contradicting rebel claims that "Reds" had burned the town using massive amounts of gasoline.

In Europe the press was divided. The free international press echoed the news coming from British and French correspondents in Gernika, describing the bombing in detail. In the United Kingdom, the *Times*,[34] *Star*,[35] *Daily Express*,[36] *Daily Worker*,[37] *News Chronicle*, *Evening News*, *Evening Standard*,[38] *Manchester Guardian*, *Glasgow Herald*, *Daily Herald*,[39] *Morning Post*, and *Daily Mail*,[40] among others, published descriptions of the massacre and its consequences. The first newspapers in Europe to report on the attack were the British *News Chronicle*, *Evening News*, *Evening Standard*, and *Star*, which all published Holmes's account on the afternoon of April 27. Following them, the *Glasgow Herald*, *Manchester Guardian*, *Daily Post*, *Daily Telegraph*, and *Daily Worker* first reported the attack on the morning of April 28. The French press followed with accounts from the Havas correspondents at the Basque front. *Ce Soir*, *Le Matin*, *L'Echo de Paris*, *Le Petit Parisien*, *Le Intransigeant*, *Le Populaire*, and *Paris Soir* published news of the bombing starting on April 28. *Regards*, *L'Aube*, *L'Ordre*, and *La Croix*[41] also included stories about the attack. The information published in *La Croix* was particularly relevant, because the Catholic ecclesiastical hierarchy had until then been openly supportive of the government led by Generalissimo Franco.

However, *Le Journal*, *Le Jour*, and *Je Suis Partout*, which all openly supported the military uprising, did not mention the event. *Le Journal* even published a front-page story on April 28 describing atrocities supposedly committed by the Spanish Republican army elsewhere. Other conservative French newspapers, such as *Le Figaro*, *Le Jour*, *L'Excelsior*, *L'Action Française*, and *Le Journal des Débats*, also ignored the event. But some European mass media supportive of the uprising—such as the *Morning Post* and *Daily Mail*; the Belgian *La Métropole*, *L'Indépendance Belge*, and *La Libre Belgique*; and the Swiss *Journal de Genève*—published accounts of the bombing. The attitude of the French press favorable to Franco's National Movement may have been an early signal of the French state's willingness to cooperate with Germany, a position that led to the creation of the collaborationist Vichy government in 1940 after the Republic's surrender to Germany.

The *Chicago Daily Tribune* and the *Bakersfield Californian* were among the first newspapers to publish news of the massacre. The *Chicago Daily Tribune* described the event as "the worst air raid yet" in an article published on April 27, the morning after the attack. The *Charleston (SC) Gazette* published an account of the bombing on April 28 that summarizes what appeared in the US press the previous day:

> Details of the Guernica's bloody desolation trickling into Vitoria tonight told a ghastly story of slaughter which even included the machine-gunning of flocks of terror-stricken sheep. Guernica was once the Basque capital and its former antiquity has been cherished by Spain. Everything lays in ruins. General Mola's insurgent planes attacked the city in groups of seven, hand-grenading its houses at first, then machine-gunning them as hundreds fled to shelters. Basque radio broadcasts described the casualties as "uncountable" with literally hundreds of Guernica's inhabitants roasted alive or torn to pieces by flying steel and drilling machine-gun bullets. The air raid lasted little more than three hours. . . . Mola's planes returned again and again to swoop low over isolated farmhouses in an area of five miles around Guernica. Anything alive, including livestock, was drilled with machine-gun bullets. . . . It was hours before fire fighters could enter the blazing city. Buildings and houses were veritable furnaces. Everywhere there was chaos with charred beams, twisted girders, broken masonry and smouldering ashes remaining where homes once stood.[42]

In the following days, many other American newspapers published stories about the massacre. In a sampling of the US press, I recorded nearly

600 news items about the bombing of Gernika between April 27 and 30, 1937 (about 100 on the twenty-seventh, 120 on the twenty-eighth, 170 on the twenty-ninth, and 210 on the thirtieth). The morning after the attack, virtually every statewide newspaper in the United States reported the bombing, most of them on the front page. On the twenty-ninth, the attack was mentioned in a significantly greater number of newspapers, and from April 30 on information and comments on the bombing appeared almost daily, allowing an estimate of 7,000 news articles on the bombardment of Gernika in the American press between April 26 and July 12, 1937. Indeed, I counted more than 2,500 news items about the bombing in the whole country during the month of May. That number drops to around 2,000 in June and, finally, about 300 more news items on the bombing until July 12, when Picasso's famous painting was first shown to the public at the Exposition Internationale in Paris.[43]

Among the American newspapers that reported extensively on the bombing were the *New York Times*, which published no fewer than 63 articles on the bombing between April 28 and July 12, 1937 ("Historic Basque Town Wiped Out," "Rebel Fliers Machine-Gun Civilians," April 28);[44] the *Lowell (MA) Sun* ("Rebels Hammer Bilbao's Gates," April 29); *New Castle (PA) News* ("Will Evacuate Citizens from City of Bilbao," April 29); *Oakland (CA) Tribune* ("Nazi Flayed," April 29); the *Portsmouth (OH) Times* ("British Foreign Office Frowns on Navy's Plan to Evacuate Women, Children from Bilbao," April 29); and the *Oshkosh (WI) Northwestern* ("Bombarded Town," April 30). Days after those stories appeared, other newspapers began to print accounts of the massacre that they had received from the major news agencies—the Associated Press, the United Press, Reuters, and the Universal News Service.[45] Most of them described the event based on information provided by the four first correspondents in Gernika.[46] The Canadian press also reported widely on the attack, and many emphasized that General Mola's air force was responsible.

## The Non-Intervention Committee Slept Through It All

A ten-year-old refugee child in East Sussex asked, "Why do the English not believe that the Germans and their planes have destroyed our towns?"[47]

The bombing of Gernika was clearly a flagrant violation of the mission of the Non-Intervention Committee, whose purpose was to stop any foreign state from participating in the Spanish war. However, both the Non-Intervention Committee and the Chairman's Subcommittee tried to avoid at all costs taking any action in response to the massacre, for several reasons. First, committee members from Germany and Italy insisted that their air forces did not bomb Gernika since their governments were officially not participating in the war. If there were German or Italian citizens involved in war actions on the Basque front, the German and Italian representatives maintained that they were "volunteers." In addition, the British and French committee members did not want to address the matter because their respective governments did not want to risk setting off a Pan-European war by generating a diplomatic crisis within the committee. Both governments needed time to continue their rearmament efforts to be ready to face Germany in the coming war that everyone expected. And finally, because the Soviet Union was exporting war matériel to the Spanish Republic, its representative could not openly condemn Germany and Italy for doing the same.

The Chairman's Subcommittee of the Non-Intervention Committee was composed of representatives from various diplomatic missions in London: from Belgium, Baron Emile de Cartier de Marchienne; Czechoslovakia, Chargé d'Affaires Vilém Èerný; France, Ambassador Charles Corbin; Germany, Ambassador Joachim von Ribbentrop; Italy, Chargé d'Affaires Guido Crolla, Ambassador Dino Grandi, and the Conte di Mordano; Portugal, Ambassador Armindo R. S. Monteiro; Sweden, Ambassador Baron Erik K. Palmstierna; and the Soviet Union, Ambassador Ivan M. Maysky and Chargé d'Affaires Samuel B. Kagan. The parliamentary undersecretary of the British Foreign Office, Lord Plymouth, presided over meetings of the committee, and Arthur F. Hemming, a well-known entomologist, acted as secretary of the subcommittee.

The British government, acting as referee of the committee, did not let things erupt. Instead, both the British and the German governments chose to adopt a mutually favorable understanding in the face of events. According to Sir George Ogilvie-Forbes, it was advantageous that British secretary of state for foreign affairs Anthony Eden noted during a debate in the House of Commons on April 28 that although Nationalist airplanes had carried out the bombings, the Republicans were also responsible for attacks of a similar nature.[48] The German government announced its regret that modern methods of war affected civilians and reminded the committee that Hitler, on May 21, 1935, had strongly urged the conclusion of an international agreement prohibiting air bombardments, but this proposal was never answered by the powers that at the time still possessed far superior air forces. Moreover, the Germans emphasized that their air force had been utilized against inhabited towns not only in the Basque Country, but also in the Abyssinian War, on the North-West Frontier, and in Aden. "If the question of air bombardments is to be satisfactorily settled in accordance with German ideas, this happy result will not be reached by reprobating individuals and falsifying facts."[49]

Under such conditions, members of the Non-Intervention Committee were informed at the May 3 meeting that the plan to control foreign access to Spain's coast and land borders had been in full operation since April 30 and that operations on a skeleton basis had begun on April 19. The control strategy must have been utterly deficient because, according to a report sent by Ambassador Bowers on April 30, four days after the massacre, about a thousand German troops had landed in Donostia at sunrise wearing khaki uniforms. Two German pocket battleships at Pasaia had apparently sent their entire crews ashore, and many of them were still on shore after the ships departed. These men were presumed to be aviators, officers, and mechanics intended for the siege of Bilbao. Also, a complete German motorized unit had recently passed through Donostia, headed for the Bilbao front, and a German submarine had been present for several days in waters off the Basque coastal city. According to Bowers, never before had so many German and Italian soldiers been seen in the Basque Country.[50]

On April 29, the Basque government proposed an international investigation into the destruction of Gernika. The next day, to silence opposition in the French parliament, Yvon Delbos, minister for foreign affairs, recommended an inquiry into the massacre before the Senate Commission on Foreign Affairs. On May 3, the Spanish Republic's foreign minister, Julio Álvarez del Vayo, declared in Paris that a commission should be formed to investigate the facts. On May 4, the first item on the agenda of the subcommittee in charge of deciding whether to launch an international investigation on Gernika was, perplexingly enough, an appeal to the two parties at war regarding the bombing of open towns.[51]

Instead of an investigation, which all representatives on the subcommittee resisted in order to avert the possible dissolution of the committee itself, Lord Plymouth asked that an appeal be addressed to the warring parties regarding the bombardment of open towns. The Portuguese representative declared that his government would support all measures to end the horrors of the war. Ribbentrop agreed that the approach should be general and designed to do whatever was necessary to end the atrocities that had marked the conflict. Everything went as planned: Ribbentrop accepted the appeal that the Germans abstain from bombing open cities because it extended to all atrocities committed during the war by both parties, not only the bombardments.

While the Portuguese and Italian representatives supported the motion, the other representatives expressed the hope of finding a way to make the conflict more humane, and members unanimously agreed to take up the matter again at the next subcommittee meeting (May 7), after having consulted with their respective governments.[52] The committee also instructed Ribbentrop, so that no precedent might be set, to describe the appeal as an effort of the governments of the Non-Intervention Committee and not of the committee itself. The only representative who spoke out against the proposal was Swedish ambassador Palmstierna, who, making tacit reference to Gernika and Bilbao, said that the Non-Intervention Committee was getting rather far away from the actual facts. He added:

> At a certain spot certain airplanes went on to shoot women and children, went down to shoot them dead on the road, and a whole town, although the military people had left it, was extinguished. I mean it is a fact upon which world conscience has been aroused. Possibly next week we might see another and larger town dealt with in the same way. Our human feelings are aroused when cruelty reaches a certain point, and then we speak up. The word "propaganda" has been used. If I may say so, if I can make propaganda against that sort of violence, I will do it, whoever has committed the crime, and I think several of us feel the same in this respect.[53]

Despite the Swedish intervention, the German ambassador was satisfied with the work done by the Italian, Portuguese, and German representatives at the meeting: they had avoided any mention of Gernika and made certain that any future action taken on the bombardment of open cities would be addressed to both parties, with no reference to foreign participation in the Spanish conflict. The forty-ninth meeting of the Chairman's Subcommittee concluded without any decision; it was one of the last clear victories of totalitarian diplomacy in Europe prior to World War II. Ribbentrop never mentioned, though, that such a diplomatic triumph was possible only because of the tacit support of Lord Plymouth.

However, the next day, on May 5, several British newspapers published articles that suggested the German representative had objected to renouncing aerial bombardments as an intrusion into internal Spanish affairs. The articles also noted that the attack on Gernika was carried out with German airplanes and incendiary bombs and thus with German complicity.[54] It was a leak, since the committee sessions were supposed to be secret and closed to the press.[55] Also on May 5, Pablo Azcárate, the Spanish Republican ambassador to London, sent a communiqué to the Foreign Office asking Great Britain to adopt whatever action was necessary to institute an international investigation to determine who bore the responsibility for the destruction of Gernika.[56]

Hans Georg von Mackensen, state secretary in the German Foreign Ministry, had instructed Ribbentrop that he should reject the creation of an investigation committee and, in line with the German ambassador's previous policy, that he should not consider the committee competent for the British proposal of initiating an investigation into the bombing of Gernika. Nevertheless, Ribbentrop was instructed to show himself prepared, "on purely humanitarian grounds," to participate in the projected appeal under the condition of not making direct or even indirect reference to Gernika.[57]

In view of the reaction in the British press, Ribbentrop and British secretary of state for foreign affairs Eden met again on May 6.[58] Ribbentrop said that he was very displeased with the inaccurate newspaper accounts, attributing to him views that he had never expressed during the meeting in connection with the bombardment of Gernika. In Ribbentrop's opinion, the source was Ivan M. Maysky, Soviet ambassador to Great Britain and a member of the committee. Ribbentrop added that if Maysky referred to Germany in relation with Gernika, he would have no other option than to abandon the committee and probably the nonintervention system.[59]

Ribbentrop also called Eden's attention to the "incorrect and tendentious allegations" in the British press and espoused by members of the House of Commons regarding the alleged bombing of Gernika by German planes.[60] Eden replied that he lacked exact information about Gernika because the Foreign Office reports were inconsistent and based on articles in the British media. However, Eden and Sir Henry G. Chilton, British ambassador to the Spanish Republic, received a conclusive report from Ralph C. Stevenson, British consul in Bilbao, on May 4.[61] Stevenson went personally to Gernika in the early hours of April 27, when the town was still burning, and reported that it had been destroyed by about fifty planes dropping heavy explosive and incendiary bombs for three and a half hours and that civilians were mercilessly machine-gunned by fighter planes. Eden was lying to Ribbentrop as well as to the House of Commons when he said that he did not have evidence that Gernika had been bombed. Moreover, he persuaded Ribbentrop to make a "suitable" declaration to the press, denying German participation in the bombing.[62] Eden was doing everything he could to prevent Germany from leaving the Non-Intervention Committee and to prevent the Spanish war from expanding into an international conflict.

Because the Soviet representative on the subcommittee was expected to raise the issue of an international investigation again, Eden asked Ribbentrop about the possibility of an investigation. The British foreign secretary wanted to know how the Germans would respond, but Ribbentrop avoided giving an answer by saying he had to consult with his government.[63]

During the next meeting of the subcommittee, on May 7, Lord Plymouth expressed his disappointment over the leak to the press after the May 4 meeting and, in a particularly severe tone, stated that "versions appeared in some newspapers which were not only tendentious, but entirely incorrect. I cannot use words strong enough to condemn those who are responsible for this information leaking out in this particular form."[64] Italian representative Grandi even read a communiqué from the rebels stating that "the National Government, who are fighting in defense of ancient Spanish traditions and world civilization, declare that non-military open cities have never been and never will be bombarded by National planes."[65] Lord Plymouth emphasized that everything discussed by the subcommittee or by the committee itself was strictly confidential. The committee then decided to ask the Foreign Office's news department to issue a special note to the press, restating that communiqués issued after the meetings were the only official reports and that any other report would be considered unauthorized by the members of the committee or the Chairman's Subcommittee.[66]

After the implicit reprimand to Maysky, and making no mention of Foreign Minister Eden's assertion in the House of Commons a day earlier that the British government would welcome an international investigation into the bombing of Gernika, Lord Plymouth offered a proposal on behalf of the British government that the Non-Intervention Committee should appeal to the warring parties to renounce the aerial bombing of open cities. The members of the subcommittee were asked to consult with their respective governments. He emphasized that the appeal was not intended to be exclusive and that other attempts to make the war more humane could also be tried. The representatives on the subcommittee agreed to submit to their respective governments the text of Lord Plymouth's proposal and resolved to consider it at their next meeting, along with any other proposal put forward with a view to securing the same end.[67]

Ribbentrop felt that he was being pressured by London, and he asked the Ministry of the Exterior in Berlin whether, if necessary, the German government would accept the creation of an investigating commission to examine the ruins of Gernika. Indeed, there was no reason to fear such an investigation. At 5:30 P.M. on April 28—the night before Gernika was occupied—General Mola had ordered the Italian command to prohibit entry to Gernika to anyone, and after being captured the town had been sealed for five days.[68] As indicated, throughout this time members of the Condor Legion performed a detailed examination of the effects of the bombing, taking photographs and movie films, while the rebel authorities organized a systematic destruction of all material evidence of the bombardment.

As a consequence, rebel authorities and the German administration were not risking much if they accepted the possibility of an international investigation.[69] Moreover, abandoning a purely rejectionist standpoint, the Spanish rebel government had organized a technical board to investigate the causes of the destruction of Gernika. Its findings were published on May 1 in the Machimbarrena-Miláns del Bosch report.[70] Obviously, the commission concluded that Gernika had been burned by the Basques. On May 8, General Sperrle, head of the Condor Legion, met with Franco to discuss the possibility of organizing a controlled examination of the ruins of Gernika, but when the German general asked Franco whether he would accept an international commission of inquiry into the bombing of Gernika, Franco snapped an "absolute no."[71] The reasons behind his position were mainly political. Franco had never acknowledged the Non-Intervention Committee and maintained that an investigation of the Gernika case would constitute interference in the internal affairs of the Spanish state.

Roosevelt was very critical of the system of nonintervention, but faced with the opposition of Secretary of State Hull, the majority in the House of Representatives and the Senate, and probably public opinion, he could not apply punitive measures on the Italian, German, and Spanish regimes—although he tried.[72] One of his first attempts in this regard was his plan to make a public statement in May about the bombing of Gernika. However, on May 15 the British Embassy in Washington asked the State Department to stop any public statement by President Roosevelt in reference to the bombing of Gernika and other cities.[73] On May 20, the first secretary at the

British Embassy, Philip Broadmead, met with Secretary of State Hull to ask that any statement by the US president on the bombing of open cities be concurrent with or subsequent to action taken by the Non-Intervention Committee in London. Broadmead predicted that the committee would approve the proposal at its next meeting with the intention of "minimizing the dangers and hardships suffered by the civilian population from various other causes besides bombing from the air."[74] In short, Eden was asking Hull to stop or delay Roosevelt's intervention in the matter and, after the committee's proposal was approved, to make a statement in support of it.[75]

At that point, Spanish Republican foreign minister Julio Álvarez del Vayo presented a booklet entitled *White Book* on foreign intervention to the League of Nations. The booklet contained about one hundred documents that showed direct Italian military intervention in the conflict. Due to diplomatic pressures, probably from the British government, there was no mention of German intervention. According to Prentiss Gilbert, US ambassador to the League of Nations, Eden wanted Álvarez del Vayo to suppress the text because he wanted to avoid at any cost an open debate on Germany at the League of Nations.[76]

Some days earlier, on May 24, the Chairman's Subcommittee met again, and the draft of the proposal on the bombing of open towns was passed. Two days later, on May 26, the full Non-Intervention Committee met to ratify the draft. The committee debated two proposals, one by Lord Plymouth and another pushed by the German, Italian, and Portuguese representatives. Plymouth redrafted his original proposal after opposition in Parliament had pressured the British government to take a more aggressive position. However, Samuel Kagan, the Soviet representative on the committee, prevented any agreement by noting that the final draft had no connection to Lord Plymouth's original proposal. Kagan said the Soviet government had no reason to think that the Spanish Republican government had violated the basic principles of humanity in its struggle against the rebels, whereas the rebels had adopted a strategy of terrorizing and persecuting civilians and destroying cities with no military significance. He concluded, somewhat sarcastically, that "the bombardment of Durango and other Basque cities, and the most outrageous bombardment of Guernica and of the most densely populated quarters of Madrid are but a few illustrations of the 'humane' activities of the rebels."[77] The committee was unable to reach an agreement on the proposals, and further discussion was deferred until the next meeting on May 28.

During debate in the House of Commons of May 26, Philip Noel-Baker of the Labour Party asked for an update on the Spanish Republican government's request to the Non-Intervention Committee for an inquiry into the bombardment of Gernika. Viscount Cramborne, the parliamentary undersecretary of state for foreign affairs, replied that the request of the Basque government for an inquiry into the bombardment of Gernika had not been communicated to the Non-Intervention Committee.[78] After deliberation, the Foreign Office had decided to submit the Basque government's request not to the Non-Intervention Committee but rather to the individual governments concerned.

At the May 28 meeting, Kagan said he had not yet received instructions from his government, so a decision was once again postponed, this time until June 1. However, on May 29 two unidentified aircraft attacked the German armored battleship *Deutschland*, which was at anchor about one and a half miles from the Bay of Ibiza. Twenty-two German soldiers died, and twenty more were severely wounded. After meeting with Eden, Hiram (Harry) Bingham IV sent a telegram to the US secretary of state describing Hitler's outrage over the attack. The British ambassador in Berlin, Sir Eric Phipps, reported that Neurath said he had spent six hours trying to calm Hitler's furious rage and urging him not to take any precipitate action. However, his efforts had met only partial success, as Hitler was determined that some act of reprisal must be made promptly and that Germany should withdraw at least temporarily from the Non-Intervention Committee and from any patrol activities.[79]

The German high command ordered an immediate retaliatory attack on Almería, a Republican city on the Mediterranean coast. On May 31, the Republican Ministry of State reported that four destroyers flying German flags had bombarded Almería for about forty minutes, firing two hundred shells, destroying thirty-nine buildings, and damaging many more. The initial report was that nineteen people had died and fifty-six were wounded, though the number of dead increased as the hours passed, all of them civilians, most of them children.[80] During the attack, government batteries returned fire, and one of the German destroyers was damaged. The same day, two merchant vessels were attacked by U-boats along the Catalan coast, and one was sunk.[81]

Germany now had an excuse to avoid discussing the bombardment of Gernika. On May 31, Ribbentrop, in a letter addressed to Captain Euan Wallace, deputy chairman of the Non-Intervention Committee, announced that the German government would not participate in the control scheme or in discussions of the Non-Intervention Committee until they had guarantees against the recurrence of such attacks on its military personnel. The German government also issued orders to its naval vessels in the Spanish theater to repel by fire any approaching Spanish Republican aircraft or attack vessels.[82]

The Italian government followed the same strategy. It informed the foreign embassies that because repeated attacks by "Red" airplanes against Italian and German ships clearly proved the existence of a premeditated plan of aggression against the naval forces sent by the two states to exercise naval control on behalf of the Non-Intervention Committee, the Italian government had decided to withdraw its ships from international maritime control and recall its representative on the committee until the latter adopted provisions to prevent further "criminal" attacks.[83] A day later, Italian, German, and Spanish rebel planes bombed Levante, the eastern Mediterranean coastal region of the Iberian Peninsula, including Valencia.

After a month of debate in both the Non-Intervention Committee and the Chairman's Subcommittee with no mention of Gernika, on June 18 the coalition approved a three-hundred-word resolution regarding the Spanish conflict:

> Deeply impressed by the sufferings inflicted upon the people of Spain by the tragic events which have marked the present conflict, and actuated by the desire to bring relief to the families and homes of the Spanish people, the International Committee for the Application of the Agreement Regarding Non-Intervention in Spain, on behalf of the Governments of Albania, Austria, Belgium, United Kingdom, Bulgaria, Czechoslovakia, Denmark, Estonia, Finland, France, Germany, Greece, Hungary, Irish Free State, Italy, Latvia, Lithuania, Luxemburg, Netherlands, Norway, Poland, Portugal, Romania, Sweden, Turkey, U.S.S.R., Yugoslavia, which are parties to the Non-Intervention Agreement, appeal to the two parties in Spain at once to take every step necessary for the protection of non-combatants, whether men, women or children, from the dangers to which they are subject, and to put a stop to the summary or mass executions of individuals for political reasons.
>
> The International Committee urge that hostages and prisoners of war, held by either party, should be treated in accordance with humanitarian principles, that for the future the system of hostages should be abandoned and that all non-Spanish nationals, held as prisoners and who have taken no

part in the present conflict, should be released. These principles should be applied equally to the civilian adherents of the opposite side in the territory under the control of the respective parties.

Lastly, the International Committee urge that both sides should abstain from the destruction of all open towns and villages and other objectives of a non-military character, whether by bombardment from the air, or by land or sea, or by fire, mining, or any other means. . . .

The International Committee for Non-Intervention in Spain earnestly hope that the present appeal which they believe corresponds with the ideals and the honourable traditions which have ever animated the Spanish people in the course of its history will evoke a response from the two parties and will help to lessen the cruel sufferings inflicted upon the civil population during the present conflict.[84]

The European powers tacitly accepted new measures after the attack on Gernika. On May 26, the committee met to address the withdrawal of "non-Spanish nationals" engaged in the conflict. Not a word was said about German aircraft. The Foreign Office did not welcome the proposal, which was estimated would cost about £1.5 million, including £300,000 from Great Britain, to remove approximately 150,000 foreigners fighting in Spain. The British Treasury objected to paying such a sum, considering that there were so few British volunteers engaged in the war. Besides, the two sides would need to show a willingness to cooperate in the evacuation of volunteers, which was unlikely.[85]

Ambassador Bowers wrote on May 18, 1937, in his weekly report to the US State Department that "the system of control provided by the Non-Intervention Committee turns out to be as much of a mockery as the non-intervention plan itself. Both men and guns have entered Spain since the control went into effect. At Bilbao a German airman was brought down and the pilot captured. On his person was found a diary. The entries in the diary show the date he went from Berlin to Rome and the date of his arrival in Spain. I attach the photostatic copy of the diary brought to me by a correspondent who talked with the aviator in Bilbao."[86]

## The League of Nations and the Bombing

After the Italian defeat in Guadalajara on March 23, the Spanish Republican army had substantial proof of the participation of regular Italian troops in the war. On March 13, 1937, Spanish foreign minister Julio Álvarez del

Vayo sent a telegram to the League of Nations, which was published in the *Journal of the League of Nations*, relating to the Italian intervention.[87] Two weeks later, on March 29, Álvarez del Vayo made public a collection of documents that left no room for doubt that Italian troops were fighting against the legitimate government of the Spanish Republic, "seriously dismissing the confidence that solemnly concluded agreements should inspire and seriously prejudicing the safety of the Western Europe and the general cause of peace."[88]

In light of the evidence, Isidro Fabela, Mexico's delegate to the league, issued a communiqué on foreign intervention in the war on March 29, stating that European problems should not be resolved by a method that, if successful, would undermine what was left of the foundations on which the league was built. He declared that his government would employ all the means in its power to promote world peace and, more especially, to bring to an end the armed conflict of which the Spanish Republic was the victim. Fabela stressed that the sole effect of attempts to apply the nonintervention policy had been to deprive Spain's legitimate government of assistance that, under international law, it was entitled to expect from states with which it had normal diplomatic relations. He also emphasized that the Spanish conflict was not a civil war but a case of military rebellion against a properly constituted government that legitimately represented the national will. He declared that no member of the League of Nations should remain at the mercy of a rebel faction supported by foreign elements and that the nonintervention system was serving only to prolong the conflict, permitting a coup d'état to turn into a war. Finally, Fabela stated that the conflict could easily lead to an open international war, as it ultimately did.[89]

On May 19, 1937, the bombing of Gernika persuaded José Giral, minister without portfolio of the Spanish Republican government, to appeal to the council for action on the issue of foreign intervention in the Spanish conflict. But the attack on Gernika was not even mentioned.[90] However, on May 28, Álvarez del Vayo presented his *White Book* on foreign intervention to the Council of the League of Nations.[91] The *White Book* included photographs of German and Italian airplanes and war prisoners, as well as a transcription of documents signed by German and Italian officers fighting under the rebels. From the statements of hundreds of Italian prisoners, Álvarez del Vayo proclaimed to the League of Nations and the international press that between November 1936 and March 1937, approximately 40,000

Italian regular troops, equipped and armed, had landed at Cádiz on Italian steamers. They gathered at the port of Santa Maria and were then conveyed to the Guadalajara front to take part in the offensive against Madrid. These facts were already known to European and non-European governments, but the precision of the information and the abundance of facts and details provided by the report were incontrovertible. For the first time, the information was disseminated to the international press.[92]

In the face of these accusations, the Italian and Portuguese delegates argued that the Spanish Republic was also violating the Non-Intervention Agreement by accepting military assistance from the Soviet Union. However, Ambassador Bowers responded that those assertions were far from the truth; since the end of 1936, the Republic had received little military aid from the Soviets, and compared to the 50,000 German and Italian professional troops present in Spain, Russia had sent no more than 2,500 men.[93]

The Spanish Republican delegation's evidence demonstrated clearly that the German, Italian, and Portuguese governments had flagrantly violated international law and the resolution of the Council of the League of Nations of December 12, 1936, which stated that every state was under an obligation to abstain from intervention in the internal affairs of other states. These three countries were also unambiguously flouting the Non-Intervention Agreement. However, again, nothing was done, and only two days later, on March 31, 1937, the Italian air force, under the command of Wolfram von Richthofen, bombed Durango, causing about 256 casualties, all of them civilians, mostly women and children.

Álvarez del Vayo appealed to the Council of the League of Nations to launch an investigation into the presence of foreign troops in Spain. He called the bombing of Gernika "open aggression" and "sham non-intervention,"[94] but he did not ask the council to discuss the destruction of Gernika, nor did he mention the attacks on Durango and Otxandio. He simply asked for some action. The bombing of the Basque towns offered the most tragic proof yet that the League of Nations was incapable of stopping the Spanish war and showed that the nonintervention system and its observation and control schemes were completely useless.

In light of the incontrovertible evidence that the Italian and German regimes had strongly increased their involvement in the war after the nonintervention system was established at the end of August 1936, the league was forced for a second time to take the issue to the council and consider a new resolution. However, similar to the meaningless resolution of December 12, 1936, the only response to the bombings in Durango and Gernika was the passage on May 29, 1937, of a weak resolution on the Spanish Republican appeal against foreign intervention. The resolution simply confirmed the general principle of the political independence of all states and observed "with regret" that the council's resolutions had not had the desired effect in Spain. It noted that the Non-Intervention Agreement was in force and expressed "the firm hope" that non-Spanish combatants would be withdrawn from the Spanish conflict. It also condemned the employment of military strategies banned by international law.[95]

The text of the resolution did not even mention Gernika. In September 1937, Álvarez del Vayo addressed the assembly again, this time about the Japanese bombing of Nanking and the rebel bombing of Madrid.[96] The council never even considered a resolution on the bombings of Gernika, Durango, Otxandio, or Barcelona, and thus never acknowledged the victims.

## The British Parliament and the Bombing

Secretary of State for Foreign Affairs Anthony Eden refrained from laying any blame for the bombings in the Basque Country. During debate in the House of Commons in April and May 1937, he skillfully parried questions from the Liberals about the air raid on Gernika. He was following the British government's official strategy of adhering strictly to the principles of the Non-Intervention Agreement and of trying to officially deny that the bombing was carried out by the German air force on behalf of Generalissimo Franco. This diplomatic policy of denying something so well known and dreadful was aimed at avoiding war by making concessions to the German and Italian aggressors. When Stanley Baldwin resigned as prime minister on May 28 and Neville Chamberlain took over, he continued the policy of appeasement of the previous administration. Most particularly, the British hoped to avoid an international investigation of the incident or even to mention German responsibility for the massacre because German ambassador von Ribbentrop had shown a strong opposition to an investigation, even threatening to exit the nonintervention system.

However, it became difficult to maintain this position, especially after Ralph C. Stevenson, British consul in Bilbao, sent a fragment from a German bomb, with German inscriptions indicating the year and location it was made, to the British Embassy, which was then delivered to London. Second, the government tried to emphasize that both sides in the war had bombed civilians, repeating claims from the rebels that the Basques themselves were responsible for the destruction of Gernika. However, it was general knowledge that the Basque government did not have any bombers and therefore could not have caused such destruction at the Basque front.

If we read the speeches of Lord Plymouth and Anthony Eden in both British chambers or before the Non-Intervention Committee on the bombing of open cities, it is difficult to find any reference to Germany in them. They both understood that it was important to prevent any action by the League of Nations. Although some members of Parliament and several delegates to the league maintained that such action would not be the best way to prevent the recurrence of war atrocities, it was difficult to claim that the League of Nations was not the place to negotiate international peace.[97]

Finally, the British government was doing everything possible to prevent further bombing by proposing before the Non-Intervention Committee a suspension of the bombardment of open cities. This was a laudable step, though—as opponents pointed out in Parliament and the League of Nations—highly useless. Many other open cities would be bombed and thousands of civilians killed by German bombers after the Non-Intervention Committee passed the resolution.

The first questions in Parliament on the subject came from a group of Liberals—Clement R. Attlee, Sir Arthur Salter, Sir Archibald H. M. Sinclair, and Nobel Peace Prize winner Arthur Henderson—on April 28. The parliamentary debate on Gernika was initiated by Attlee. He asked Eden whether he would take immediate steps to address a collective protest with other powers to Franco and Hitler against the bombardment of the civilian population of open towns. Eden's responses to this and subsequent questions were generally evasive. He answered that His Majesty's Government "deeply deplored" the bombardment of any civilian population wherever it might occur and whoever might be responsible, and he insisted that the British government was open to making its attitude on this subject clear to both parties and to promoting agreements to safeguard the civilian population.[98] Eden's responses to related questions from other Liberal members were similarly evasive and noncommittal. When Arthur Henderson insisted that the massacre was committed by German planes flown by German pilots and asked whether it was not possible for the Council of the League of Nations to take action in response to the massacre in Gernika, Eden replied that "the House would prefer, as far as Government action is concerted, to leave the matter as I have just stated."[99]

Eden also tried to emphasize that both sides in the Spanish conflict were equally guilty of attacks on civilians. When he mentioned a second report in the *Times* on April 28—on the same page as the report on the bombing of Gernika—which detailed the bombing of the open town of Motril by Spanish Republican government planes, Katharine Marjory Ramsay, Duchess of Atholl, had a biting response. She had visited Spain in April 1937 to observe the effects of the bombings on the civilian population and had even visited prisoners in government prisons.[100] As a result of her investigations, she became an ardent opponent of the British policy of nonintervention.[101] In response to Eden's suggestion that both combating parties were bombing open cities, Ramsay pointed out that there was a big difference between bombing a city as part of a war experiment and deliberately destroying it, not to mention machine-gunning women and children fleeing in panic.[102]

The House of Commons scheduled a further inquiry into the subject for May 3, and Eden hurried to request more information from British diplomats, especially Sir Henry G. Chilton, ambassador to the Spanish Republic. On April 30, Eden received information from the Reuters correspondent at Donibane Lohitzune[103] that Franco's government officially denied any knowledge of the bombing. He had also read the report in the *Times* on April 28 by George L. Steer, who had been in the city and wrote that the town had been bombed by German planes of several types.[104] In addition to press accounts, the Foreign Office began to receive information from its embassies in Hendaia,[105] Paris, Rome, and Berlin starting on April 28, two days after the attack. Chilton also reported by telegram to the Foreign Office on April 29 that the press controlled by the rebels had denied involvement in the bombardment and that Colonel Julián Troncoso, military governor of Irun, had assured him that airplanes were unable to fly on April 26, 27, and 28 because of low clouds. In a dispatch a day earlier, Chilton had referenced the reports by Steer and President Agirre concerning German responsibility for the massacre, but focused on the news that appeared in the press controlled by the rebels.[106] However, Chilton's dispatch was not officially received by Eden until May 3.

In the House of Lords, Robert Gascoyne-Cecil, 1st Viscount Cecil of Chelwood and winner of the Nobel Peace Prize in 1937, raised the issue of Gernika. Lord Cecil, who had devoted his political career to the creation of international institutions as a way to guarantee peace,[107] expressed on April 29 his concern about what he described as "a piece of terrorism" with no precedent in history. He emphasized that the best course of action was to pressure Germany through the League of Nations to ensure that such a massacre never happened again.[108]

Lord Plymouth responded that he had no official information regarding the bombing of Gernika and that he could not confirm or deny that German planes had destroyed the city. He reiterated Eden's earlier statement that the British government deplored the bombing of open cities, wherever it might occur and whoever might be responsible.[109] Lord Plymouth added that the British government had no information on the bombardment of Bilbao[110] and said that Lord Cecil's plea for action by the League of Nations was not the best way to prevent further bombings and safeguard civilians. Cyril Forster Garbett, Lord Bishop of Winchester, repeated Lord Plymouth's contention that the government had no official information as to whether this bombardment had taken place but added that "if it is accurately reported, [it] is an appalling outrage against all the laws of civilization."[111]

One day later, on April 30, Sir Archibald Sinclair remarked in the House of Commons that on April 29, Bilbao, Durango, Getxo, Zaratamo, Zeberio, and Zestao were reported to have been bombed by German, Italian, and Spanish rebel planes. Sinclair pointed out the serious threat of such actions to the existence of the nonintervention system and international peace. Eden answered that he was aware of the seriousness of the situation but that he should be given more time to determine the British government's strategy. Requests from other members of Parliament for further information and a plan of action from Eden met with similar evasions.

On May 3, Reginald William Sorensen, Baron Sorensen, asked Eden whether he would help launch an international commission to investigate the circumstances of the air attack on Gernika. Eden replied that he did not have complete information and emphasized again that Gernika was only one of the open cities that had been bombed.[112]

It was untrue that Eden did not have "complete information." On May 3, before he addressed the House of Commons, he had received a telegram from Consul Stevenson, who had visited Gernika the day after the raid. The telegram contained Stevenson's emphatic assertion that Gernika had been bombed by the Condor Legion. Stevenson also sent Ambassador Chilton two unexploded incendiary bombs with inscriptions in German that he had picked up in Gernika. Moreover, Chilton had photographs of identification documents from downed German pilots, diaries, credentials, and other evidence that Stevenson had sent him in April, after the spring offensive started on March 31. Stevenson was very precise in his dispatch to Eden on

May 3 when reporting that the Basque government's observers had recognized German airplanes and that unexploded incendiary bombs identified as German had been picked up in Gernika and Galdakao. According to Stevenson, an inquiry into the events could do no more than confirm the facts.[113]

Hugh Dalton, another member of Parliament, asked if Eden was aware that a Heinkel He111 had been shot down over Bilbao two weeks earlier and that the crew was found to be carrying German papers. Moreover, there was a diary showing that the pilot of the plane had left Berlin on April 5, 1937, and traveling via Rome had reached the Basque Country through Seville. He asked whether that was not a clear violation of the Non-Intervention Agreement. Eden again stated that he had no information regarding this particular incident. When Labour Party member Frederick J. Bellenger asked whether Parliament would have assurance from the Foreign Office that if the facts were demonstrated, the British government would take action, Eden did not reply.

It appears that the Spanish rebel government was making its own efforts to influence British public opinion. Following the discussion on Gernika in the House of Commons, Communist Party member William Gallacher asked Eden whether Frederick Ramon Bertodano, 8th Marqués del Moral, had been asked to refrain from political activities while in the United Kingdom. When Eden offered a vague answer, Gallacher asked whether Eden knew that Bertodano was trying to influence members of the British Parliament in connection with Spanish affairs. Eden was silent. On May 4, Eden received Stevenson's full report. Stevenson testified that, beyond any reasonable doubt, Gernika had been attacked by planes that dropped heavy bombs and incendiary bombs, destroying nine out of every ten buildings in town.[114] On May 5, Eden was forced to answer several questions from members of the Labour Party, and his responses were closely tied to the government's official line: try to avoid an international investigation or any other action that could provoke a diplomatic crisis. To achieve such a goal, Eden was forced to be untruthful to both chambers of Parliament.

On May 5, Arthur Henderson[115] asked Eden whether he would call for a meeting of the League of Nations' Council to avert the threat of Bilbao being razed to the ground. Eden said that this was a decision for the Spanish Republican government to make. He also noted that, at the urging of the Foreign Office, the Non-Intervention Committee would consider a resolution on the bombardment of open cities on May 7. Henderson insisted that without action from the committee, the situation could worsen, as the rebel general staff had declared its intention to launch air attacks on Bilbao and Madrid on an unprecedented scale. Again, Eden said he was aware of the gravity of events, which was the reason for the initiative to the Non-Intervention Committee.[116] At that point, Conservative Victor A. Cazalet, known as one of the "British friends of Franco," asserted that Steer's report on the bombing in the *Times* was entirely inaccurate. Not even Eden responded to this remark.

When Labour Party member Lauchlin MacNeill Weir and Sir Geoffrey Le Mesurier Mander, a Liberal Party authority on foreign policy and one of the strongest opponents of the policy of appeasement, asked Eden whether the Non-Intervention Committee had received any information on the number of foreign nationals serving in the war, Eden answered, "Not so far as I am aware." However, he had actually received hundreds of reports on this subject, with accurate information on the names of boats, their ports of origin and destination, the number of troops per shipment, and the day of arrival of every one of the Italian "volunteers." According to the Fisher Memorandum, which was submitted to Eden in February 1937, fifteen thousand Italian troops had been transported to areas controlled by the rebel army during the first three weeks of January. Eden knew that approximately fifty-one thousand Italian and five thousand German troops were present in Spain and engaging in the war at the time.[117] The secretary was lying once again to his own Parliament.[118] More specifically, Mander asked Eden whether he could address the landing of about fifteen hundred more German troops at Donostia on April 27, 1937, only a day after the massacre at Gernika. Eden responded that he only had reports from the press, although, as I have already mentioned, the US and British Embassies were aware that Germany had sent one hundred more aircraft to Franco,[119] and the secret services reported on May 1 that fifteen hundred more German soldiers had landed in Donostia a day earlier and a U-boat had arrived in Pasaia.[120] Mander, visibly disturbed by Eden's open duplicity, asked whether he should conclude that German intervention in the war was limited to the massacre at Gernika and whether the British government would consider the advisability of participating in an investigation on the destruction of the Basque town. Eden did not respond.[121] However, Conservative Henry P. Croft, 1st Baron Croft, another of the "British friends of Franco," noted that if an investigation was to be conducted on Gernika, others would have to be undertaken on Eibar and the cities burned by the "Reds."

On May 6, Labour Party member John J. Tinker told Eden that numerous religious bodies and social organizations had passed resolutions asking the British government to bring the massacre to the attention of the League of Nations so that it could be dealt with. Croft insisted again that the responsibility for the bombing had not yet been established, and Conservative Sir Patrick W. Donner stated that the Spanish Republican forces had also bombarded three open cities in the same week that Gernika had been bombed. When Major-General Sir Alfred W. F. Knox, an Ulster Conservative, mentioned that Generalissimo Franco's treatment of civilians was just as humane as that of any sentimental supporter of the Spanish Republican government, Mander replied that Franco's handling of civilian populations had been demonstrated in Gernika[122] and that the conclusion that he himself had reached was that German airplanes had carried out a systematic bombing of the city. He added, "I see no evidence anywhere to suggest that this is a case of mass suicide by the Basque people."[123]

The discussion in Parliament continued into June, with members pressing Eden for information about the destruction of Gernika and the role of German airmen and planes in the attack. Members also persisted in their insistence that the matter be referred to the consideration of the Non-Intervention Committee or to an international investigation into the bombing. Eden continued to maintain that no British official was present at Gernika at the time of its destruction and that the British ambassador at Hendaia had, therefore, received no firsthand evidence from any official under his jurisdiction on which he could base a considered report on the circumstances in which the destruction of Gernika took place.[124] That, too, was not true. On May 8, Eden had declared to Portuguese ambassador to Great Britain Armindo Monteiro that German planes had bombed Gernika. Clearly, Eden's reluctance to acknowledge publicly the role of the Germans in Gernika had little to do with his ignorance of the facts and everything to do with his government's official stance on the matter of foreign intervention in the Spanish conflict.[125]

That was one of the last times Gernika was mentioned in the British Parliament. During the following months, debates on the Basque issue focused on the evacuation of refugee children to Great Britain. However, the Labour Party made one last effort to investigate the cause of the destruction of Gernika, sending a group of experts to Bilbao, including Robin McKinnon Wood, a former member of the aerodynamics department of the Royal Aircraft Establishment; Geoffrey H. C. Bing, a lawyer; and Commander Harry

Pursey, a mine and ship construction expert. All of them were Labourite members of Parliament. By the time they reached the Basque Country, Gernika was already in the hands of the rebels, and the town was closed for some weeks to the international press while all evidence of the bombardment was erased. Despite the impediments, the Labour Party investigators collected damning evidence and testimony in Bilbao. Among others, they interviewed a German pilot captured by the Basque forces, Hans Joachim Wandel, who confessed that his orders were to machine-gun from the air "anything moving." After some weeks in the Basque Country, the team concluded that "the air operations in the Basque country are being conducted by German airmen and Germany has sent both pilots and planes after the imposition of the ban on volunteers and the control. They ratified that there can unfortunately be no doubt that the German flyers have orders to wage indiscriminate warfare."[126]

In February 1938, the British chargé d'affaires at Hendaia, Geoffrey H. Thompson, went to Gernika to examine the town, and he reported his findings to Sir Robert Hodgson, the British representative to the rebel government. He wrote that Eibar, Durango, and Gernika were sad monuments to the ruthless efficiency of the German and Italian air forces. By the time he passed through Gernika, there was not a single building left standing, and it was "clear from the pitted and pockmarked condition of the walls still standing that it was heavily dosed with high explosive [bombs] and that incendiary bombs completed the destruction. I know, as a matter of fact, that H.M.G. [His Majesty's Government] have full details of what occurred in Guernica from German sources; and if I seem to labor the point it is because I feel myself that the proofs so frequently furnished by this war of the extent to which the Germans and Italians believe in 'frightfulness' afford perhaps the most menacing lesson the English people can learn from it."[127]

Years later, Thompson recalled his visit to Gernika: "The ruins of Guernica . . . presented a melancholy tribute to the Luftwaffe, whose first experiment it had been with tactics to become only too familiar to the inhabitants of Britain less than three years later. . . . Although at the time George Steer wrote the story movingly for *The Times*, there were all too many in Britain, especially on the right amid the Tory back benches, who chose to believe the Nationalists' allegations that the town had been destroyed not by German bombs, but by the retreating 'Reds.'"[128]

## Gernika in the US Congress

After the Italian defeat at Guadalajara in March 1937 and the first bombings of open towns in the Basque Country, foreign intervention in the war became obvious, and the US Senate started to discuss the possibility of an embargo on Germany and Italy. Secretary of State Hull and Senator Key Pittman of Nevada, chairman of the US Senate Committee on Foreign Relations, were opposed to taking that step. Basically, both Hull and Pittman saw in Francoist Spain a strong anti-Communist regime and, following British policy, understood that any action on the part of the United States that would accentuate the differences between the nations and forces engaged in the Spanish conflict might have the effect of precipitating the United Kingdom into a position where it would have to make broad concessions to the German-Italian-Spanish group.[129] As a basis for compromise, it was suggested that the Germans and Italians agree to Franco-British naval control of the entire Spanish coast in exchange for recognition by the British and the French of Franco's belligerent rights.[130] Declaring an embargo on Germany and Italy was not going to help this position, so Hull and Pittman chose to follow the same strategy as Eden and Lord Plymouth—they opted to maintain that there was no evidence of German and Italian participation in the war.

However, Congress had ample evidence of the dominant presence of foreign troops in the conflict. The Spanish Republican government, which enjoyed full US diplomatic recognition, had asserted to the League of Nations that foreign troops were assisting the rebels with reinforcements of aircraft and infantry. The British and French press had also reported foreign intervention, and Senator Gerald P. Nye quoted Robert Lasuet of the French army, who had declared that no fewer than one hundred thousand foreigners were fighting in the war. *New York Times* overseas correspondent Frank L. Kluckhohn had reported that the backbone of Franco's army was small and that foreign assistance had made rebel success possible.[131] The Italian press had even boasted that the rebel army's advance had been chiefly due to support provided by the Italian regime. The US ambassador to Italy, William Phillips, also informed Hull repeatedly about substantial foreign assistance, in the form of both supplies and men, coming to the rebels from Germany and Italy. On May 29, the State Department received a detailed report on the bombing at Gernika from Phillips, stating that the German Luftwaffe was responsible for the massacre.[132] A second report from the Spanish Republican embassy in Washington was received on June 12.[133]

There was also information available on the landing of at least three thousand Reichswehr troops from Bavaria in Spanish territory on January 10, 1937. Bowers had informed Hull: "Now with a full knowledge that as many as 17,000 German and Italian soldiers landed at Cadiz within two weeks, beginning Christmas week, the British policy is to shut off 'volunteers' . . . and I shall be much astonished if anything is done that will stop Germany and Italy from continuing to send in soldiers."[134] In response to Hull's position, Congressman Jerry J. O'Connell of Montana said:

> No evidence! Mr. Speaker, I ask you, what is the meaning of "evidence" in the vocabulary of the State Department? The correspondents of many newspapers both for this country and for England signed their names to stories which recited in detail the "evidence" the State Department chooses to ignore. One of those correspondents, G. L. Steer, cabled to *The New York Times* from Bilbao on April 28. I have seen and measured the enormous bomb holes at Guernica, which, since I passed through the towns the day before, I can testify were not there then. Unexploded German aluminum incendiary bombs found in Guernica were marked "Rheindorf Factory, 1936." The types of German airplanes employed were the Junker Ju52/3M heavy bombers; Heinkel He111 medium fast bombers, and Heinkel He51 pursuit planes. Steer went on to quote statements of German pilots who, when captured early in April, admitted that the insurgent airplanes are "manned entirely by German pilots, while nearly all the crews are German." It seems that the State Department does not regard reports by responsible eyewitnesses as "evidence." But to the man on the street evidence that Germany and Italy are engaged in the most brutal slaughter of all history appears incontrovertible.[135]

Senator Nye also believed there was no doubt that Italy and Germany were helping wage undeclared war on the Spanish Republic. On April 9, he asked the secretary of state to counsel the Senate on whether existing neutrality laws were sufficient to allow the United States to initiate an embargo against states intervening in a civil war.[136] Nye also asked the State Department to provide a legal analysis of such foreign intervention.

Senator Pittman objected to Nye's statements and claimed as chairman of the Senate Committee on Foreign Relations that there was no evidence to indicate that the Italian regime was supporting the Spanish rebels.[137] His objection, and that of Senator Joseph T. Robinson of Arkansas, suggests that the State Department and the Committee on Foreign Relations wanted to prevent discussion of the issue. Moreover, the *Washington Post* pointed out that Secretary Hull was keeping some information from coming to light. Ambassador Bowers had been sending weekly reports that removed any doubt that German and Italian troops were engaged in the war. In addition, Horace H. Fuller, military attaché at the US Embassy in Paris, had reported to the State Department on February 23, 1937, that his counterpart at the German Embassy had told him that there were between forty and fifty thousand Italian and about thirty thousand German troops fighting with Franco's armies.[138] Bowers had tallied about thirty-one thousand Italian troops who arrived in Spain through January 1937,[139] and William C. Bullitt, US ambassador to France, had sent a dispatch to Hull on February 22 containing similar data on the transport of Italian troops.

In light of the quality and clarity of the information available to Hull, we can only conclude that he was lying to Congress when he stated that he had no evidence of foreign intervention. It is uncertain if Pittman or Robinson had the opportunity to read any of Bowers's, Chapman's,[140] or Bullitt's dispatches or, in general, any of the weekly reports sent by US ambassadors and attachés in Europe (mainly those in Spain, France, Italy, and Germany). A *Washington Post* editorial suggested on March 27 that if Pittman and Robinson did not bother to read these reports, they were shirking their duties. The editorial added that there was a widespread realization that the government's policy of nonintervention was not neutrality at all but merely disguised assistance to a Fascist rebellion. It concluded, "If, on top of that, the administration is now openly aiding the Spanish rebels, the deep-rooted American sense of fair play will be deeply outraged. The Post . . . is no believer in the efficacy or desirability of a mandatory neutrality policy. But when such a policy has been decided upon, it must be vigorously and consistently applied."[141]

One article in the *Pittsburgh Press* on March 29, 1937, two days before the bombing of Durango, declared that this was too serious a crisis "to play blind man's buff." The only logical explanation for the apparent lies of Hull, Pittman, and Robinson was that, rather than hoping to aid a dictatorship or cover up the massacres of the rebel air force in the Basque Country, they feared the rise to power of a Communist government in Spain. This seems the only way to comprehend statements like Pittman's to the Senate on April 9: "As to whether or not any armed forces, under the definition of 'armed forces' generally recognized in military matters, are engaged in war in Spain, I have no evidence."[142]

The spring offensive in the Basque Country and the bombing of Durango (March 31) and Gernika (April 26) expedited the debate in Congress regarding foreign intervention in the war. Senator William E. Borah of Idaho, former chairman of the Senate Committee on Foreign Relations, discussed the bombing of Basque towns on May 6, pointing out that fighting communism did not necessarily entail helping Fascism. It was not a fight between communism and Fascism, he said, but between all forms of totalitarianism and democracy. According to Borah, Fascism in the Basque Country had presented to the world its masterpiece, the most revolting instance of mass murder in all history. The Fascists had shown the world how thorough and effective modern weapons were when used for the destruction of women and children; how effective airplanes were when dropping bombs and hand grenades into homes; how airplanes, "swooping low like winged monsters," could massacre thousands of innocent children without endangering in the slightest the lives of the assailants; and how at the same time they could set a noncombatant city on fire and leave the streets covered with the charred bodies of the slain. He added, "No language can describe the scene at Guernica and Guernica was not a single instance, it was simply a culmination of a long line of unspeakable atrocities. It was not a military maneuver. The city was a long distance from the battle line. The attack had no legitimate military objective. An unarmed, noncombatant city was singled out for the most revolting instance of mass massacre of modern times. It was Fascist strategy."[143]

On May 10, the *New York Herald Tribune* published an article entitled "Guernica Raid Denounced by 76 United States Leaders." The article refers to a document entitled *Appeal to the Conscience of the World,* written and circulated by Bishop Francis J. McConnell of the Methodist Episcopal Church of New York and chairman of the North American Committee to Aid Spanish Democracy. The appeal, which publicly denounced the slaughter of noncombatants in the bombing of Gernika, was signed by seventy-six eminent politicians (including seven US senators,[144] five congressmen, and four former cabinet members), as well as prominent scientists, clergymen, journalists, and academics. As Bishop McConnell announced, the text was cabled to Generalissimo Franco, Secretary of State Hull, and five thousand clergymen throughout the United States, with the request that it be read from the pulpit. McConnell himself referred to the massacre when he spoke from the pulpit at the General Conference of the Commission of Evangelism held in Minneapolis on May 19, 1937. Senator Nye had it printed in the *Congressional Record* on May 20.[145]

On May 11, Congressman Jerry O'Connell and three other members of the House of Representatives announced in the Senate that they had sent a letter to the State Department, stressing that, because the Italian and German regimes were fighting on the Basque front and that the bombing of Gernika had been carried out by the German regime in collaboration with the Spanish rebels, Germany and Italy came under the arms embargo as set forth in the neutrality laws.[146] Secretary Hull replied that he agreed with Senator Pittman that there was no evidence that the Germans had destroyed Gernika.

Not even children who were victims of the attack were beyond the range of this controversy. It is remarkable that, considering that the Basque population is mostly Catholic, the bombing of Gernika by German planes was denounced by the Commission of Evangelism (a Christian but non-Catholic organization), while, at the same time, in May–June 1937, several important Catholic leaders from Massachusetts—William Cardinal H. O'Connell of Boston, Congressman John W. McCormack, Senator David Ignatius Walsh, and Governor Charles Francis Hurley—were lobbying to stop admission into the United States of five hundred refugee children, the first victims of the bombings in Gernika, Durango, Bilbao, and other places.

On May 10, Senator Nye raised another issue regarding a possible violation of the Neutrality Act. Nye had acquired documents that showed that the owners of the New York firm García & Díaz and their employees were part of a Spanish espionage network serving Franco. Manuel Díaz and Marcelino García, the owners, operated steamships that ran between New York, Cuba, Mexico, Central America, Italy, and Spain. Neither Díaz nor García was a US citizen. Their activities consisted of exporting materials from the United States to the Spanish Nationalist regime, which was a flagrant violation of the Neutrality Act of January 1937.

The documents showed that Díaz and García had been in a relationship with Juan Francisco de Cárdenas, Spanish ambassador to the United States until 1934, when he was transferred to Paris, where he served as ambassador until the outbreak of the civil war in 1936. Then Cárdenas returned to the United States and occupied headquarters in the Ritz-Carlton Hotel in New York in the service of General Franco. Associated with him was José de Gregario, a former secretary at the Spanish Embassy. They were in charge of collecting funds for the Francoist cause.[147]

It was clear from the García-Díaz correspondence that the firm was involved in activities that violated and threatened American neutrality.[148] Civil rights activist John T. Bernard, a congressman from Minnesota of Corsican origin, implied that the company was more than willing to contribute to the destruction on the level of Gernika. According to Bernard, there were reasons to believe that Garcia & Díaz had purchased goods for shipment to Italy, Portugal, and Argentina and that these purchases had been transshipped to rebel ports in Spain. He added, "I am not alone in calling them murderers, Franco, Hitler and Mussolini together stand condemned by all the civilized world. They have outraged all human decencies. They have violated all principles on which our government was founded and which our people cherish. . . . As a Catholic and as a man I am doubly appalled by the destruction of Guernica, the holy city of the Basque Catholics. The parliaments of every democratic country have sounded the world's indignation at the massacre of Basque women and children by German bombs." In ringing words, Senator Borah voiced the abhorrence that Americans felt for this slaughter: "So long as men and women may be interested in searching out from the pages of history outstanding acts of cruelty and instances of needless destruction of human life they will linger longest and with the greatest horror over the savage story of the Fascist war in Spain."[149]

On May 17, Senator Nye submitted Resolution 131 to the Committee on Foreign Relations, proposing that the committee investigate the activities within the United States of aliens acting for or on behalf of either party at war to determine whether such activities constituted an interference with or obstruction to lawful commerce between the United States and ports within the Spanish Republic. Nye also recommended that the committee investigate the purchase within the United States of war matériel for the use of either party at war, in violation of the neutrality laws or treaties of the United States, and examine the amount and sources of all funds expended for these activities as well as the means by which any aliens engaged in such activities secured entry into and remained within the United States.[150]

The same day, Senator Matthew M. Neely of West Virginia asked consent to have printed in the *Congressional Record* an editorial entitled "The Unmasking in Spain" from the *Wheeling (WV) Intelligencer* of May 7,

1937. The article was a denunciation of the attack against Gernika and, in general, of Francoism:

> It is no longer war in bleeding Spain. It is slaughter; cruel, cold, calculated extermination of men, women, and children. There has been terror in both sides, as always in such a conflict, but nowhere in all the shocking records has one read of such fiendish ferocity as that exhibited by the Nazi aviators at Guernica and Durango, with their leaden hailstorm, poison gas, and incendiary bombs let loose on the fleeing population of the peaceful and piously Catholic Basque country. Dictatorship, as represented by Hitler and Mussolini, and the would-be dictator, Franco, has left a fitting memorial before Bilbao, before which liberty-loving and humane people everywhere must stand aghast. The worst of the Moors, or the most vicious Spaniards, could not have been capable of such diabolic deeds. Only dictatorship, as we have come to know it in present days, could have conceived such a plan of stopping short of a military objective to provide "education" for innocent civilians.[151]

On May 17, Bishop Francis J. McConnell sent Secretary Hull, on behalf of ninety distinguished citizens, an appeal to the conscience of the world, "evoked by the anguishing news of the ruthless bombardment of non-combatant men, women and children at Gernika." The signatories asked Hull "to mitigate the suffering of thousands of non-combatant Basques enduring the calamity of war in defense of their native soil."[152] This was one of the first appeals to Hull calling for US mediation in the Basque conflict. A few days earlier, the Women's International League for Peace and Freedom had written to the State Department to press for the withdrawal of foreign forces from the war. At the league's annual meeting, held from April 30 to May 3, 1937, the association passed a resolution to be sent to President Roosevelt regarding the conflict's threat to world peace.[153]

Three weeks later, the Women's International League sent a second letter to Roosevelt, asking that the proclamation prohibiting export of arms, ammunition, and implements of warfare from the United States to the Spanish Nationalists be extended to the regimes that had invaded Spain with troops and implements of war, "as they are belligerent countries engaged in this conflict and come within the scope of this same neutrality law."[154] Also, Democratic senator Robert J. Bulkley of Ohio wrote to Hull on behalf of the Inter-Professional Association, urging that the Neutrality Act be invoked against Germany and Italy.[155] Many other US government agencies were receiving letters of protest.[156] Arthur A. Bolsterli wrote to

Senator Augustine Lonergan of Connecticut, urging the immediate application of the neutrality laws against Germany and Italy. Bolsterli finished by declaring, "No Helium to Germany! Certainly not, American Helium for American use only!"[157]

The shelling of Almería on May 30, on top of the bombings of Durango, Gernika, Otxandio, Bilbao, Madrid, and Barcelona, prompted Montana congressman O'Connell to introduce Joint Resolution 390 to the Committee on Foreign Affairs on June 1, asking the president to declare Germany and Italy to be at war with the Spanish Republic under the terms of the Neutrality Act of 1937 and to invoke penalties against the German and Italian regimes.[158] The resolution passed the Senate, and on June 2 a group of seven congressmen,[159] led by O'Connell and John T. Bernard, sent a letter to Secretary Hull, requesting that President Roosevelt adopt the resolution.[160]

On June 8, 1937, Washington congressman John M. Coffee also requested that the Neutrality Act be enforced against Germany and Italy. He stated that "recently the world was shocked by the unspeakable infamy of wholesale slaughter of innocent women and children by bombs dropped mercilessly from German military planes upon the holy city of Guernica. Here noncombatant women and children, amid ineffable agony, were blown to bits or maimed for life in a civil war prolonged and magnified from a mere skirmish into a major conflict by the wanton intervention of Nazi Germany and Fascist Italy under the control of megalomaniac dictators."[161] Coffee added that Secretary Hull appeared unwilling to apply the law, which was drafted for such purposes, and requested, under the terms of the act, that Americans be prohibited from traveling as passengers on ships flying the flags of Germany and Italy. He asked Hull to put consideration of humanity and fair play above consideration of profit.[162]

The US government never invoked the Neutrality Act of 1937 against Germany or Italy. However, the State Department had to give an explanation of why it was opposed to invoking the act. Between May 31 (the shelling of Almería) and June 8, 1937, the State Department received 322 letters and telegrams protesting the bombardment of Almería and demanding that the arms embargo be applied to Germany and Italy. Until June 8, an additional 2,219 letters and telegrams pressing that same demand arrived. As a consequence, the Office of Arms and Munitions Control of the US Department of State prepared a memorandum on June 8 setting down some of the effects that it expected would result from the application in mid-1937 of American neutrality legislation on Germany and Italy. The office maintained that placing an embargo on the export of arms to Germany and Italy would have no appreciable effect either on the armament of those two countries or on the supplies of munitions that they shipped to the rebels. US exports of arms, ammunition, and implements of war to Germany from January to June 1937 were valued at $442,437.47 and those to Italy at $169,260.18. However, exports to Germany of engines and propellers valued at $392,735 were intended for installation in planes being sold to South African, Danish, and Bolivian commercial airlines. Of the exports to Italy, engines valued at $51,000 were for installation in planes being sold to the Yugoslav government. The conclusion was that a total embargo on exports of this sort would have little or no effect on these two countries.

Of other provisions of the Neutrality Act that would become effective upon the proclamation that a state of war existed, the most important was the provision that prohibited the purchase and sale of bonds and securities of belligerent governments. As the memorandum indicated, the prohibition of the purchase and sale of Italian and German government bonds would not have any significant effect and would prove inconvenient to American holders of these bonds. US exports to these two countries were valued at $65 million during the first four months of 1937, but new loans to Germany and Italy were already prohibited by the Johnson Act. Invoking the Neutrality Act against Germany and Italy would press these two countries to make their purchases elsewhere. The application of the act would also force German and Italian vessels to withdraw from North Atlantic commerce.

Apart from these three direct effects, the State Department observed some secondary effects that discouraged the application of the Neutrality Act. The Ethiopian experience suggested that the effect on Mussolini and Hitler of the application of the neutrality laws would not induce them to withdraw, but rather would impel them to push their Spanish adventure. The United Kingdom might be induced to compromise with Germany and Italy in order to remove the growing menace to a general war, for which Great Britain did not believe itself prepared at that time. As for France, the memorandum suggested that applying the Neutrality Act would promote an active policy of aiding the Spanish government or, if the French cabinet refused to take the risk of such a step, the breakup of the Popular Front through the withdrawal of the Communists. The conclusion of the State Department was that the application of the Neutrality Act, far from having a sobering effect on Germany and Italy, might encourage extremists in all European states, seriously endanger the success of conciliatory efforts being made by British and French diplomats, and increase the likelihood of an international war.[163]

The document omitted any reference to the effect of the Neutrality Act on the export of petrol by the Texaco Company to Germany. It avoided the main point—that a state of war did indeed exist and that no matter the poor consequences of the application of the Neutrality Act against Germany and Italy, it had to be done because it was the law.

On March 17, 1938, Cardinal O'Connell arrived in New York City from his vacation in the Bahamas and was interviewed regarding the bombing of Barcelona by rebel planes. He told the *Boston Post* and the *Boston Record* that the story was a "tall tale," Red propaganda from the pro-Republican American press. In vague reference to Gernika, he claimed that when a city had been bombed in the past by rebel planes, it had always been a "military maneuver" and not an attack against open, defenseless cities. However, "war is war," the cardinal added. He also emphasized that Generalissimo Franco could no longer be considered a "rebel"; he was, rather, the leader of a national movement involved in a "saintly crusade" for the preservation of Christian civilization.[164]

However, by the end of the Spanish war in early 1939, Catholic public opinion in the United States had shifted. On January 23, 1939, *Time* published an article on US public opinion toward the war, reporting that, according to a Gallup poll, Franco partisans totaled only 38 percent of US Catholics, a minority.

Nonetheless, pro-Francoist US Catholics remained strong and vocal. They vigorously opposed the "Lift the Embargo Campaign" that US supporters of the Spanish Republican government in the United States—among them Senator Nye, Senator Borah, Senator Bob Reynolds of North Carolina, and Congressman James H. Lewis of Illinois—had initiated. President Roosevelt himself seemed to be in favor of lifting the embargo until, during an address to Congress, he referred to the injustice of such a measure. Both Archbishop Michael Joseph Curley of Baltimore and Cardinal O'Connell in Boston opposed the campaign, as did Congressman John W. McCormack of Massachusetts. Senator Pat McCarran of Nevada, according to *Time*, "a good Roman Catholic and father of two nuns (but also a divorce lawyer)," declared that any attempt to lift the embargo "will be met by Senate opposition that will be remembered for a long time to come."[165]

But the embargo was never lifted. On April 1, 1939, the military government of Generalissimo Franco assumed control of Spain and received the official recognition of the US government. Roosevelt then declared the end of civil strife as described in the Neutrality Act of January 8, 1937, which would lead to the end of the embargo on the shipment of war matériel to Spain.

## Further Bombings and the End of the War

While the Non-Intervention Committee and Chairman's Subcommittee continued to deliberate, the Luftwaffe continued its attacks on civilian targets. It bombed Bilbao four times on May 20 and 21, machine-gunning civilians; on May 24, Bilbao was bombed again; a day later, on May 25, Bilbao and Sestao were bombed nine times: twelve women and six young children were killed that day. Mungia was bombed on May 25, and on May 29 Bilbao, Larrabezua, and Lemona were attacked by German planes. The Basque government issued a report on the number of casualties caused by the combined air forces—2,445 civilians dead and 1,601 wounded.[166]

The bombardment of Basque open cities did not stop until Bilbao was captured by the combined troops on June 19, 1937.[167] According to Bowers's report on June 15, it was impossible to believe that the Basques could successfully defend themselves, "despite their almost super-human bravery, against an extraordinarily large fleet of bombing planes when they are without planes for air defense." He reported that in the advance of the insurgents and their allies, planes swooped down on villages, machine-gunning the people. Wilfred Jones, representing the Society of Friends of America in their humanitarian work, who had just returned from Gasteiz and Salamanca, told Bowers that on June 13, he counted sixty planes going toward Bilbao. Jones also reported that the country between Salamanca, Gasteiz, and Burgos was swarming with Italian soldiers, many on their way to the Bilbao front.[168]

The war in Euskadi was over. Lehendakari José Antonio Agirre transferred the Basque government to Turtzios, a small town in the western end of the Basque Country. From there the government had to move again, through Santander to the Catalan front, where the remaining Basque contingents continued fighting for the Republic until April 1939. Italian foreign minister Galeazzo Ciano telegraphed General Bastico on August 27, 1936, a few days after Santander was occupied by the combined army, "to secure for us, tactfully, flags and guns captured from the Basques. I envy the French their Invalides and the Germans their Military Museum. A flag taken from the enemy is worth more than any picture."[169]

On April 16, 1938, the British and Italian governments, both members of the Non-Intervention Committee, signed the British-Italian Agreement, which required that Italian troops leave the Iberian Peninsula at the end of the war in exchange for British recognition of Italian sovereignty in Abyssinia.[170] Eden resigned in protest and was quickly replaced by Lord Halifax,[171] who a few months later signed the Treaty of Munich with Germany on September 29, 1938.

By May 26, 1938, most of the troops from the Condor Legion had returned to Germany. On May 19, 1939, the Condor Legion participated in a victory parade that took place in Madrid, though Generalissimo Franco avoided inviting Reichsmarschall Hermann Göring to participate. A few days later, on May 22, Franco saw the legion off at the air base in Virgen del Camino, near León. When the troops arrived in Hamburg, they were received by Göring and marched through the city behind Wolfram von Richthofen. Later, as part of the celebrations organized for Hitler's fiftieth birthday on June 6, 1939, the führer and Göring led a victory parade in Berlin, marching through the Brandenburg Gate. At the Lustgarten, Hitler spoke before the 14,000 troops of the Condor Legion and the German Ministry of Air.

Göring decorated the soldiers with the Spanienkreuz (Spanish Cross), while blonde members of the Bund Deutscher Mädel (League of German Girls) filled their belts with flowers. On October 1, 1937, Franco gave Hitler the title of "Gran Caballero de la Gran Orden Imperial de las Flechas Rojas" (Great Knight of the Grand Imperial Order of the Red Arrows) and the "Collar de la Gran Orden Imperial de las Flechas Rojas" in recognition of his military assistance.[172]

Altogether, 15,000 to 16,000 soldiers participated in Operation Rügen, which resulted in 226 German deaths. As General of Artillery Walter von Reichenau wrote, two years of war experience was more useful than ten years of training in times of peace.

The Non-Intervention Committee had tried all along to emphasize the internal nature of the conflict on the Iberian Peninsula. The press supported that idea, and most historians use the term *Spanish Civil War* to describe the conflict, even though all the men who participated in the massacre at Gernika were Italian and German. Narcissus Bassols and Isidro Fabela, representatives of the Mexican government at the League of Nations, criticized the categorization of the war as a "civil" conflict, and Congressman O'Connell of Montana offered a similar critique, calling Germany and Italy "belligerents in the war of invasion now going on in Spain."[173] In one of his reports, Ambassador Bowers called the conflict "a war of foreigners"—that the real fighting was being done by foreigners, mostly professional Moorish, German, and Italian troops. Moreover, he stated that the Germans, due to their advantages in armament, training, and ammunition, had assumed leadership over many aspects of the war.[174]

Nonetheless, many American observers continued to consider the conflict as no more than a civil war. When Hull defended the enactment of the joint resolution on the exportation of arms and munitions to Spain, he was asked by Congressman O'Connell whether the conflict was a civil war. Pittman answered that the question was not relevant for passage of the resolution, but he was forced to admit that "two forms of government are fighting in Spain in what is called a 'civil war,' but it is a fight of foreign theories of government, not involving democracy, in which the opposing forces are aided and sympathized with by great, powerful governments who espouse one cause to the other."[175]

Nye also thought the war was an international conflict. On June 28, 1937, he asked that the *Congressional Record* print an article entitled "Out in the Open" from the *Washington Post,* which pointed out that the Fascist newspaper *Il Popolo d'Italia* had reported that Italian forces had been fighting for Franco's armies. The article maintained that it was not a secret that Mussolini and Hitler had been furnishing Franco's army with troops, ammunition, and supplies for months. On April 9, 1937, Nye insisted that Italy was engaged in an undeclared war on the Spanish Republic and that the Spanish government had stated at the League of Nations that foreign professional troops were fighting against government troops on the battlefield. Julio Álvarez del Vayo had sent the secretary-general of the League of Nations his *White Book* containing documents citing blatant violations of the Non-Intervention Agreement by Germany, Italy, and Portugal, which was distributed to members of the league. Nye also quoted reports by journalists, such as *New York Times* correspondent Frank L. Kluckhohn, who asserted that the "backbone" of Generalissimo Franco's army was foreign and that his success was due to foreign assistance and supplies. Nye also mentioned correspondents Robert Lasuet (Associated Press), Hubert R. Knickerbocker (European correspondent for the International News Service), Charles A. Selden (former special correspondent for the *New York Times* in Paris), and Edwin L. James (reporter for the *New York Times*), all of whom agreed that the conflict was not a "Spanish Civil War" but an international conflict.[176]

The US Congress finally accepted the argument from Nye, Borah, and O'Connell that the conflict was international and that Germany's and Italy's support for the National Movement was far beyond doubt. Joint Resolution 390, which declared Germany and Italy to be at war with the Spanish Republic, constituted an acknowledgment of the unquestionable international character of the war.[177]

Ambassador Bowers seems to have had no doubt about the international nature of the conflict. He considered it a trial run for World War II: "It was . . . clear that it was not a 'civil war' in the usual meaning of the term, but a war of aggression openly waged by Hitler and Mussolini. And it was clear that it was not a war for the church, supported by hordes of Mohammedans from Morocco, and the persecutors of the church from Germany, since the Basques, the most devout Catholics in Spain, had written their denial with their heart blood while fighting like tigers for democracy."[178]

The Non-Intervention Committee did not stop the war, nor did it prevent the atrocities in Durango and Gernika. And the Germans used the skills they had mastered in Spain in their assaults on other civilian populations during World War II. Richthofen himself led one of the Luftwaffe's units during the attack against Warsaw, which was bombed following the same strategy as in Gernika, but on a stunningly larger scale. On May 14, 1940, German bombers leveled Rotterdam under the same "terror-bombing" scheme they had perfected in the Basque Country. The populations of London, Coventry, Liverpool, and countless other cities would suffer the same effects of war experiments as the people at the Basque front. Years later, Anthony Eden recalled the bombardment of Gernika as "the first blitz of the second world war, carried out, according to our reports, by German aircraft."[179] As David R. Davies wrote for the *Times*, the British people were indebted to George Steer for his articles describing the fate of Gernika: "Now we know beyond peradventure what to expect when the squadrons of the air are let loose to work their havoc upon the capitals of Europe."[180]

However, today most historians still persist in calling this unmistakably international conflict the *Spanish Civil War*.

# 6

## Rebuilding Gernika

Those who survived the attack on Gernika had lost everything—their homes, their work, and often members of their families. Gernika became a ghost town, a village without houses, without a school, without supplies, without electricity or running water. On April 29, at about 12:30 P.M.,[1] when the first rebel troops entered the city, it was almost empty. In Margarita Lauzirika's words, "So our town disappeared and another battle began, that of survival, with no home, no money, no job."[2]

Some people were shot, such as the former mayor of Kortezubi Jose B. Ikazuriaga.[3] Others were taken to prison for years or went into exile. As Mayor Jose Labauria reported, the rebels shot at least two people after capturing the town, Juan Carlos Iturri and Víctor Alberdi, and ordered the imprisonment of many more, including Jose Alegria, Paco Alegria, Eulogio Arrien, Braulio Arzanegi, Cornelio Basabe, Juan Basabe, Juan Gezuraga, Elias Ezkurdia, and Carmelo Uribe.[4] Basque poet Esteban Urkiaga (Lauaxeta) was captured, along with French journalist Georges Berniard, by rebel troops in Gernika on April 29. Lauaxeta, sentenced to death after a summary trial, was executed on June 25 in Gasteiz.[5] Under threat of being shot like Lauaxeta, Berniard agreed to write an article, published on May 8, 1937, in *La Petite Gironde,* claiming that Gernika had first been "horribly mutilated" by aircraft serving Franco and then burned by anarchists.[6]

Because of the terrible living conditions, bad food, and fatigue, the death toll among wounded prisoners of war confined in Gernika after the war was extremely high. From June 1938 to May 1940, there were 265 deaths at the Hospital Militar Nacional de Prisioneros de Guerra, which was located in the former building of the Augustinians' school in Gernika.[7] That makes an average of almost 1 death every three days during a period of two years. It was called a hospital, but the wounded were so poorly cared for that they died mostly from deadly illnesses such as pulmonary tuberculosis, typhoid fever, meningitis, and septicemia.[8] The corpses were taken by night to the cemetery in the nearby town of Zallo and buried in unmarked graves on a piece of land called *la ampliación* (the enlargement).

For half the people in Gernika, April 26, 1937, was their last day at home. The families of Gernika had to abandon their normal lives after the bombing. Most fled to Bilbao in military trucks or trains sent by the Basque government, or in their own oxcarts or on foot, and they were housed in large barracks. Some witnesses recall a daily ration of rice with salt, black bread, and milk. Eventually, they found places to stay in the homes of friends and relatives and started to rebuild their lives away from their place of birth.[9] So many people fled to Bilbao that within a few days after the bombing of Gernika, the number of refugees in Bilbao rose to 150,000.[10] According to data provided by US consul William E. Chapman, by May 2, 1937, six days after the bombing of Gernika, there were already around 250,000 refugees in the city.[11]

Many of the evacuees never returned to Gernika. Some women and children were sent to refugee colonies that the Basque government established in France, Great Britain, Belgium, and other European countries. In most cases, it was not possible to support entire families in one place, so many refugee children were housed in colonies or camps under the supervision of Basque nuns and priests, all of them volunteers. More than 32,000 Basque children were evacuated during the spring and summer of 1937, among them many children from Gernika.

Some refugees stayed in the Basque Country, and when Bilbao was captured by the rebels two months later, on June 19, some of them tried to return to Gernika. They found guard posts and signs warning them away. When authorities eventually allowed them to return with approved safe-conduct documents, there was very little they could recover from the ruins.[12]

Immediately after the fall of Bilbao in July 1937, a deep process of ideological purgation took place in the Basque Country. A new mayor was named in Gernika, and all public servants were investigated and, if their political views were unacceptable, removed from their jobs. This included any public officer such as the mayor and the city counselors, but also any officials working on the city council, such as secretaries and assistants, the staff at the municipal courts of justice, the doctor, the municipal architect, and the veterinarian. The Provincial Court of Bilbao circulated a series of orders, including one concerning Gernika, on July 6, requiring municipal judges to send the provincial court a list of the secretaries, deputies, and officers of the various municipal courts so their ideological affiliation could be examined. If they failed to meet the required standards, they were removed from their jobs.[13] There were thousands of officials purged during the months following the occupation of Bilbao. The Order of November 5 and the Decree of September 2, 1936, required every city council to send a short list of people "fit" for the performance of municipal justice services—that is, municipal judges and prosecutors and their alternates. Among the factors taken into account when naming a new authority were his political or ideological affiliation from July 1936, public events attended by that person "until the liberation of Bilbao," his religious beliefs, "public ostentation of pro-Spanish convictions," and affiliation with the National Movement.[14] It was thus essential for municipal employees to obtain a certificate of good conduct issued by the new authorities as official proof of loyalty to the regime.[15] Some people were fired from their public offices under suspicion of having been Basque nationalists or republican.[16]

According to witnesses, all people over eighteen years of age who were not considered sympathetic or supportive to the Francoist regime could be ordered to work in the ruins removing debris and recovering corpses. As Pedro Agirre, one of those who was forced to work in Gernika's ruins, reported, they found partially decomposed bodies and body parts buried in the rubble. Unidentifiable or not, these victims were never registered. The bodies were simply placed in bullock carts and moved elsewhere.[17] According to Alisa Jaio, women were forced to work cleaning the military barracks:

> After the bombing, General Cabanellas [president of the Board of National Defense, the institution that assumed all powers of the state] of Franco's army came to Gernika for about three days. He was old, big, tall but not fat, and had whiskers. Franco's men forced me to cut my hair. I was punished for not being Francoist. They came to my home and forced me to work. They came every day looking for me. They took me to work with their rifles. They forced me to clean Cabanellas's bathroom and barrack. They took us to the Augustinians, they shaved our heads and forced us to walk through Gernika with nothing to cover our bald heads.[18]

The movable and real estate property of people officially identified as Basque nationalists or as somehow opposed to the regime was confiscated and auctioned by public officers.

After the summer of 1937, evacuees with relatives in the area began to return to the little towns in the valley, Albiz, Axuria, Astelarre, Elexalde, Muxika, and Zelaieta. The children began to return to school, sometimes ten miles from home, for just two hours per week. Many of them attended just enough school to learn how to read and write and understand some basic math.[19] However, all eighteen-year-old men were conscripted into military service for four years. Most children devoted the bulk of their time to helping at home, working as hard as their parents to help the family survive. The war had stolen their childhood.

By late 1937, the first groups of prisoners of war began arriving to work on reconstruction as a way to avoid prison. The rebuilding of Gernika was to take ten long years. The economic depression in the postwar period, which affected the entire Basque Country, had a heavy impact on the citizens of Gernika, who, apart from facing new economic, political, and social realities, had to start rebuilding their own homes. The postwar depression struck the most destitute families the hardest, especially those who were accused of having collaborated with the Basque government or of being Basque nationalists. As a result, many Gernikans were forced to flee to Australia or the United States, where some already had relatives, especially in the state of Idaho.

In 1937 Gernika had about 5,600 residents. In 1940 the town recorded 2,249 fewer inhabitants. In fact, the population of Gernika had shrunk to what it was forty years earlier, at the beginning of the twentieth century. The town did not reach the population it had in 1937 until 1947, ten years after the bombing, once it was finally rebuilt and normal life had returned.[20]

At the orders of General Mola, on April 28 Gernika was immediately closed to the international press, to the Red Cross, and, in general, to anyone who did not have a pass issued by the rebel authorities, although a few outsiders, such as George Steer, were able to evade the ban and enter the town.[21] The first orders of the rebel officers were to occupy the armament factories of the city,[22] which remained untouched, and to destroy any evidence of the bombing.[23] The troops filled in the immense bomb craters and collected and destroyed any bombs that had not exploded, as well as any trace of German incendiary shells. Only after troops had cleared the city were international authorities allowed to visit the altered ruins of Gernika.

The material devastation of the city was substantial: 100 percent of the buildings in the city center were reduced to rubble. As mentioned, Gonzalo Cárdenas Rodríguez, general assistant director of Regiones Devastadas (Devastated Areas), the Spanish administrative body in charge of the reconstruction of cities and towns after the war, issued a report on the damages caused by the war "actions."[24] His data indicated that 271 buildings had been completely destroyed, representing 85.22 percent of the total 318 buildings in Gernika at the time (meaning 100 percent destroyed, to which we have to add the 13.78 percent of the buildings that were only damaged).[25] Only 1 percent of the buildings in Gernika remained untouched, most of them the property of well-known Francoist families. Moreover, those buildings destroyed by the bombing of Gernika constituted 67.58 percent of the 401 buildings completely destroyed in all of Bizkaia (excluding Bilbao) during the war in the Basque Country.[26] Cárdenas estimated that the value of the buildings completely destroyed amounted to 11,940,791 pesetas, roughly US$1 million, which represented 34.1 percent of the total costs of rebuilding Bizkaia (which as we have seen was estimated at 35 million pesetas), excluding Bilbao.

The rapid reconstruction of the city was a political and diplomatic goal of Franco's government for three reasons. First, it was important to erase as soon as possible any traces of the bombing. Second, the reconstruction of Gernika would be used as an argument to prove the rebels' claim that, while Basque nationalists and Asturian miners (dynamiters) had set Gernika and other towns on fire, the new Francoist state was the one rebuilding the country from the ashes. Finally, the reconstruction of the city would be used by the new regime to show that it was achieving peace in a place where political instability and war had reigned.

On July 6, 1937, a little more than two months after the attack, Salustiano Olazabal, who had been appointed the new mayor of the city, met with the Junta Técnica de Reconstrucciones (Technical Board of Reconstruction) in Burgos to start the rebuilding work as soon as possible. In December the Technical Board unveiled a reconstruction project that was approved by General Franco, but nothing was done. Indeed, the Technical Services of the Falange Española, the only official political party of the regime, proposed in 1938 the reconstruction of Gernika as the National-Syndicalist capital of the Basque Country. In line with Albert Speer's projects for the Reich Chancellery and the Zeppelinfeld Stadium in Nuremberg, the plans included a colossal stadium for military parades, a Plaza del Imperio (Plaza of the Empire), a memorial for the "Francoist crusaders" dead in combat, and a War Garden.[27] The project never materialized.

The Servicio Nacional de Regiones Devastadas y Reparaciones (National Service of Devastated Regions and Preservation) was created in January 1938, and in February Olazabal presented a report demanding more speed in the proceedings. However, nothing was done until the war ended with the Francoist victory in April 1939. In August the National Service was renamed the Dirección General de Regiones Devastadas y Reparaciones (General Division of Devastated Regions and Preservation) and was included within the Ministry of the Interior under Jose Moreno to monitor and direct reconstruction projects.

In order to counter the response to the bombing of Gernika and other cities in the international arena, the regime tried to show the rebuilding of these places as a postwar humanitarian effort led by Franco himself. Accordingly, a Ley de Adopción (Law of Adoption) was passed on September 23, 1939, providing that any city or town to be rebuilt had to be adopted by the generalissimo, showing him as the benign father of his distressed people. Gernika was "adopted" on October 12, 1939, together with other cities, so each city could obtain special funds for a rebuilding plan. By December 1939, Gonzalo Cárdenas and Luis María Gana's reconstruction project was finished. As of July 17, 1940, cities like Gernika that were adopted under the law became subject to a transient municipal governing system, allowing the intervention of the state in local issues as a controlling body, the annexation of adjacent neighborhoods, and, most important, the application of a special fiscal regime, with certain tax exemptions when applicable.[28]

According to the new decrees, prisoners of war would be utilized as the main source of labor, in violation of the Geneva Convention.[29] From 1939 to 1942, the POWs were grouped into labor battalions under the jurisdiction of the Jefatura de Campos de Concentración y Unidades de Soldados Trabajadores (Head Office of Concentration Camps and Units of Working Soldiers) within the Ministry of War.[30] In 1942 the Jefatura was dissolved, as were most of the labor battalions, except for special units of "punished" prisoners who remained in the labor fields until the end of 1946 and even the beginning of 1947.

In 1940 there were about 280,000 prisoners of war in Spanish prisons and concentration camps. By 1941 at least one-third of the approximately 10,000 workers of the Division of Devastated Regions were POWS. In July 1942, the Jefatura de Campos de Concentración released a statistical report on the labor fields and battalions, which revealed that there were almost 50,000 prisoners being used as a source of labor. By 1945 there were still nearly 3,000 prisoners in forced labor.

According to the Ley de Redención de Penas por el Trabajo (Law of Sentence Reduction by Laboring),[31] prisoners could voluntarily choose to work in the labor fields and reduce their sentences by one day for every two days of labor. Some chose to join labor battalions to escape the confinement of the jails and concentration camps and at the same time reduce their sentences. Accordingly, starting in May 1938, hundreds of prisoners were taken to Gernika from all over Spain. At first, they were housed in the school at the Plaza de Pasealeku, but the building was soon too small for the growing number of prisoners, so starting in December 1938, they were held in the former Augustinians' school, which had been converted into a prison. This building also quickly became overcrowded, unable to adequately house nearly a thousand prisoners.

The working day began at about 6:30 A.M., with formation, roll call, patriotic hymns, and the raising of the Spanish flag. After breakfast the prisoners were taken in formation to the city center about five hundred yards from the prison. They worked from 8:00 A.M. until noon, when they returned to the prison to have lunch. They went back to work from 2:00 until 6:00 P.M. Finally, they returned to the military prison, and after roll call, lectures, hymns, and the lowering of the flag, they had dinner.[32]

The first projects for the reconstruction of Gernika were drawn up by Gonzalo Cárdena, subdirector of the General Division of Devastated Regions and Preservation, who was in charge of the reconstruction of Gernika. Cárdenas worked with Luis Gana, director of the Comisión Provincial de Vizcaya (Provincial Commission of Bizkaia). The plans were designed according to the old morphology of the town, but included some minor improvements, such as the straightening and widening of the streets, the construction of a new marketplace, and the renovation of the water and the public lighting systems. The project was planned for a new city that was expected to increase its population to 12,000 inhabitants in the course of two decades.[33] The San Juan Church and the 1925 pelota court, or *frontón*, one of the largest and most modern of the Basque Country at the time, were never rebuilt. Indeed, a new covered *frontón* was not built until the 1960s.

The new parceling of Gernika created serious legal problems and complicated paperwork. When some streets were straightened and widened, private parcels belonging to homes before the bombing became in many cases part of the new streets and therefore public property. In addition, houses that in the past were thirteen feet wide by eighty-two feet deep were also widened, and new construction required blocks with an interior courtyard, allowing all rooms access to light and ventilation. As a consequence, the number of homes in the central area of Gernika was significantly reduced, and a complex process of expropriation was organized.

Authorities of the new regime soon began to expropriate without compensation the homes and land of people who, not being supporters of the regime, were imprisoned or exiled or had been killed during the bombing. Former residents were given a minimum period of time to claim their property, and people in prison or in exile did not have time to make their claims. Moreover, all kinds of bureaucratic obstacles were created to obstruct those who could not show "allegiance" to the regime, while affiliates to the National Movement were privileged. This administrative framework gave rise to a corrupt market of concessions and favors, while the property of former residents who did not or could not file their claims within the time fixed by the law was in many cases expropriated without compensation. As architect Gonzalo Cárdenas put it, "faithful to the slogans of social justice of the New State," the difficulties created by the expropriations were remedied "thanks to the goodwill of the citizens of Gernika, who thinking only of seeing their city rebuilt, accepted the new parcel, sacrificing individual interests for the common good."[34]

On February 27, 1947, almost ten years after the attack, the National Service of Devastated Regions and Preservation officially presented to the city council of Gernika-Lumo a final report on the reconstruction.[35] Once rebuilt, the houses were sold to new residents who bought them at a fixed price. As a consequence of this policy of reconstruction, most exiles or imprisoned people never had the opportunity to return to their homes.

The industrial part of Gernika was not bombed, and the regime was interested in maintaining the Talleres de Guernica and Astra-Unceta, among other factories in the industrial part of the town, in full production. Thus, apart from the reconstruction of old Gernika, the Bizkaia Commission of Devastated Regions in charge of the reconstruction prioritized the erection in newly urbanized areas of cheap houses for workers. Originally, these houses were to be rented at modest rates, but by the time the buildings were completed, the prices were too high and the quality too poor. Between 1940 and 1943, the Talleres de Guernica had already built twenty houses in the industrial area of the town, and the Division of Devastated Regions undertook the construction of eighty-four more houses for workers. By late 1943, more than a hundred low-quality homes had been built in Gernika for the families of industrial workers.

Since the state did not have qualified workers for many specialized tasks, Devastated Regions had to hire the services of private companies, which made considerable profits. These companies had to meet the requirements of Devastated Regions and the institutions and personnel attached to it, such as the municipal architect of Gernika, who was in charge of supervising reconstruction. This system gave rise to bribery and more corruption.

The reconstruction effort was used for propaganda purposes from 1937 until 1947. In August 1939, the provincial council of Bizkaia decided to build three crucifixes made of the wood from the old Oak of Gernika, designed by sculptor José María Garrós. The first was sent to Pope Pius XII, the second given as a gift to Franco, and the third remained in the council. Pilar Primo de Rivera, head of the Spanish Falange Women's Section and the sister of Jose Antonio Primo de Rivera, founder of the Spanish Falange, and daughter of Miguel Primo de Rivera, Spanish dictator of the 1920s, visited the works on April 14, 1941. José Moreno, minister of the interior and general director of the National Service of Devastated Regions and Preservation, toured the project on October 16, 1944. Blas Pérez González, minister of the interior, also came to Gernika on October 31, 1945. Seven years later, on February 13, 1946, Franco was named *hijo predilecto* (preferred son) of Gernika, an honor the dictatorial government forced upon the residents of the town.

Twelve years after the bombing, on October 27, 1949, the civil governor of Bizkaia, Genaro Riestra, passed a decree requiring the proprietors of tombs and sepulchers that bore inscriptions in Basque to remove the epitaphs and replace them with inscriptions in Spanish.[36] The mayor of the city, Vicente Rojo Cubillo, immediately carried out the order, which applied to all families whose relatives were buried under headstones with Basque inscriptions.

# 7

## Gernika in the Courts of Justice

The war began in 1936 as a military uprising against the legitimately constituted democratic government of the Spanish Republic. As such, it was against the law, and pursuant to the provisions of Articles 237 and 238 of the Spanish Republican Military Code, organizers or participants in the coup were guilty of conspiracy against the Republican government and of rebellion. Also, those involved in mass killings could be charged with murder. German citizens or citizens of other nationalities involved in espionage or cooperation in the rebellion could be prosecuted under Article 222 of the code. Finally, a handful of German pilots captured by the Basque troops were tried by the Tribunal Popular de Vizcaya (People's Court of Bizkaia) on charges of murder and rebellion, and for participating in the bombing of open cities and for strafing civilians of all ages from the air they were tried under the charge of murder.

In the course of a minor attack against the Castle of Izuzkitza near Otxandio on October 5, 1936, eleven rebels were taken prisoner by Basque troops, among them three soldiers fighting with the German army. The men were taken to prison in Bilbao. According to information provided by the Basque army, the three were Wolfgang Ludwig V. Eynatten, a doctor born in Eynatten (Euppen), Wallonia, Belgium, on May 16, 1901; Lothar Gudde, a teacher of languages born on October 9, 1917, in North Rhine, Westphalia, Germany; and Herman Maurer Lehmann, a hairdresser born in Zurich, Switzerland, on January 6, 1919.

The three were charged with military rebellion as described in Articles 237 and 238 of the Spanish Republican Military Code and with treason as described in Article 222. The prosecutor asked for the death penalty for Gudde and twelve years of military imprisonment for Eynatten and Maurer. The defense argued that there were mitigating circumstances, as described in Article 239 of the code, and asked for a penalty of six years of military imprisonment. The court found them all guilty. Lothar Gudde, as the leader, was sentenced to death. Eynatten and Maurer were condemned to imprisonment for life. Gudde's execution by firing squad took place at 6:00 A.M. on November 11, 1936, and was recorded in the municipal register of Zamudio.

On October 28, 1936, the consuls of Argentina, Austria, Belgium, Great Britain, and Switzerland left Bilbao on the British warship *Exmouth* to Donibane Lohitzune at 7:00 A.M. Most embassies, such as the British and the American, had moved their headquarters in the northern Basque Country in France, because it was very close to the Spanish border and away from the war, so the embassy staff was safe. When they were asked to show the contents of their bags as part of a routine inspection, all of them cooperated readily until the Austrian consul, Wilhelm Wakonigg, refused. He eventually relented, and when the contents were examined, they proved to be highly incriminating. There were several documents with information about the defenses of Bilbao, including details about the fortifications surrounding the city, the exact location of factories making shells and fuses for artillery and rifle ammunition, and information about the gunpowder used by the Basque army.

The bag also contained two maps of the estuary of Bilbao and numerous letters, one of them addressed to the chief of staff of the rebel Northern Army, another to the rebel civil governor of Donostia, and another to Colonel Solchaga, commander in chief of the rebel army in Gipuzkoa, containing information on the status of the war and signed by captain of engineers Pablo Murga. One of the letters, signed by Emilio Schaeidt, included highly derogatory descriptions of members of the Basque government.[1] Wakonigg also carried a report by José Anglada with a list of officers of the Basque army according to their sympathies for or against the Francoist regime, a report by Julián Munsuri entitled "Information on the Basque Nationalist Movement," letters signed by banker Julio Hernández Mendirichaga containing sums of money, notes from the Bank of Spain, details on Basque banking interests, and two small bags containing jewels (it was illegal to take jewels out of the country). Among the letters was one addressed to General Emilio Mola.[2]

Wilhelm Wakonigg was sixty-two years old; married; a native of Litija,

Slovenia; and living in Bilbao, where he served as consul for Austria and Hungary. As was later revealed, Wakonigg had been head of German espionage in the Basque Country during the Great War. Indeed, there had been German spies in the Basque Country ever since the Great War, mainly concentrated in Bilbao, where they focused their attention on the production of raw materials and, more specifically, of iron ore.[3]

The documentation carried by Wakonigg revealed to the Basque police the names and addresses of several German agents collaborating with the Spanish rebels, among them Emilio Schaeidt, who passed information to the German air force recommending buildings to be bombed or spared. Schaeidt confessed during the trial that the buildings he cataloged had suffered the consequences of the bombardment carried out with German personnel and matériel on September 25, 1936. In another letter from Schaeidt, dated October 26, 1936, there was evidence that the houses of Germans resident in Bilbao had suffered no damage. Schaeidt affirmed that German property was spared because of information he had provided. In one of the letters, Schaeidt discussed the aim and results of the German bombings.[4]

Another agent involved in this effort was Federico Martínez Arias, consul of Paraguay in Bilbao. In the end, police investigations revealed six people involved in the German spy network in Bilbao. During the proceedings, the prosecutor, Jose Miguel Gomendio, established that all of them had disseminated information about the war industry, defenses, and positions of artillery in the port of Bilbao to the forces of the Luftwaffe operating in the Basque Country. Wakonigg, Martínez, and Anglada were accused of treason and espionage as defined by Article 222 of the Military Code. The prosecutor demanded that a death sentence be applied against all three, and they were sentenced to death by firing squad.[5]

Despite international pressure to spare Wakonigg, the execution of all three men took place at 7:15 A.M. on November 19, 1936. Their deaths were recorded at the Municipal Court of Zamudio. George Steer reported that Minister of Justice Leizaola and Wakonigg's son-in-law, the chief of the Basque police, Luis Ortuzar—both of whom were close friends of Wakonigg's but had previously been unaware that he was a spy—visited him to comfort him in the evening and as in the old days had a long and friendly talk.[6] Wakonigg was buried in the cemetery in Begoña. Martínez and Anglada were buried in Derio. Captain Pablo Murga was also sentenced and shot.

More German pilots were taken prisoner in the spring of 1937 after their airplanes were shot down.[7] One of them, Walter Kienzle, confessed that he was a German soldier, but like most of the other captured pilots, such as Gunther Schulze-Blank, who also confessed to being a German soldier fighting with the German army, he denied having taken part in the bombing of Gernika.[8]

Basque forces shot down their first enemy aircraft, a Junker Ju52, on January 4, 1937. As Steer noted, no insurgent pilot of Spanish nationality and no machine of a Spanish type was ever brought down or captured in Basque territory.[9] Ten German pilots were captured, five of them alive, while the other five were killed when their planes crashed. On April 12, a German Heinkel He111 was shot down over Bilbao. Hans Sobotka was one of the members of the crew who died in the crash.[10] His passport showed German and Italian stamps, indicating that he had left Germany on April 5 and reached Seville via Rome on April 6.

Some days earlier, on April 5, Captain Walter Kienzle and Lieutenant Günther Schulze-Blank were captured near the Urkiola Pass, together with two other German soldiers, when by error they motored into the Basque lines during a ground reconnaissance in their car. Kienzle and Schulze-Blank were brought to a court of justice on May 21. Jesus Monzon, the public prosecutor of the Tribunal Popular de Vizcaya, said that the case was quite simple: "This country, the oldest and most democratic in the world, is being brutally attacked by German aircraft. These men are German military pilots who admittedly came here as volunteers and took part in actions against our lines."[11] Monzon further denounced what he described as the German massacre of priests, women, and children at Basque cities and towns and demanded the death penalty under the charges of rebellion and murder. Florencio Arostegi, the lawyer for the defense, pleaded for clemency by pointing out that the men were not guilty; responsibility for the attacks lay with the governments that had sent them to war: "You cannot make the prisoners responsible for the actions of Germany or for the terrible crimes committed by German aircraft since they were captured."

When examined by the prosecutor, Kienzle, who was twenty-four years old, from Ludwigsburg, stated that he had been a lieutenant in the German air force before joining the Condor Legion. When asked what motives prompted him to serve in Spain, he replied that he had "heard and read a lot about Spain that everything was in a mess, churches being destroyed, nuns killed and saw photographs in the newspapers."[12] He thus engaged himself for Spanish service at a certain office in Berlin, and, as Steer noted, no difficulty was made about his getting a passport to Spain. "It was very easy," he underlined. On March 31, he flew to Gasteiz, where he became commander of one of the two squadrons of nine Heinkel He51 pursuit planes. He denied that he had taken part in the bombing of Durango[13] or that he knew of the bombing until the day he was taken prisoner: "I was not aware before I came to Spain that the Republican Government exists as it does, only reading in the newspapers of disorder on the Government side and order on Franco's. I have changed my opinion of the Republic. I see that order reigns, priests walk about normally, Masses are said, and the people here are very nice to us. I myself was shocked when shown pictures of the air raid."[14]

Schulze-Blank, aged twenty-two, from Magdeburg, was a professional test pilot who had done two years' service in the German air force until he retired as a lieutenant. He testified that he had acted under Kienzle's orders as a Heinkel He51 pilot. He joined the Condor Legion at the end of December, and by March 27 he was in Gasteiz to prepare the airfield for the German and Italian pursuit planes serving on the Basque front. He stated that he did not know anything about the bombing of Durango and that he considered it "wrong to machine-gun women and children, and it was never suggested in Germany that that would be our job."[15]

German airman Hans Joachim Wandel, aged twenty-three, from Silesia, an architect and amateur flier, was captured on May 13 when a Basque machine gunner in a small pinewoods behind Mount Bizkargi, near Larrabetzu, shot down his Heinkel He51.[16] Wandel landed by parachute and was called as a witness in the trial against Kienzle and Schulze-Blank. He testified that he belonged to the same squadron as the defendants. Moreover, his diary showed the word *Guernica* on April 26, the day when the town was bombed.[17] Wandel admitted that Gernika had been bombed, but said that he, as the pilot of a pursuit plane, did not take part. He had accompanied German bombers on other expeditions when they destroyed "Basque pinewoods with incendiary bombs," which, he said, were highly efficient. However, later and during his trial on May 26, he admitted under oath to taking part in the bombing of Gernika.[18] His diary further showed that he was recruited in Berlin in April for service in Spain, signing on in an office near the Wilhelmstrasse. The offer was for six hundred pesetas a month, the normal pay for a member of the Condor Legion, and a bonus upon returning to Germany. He told his captors in the presence of George Steer that he left Berlin on April 22 for Rome in a commercial airplane. Two days after arrival, he handled a Heinkel He51 for the first time, practicing machine-gun fire at a fixed target from altitudes from three thousand to three hundred feet. On April 25, he went to Gasteiz, where he joined a squadron of German fighters, consisting of twelve pursuit planes. On April 26, he participated in the strafing of civilians in Gernika. After testifying against Kienzle and Schulze-Blank, Wandel was sent to prison to await his own trial.[19]

Wandel's testimony implied that the fighter squadron of twelve Heinkel He51s of which he was a member had indeed participated in the attack against Gernika. We know that there were only two squadrons of Heinkel He51s stationed at the air base in Gasteiz in April 1937, totaling twenty-one aircraft. It is difficult to believe that Wandel, lacking any training, was sent to Gernika while his squadron leader remained in Gasteiz, a twenty-minute flight from the target.

The trial of Kienzle and Schulze-Blank lasted four hours. The jury of sixteen citizens found them guilty on both charges after fifteen minutes' deliberation on May 21, 1937. A plea for revision of the sentence was presented but refused. The trial took place in the presence of foreign press correspondents and many members of the public and appeared to be wholly fair. Wandel was also tried and sentenced to death before a firing squad on May 25 under the same charges.[20]

As a reporter for the *Nevada State Journal* stated, Wandel's "chances of escaping death were regarded as meager after he admitted participating in the destruction of Gernika."[21] The question of execution was considered by the Basque Council of Ministers at their meeting on May 26, just after Wandel's trial.[22] After deliberation, the government announced the postponement of the execution of death sentences.[23] The official announcement said that the government had deferred the executions in order to facilitate calmer discussion about the political situation and to prevent any actions that might prolong the intervention of totalitarian governments in the war in the Basque Country.[24] Also, these pilots were scheduled to be released in exchange for a number of prisoners held by the rebels.[25] The release of the pilots was exploited by the Nazi propaganda machine when German official sources pointed out that Germany's warm approval of General Francisco Franco's action in releasing a group of foreign volunteers reflected Germany's support of "every move in the direction of humanization of the war."[26]

The three pilots were never shot. Indeed, all Basque nationalist members of the Basque government, including President Agirre and Minister of Justice Leizaola, were openly opposed to any death sentence. The prosecutor's office also opposed the application of death sentences, as confirmed by prosecutor German Iñurrategi in his memoirs: "I thought about it for a long time before accepting the position. I was not born for demanding death sentences, and in that situation something told me that I had to demand some."[27] Moreover, Manuel Irujo, a member of the Basque Nationalist Party and minister of justice of the Spanish Republic from May 17, 1937, was strongly opposed to the application of the death penalty in the Basque Country, in Catalonia, and in Spain. Irujo obstructed all executions by firing squad during his tenure and favored the exchange of prisoners of war and political prisoners, among them German pilots involved in the bombings in the Basque Country. Starting on May 17, no more pilots were shot in the Basque Country. Thousands of people owed their lives to this minister.

Kienzle, Schulze-Blank, and Wandel were among the very few German pilots taken to Basque prisons, tried, and sentenced by Basque courts of justice under the charges of murder and rebellion. They were the only people ever tried and sentenced for atrocities committed by the combined Nationalist aviation during the campaign against the Basque Country. Wandel was the only person involved in the bombing of Gernika ever tried and sentenced for murder. As I said, all three were pardoned by the Basque government and later liberated. In fact, before the capture of Bilbao by the combined forces, Jesús Leizaola, minister of justice of the Basque government, ordered all the prisoners to be liberated and driven safely to the enemy's positions to save them from being killed by an angry mob during the interval between the retreat of the Basque troops and the advance of Spanish Nationalist troops into Bilbao. As stated by Claude Bowers, Leizaola remained at the prison throughout the night, "personally to protect them against the possible fury of the crowd. As these prisoners emerged and started down the road, a crowd collected, and Leizaola appeared upon the scene, placing himself between the prisoners and the crowd, and announced that he had ordered their liberation. They were untouched. And then, his work done, the city preserved from wanton damage, the tired minister drove out of the city toward Santander in the nick of time."[28]

In any event, the cases against Kienzle, Schulze-Blank, and Wandel represent an important law of precedent in the field of terror bombing. The international law on aerial bombardment prior to 1937 is included in articles of the Hague Conventions of 1864, 1899, and 1907. Subsequently, a meeting of representatives of Britain, the United States, France, the Netherlands, Italy, and Japan met in The Hague from December 1922 to February 1923 to draw up a pact on the laws of war in the air. The committee drafted *The Hague Rules of Air Warfare,* which were completed on February 19, 1923, but never ratified.[29] As a consequence, the Hague Conventions of 1907 were the last treaty addressing aerial bombardment ratified prior to the war in the Basque Country.

Although the *Rules of Air Warfare* were never adopted in any legally binding form, in May 1937 the Non-Intervention Committee used them to bluntly denounce the bombings and other atrocities committed during the war—specifically referring to the bombing of Gernika, but omitting an explicit reference to it: "Deeply moved by the horrors associated with the use of certain methods of warfare, [the committee] condemns the use in the Spanish struggle of methods contrary to international law and the bombing of open cities."[30]

The bombing of Gernika demonstrated the pressing need for legal measures regarding international humanitarian law and aerial warfare. The first of these resolutions was passed by the Non-Intervention Committee in June 1937. The attack against Gernika completely ignored the international customary law and aerial warfare practices enforced by the Geneva Conventions of 1899 and 1907, the procedures for bombardments that the Greco-German arbitration tribunal of 1930 had recognized, and the covenant of the League of Nations and its derivative conventions. Concretely, the Greco-German tribunal examining the legality of the air raid against Salonika in January 1916 considered that the occupation of Salonika by the armed forces of the Entente in the autumn of 1915, at a time when Greece was not yet at war, constituted a violation of that country's neutrality and was an unlawful act of hostility. The bombardment of the area was further considered a violation of the fair practices of war.

The bombing of Gernika provided a new example of the persistent violation of human rights and laws of war, a practice that entailed the risk of such acts being adopted as customary practice. In this sense, it was understood that the establishment of rules for aerial bombardment and—along with the League of Nations' declaration against bombardment from the air—the provision of specific definitions for what should be considered an open or undefended city, an indiscriminate raid, or an appropriate warning was an urgent task.

Only ten days after the bombing of Gernika, German ambassador Joachim von Ribbentrop called on British foreign secretary Anthony Eden to protest the "incorrect and tendentious allegations" in the British press regarding the "alleged bombing of the Basque city by German planes."[31] After a month of debate, on June 18, 1937, the Non-Intervention Committee passed a resolution regarding the bombing of open cities, avoiding any mention of Gernika and equally directed at both warring parties. However, it was clearly not enough.

The bombing had caused a strong international reaction. The November 6, 1936, London Procès-Verbal on submarine warfare against merchant ships was regarded by various states as also being applicable to military aircraft in operations against merchant shipping.[32] Among the many initiatives in the United States by congressmen and journalists, one of the most striking was published on May 10 in the *New York Herald Tribune* as "Guernica Raid Denounced by 76 United States Leaders," which was added to the *Congressional Record* by Senator Gerald P. Nye on May 20,[33] stating that "we call upon all men of good will to protest this immense crime in the name of all that is sacred to human morality and human decency and in the name of Almighty God."[34]

The Roosevelts were keenly aware of the plight of the Basque people. Eleanor Roosevelt was honorary president of the American Board of Guardians for Basque Refugee Children, officially created in May 1937 to give refuge in New York to five hundred Basque children known as the "Children of Gernika," who were evacuated from the Basque Country after the Luftwaffe's bombing campaign. Immediately after Bishop Francis J. McConnell wrote and circulated his *Appeal to the Conscience of the World* on May 15, and President Roosevelt revealed his intention of making an international appeal on the bombing of open cities,[35] Philip Broadmead, first secretary of the British Embassy in Washington, met with Secretary of State Cordell Hull on May 20 and asked him to prevent the president from undertaking any independent intervention on Gernika.[36] The US administration acted accordingly, but the White House did not remain silent for long.

The bombing of Gernika and the attacks on Barcelona that followed, as well as the brutal bombardments carried out by the Japanese air force in China in 1937 and 1938, motivated the Unanimous Resolution of the League of Nations Assembly of September 30, 1938, on the Protection of Civilian Populations Against Bombing from the Air in Case of War.[37] The resolution was adopted along with the principles laid down by British prime minister

Neville Chamberlain in Parliament on June 21, 1938. He stated that there were three principles of international law that were as applicable to warfare from the air as they were to war at sea or on land. In the first place, it was against international law to bomb civilians as such and to make deliberate attacks upon civilian populations. That was undoubtedly a violation of international law. In the second place, targets attacked from the air must be legitimate military objectives and must be capable of identification. In the third place, reasonable care had to be taken in attacking military objectives so that by carelessness a civilian population in the neighborhood was not bombed.[38]

Like any other declaration, the resolution did not have binding force. Therefore, in response to the lack of an international covenant on the matter and following these principles, the contracting parties in the League of Nations organized a committee that drafted the Convention for the Protection of Civilian Populations Against New Engines of War that was completed in Amsterdam in 1938, declaring that this way of carrying out war was illegal and inhumane and concluding that "the civilian population of a state shall not form the object of an act of war." It added:

> The bombardment by whatever means of towns, ports, villages or buildings which are undefended is prohibited in all circumstances (art. 2)
>
> The bombardment by whatever means of towns, ports, villages or buildings which are defended is prohibited at any time (whether at night or day) when objects of military character cannot be clearly recognized (art. 3).
>
> Aerial bombardment for the purpose of terrorizing the civilian population is expressly prohibited (art. 4).
>
> . . . The use of chemical, incendiary or bacterial weapons as against any State, whether or not a party to the present Convention, and in any war, whatever its character, is prohibited (art. 6).[39]

But the convention was never ratified.

Roosevelt's presidential statement did not come until the outbreak of World War II.[40] When war broke out on September 1, 1939, at 4:00 A.M., President Roosevelt issued the *Appeal on Aerial Bombardment of Civilian Populations*, which had been blocked by the British in May 1937, in the following terms:

> The ruthless bombing from the air of civilians in unfortified centers of population during the course of the hostilities which have raged in various quar-

> ters of the earth during the past few years, which has resulted in the maiming and in the death of thousands of defenseless men, women, and children, has sickened the hearts of every civilized man and woman, and has profoundly shocked the conscience of humanity.
>
> If resort is had to this form of inhuman barbarism during the period of the tragic conflagration with which the world is now confronted, hundreds of thousands of innocent human beings who have no responsibility for, and who are not even remotely participating in, the hostilities which have now broken out, will lose their lives. I am therefore addressing this urgent appeal to every government which may be engaged in hostilities publicly to affirm its determination that its armed forces shall in no event, and under no circumstances, undertake the bombardment from the air of civilian populations or of unfortified cities, upon the understanding that these same rules of warfare will be scrupulously observed by all of their opponents. I request an immediate reply.[41]

It had taken twenty years since the end of the Great War and so much bloodshed to proclaim such principles, enclosed in four brief and transparent points. But once again, the declaration did not promote the ratification of an international binding covenant, and during World War II Europe and the world would suffer the worst horrors of aerial bombing.

Terror bombing as such is not today a violation of positive international law. We may infer, therefore, that it may not be considered in this light a war crime. The assumption of this principle means, however, the assumption of a principle that goes against the spirit of criminal law: to assume that the way in which an atrocity is perpetrated absolves the aggressor—in other words, that killing civilians by dropping bombs on them from the air or killing them by other means on the ground are two different issues that warrant different legal treatment, leaving aside the main fact that both cases involve the loss of lives. This assumption contradicts the principle established by the 1927–30 Greco-German arbitration tribunal subordinating the laws of war in the air to the laws of war on the land, under which causing the deaths of civilians during a war is a violation of the laws of war, regardless of the method used.[42]

Taking into account the lack of a positive norm in 1937 regarding aerial warfare in general and terror bombing in particular, the cases against Kienzle, Schulze-Blank, and Wandel represent some of the very few examples of sentences based on the principles expressed above. These pilots were sentenced to death under the charge of murder for bombing (a Heinkel He51 could carry six 22-pound bombs) and machine-gunning civilians in Gernika and in other towns and cities in the Basque Country—in other words, for practicing terror bombing. Wandel was the only person ever convicted for his participation in the massacre. Moreover, Kienzle, Schulze-Blank, and Wandel were among the few persons ever specifically convicted of terror bombing in a court of justice.

## Gernika in the Nuremberg Trials

The Luftwaffe had bombed Gernika to bring the Basques to submission, but it would take almost two more months for the rebel troops to cover the twenty-five miles that separate Gernika from Bilbao. After the capture of Bilbao on June 19, 1937, the war in the Basque Country was over. After the Spanish Republican army was defeated in April 1939, the Basque government had to make a decision about its future: to dissolve and renounce fighting or to act from exile and face, together with the rest of the European and American democracies, the totalitarian forces. The decision to go on fighting seemed obvious to the Basque government, which was among the first in Europe to face the German Nazis and the Italian Fascists. By 1939 the Basque government considered itself at war with all the enemies of democracy in Europe.[43] The Basque government was committed to taking an active role in the upcoming world war, both politically and militarily. So the Basque government, led by Lehendakari José Antonio Agirre, went into exile and transferred its central offices from Barcelona to Paris. One day after the German occupation of Poland, the Basque government declared that it was virtually at war with the German, Italian, and Spanish regimes and on the side of the democratic states. After the German occupation of Paris in June 1940, the Basque government was forced to evacuate its office there.

President Agirre disappeared at Dunkirk in June 1940, and Manuel Irujo assumed the temporary presidency of the Basque National Council, an institution that replaced the Basque government until Agirre reappeared in Montevideo, Uruguay, in October 1941. After fleeing the Gestapo, Agirre escaped to the Americas via Berlin, in what became one of the odysseys of Basque exiles.[44] The Basque government was reinstituted in October 1941, and its central offices were transferred from London to New York until the liberation of Paris in 1944. After the bombing of Pearl Harbor on December 7, 1941, Roosevelt was no longer under Hull's directives against intervention, and the Basque government initiated diplomatic and strategic negotiations with President Roosevelt's administration.

Two weeks before the Japanese attack on Pearl Harbor, on November 20, 1941, Lehendakari Agirre met William S. Stephenson, head of the British Security Council, at the British Embassy in New York.[45] The following day, he met with several secret service agents from the American Office of the Coordinator of Information to advance institutional cooperation.[46] Roosevelt had created the OCI on July 11, 1941, at the suggestion of Stephenson and John H. Godfrey, director of British Naval Intelligence, as a means of coordinating the work of the different US intelligence services. On January 8, 1942, Frederick P. Keppel, president of the Carnegie Corporation, wrote to William Joseph Donovan, head of the OCI, in favor of using Basque agents in the Americas and in the Philippines. Secretary of State Cordell Hull and US ambassador in Madrid Carlton Hayes opposed such cooperation. Whatever the case, after the final round of meetings in May 1942, as well as the creation of the Office of Strategic Services and the Office of War Information within the OCI in June, the Basque government and the US intelligence services began cooperating. The two administrations agreed to initiate a partnership between the Basque Secret Service and the OSS, which would continue from May 1942 until the end of 1949. The Basque-American agreement comprised four main points: the Basque secret services would collaborate with the US Office of Strategic Services; the Basque secret services would operate under direct Basque command; the Basque secret services would operate in South and Central America, in Europe, and also in the Philippines; and the main objective was to dissolve the German and Spanish spy networks in Latin America and the Japanese in the Philippines.[47]

The Basque government denounced the excesses and the violation of human rights by the Franco regime before the British, French, and American administrations. At the end of World War II, Franco's government was sanctioned for its association with the German and Italian totalitarian regimes. Between July 17 and August 2, 1945, representatives from the chief Allied governments—Great Britain, the Soviet Union, and the United States—met in Potsdam and decided to deny Spain's admission to the international organizations to be created after the war. Accordingly, the Spanish state would not be accepted into the United Nations, which would result in the withdrawal of all of Madrid's ambassadors, consuls, and international diplomats. The UN approved the Project of Resolution on Spain (Document A/40), by which the General Assembly recommended that the members of the United Nations withdraw their diplomats from Spain.[48] On March 4, 1946, the British, French, and American governments, all members of the UN Security Council, signed a public denunciation of the Spanish regime, although they declared their refusal to interfere in Spain's internal affairs.[49]

As part of this strategy of denouncing the Francoist regime's association with the Axis powers, the Basque government tried to act as a particular plaintiff during the Nuremberg Trials in the cases against Hermann Göring, head of the Luftwaffe as reichsminister of aviation and therefore one of the main culprits in the bombing of Gernika, and in the case against Major General Hugo Sperrle, head of the Condor Legion, who was tried as part of Case 12, heard from November 28, 1947, to October 28, 1948.

The attack described as a "complete success" in 1937[50] turned out to be just a prelude to what the Luftwaffe did in Barcelona,[51] Rotterdam,[52] Warsaw, and elsewhere.[53] The massive carpet bombing of civilians and nonmilitary targets became a standard part of the Nazi regime's offensive strategy. This policy was responsible for countless wartime atrocities.

On February 4, 1945, Winston Churchill, Franklin D. Roosevelt, and Joseph Stalin met in Yalta and agreed that Germany would have to undergo a process of demilitarization and denazification. Part of this process would consist of the prosecution of the primary German leaders and other persons responsible for atrocities. Three months later, on May 2, President Harry S. Truman proposed Robert Jackson as chief US counsel for the prosecution of German war criminals, and on October 14 British judge Sir Geoffrey Lawrence was designated president of the International Military Tribunal. After visiting Nuremberg, Robert Jackson decided to locate the court in the city's Palace of Justice.

The authority for the proceedings was built on several agreements, among them the Moscow Declaration on German Atrocities, signed on November 1, 1943; President Truman's Executive Order 9547, Providing for Representation of the United States in Preparing and Prosecuting Charges of Atrocities and War Crimes Against the Leaders of the European Axis Powers and Their Principal Agents and Accessories, of May 2, 1945; the London agreement enabling the prosecution of war criminals of August 8, 1945; the Charter of the International Military Tribunal of August 8, 1945; and, finally, the Berlin Protocol of October 6, 1945.[54]

On November 20, 1945, the trial of the major German war criminals began, and on October 1, 1946, the verdicts against the convicted war criminals were delivered: eleven of the twenty-one defendants were sentenced to death. Two weeks later, on October 16, ten of the war criminals were hanged. The eleventh, Hermann Göring—the leader most responsible for the massacre at Gernika—committed suicide. Göring was interrogated before the trial by Joseph Maier, chief of the Briefing Analysis Section, and by Sander, chief of the Analysis Interrogation Section, about the Gernika massacre. The German officer answered indifferently: "a lamentable event. But we could not do otherwise. At that time, such experiments could not be carried out elsewhere."[55] Wolfram von Richthofen, commander of the Condor Legion during the attack and therefore one of the massacre's main instigators, died of a brain tumor in captivity on July 12, 1945. He thus never faced trial.

But the case against many other people implicated in atrocities went on. Indeed, Major General Hugo Sperrle was among the German officers who were tried as part of Case 12, which took eleven months to decide. In addition to the five major legal sources mentioned above, the authority for the proceedings of the twelve subsequent cases in Nuremberg derived from five agreements: Control Council Law 10 of December 20, 1945; Executive Order 9679 of January 16, 1946; US Military Ordinance No. 7 of October 18, 1946; US Military Ordinance No. 11 of February 17, 1947; and US Forces of the European Theatre Order 301 of October 24, 1946.

The Basque government prepared a list of charges to be added to the accusations against Sperrle, which was given to Edgar Faure, adjunct prosecutor at the international tribunal of the French Republic. The document described the participation of the German Luftwaffe at the Basque front and its participation in the massacres at Durango, Otxandio, Gernika, and other cities in the Basque Country. The report included evidence and testimony and was signed by the president of the Basque government in exile, José Antonio Agirre.

The prosecution in Case 12 indicted fourteen former German officers on charges of crimes against humanity, war crimes, crimes against peace, and ill-treatment and murder of prisoners of war. Most of the defendants were acquitted of crimes against peace and conspiracy, but almost all of them were found guilty of crimes against humanity and of war crimes as well as of crimes committed against civilians.

Only two of the defendants were acquitted of all charges, Admiral Otto Schiniewind and Major General Hugo Sperrle. Indeed, Sperrle was never charged with crimes against humanity for his participation in the bombings committed in the Basque Country, since the trial focused only on crimes committed in the invaded countries of Europe, as stated by the Moscow Declaration on German Atrocities.

The bitter war in Spain therefore lay outside the court's jurisdiction. As a result, no one was ever tried in Nuremberg or anywhere else for the massacre in Gernika. Hugo Sperrle died in Munich in 1953. Second Lieutenant Hans W. Asmus,[56] Colonel Hans Henning Freiherr von Beust, Lieutenant Colonel Karl von Knauer, and First Lieutenant Rudolf von Moreau, the German officers in command during the bombing, were never tried for their participation.

Nor were any of the principal instigators of the attack in the Spanish or Italian armies ever tried for the atrocity, including General Francisco Franco, General Emilio Mola, General Alfredo Kindelán, Colonel Juan Vigón, and General Vincenzo Velardi. German foreign minister Konstantin von Neurath (tried in Nuremberg and sentenced to fifteen years' imprisonment for his diplomatic maneuvers as head of the Reich's Foreign Ministry), German ambassador to the United Kingdom Joachim von Ribbentrop (tried, sentenced to death, and hung in Nuremberg), and German ambassador to Franco General Wilhelm von Faupel (died in May 1945) were never tried for their participation in the denial of the massacre. Unlike the German government, the Spanish and Italian governments have never assumed responsibility for the participation of their soldiers in the massacre.

# 8

# Gernika as an Icon of Terror Bombing

Vicente Talón maintained that if Picasso had not painted the *Guernica*, what happened in Gernika on April 26, 1937, would have been forgotten.[1] However, Picasso made the first sketches of his painting on May 1 and finished it on June 4. It was first exhibited to the public inside the Spanish pavilion at the World Exposition in Paris on July 12, 1937.[2] After the German occupation of Paris in 1940, a Gestapo officer who visited Picasso in his studio saw a sketch of the painting and asked him, "Have you done this?" Picasso responded, "No, you did it."[3]

But news of the bombing had covered the front pages of most of the free-world press since the morning after it happened. It was not Picasso who first gave the massacre its international notoriety, although the aesthetic value of his canvas and the international infamy that the attack on Gernika had attained in the preceding months secured resounding critical success for the canvas and made Gernika an international icon of terror bombing and by extension of the human suffering caused by wars. Even before the attack, Gernika—the city of the Basque Tree of Liberties—had long served as a symbol of freedom in Europe and the Americas.

Despite the testimony of scores of eyewitnesses to the event, the massacre became known internationally mainly from the reports of Steer, Monks, and Holme. Their articles constituted the main sources of information for the international press at the time and caused the most significant impact in the international political arena and on public opinion. It is also unquestionable that Picasso's painting later provided an unforgettable visual image of the atrocities described in Steer's and Monks's reports and made Gernika a universal icon.

Gernika was not the first city to be bombed in the Basque Country or in the world. There is an appallingly long list of bombed cities that includes about a thousand places in the century that preceded the attack on Gernika. One of the first bombings from the air occurred on August 22, 1849, during the First Italian War of Independence (1848–49). On that occasion, the Austrian general of artillery and inventor Franz von Uchatius launched several balloons against Venice from vessels moored offshore. The balloons, each armed with thirty-three pounds of explosives, were designed to deflate automatically when they were over the target, dropping their shells.[4] This was the only way possible to lay siege to the city, which was otherwise well protected from attack by its sheltering lagoon.

However, the destruction of Gernika had an unprecedented impact in the diplomatic arena and in the international press explainable only in terms of panic. The Western powers were terrified that the German Nazi regime, by then so obviously committed to a Pan-European war, would make use of such destructive power against other European cities and reduce them to ashes as Gernika had been—as indeed happened in 1939 and 1940.

This fear pervaded the League of Nations and was reflected in the messages of US ambassadors and observers in Europe. As Emperor Haile Selassie had stated on June 30, 1936, before the League of Nations, "It is us today. It will be you tomorrow."[5] In view of the attitude of Hitler and Mussolini in Germany and Italy, Hugh R. Wilson, US ambassador to Germany (1938–39), and later adviser to the secretary of state (1940–41), also expressed his serious concerns about the fate of a peace agreement to the Bureau of the Disarmament Conference in Geneva on May 31, 1937. According to Wilson, Germany's absence from the League of Nations rendered much of the work done to achieve international peace illusory, and the apparent determination of most of the industrialized nations to carry out their various rearmament programs gave little promise for a reversal of the situation.[6] John C. Cudahy, US ambassador to Poland, was also profoundly pessimistic about the possibilities of a peace agreement on the subject of disarmament at the League of Nations in 1937, so long as Hitler and Mussolini were in power. Indeed, Cudahy was much more distrustful and skeptical than Wilson about the possibility of peace and was concerned about a possible German invasion of Poland. "Germany is the outstanding threat. The whole impulse of the country is war preparation. The economy is a war economy and if this were suddenly stopped, from four to six million people would be thrown out of employment. But it must be stopped or the end is a certain conflict." So concluded Cudahy in May 31, 1937, a month after the attack on Gernika.[7] In sum, every European and American statesman was aware that Germany was preparing to bring war to the rest of Europe, that the bombing of Gernika was a rehearsal, and that if war broke out as expected, Warsaw, Rotterdam, London, and any other European city the Germans chose were likely to be bombed in the same way that Gernika had been.

But apart from the reasonable panic, Gernika became front-page news in the international press because the bombardment was in many ways a turning point in the history of terror bombing. The bombing of Gernika was a tragic event for a number of reasons, but it also represented a unique episode involving new and for the most part experimental bombing techniques. Its success made it the canonical strategy for terror-bombing attacks during World War II, until the dropping of the atomic bomb on Japan in 1945.

The differences between tactical, strategic, and terror bombing lie in the goal or intention of the bombing. The aim of tactical bombing is to destroy army units at or near the front as part of a combined attack and mostly in support of ground or naval forces. Tactical bombing in the 1930s was mostly subordinated to ground or naval command and was intended to subdue land or naval targets. Area or saturation bombing, on the contrary, primarily targeted sites of industrial or military production far behind the front lines.

In this sense, dive-bombing should have become the essential tactic of strategic bombing. Precise and specific, the warplane swooped down on the target at an angle from 45 to even 90 degrees and dropped a single heavy bomb with a high degree of accuracy on a defined target (a bridge, a tank, a ship, or any other moving or unmoving target). Even so, the maximum average load of ordnance for a dive-bomber in 1937 was limited to a single bomb of 1,100 pounds, obviously not enough to destroy a factory. Consequently, dive-bombers were mostly used in tactical operations to destroy batteries, tanks, or other heavy movable units, bridges, strongholds, or ships. Concentration bombing schemes were primarily intended to destroy factories or large production centers far behind the enemy lines. The system was not as accurate as dive-bombing, but by increasing the number of planes and bomb loads the effect was much more devastating.

However, by increasing bomb loads—especially when bombing by night—the bomb strikes were far from precise. Soon these indiscriminate saturation bombings became terror bombings when affecting entire cities in industrial areas or isolated war-matériel production zones. Indeed, the command of the Condor Legion soon confirmed that the early bombings of Elorrio, Otxandio, and Elgeta did not achieve great tactical results. Only a month after the offensive in the Basque Country began, Durango was bombed by the Italian air force under German command with the sole intention of spreading terror. But this strategy did not work either. Gernika came next, but only after a whole month of aerial experimentation and theoretical development in other areas of the campaign against the Basque Country. In Gernika the German air command experimented with a new type of terror bombing, based on a new and complex scheme of saturation bombing in successive waves and clusters and a new flight formation.

The Condor Legion had two main objectives in the war: to prepare soldiers and pilots for the impending world war and to develop a strategy for combining air raids with land and naval attacks to produce rapid advances (*Blitzkrieg*). Thus, according to Richthofen, the basic strategic objectives of combat raids in the Basque Country where the Basque militia did not have pursuit planes were to attack the enemy's positions and strongholds (to be achieved through tactical bombing), to destroy the main means of communication and consequently cause a collapse in the transportation of troops and war matériel and to destroy the sources of ammunition and food supply (to be achieved through strategic bombing), and, finally, to destroy the enemy's population (to be achieved through terror bombing). In other words, terror bombing was intended to destroy the enemy's morale by frightening and demoralizing the civilian population and the nonprofessional militia. Gernika fell under this last category.

The most direct way of breaking the enemy's morale was through a heavy air raid over a meaningful city with the sole aim of razing it to the ground. The plan was thus to frighten the enemy into submission through a rapid, overwhelming attack, "un successo rápido e decisivo," in General Pietro Pinna's own words.[8] Erwin Jaenecke, a member of the Condor Legion general staff, considered the bombing "a total success of the German air force."[9] However, even though the general staff of the Condor Legion considered it a masterpiece of terror bombing, the bombing of Gernika did not achieve its main goal, which was to bomb the enemy into submission.[10] The war in the Basque Country did not end until the capture of Bilbao, which was twenty miles by road from Gernika and did not fall until June 19, 1937.

However, the complete destruction of a city by making it uninhabitable forced a massive migration of people, increasing the feeling of insecurity and frustration among them and generating in the enemy's field the complex and expensive task of taking care of a moving human mass (up to 250,000 noncombatants took refuge in Bilbao during the campaign in the Basque Country).

Carpet bombing, an indiscriminate system of area bombing, became the perfect program for terror bombing—the most National Socialist way of fighting wars, in Göring's view—because of the enormous destruction that this system of bombardment makes possible. Accuracy is not an essential element of terror bombing. Indeed, the main elements of this type of bombing are quantity, quality, and density, all three elements increasing inaccuracy. The quantity and quality of the ordnance are proportional to the desired extent of destruction, and greater destruction is achieved by concentration. In order to drop a vast amount of ordnance on a certain compact area, the most effective strategy was for the planes to fly in compact groups, following each other closely and launching their cargoes along the same aerial path. The Luftwaffe's application of this bombing method at the Basque front drew a line between the different methods of bombing and the various schemes of saturation bombing. Terror bombing, conceived as an independent action performed through a specifically designed and distinctive system of bomb delivery, was executed in Gernika for first time in history.

The new theoretical or strategic conception of bombing led to the development of new specialized bombers. Unlike World War I, when the German Giant and Gotha bombers were almost inaccessible to British fighters, after 1937 pursuit planes gained speed and maneuverability, and slow, heavy bombers needed a protective escort of fighter planes. The mechanical army of the 1920s led to the conception of a highly specialized aerial machine of war by the end of the 1930s. Thus, the heavy, low-soaring Junkers Ju52s that bombed Gernika were specialized in area bombing or transportation tasks, while the Junker Ju87 Stukas became the par excellence German dive-bomber, or Sturzkampfflugzeug, of early World War II.

Moreover, the Stukas had a whistling device attached to their fuselage, the *Jericho-Trompete* (Trumpet of Jericho), which was intended to terrify the adversary with a high-pitched siren sound that was activated by the air when the plane was swooping down. The Stuka was used for first time in the experimental air unit led by First Lieutenant Rudolf von Moreau on the Basque front in 1937 and would later be known on the Russian front as the "tank cracker."

By 1937 terror bombing had become the most important tool of a new way of considering and conducting war. As Günter Grass accurately described it, the bombing of Gernika was the tragic prelude of a new era of terror bombing.[11]

Certainly, this was not the first time an open city with no strategic or military interest was bombed. London, Paris, and several southeastern English coastal cities (King's Lynn, Sheringham, Great Yarmouth, and Boston) were exposed to indiscriminate bombing for two years during World War I. By the end of the Great War, the German Imperial Navy's Zeppelin "baby killers" had completed more than fifty raids against English cities and killed nearly 600 people, mostly civilians.[12] By the fall of 1915, fifty-eight explosive and incendiary bombs had been dropped on Paris, resulting in 6 people killed and 34 wounded. London suffered the first Zeppelin attack in May 1915 and the first attack by German Gotha bombers in June 1917, resulting in 157 deaths and 432 wounded. On July 7, twenty German warplanes raided London, causing a further 594 casualties.[13] The magnitude and nature of the German campaign against England led to lively public and political debates about terror bombing and created many new problems regarding the protection of the civilian population, civic order, and the state of public morale.

By 1937 the techniques of terror bombing had developed in many ways. Even if Gernika was not the first time an open city with no strategic or military interest was bombed or the first time a terror-bombing campaign had been launched or the first time a mixture of incendiary and explosive bombs had been dropped or civilians machine-gunned from the air, in Gernika the German war machine opened a gate for future improvements in bombing tactics and aerial strategies. The bombing of April 26, 1937, is unique for several reasons, and this explains why Gernika became an icon of terror bombing.

This was the first bombardment ever deliberately intended to cause the maximum number of civilian casualties as part of a war experiment. The attack was carefully planned and meticulously performed with that sole aim. It was also thoroughly recorded, and the ruins of the city were carefully examined by the Germans for more than two weeks before the city was opened to international observers. Alfons Kössinger, the reconnaissance officer of the Condor Legion, recalled that his unit was ordered to photograph the bombing of Gernika from the air and to photograph and make motion-picture records of the results once the city was captured, in order for the experts to carefully analyze the effectiveness of their weapons and strategy. Gernika remained strictly closed to the public until the examination of the city and the removal of evidence of the bombing were completed. This is certainly the most macabre part of the bombing of Gernika—the whole operation was all merely a military experiment.

The bombing of Gernika was planned according to a new strategy. Condor Legion general staff member Adolf Galland described the new system of carpet bombing in his memoirs, although he did not refer to the attack on Gernika.[14] Although this was not the first time the technique of concentration bombing was applied—flying in close formation, successive waves of Japanese bombers had dropped their cargoes on Shanghai in 1932—it was the first time an attack occurred based on a very specific and complex version of "carpet bombing" or "saturation bombing" in combination with the "shuttle bombing" technique. Flying three abreast in close formation and following the same north-south direction, successive bomber groups dropped their cargoes on Gernika. However, in Gernika each of the three bomber groups performing "carpet bombing" was followed by a group of pursuit planes that performed air-to-ground attacks in the intervals between bomber attacks. As a consequence, Gernika was assaulted nonstop for three and a half hours by four successive waves of bombers and pursuit planes. During the interludes between bomber attacks, pursuit planes machine-gunned survivors who were trying to escape the flames scorching the city center.[15] Because the Gasteiz airfield was so close to the target, it was easy for the fighters to return to base after an initial attack to rearm while another flight squadron was bombarding the position. By the end of the fighters' attack, a new group of bombers carpeted the town, followed by other fighters' attack. This bombing tactic had the advantage of keeping the enemy under continuous attack for hours, dramatically increasing the psychological stress of the victims, as in the case of Gernika. This bombardment process was known as "shuttle bombing"[16] or "chain bombing," and it was rehearsed, en masse, in Gernika.

As noted, the first wave of bombing, carried out by two Heinkel He111s, a Dornier Do17, and three Savoia-Marchetti SM.79s, was intended to bring people into the city center, because after this first bombing no one would expect a second and much more destructive wave of bombers. It was correctly calculated that the natural reaction of most people in that situation was to assist the wounded. Once the pursuit planes circling the city had herded people inside their ring of fire, the second group of bombers would appear to loose another wave of bombs on the population. This deadly logic was performed on such a scale for the first time in Gernika.

Accordingly, for the first time pursuit planes were used not only to escort the bombers but primarily to contain the victims within the target area, referred to as the "fire ground" or "ring of fire." The purpose of the "aerial corral" was both strategic and tactical. First, by confining the victims within the target area, those not killed by the detonations would be asphyxiated, scorched, or crushed by debris. The second purpose was tactical: to prevent the enemy from reorganizing before a ground attack was launched, allowing the capture of a position by an aerial knockout blow. Indeed, the fire ground—the Wagnerian ring of magic fire in which Brünnhilde was held captive—gave its name to the whole Operation Feuerzauber of the Condor Legion. As stated by eyewitness Alberto Onaindia, "The method of attack was always the same. First there was machine-gun fire, then ordinary bombs, and finally incendiaries."[17] As mentioned, this pattern, first used in Gernika, would be followed by the Germans when they bombed Warsaw (September 17, 1939) and Rotterdam (May 14, 1940).[18]

The path followed by the successive waves of planes was prearranged: the first group of experimental aircraft (Heinkel He111s and Dornier Do17s) followed a west-to-east path, while the rest of the bombing waves (Junker Ju52s) raided from north to south. Both paths crossed exactly over the middle of the city, thus causing major material damage.

The Junker Ju52s used a mixture of incendiary bombs (probably close to 70–80 percent) and different types of high-explosive shells. Both the quantity and the quality of the shells and the order in which the bombs were dropped were methodically calculated. And thc calculations proved to be utterly effective. A mixture of different types of heavy explosive bombs and incendiary bombs dropped in a certain order was essential to achieve the maximum destruction. In the Basque Country, the German air command had discovered that small incendiary bombs did not fracture the solid tile roofs of the Basque stone houses. They realized that the incendiaries had to be dropped only after the heavy high-explosive bombs were dropped, so that the inflammable liquid penetrated the cracks, allowing fire to spread through the wooden structures of the centuries-old Basque houses. Accordingly, the German air command launched the different types of bombs according to a predetermined scheme: first, a wave of explosive shells in huge quantities and, afterward, the incendiaries to generate a larger fire.

Shells with timers that exploded later to generate subsequent fires, extremely high temperatures, and hot-air whirlpools contributed to the hellhole effect described by Steer in Gernika and severely increased the damage caused by the denotations. Some bombs were still exploding days after the attack (three days in the case of Gernika). Both the bombing and the following firestorm (the long-lasting effect described by Galland)[19] were highly uncontrolled and indiscriminate, perfect for terror bombing.

Gernika represents one of the first large-scale bombardments in which a significant number of planes concentrated their fire on a relatively small single target. During the Great War, the largest raids on London had involved as many as thirty-six planes.[20] The comparative intensity of the raid on Gernika, which had a significantly smaller population than Greater London, was unprecedented. Fifty-nine planes struck downtown Gernika, an area of less than one square mile, dropping from 68,000 to 90,000 pounds of explosive and incendiary projectiles for almost three and a half hours. Such dense carpet bombing was unknown in 1937. For instance, during the attack of September 8, 1915, carried out by three Zeppelins against London, a total of 4,000 pounds of mixed explosive and incendiary bombs was dropped.[21]

Gernika represents one of the first long-endurance bombings ever recorded. The closest similar attack was in Shanghai, where on August 28, 1937 (Bloody Saturday), Japanese bombers dropped bombs in successive but independent waves, none of them lasting longer than a half hour. Gernika is the first city ever completely razed by a bomb attack that destroyed 100 percent of the stone buildings in the downtown area and 85.22 percent of the buildings in total. Only 1 percent remained untouched. As one reporter in Gernika asserted, “The buildings left standing can be counted almost on the fingers of one hand.”[22] It is very difficult to find entire villages, towns, or cities completely destroyed during an air raid before 1937.[23] As a result of this extensive damage, the reconstruction of the city—carried out by POWs who worked in the ruins of Gernika in the worst possible conditions—took ten years.

As Noel Monks said, “Both my colleagues went through the Abyssinian campaign with me and all three of us have spent six months in Franco’s territory, where we had every opportunity of seeing Franco’s entire squadron of German and Italian planes."[24] However, Steer, Monks, and Watson described the bombing of Gernika as "the worst bombing effect" ever seen, and they all emphasized that they were well used to the sight of heavy bombardments. "I have seen many ghastly sights in Spain in the last six months, but none more terrible than the annihilation of the ancient Basque capital of Guernica by Franco's bombing planes," Monks wrote.[25]

The destructive capacity of the Luftwaffe and more specifically the high number of fatalities (nearly 20 percent of the people in town), the unparalleled level of physical destruction, and the strategy of the attack were stressed by the reporters because all this was a novelty in the field of aerial bombardment in 1937. Most newspaper accounts made reference to the capability for destruction of the new airplanes within the context of a new and unknown "modern warfare." Of the first six articles in the *New York Times* regarding the attack, five referred specifically to the massive destruction of the city and the indiscriminate mass murder of innocent civilians. The German air command elected to bomb Gernika on a market day to guarantee a maximum number of people gathered in the streets, and the first bombs were dropped on the marketplace, causing the first casualties of the day. The Spanish and German general staffs knew the precise location of the three war hospitals in Gernika, and they knew that the city was a place where wounded or ill troops were taken to receive care. The hospital at the Calzada Asylum was bombed, while the factories remained untouched. Indeed, all the newspapers based their early reports on these or similar facts because they were the most groundbreaking and shocking aspects of the bombing. A typical report was that published in the *London Morning Post:* "It was hours before the fire-fighters and salvage crews could think of venturing into the blazing, crumbling streets. In one bomb shelter over fifty women and children were trapped and burned alive. Everywhere is a chaos of charred beams, twisted girders, broken masonry and smouldering ashes with forlorn groups of inhabitants wandering in search of missing relatives. The survivors spent a night of horror sleeping where and if they could, awaiting with dumb resignation their evacuation today."[26]

Forty out of the sixty-three articles published by the *New York Times* between April 27 and July 4, 1937, made reference to the total destruction of the Basque town. And 80 percent of the newspapers published these accounts on the front page. Paraphrasing Anna R. Mask, the bombing of Gernika gave eloquent expression to the intensity and immensity of what was the tragedy not only of Gernika but of the world, because it showed how ruthless the drive for power could become and how efficient the Luftwaffe was.[27]

Certainly, it is not easy to find examples of such massive and prolonged strafing of helpless civilians prior to 1937 or of attacks that provoked such genuine and abundant moral indignation in the free world. As Canon Alberto Onaindia stated, "The planes descended very low, the machine-gun fire tearing up the woods and roads, in whose gutters, huddled together, lay old men, women, and children. Before long it was impossible to see as far as 500 yards owing to the heavy smoke. Fire enveloped the whole city. Screams of lamentation were heard everywhere, and the people, filled with terror, knelt lifting their hands to heaven as if to implore Divine protection. The aeroplanes descended to 600 Ft., letting loose a terrible machine-gun fire."[28] In the letter that a group of Basque priests sent to the pope, they described how planes had machine-gunned the inhabitants pitilessly as they ran in terror, fleeing the explosions and fires that surrounded them, causing many deaths: "The aeroplanes which flew with impunity almost at ground level, saw perfectly the ruin and casualties which they were causing. Nevertheless they continued to attack in full knowledge of what they were doing."[29]

The raid showed for the first time the consummate brutalities of which modern warfare was capable. The ferocity of the terror-bombing campaign described by George L. Steer and reported by British eyewitnesses of the raids in the Basque Country enhanced the preexisting concern and alerted Europeans to the probability of further attacks by the German air force.[30] *New York Times* columnist D. W. Brogan expressed these concerns clearly when he wrote that the bombing of Gernika had taught the world that Great Britain was no longer an island. "Her age-old security" was threatened by German planes to a degree unknown in previous history. Indeed, according to Brogan, the air raids of the Great War had been more important as an augury of future menace than as a real threat to British security; they had been irritating but not as deadly as the last German raids in the Basque Country. The British people had to adapt themselves to the new psychology of a people who had to realize that if there was a war, it would not be fought abroad but in large part take the form of "making a hell of England's green and pleasant land."[31]

Linked to the nature of the attack, the denial of responsibility for the raid was also highly shocking and disquieting because it indicated that the German regime was preparing for further attacks against other European or American targets that could expect equal treatment within the framework of an increasingly certain new world war. This was the first clear announcement of what the Nazis would inflict on Europe in the context of another war. As the anonymous author of the prologue to *Foreign Wings over the Basque Country* wrote in 1937:

> The episode of Guernica, with all that it represents both in the military and the moral order, seems destined to pass into History as a symbol. A symbol of many things, but chiefly of that capacity for falsehood possessed by the new Machiavellism which threatens destruction to all the ethical hypotheses of civilization. A clear example of the use which can be made of untruth to degrade the minds of those whom one wishes to convince. And so, over against the truth, the legend of what happened in Guernica is being formed. And whatever it lacks in poetry this legend is at least a revelation of dark corners in the human mind.[32]

Gernika thus represents a preamble of what would be launched over the rest of Europe in the following years. Wilfred von Richthofen, commander of the attack against Gernika, also took part in the raids on Warsaw (September 1939) and many other targets during the operation in Crete (May 1941) and in the campaign against the Soviet Union (June 1941–43). Indeed, Richthofen and Hugo Sperrle, who was in command of the bombing of Gernika, would be two of only six Luftwaffe generals promoted to the rank of *generalfeldmarschall* during World War II.

Even after the Spanish war ended and the Germans went home, the Franco regime imposed the cruelest punishments and repression on the survivors. That uncivil period, which was marked by atrocities, dictatorship, and the violation of the most elemental human rights, did not end until 1945 in the northern Basque Country and until 1975 in the southern Basque Country.

There are no precedents in modern European history for the mass evacuation of children such as the one undertaken by the Basque government as a consequence of the bombing campaign started by the Condor Legion. Consistent with the data given by US consul William E. Chapman, the media accurately estimated that there were about 250,000 refugees in Bilbao in early May, after the initial air offensive of April.[33] The evacuation of 32,000 children—totaling 20 percent of the children living in the area controlled by the Basque government—between May and August 1937 was the first large-scale operation for the evacuation of children in contemporary European history. It was also the first time that the possibility of evacuating hundreds of thousands of civilians to foreign countries had been considered. The evacuation campaign generated great concern in Europe, particularly in England, because it evoked the evacuation campaign undertaken by the British government in London during the Great War and warned of the immediate consequences of a terror-bombing campaign during World War II.

# 9

## Gernika in Modern Memory

Picasso's *Guernica* has become a symbol of the atrocities of war. However, even before Picasso's masterpiece was first exhibited in Paris, the bombing of Gernika had become a subject of worldwide outrage. As soon as news of the bombardment became public, it became the focus of international shock, panic, and indignation, as it revealed the German regime's contempt for human life.

Besides the diplomatic and political actions that occurred as an immediate response to the attack on Gernika, the bombing also had an impact at the social level, and it soon became an icon for the atrocities of war. The Basque battalion that took part in the liberation of the Bordeaux area in 1945 was named Gernika after the victims of the bombing, and some of the Basque soldiers I have interviewed or whose works I have read, such as José Elizalde and Joseph Eiguren, had Gernika on their minds when they declared their intention to join the Resistance or the US Army to fight European totalitarianism.[1]

In 1943 the dedication of squares, streets, and parks named after Gernika was first broached in the United States. The devastated Basque town was about to become one of the symbols of the Basque resistance in exile and, by extension, an icon of the suffering of innocent civilians in the course of modern warfare. But the tradition of dedicating public sites under Basque names was not new in the Americas. There were substantial populations of émigré Basques and their descendants in the United States, Mexico, and several South American countries, and most of these communities worked hard to preserve their Basque culture and ties with the homeland. On November 1, 1882, during a celebration of the Fiestas Euskaras (Basque

Festivals) in Buenos Aires, the Plaza Euskara (Basque Square) was inaugurated, a seed from the Tree of Gernika was planted, and the Basque flag was raised while the crowd sang Iparragirre's "Gernikako Arbola" (Tree of Gernika). The participants used three national symbols with obvious political connotations: the Basque national flag, the "Gernikako Arbola" as the Basque national anthem, and the use of the terms *euskaros* (Basques) and *Euskaria* as a reference to Euskal Herria (Basque Country). Nearly a century before the bombing, Gernika was already recognized in the Americas as a symbol of the liberties and political rights of the Basque nation. In July 1943, at the National Congress of Mayors of Uruguay, the mayor of Cerro Largo, Giordano B. Etcher, proposed that the mayors inaugurate public squares in honor of Gernika in each of Uruguay's state capitals[2] as a tribute to the Basque people in their fight for freedom against German Nazism, Italian Fascism, and Spanish National-Catholicism.[3] The congress unanimously approved Etcher's motion. Consequently, the city council of Mercedes in the Department of Soriano decided to inaugurate a park in honor of the bombing victims at a meeting on September 17, 1943. At the urging of Rogelio C. Sosa, mayor of Mercedes,[4] nineteen Uruguayan mayors met in that city in November 1943 to inaugurate the first monument to commemorate the massacre. Town councillor Zoilo Chelle declared in his address that Gernika was more than just a symbol of mass execution; it was a beacon of liberty and democracy.[5] The red granite monolith still stands under an oak on the bank of the Río Negro. In April 1944, Pedro Artetxe and Gabriel Damboriana—a member of the City Council of Montevideo—proposed to Mayor Juan Pablo Fabini that a square at the intersection of Ramón Anador and Catalonia Streets be renamed Plaza Guernica. The city council voted unanimously in favor of the proposal, and Basque artists Nestor Basterretxea and Félix Muñoa were appointed to design a bronze plaque depicting a Basque couple, to be placed in front of the Parliament, and another plaque depicting the Oak of Gernika to be placed on a red granite monolith in the square. Carlos G. Mendilaharzu, a member of the Basque Center Euskal Erria in Montevideo, carved the mold, and the Plaza Gernika was inaugurated on May 13, 1944. The presence at the dedication ceremony of such a large number of members of the Uruguayan government and international diplomats gives us an idea of the importance of Gernika as a symbol. The mayor of Montevideo, Juan Pablo Fabini, and several members of the city council were present. So were the president of the High Court of Justice of Uruguay, Julio Guani;

Minister of War Hector Luisi; Minister of Agriculture and Livestock Arturo González Bidart; Minister of Industry and Labor Javier Mendivil; Minister of Economy Héctor Álvarez Cina; the ambassador of Mexico, Mariano Armendariz del Castillo; the ambassador of Venezuela, Gustavo Tejería; the ambassador of Belgium, Joseph de Neef; and the general consuls of Czechoslovakia, Great Britain, Greece, Mexico, Norway, and Poland. Senators Justino Zabala Muniz, Martín Etchegoyen, and Dardo Regules were also present, as were the former Uruguayan ambassador to the United States José Pedro Varela Acevedo; the director of the Linguistics Department at the Instituto de Estudios Superiores, Adolfo Berro García; the director of the Museum of Fine Arts, Carmelo Arzadun; and the Uruguayan consul at Iruñea-Pamplona, Gabriel Biurrun. Apart from the political representatives, the attendees included delegations from the two Basque Centers in Montevideo, Euskal Erria and Centro Euskaro, and representatives of the Catalan (Casal Català), Galician (Irmandade Galega and Casa de Galicia), Andalusian (Peña Andaluza), Asturian (Centro Asturiano), Spanish (Centro Republicano Español, Centro Democrático Español, Casa de España, and Asociación Española Luis Tuya), French (Comité de Liberación Francés), and Italian (Allianza Internacionale Giusepe Garibaldi and Asociación Italia Libera) associations in Montevideo. The delegate of the Basque government in exile in Uruguay Joseba Bingen Ametzaga delivered the keynote speech. On June 2, 1944, the board at the Euskal Erria Basque Center sent a letter of thanks to Mayor Fabini for the decision to erect a monument.[6] In a letter to President José Antonio Agirre, Bingen Ametzaga also reported that Juan José Amezaga, president of the Republic of Uruguay, who had initially accepted an invitation to the event, did not attend because of diplomatic pressure from the Spanish delegation in Uruguay, which naturally opposed the erection of a monument honoring the victims of the bombing. The official position of the Spanish government was still that Gernika was never bombed and that it had been reduced to ashes by the Basques themselves.[7]

Following the inauguration of the Plaza Gernika in Montevideo, the National Congress of Mayors of Uruguay decided in April 1945 to dedicate a third square in Colonia:

> The National Congress of Mayors held in Uruguay agreed that all cities in the Republic should bear the name of Guernica in some of their streets or squares to disseminate and thus preserve the memory of the martyred city. . . . Fulfilling the resolution a square with the name of Guernica was inaugu-

> rated in the city of Colonia. A seed of the historic oak was planted there; as a memento of the destruction of the Holy Town, a street with cypresses at both sides leads to the square. At the centre of the square stands the stem of the Tree of Guernica.[8]

Five months after the inauguration of the Plaza Guernica in Montevideo, a large delegation of Basques from Argentina arrived in Montevideo on September 10, 1944. Among them were Ramón M. Aldasoro and Joxe Mari Lasarte, members of the Basque government-in-exile delegation in Argentina; Joaquín Ganboa, president of the Laurak Bat Basque Center; Germán Ibieta, president of the Euzko Txokoa Basque Center; and a delegation from the Euzko Emakume Batza (Basque Nationalist Women's Union). Bingen Ametzaga attended on behalf of the Basque government delegation in Uruguay, and Ricardo Gisasola represented the Basque centers in Montevideo. The mayor of Colonia, Rostagnol Bein, as well as the elected representatives of the city and the police chief, Pedro Aranbillet, who was of Basque origin, were also present at the ceremony. Minister of Agriculture and Livestock Arturo González Bidart, also Basque, represented the Uruguayan government. The president of the Basque Center in Colonia, Alejandro Otaegi, and an exiled priest from the city of Carmelo, Tomás Yoldi, presided over the event.

After a banquet that included four hundred guests, the Plaza Gernika of Colonia was inaugurated.[9] In the course of the ceremony, Father Yoldi stated that "the bombs that sank and destroyed Gernika were equal to those robots that sow death on the outskirts of London" and concluded that "we long for freedom for all and democracy for all peoples."[10] As he had done with previous dedications, the Spanish diplomatic representative in Uruguay did not attend but sent a note protesting the event.[11] In spite of Spanish protests, a new Oak of Gernika was planted in the city of Piriápolis (Uruguay) in 1950.

Apart from the renaming of streets, squares, and public sites, the Day of the Bombardment was inaugurated on April 26, 1944, as an annual commemoration of the massacre all over the Americas. In 1947, during the celebration in Montevideo, Mayor Fabini approved, in agreement with the city's director of promenades and gardens, the erection of a stand of oak trees from Gernika along Prado Avenue. Seeds from offshoots in the gardens at the two Basque Centers in Montevideo, Euskal Erria and Centro Euskaro, were planted there.[12]

The Department of Basque Studies at the University of the Republic celebrated the Day of Gernika annually on April 26. In 1948 the department approved the planting of a seed from the Holy Oak in Montevideo's Plaza Gernika. The mayor of Montevideo and other city representatives attended the event. Arantzazu and Joseba Bingen Ametzaga planted the seed,[13] and the gathering was enlivened with Basque folk dances and music. Bingen Ametzaga delivered a speech, and Father Pedro Goikoetxea offered a mass in honor of the victims.[14]

There are public places named after Gernika in Uruguay, a town named Guernica outside Buenos Aires, and Plaza Guernica Squares in Santiago de Chile, Mexico City, Bogotá, and Rosario (Argentina). There is also a Calle Guernica in Mar del Plata (Argentina) and a Guernica Street in San Marcos (California). An offshoot of the Tree of Gernika stands in the Plaza San Martin of Mar del Plata (Argentina), and another one stands in the Plaza Moreno of La Plata (Argentina). In 1992 the City of Trees, Boise (Idaho), established a sister-city relationship with Gernika, the Town of the Tree, and a seed of the Oak of Gernika was planted in front of Boise's capitol building.

And the remembrance continues. To commemorate the seventieth anniversary of the massacre, the Basque government's minister of justice, Joseba Azkarraga, dedicated the Plaza Roble de Gernika in Sunchales, Argentina, on August 27, 2007; on October 11 Lehendakari Juan Jose Ibarretxe and Lucho Garzon, mayor of Bogotá, Colombia, dedicated a sculpture by Xabier Santxotena in that city's Plaza Guernica.[15] The original sculpture standing in Plaza Gernika was designed by Basque sculptor Jorge Oteiza in 1945, a year after the Plaza Gernika was inaugurated in Montevideo.

The tradition of naming public places after Gernika has not died in the Americas. In 2002 the city council of Mar del Plata in Argentina voted unanimously to give the name Euskal Herria (Basque Country) to the neighborhood surrounding the Calle Guernica.[16] On April 27, 2007, during the celebration of the Day of Gernika in Montevideo, Miguel Asqueta Sóñora, a representative of Basque origin in the House of Representatives, spoke for a half hour on Gernika as a universal symbol for peace.[17]

When the Spanish Republican government commissioned Pablo Picasso to produce a large canvas for the Paris Exposition Internationale des Arts et Techniques dans la Vie Moderne in 1937, he painted his 250-square-foot canvas as his comment on the bombing of an open city that was slowly and systematically pounded to rubble, intending it to shake the conscience of the democratic world.[18] It soon became a universal symbol of the suffering of innocent civilians at war. As Picasso himself stated in March 1945:

> What do you think an artist is? An imbecile who has only eyes, if he is a painter, or ears if he is a musician, or a lyre in every chamber of his heart if he is a poet, or even, if he is a boxer, just his muscles? Far from it: at the same time, he is also a political being, constantly aware of the heartbreaking, passionate, or delightful things that happen in the world, shaping himself completely in their image. How could it be possible to feel no interest in other people, and with a cool indifference to detach yourself from the very life which they bring to you so abundantly? No, painting is not done to decorate apartments. It is an instrument of war.[19]

Picasso's symbol continues to shake the world's conscience. A tapestry reproduction of Picasso's masterpiece donated by Nelson A. Rockefeller has hung over the entrance of the Security Council of the United Nations since 1985. The antiwar metaphor was considered by some too bitter, and in February 2003, when the council was discussing the invasion of Iraq, the tapestry—which formed a backdrop for television interviews—was conveniently covered by the blue flag of the UN. Six years later, in the aftermath of the war in Iraq and Afghanistan, the tapestry was moved to the Whitechapel Gallery in London "as a precautionary action" while the UN headquarters were undergoing renovations.[20]

Picasso's *Guernica* also shakes the Basque Country and today represents the fight of the people of Gernika to preserve their historical memory. The enduring demand that Picasso's *Guernica* be permanently displayed in an art museum in Gernika is a key point toward understanding how the Basque people in general and the people in Gernika in particular feel about the bombing of the town.

In May 1939 the masterpiece was brought to the United States and exhibited in the Valentine Gallery under the auspices of the American Artists Congress. At Picasso's request, the canvas was kept at the Museum of Modern Art (MOMA) in New York City. In accordance with the artist's will, the painting was to remain in New York until the Spanish Republic was restored. This never happened. When Franco died in 1975, public liberties in Spain were restored after thirty-nine years of dictatorship. However, the new government was not a republic but—according to Franco's will—a constitutional monarchy under King Juan Carlos I. Still, the directors of MOMA agreed that *republic* was a synonym for *democracy*, so after forty-four years in New York, following the instructions of the Spanish minister of culture, Iñigo Cavero, in October 1981 Picasso's masterpiece was secretly transported to Madrid instead of to Gernika, in order to "avoid political conflicts."

But political conflict was not avoided. The city council of Gernika has repeatedly requested that the painting be housed in Gernika. In this sense, the council of Gernika, acting unanimously at the meeting of January 26, 1995, required the Basque Parliament to initiate appropriate procedures for the transfer of the canvas from Madrid. Under the motto "*Guernica* Gernikara" (*Guernica* to Gernika), a popular platform composed of intellectuals, artists, and sportsmen has demanded from each of the Spanish ministers of culture[21] the transfer of Picasso's canvas to the people of Gernika, and a ceramic mural representing Picasso's *Guernica* was erected in 1997 on Allendesalazar Street in Gernika under the slogan "*Guernica* Gernikara." The debate continues. The Basques maintain that the painting belongs where the victims of the massacre lie. The Spanish government, however, sees the economic benefits of keeping the painting in Madrid, where it attracts tourists. Moreover, a transfer would imply that the current Spanish government is acknowledging the responsibility of the Francoist regime for the attack, an acknowledgment that the government is still not prepared to make.

The Spanish Ministry of Culture initially objected that Gernika did not have an adequate place to display Picasso's canvas. So the city council took over the Montefuerte Palace next to the Tree of Gernika to house the painting. Then the Ministry of Culture alleged that Gernika lacked the necessary security equipment and facilities to protect the painting. In response, the Basque government promised round-the-clock protection by the Basque autonomous police and other necessary security procedures. Finally, the ministry has argued that moving the canvas to Gernika could damage the painting, even though it had been previously moved from Paris to New York, from there to the Casón del Buen Retiro in Madrid, and subsequently from there to the Reina Sofía Museum, where it remains today.

All the mayors of Gernika have repeated the request that the painting be moved to the town it memorializes. As former mayor Eduardo Vallejo stated, "We are the moral owners of this canvas, and we will not give up." The current mayor of Gernika, Jose Mari Gorroño, told me that "while Picasso's *Guernica* is kept out of Gernika, the artist's indictment of the horrors of war and its symbolism remains confined." On July 1, 2007, the president of the Basque government, Juan Jose Ibarretxe, requested once again that the Spanish government transfer the *Guernica* from Madrid to the Basque Country. Moreover, in June 2009 the Board of Trustees of the Solomon R. Guggenheim Foundation included in the Guggenheim Museum Bilbao Strategic Plan 2009–12—approved by its Executive Committee and Board of Trustees in December 2008—the creation of the Guggenheim Urdaibai Museum in the Gernika area and approved the signing of a collaboration agreement with the Executive Council of Bizkaia to finance it.[22] It seems this would be an excellent place to display Picasso's canvas.

# Epilogue

## Gernika, World Capital for Peace

*Jose Mari Gorroño Etxebarrieta, Mayor of Gernika-Lumo*

On April 26, 1979, at the start of the long path toward democracy, the city council of Gernika decided unanimously to retire all honors that Fascist authorities in the city council had granted to Generalissimo Franco under his dictatorship. The council also voted to ask that the new Basque government make an official declaration stating that the destruction of Gernika was due to an aerial bombardment ordered by rebel troops under Franco's command and to require the Spanish, German, and Italian governments to acknowledge their moral and material responsibility for the bombing. The memory of people such as former mayor Jose Labauria, who had exposed the true nature of the bombing and thereby suffered exile, was to be honored. The Basque government was also asked to organize a Committee of Inquiry on the Bombing of Gernika with three main objectives: to encourage historical research to help clarify the details of the bombing, to create a peace museum in Gernika, and to obtain Picasso's *Guernica* and install it in the museum.

Four years later, on July 11, 1983, the city council also decided to restore the Basque spelling, "Gernika," for the town, which had been spelled "Guernica" in Spanish because of the dictatorship's prohibitions against writing in Basque or with Basque characters.[1]

The Basque Jesuit Jesús Arana embarked on the first attempt at reconciliation between Gernika and Germany in 1979, when he initiated the establishment of the Committee of Inquiry on the Bombing of Gernika. For many years, he asked in vain for a gesture of reconciliation from the German federal government. As Lothar Lahn, the German ambassador in Madrid, suggested on October 22, 1981, this was a difficult diplomatic issue since it could start a long list of demands over actions by the Condor Legion during the Spanish war.

However, Arana's effort was embraced by two Green Party members in the Bundestag, Petra Kelly and former general Gert Bastian. On the fiftieth anniversary of the bombing on April 26, 1987, Kelly placed a bouquet of flowers beneath the Tree of Gernika in memory of the victims of the massacre and described the town as a symbol of peace and democratic liberties. She also pushed for the creation of a Center for Peace and Reconciliation in Gernika as a gesture of goodwill from Germany. At the same time, the Basque Parliament unanimously approved the establishment of a Peace Research Center on April 10, 1987, to preserve the memory of the tragic historical event.[2]

As a result, Juan Gutiérrez, who had been engaged in the peace movement since 1968, was appointed in 1987 to design the Gernika Gogoratuz (Remembering Gernika) Peace Research Center.[3] The major objective of the museum was to contribute to a sustainable world peace and to promote its realization within the Basque Country. Kelly brought the idea to the Bundestag, though Heinrich Pohlmeier, a member of the German Christian Democratic Union, expressed unfounded concern that behind the gesture of reconciliation Basque politicians might be hiding the covert aims of the terrorist group Euskadi ta Askatasuna (ETA, Basque Country and Freedom).

Meanwhile, Gernika Gogoratuz helped the survivors of the Gernika bombing contact survivors of the bombings in Dresden and Hiroshima and victims of the political struggles in Colombia and Guatemala. In 1990–91, Juan Gutiérrez,[4] by then the director of the Peace Research Center, acted as the European coordinator of the International Week for Science and Peace, proclaimed in 1988 by the United Nations General Assembly, and in 1992–93 he served as world coordinator of the event. After initial difficulties, on April 29, 1989, a partnership between the cities of Gernika and Pforzheim, which was nearly destroyed by an air raid on February 23, 1945, was signed.[5] The protocol had an important symbolic value because many of the pilots of the Condor Legion were from that city. But on April 24, 1997, the German Bundestag again rejected an official declaration of German participation in the destruction of Gernika.

In 1997, on the sixtieth anniversary of the bombing, Gernika Gogoratuz collected and published the remembrances of four hundred survivors of the Gernika massacre and organized the first public meeting. The president of Germany, Roman Herzog,[6] sent a message to the survivors on April 27, 1997, acknowledging German responsibility for the bombing. The message was read in Gernika by Henning Wegener, German ambassador to Spain. Herzog, expressing regret and extending "a hand of friendship and reconciliation" on behalf of all German citizens, wrote: "I would like to place myself in the past and admit the culpable involvement of German fliers expressly. To you as survivors of the attack, as witnesses of the horror, I address a message for the memory, the sympathy, and the mourning. . . . To those who carry the wounds of the past still in themselves, I offer my hand with a request for reconciliation."[7] Migel A. Aranaz, the mayor of Gernika, said it was poignant to see the survivors embracing Wegener after he had read the declaration.

A year later, the lower house of the German parliament voted to erase the names of Condor Legion soldiers from German military sites and bases. After many years of debate, chancellor and historian Helmut Kohl approved a grant of three million deutsche marks for the construction of a museum in Gernika, which was disbursed between 1997 and 1999.

On April 7, 1998, the Gernikako Bake Museoa opened near the city hall in Gernika, the first peace museum in the Basque Country and in Spain.[8] The mission of the Gernikako Bake Museoa (Gernika Peace Museum Foundation) is "to preserve, display, publicize, conduct research, and educate visitors in the basic ideas of the culture of peace, and the past and present relation of this culture to the history of Gernika-Lumo, so that, together with other history and peace organizations, Gernika-Lumo, the province of Bizkaia, and the Basque Country be used as local, regional, national, and international references in the search for peace and culture."[9]

The seventieth anniversary of the massacre was commemorated in April 2007. "Gernika shall be the world capital for peace," proclaimed Migel A. Aranaz, the mayor of the city. Simultaneously, under the motto "Bakea Gogoratuz" (Remembering Peace), the Gernika Association and the Cervantes Institute of Berlin, with the support of the Basque Filmoteca, the Cinema Arsenal, and other Basque and German institutions, organized a series of activities to commemorate the bombing.

On April 26, 2007, the president of the Basque Country, Juan Jose Ibarretxe, read the "Gernika Declaration." The mayors of several cities that had suffered bombings during World War II, including Volgograd (formerly Stalingrad), Hamburg, Dresden, Pforzheim, Coventry, Auschwitz, Warsaw, and Hiroshima,[10] also participated in the event. Nobel Peace

Prize Laureate Alfredo Perez Esquivel and the winner of the Nobel Prize in Chemistry Mario Molina also took part in the ceremony. The ceremony was broadcast that day in Mexico City, Santiago, Buenos Aires, Rosario, La Plata, Bahía Blanca, Montevideo, Boise, New York, Sidney, and Madrid.

Mayor Aranaz spoke about the transfer of Picasso's *Guernica* to the place where it belongs and reiterated that the city would not accept sketches by Picasso, offered by the Spanish minister of culture in lieu of the actual painting. The Reina Sofía Museum in Madrid continues to reject requests that the painting be moved to Gernika. And unlike the German government, the various Spanish democratic governments since 1975 have never expressed regret or made any declaration about the responsibility of the Spanish army in the attack. Neither has the Italian government.

In Gernika war has taught us to promote peace and understanding. Forgiveness, dialogue, memory, respect of human rights, and the practice of democracy are the only ways to achieve human understanding. We, the people of Gernika, will work to make our city an international symbol for peace. This book is a detailed account of the massacre based primarily on archival documents and the written testimony of eyewitnesses. It is a tribute to the victims of the raid against Gernika and to all the cities bombed in the course of war. This is the only way we can give the victims back their right to be remembered and make a claim for compassion, reconciliation, and tolerance. In the words of Basque minister Telesforo Monzon, Gernika was our town, but after the massacre it became a universal symbol of freedom now inherited by humankind.

# Appendix 1

## The Number of Planes Involved in the Attack on Gernika

With respect to the German bombers involved in the attack on Gernika, twenty-six Junker Ju52s were stationed at the air base in Burgos, divided into three squadrons, led respectively by Lieutenant Colonel Karl von Knauer (who flew with Major Robert Fuchs), Colonel Hans Henning von Beust, and Captain von Krafft Ehrhart Dellmensingen. The three Ju52 squadrons attacked in numerical order, based on their official numbers. Colonel Beust said in 1955 that "they flew in four squads of attack of six aircraft each," making a total of twenty-four Junker Ju52s.[1] Apparently, this is a transcription error, because the original German version of this document mentions three groups of six units each, or a total of eighteen Junker Ju52s, and Maier also refers to eighteen bombers in his Spanish translation of the testimony.[2]

There are some German documents that provide information or figures but lack credibility. For example, the Scientific Section of the German Air War Weapon stated that the raid ordered over the bridge and road junction east of Gernika on April 26 was carried out by nine aircraft from 7,545 feet in a single pass over the town. The report states that only 9 551-pound bombs and 114 110-pound bombs were dropped (the report does not mention the incendiaries), or a total of 17,527 pounds of explosives.[3] The document states that Gernika's situation as an open city was respected by the German airmen, who did not drop bombs on the city center, and that the destruction was due to the incendiary action of the "Reds." The same Scientific Section had even denied in a previous report that Gernika had been bombed at all. The lack of credibility of these documents requires that we reject the data based on their propagandistic nature.

Karl von Knauer never mentioned how many Ju52s took part in the bombing, but he specified that the K/88 bomber unit bombed Gernika, as a group, and never mentioned that only some of the bomber planes participated in the attack.[4] Knauer said the two Heinkel He111s and Dornier Do17s of the VB/88 experimental squadron led by von Moreau did not fly that day, but Richthofen's testimony is conclusive on this point—he states that Moreau actually flew that day over Gernika.[5] Also, some of the eyewitnesses confirmed that they saw Heinkel He111s over Gernika.[6] From Knauer's testimony, we follow that the Junker Ju52s bombed Gernika in close formation, clustered in groups of three aircraft each, so it is logical to assume that the total number of Ju52 bombers was a multiple of three. Since General Pinna mentions in his report that there were twenty-three Junker Ju52s at the air base in Burgos, and Maier mentions twenty-six Junker Ju52s in Burgos after April 17, we conclude that between April 17 and 21, three Ju52s were sent to Burgos to participate in the attack. Like Knauer, Richthofen also mentions that he sent "the" K/88 bomber unit in Burgos to Gernika and never indicates that only some of the Ju52s took part in the attack. We do not have any information available showing that the K/88 bomber squads did not participate in the attack with all their units available, so there is no reason to suppose that the twenty-six Junker Ju52s in the K/88 unit were not sent to bomb the target. Moreover, we know that between April 17 and 25, at least two Heinkel He111 bombers and a Dornier Do17 were sent to Burgos from Seville, thereby increasing the number of bombers that would take part in the attack on Gernika. It would not make any sense to send extra bombers from Seville to Burgos to bomb Gernika and then leave at the air base some of the bombers that were already there.

Finally, Jesús Salas stated that, between March 31 and June 14, 1937, Richthofen sent between nineteen and twenty-one Junker Ju52s to bomb Basque positions at least thirteen times, and on eight occasions he sent twenty-one Ju52s (61.5 percent), on three occasions twenty Ju52s (23 percent), and twice nineteen Ju52s (15.3 percent).[7]

With the information that we have, and lacking the flight diaries of the K/88 bomber squads, I conclude that one Dornier Do17, two Heinkel He111s, and at least twenty-one (and a maximum of twenty-four) Junker Ju52s participated in the bombing of Gernika, grouped into three squads and distributed into seven waves of three aircraft each, flying in close formation. All this gives us a minimum number of twenty-four German bombers over

Gernika on April 26: twenty-one Junker Ju52s, two He111s, and one Dornier Do17.

With respect to the German pursuit planes, there were three J/88 squadrons at the airfield of Gasteiz: the first squad of twelve Heinkel He51s led by Harro Harder, the second squad of seven Messerschmitt Bf.109s led by Günther Lützow, and the third squad of twelve Heinkel He51s led by Douglas Pitcairn. We know the number of planes in Gasteiz from General Pinna's report of April 17, 1937, and the rest of the reports mentioned elsewhere in this book. These data match the eyewitnesses' reports that we have. According to information provided by George Steer in an article reprinted by the *New York Times* on May 22, Captain Walter Kinzle said that when he reached the airfield in Gasteiz on the last day of March, he was appointed leader of one of the Heinkel He51 squads composed of nine planes.[8] Hans Joachim Wandel, a Heinkel He51 pilot who participated in the bombing of Gernika, testified during his trial in Bilbao on May 25, 1937, that in Gasteiz, where he arrived on April 25, there were two Heinkel He51 fighter squads composed of twelve planes each.[9] Patrick Laureau states that "the ten planes available to the first squadron took part in the bombing of Gernika" and adds that the Condor Legion pilots were very reluctant to admit their participation in the bombing.[10] In fact, we know from the testimony of Beust, leader of the second squadron of Junker Ju52s, that they were given orders not to talk about the bombing and to deny the facts. The documentation indicates that on April 17, there were twenty-one Heinkel He51 fighters and seven Messerschmitt Bf.109s in Gasteiz, plus six Heinkel He51 fighters in Burgos. This means that between April 17 and 25, at least three Heinkel He51 fighters, one of them piloted by Wandel himself, were transported to Gasteiz to participate in the bombing of Gernika, making a total of twenty-four Heinkel He51 fighter planes in Gasteiz on April 26. Wandel testified that he flew alongside Kramay to Gernika, but Kramay is not on the list of pilots of the first squadron of Heinkel He51s led by Harder, so he might have been a member of the third squadron led by Douglas Pitcairn.[11] Richthofen himself wrote in his diary that he sent "the" J/88 fighter squads over Gernika to act "with strength and determination." He did not specify having sent only some planes and emphasized that he wanted to act with much power to achieve a complete and definitive success, which means that he probably sent most of the planes of the various squadrons in Gasteiz. Indeed, he decided to involve Italian fighters and bombers in the attack against Gernika, although he felt no respect whatsoever for the Italians, as he stated explicitly several times in his diary.[12] Why would Richthofen employ Italian fighters and leave his own units on the ground?

It is likely that the third Heinkel He51 squadron led by Pitcairn and stationed in Gasteiz also participated in the bombing of Gernika. This unit, composed on April 26 of twelve planes, according to Wandel's testimony, participated at noon on April 26 in the machine-gun attacks that took place in the area. Reporters Steer, Corman, and Monks were eyewitnesses and victims of these attacks.[13] Based on Monks's testimony, Salas said seven fighters were involved in these actions.[14]

With respect to the Heinkel He51 fighter squad stationed at the airfield in Burgos, if we conclude that they did not participate in the attack, it is extremely difficult to explain why Italian fighters from Gasteiz should escort the German Junker Ju52 bombers departing from Burgos, instead of the Heinkels, because this kind of action was precisely their mission. On the other hand, if we conclude that one of the two squadrons of Heinkel He51s in Gasteiz was not involved in the attack, it would also be difficult to explain why a Heinkel He51 fighter squad stationed in Burgos would take part in the bombing while the Heinkel He51 fighter squad remained motionless at the air base in Gasteiz, which is only fifteen to twenty minutes from Gernika, much closer than Burgos.

In sum, the documentation we have is very limited, and we can only conclude that the twelve Heinkel He51 fighter planes of the first J/88 squad available on April 26, 1937, did indeed participate in the attack. We can also be quite certain, based on the documentation of General Pinna, that the second J/88 squadron was composed of seven Messerschmitt Bf.109 pursuit planes and that, led by Günther Lützow, they participated in the attack on Gernika.[15] That makes a total minimum of nineteen German pursuit planes (twelve Heinkel He51s and seven Messerschmitt Bf.109s) and a maximum of thirty-seven (if we add the twelve Heinkel He51s led by Pitcairn stationed in Gasteiz and the six Heinkel He51s stationed in Burgos).

As regards the Italian bombers, three Savoia-Marchetti SM.79s took part in the bombing of Gernika—as recorded in the dispatch signed by Vincenzo Velardi on April 26, 1937. This document mentions that the SM.79 bombers flew for five hours and twenty minutes (total flight time for the three planes, or one hour and forty-five minutes per plane), enough to make two passes over the town.[16] The flight diary of Castellani, squad leader of the unit of three SM.79s that bombed Gernika that afternoon, mentions a shorter flight, of one and a half hours between 3:30 and 5:05 P.M., but the flight diary lacks credibility on many of its points—for example, when it states that they bombed from an altitude of 11,811 feet (3,600 meters), which has been denied by almost all the witnesses of the bombing and is completely absurd, since this height triples the normal bombing altitude taken at that time in the absence of air defenses.[17] Also, Richthofen declared that the planes bombed from an altitude of 800 meters (2,624 feet), and we know from the meteorological reports of April 26 that there were heavy clouds at an altitude of 900 meters. In any case, we may say that at least three Italian bombers took part in the bombing of Gernika.

We have much archival information on the participation of Italian fighters. The report of the Italian Foreign Ministry on the intervention of the Italian air force in the war, covering the actions of the Aviazione Legionaria from the beginning of the war until May 16, 1937, states that three Italians bombers acted on Gernika but that the participation of the Italian Fiat CR.32 fighters happened to be very active (*attivissima*) while escorting German bombers and making flights along the front line in the area of Durango.[18]

In fact, the activity of the Italian fighters was very intense. The bulletin of the Aviazione Legionaria mentions the participation of fifty-seven Fiat CR.32 fighters on the Basque and Aragonese fronts (Bilbao and Zaragoza) that day, with a total of eighty-two hours of flight performing escort and cruising duties, but the document does not specify how many of these fighters acted on each of the two fronts and what specific tasks each of them performed.[19]

The document included in the Attivitá Giornalera dell'Aviazione Legionaria del Continente report records the activity of five Fiat CR.32 fighters stationed in Gasteiz with a total of seven hours and fifty-five minutes of flight on the Basque front, making "a cruise flight along the front line." In addition, the document records the activity of two groups of five Fiat CR.32 fighters stationed in Gasteiz, escorting the German Junker Ju52 bombers for nine hours and forty-five minutes (which is more time than required to fly to and from their airfields). That document also records the flight of a solitary Fiat CR.32 fighter that flew from Gasteiz to Logroño and back, for a period of fifty minutes.[20]

From the flight diary of the Fiat CR.32 fighter squad No. 26 of Gasteiz, we know that the return flight between Logroño and Gasteiz was made by Lieutenant Rocca (pseudonym of Corrado Ricci). The squadron of five fighters that escorted the German Junker Ju52 squad from Burgos was led by Lieutenant Maggi (pseudonym of Vincenzo Vanni), and the group of five Fiat CR.32 fighters that made a cruise "along the front of Durango" was led by Captain Violti. When he returned from his flight to Logroño, Lieutenant Corrado Ricci led the group of five Fiat CR.32 fighters that made the second cruise flight "along the front of Durango."[21] All these data are corroborated by the report signed by Lieutenant Colonel Pilota, commander of the air base, signed on April 26 at Salamanca.[22]

In short, the documents show that ten CR.32 fighters escorted the German Ju52 bombers and that another five Fiat CR.32 fighters participated in the bombing by machine-gunning the front in the Durango area (about a one-minute flight from Gernika) for seven hours and fifty-five minutes. To these, we have to add Lieutenant Ricci's return flight of fifty minutes in his Fiat CR.32 from Gasteiz to Logroño. Without more data, it seems that sixteen Italian Fiat CR.32 fighters from the air base in Gasteiz were involved in the attack (but we have to take into account that Ricci, Constantini, and Pongiluppi flew twice that day). This information matches the information of General Pinna, who reported that there were ten CR.32 fighters in Gasteiz and twenty-five in Logroño, or a total of thirty-five Fiat CR.32 fighters in the area.[23] From this information, we can deduce that a total of forty-one Fiat CR.32 fighters acted that day over Zaragoza (sixteen fighters over the Basque Country and forty-one in Aragon, making a total of fifty-seven Fiat CR.32s totaling eighty-two hours, which represents an average flight of more than one and a half hours). This represents sixteen flight operations conducted by thirteen pilots. In other words, thirteen Fiat CR.32 fighters participated in the bombing of Gernika performing various tasks. That is, there was a total of about fifty-nine aircraft involved in the attack on Gernika, about twenty-seven bombers and at least thirty-two fighters, some of which made more than one flight that day over Gernika.

# Appendix 2

## The Quantity and Type of Bombs Dropped on Gernika

We do not have the records of the bombs used that day on Gernika, so it is difficult to calculate the exact number that were dropped, but we do know how many bombers took part in the bombing, and we have some documents that help us calculate the number of tons dropped.

Lieutenant Colonel Karl von Knauer wrote an interesting report on the type and quality of the bombs used by the Condor Legion.[1] The legion's planes were equipped with ESAC-250 cartridges that held the bombs vertically instead of horizontally. Junker Ju52 bombers could carry six 551-pound bombs (totaling 3,306 pounds) in the ESAC-250 cartridges, or alternatively twenty-four 110-pound bombs (totaling 2,640 pounds) or ninety-six 22-pound bombs (totaling 2,112 pounds). Also, Richthofen, Beust, and Steer mentioned a cargo load of 3,300 pounds of bombs per Junker Ju52 and stated that most of the high explosives used were 551-pound and 110-pound shells. However, these statements do not exclude the use of other type of bombs.

The Heinkel He111 was able to carry about 3,306 pounds of bombs in the ESAC-250 cartridge, although von Krafft Ehrhart Dellmensingen remembered loading thirty-two 110-pound bombs—that is, a total of 3,520 pounds (1,600 kilos). And it is important to emphasize that all the bombers for which we know the bomb capacities flew with their maximum loads.

The Dornier Do17 1937 had a smaller bomb-load capacity of about 2,204 pounds.

The Junker Ju52s and the Heinkel He111s could carry more than 3,300 pounds. Therefore, apart from the bombs held in the ESAC-250, the German bombers also carried bomb shells in boxes (and occasionally barrels of gasoline) in the interior of the planes and dropped them out the doors of the planes while other shells were being dropped from the ESAC-250s.

As for the Italian bombers, Italian Air Command dispatches mention the participation of three Savoia-Marchetti SM.79 bombers, which dropped thirty-six 110-pound bombs, or a total of 3,960 pounds of explosives.[2] However, this does not seem credible, since in 1935 the Savoia-Marchetti SM.79 could carry a total bomb load of nearly 4,409 pounds. It is questionable that the Italian command would have decided to send three bombers with a total bomb load that a single plane could have carried, especially if we consider that there were no enemy planes in the air to interfere with their flight. The dispatch does not specify whether this was the total cargo or the cargo of each of the three planes. Moreover, Richthofen referred in a report written on May 28, 1937, titled *Effect of the Bombing of Spanish Cities*, that the Italians used 226.46-pound (100-kilogram) bombs that "completely destroyed four-story buildings."[3] These bombs are not mentioned in the Italian report.

We know, then, that the two Heinkel He111s dropped a total of 6,612 pounds of bombs and that the Dornier Do17 dropped an approximate total of 2,204 pounds of explosives. Twenty-one Junker Ju52s and three Savoia-Marchetti SM.79s also took part in the attack, so therefore we have a total of approximately 68,343 pounds of bombs (31 tons), if we consider an average load of 2,645.5 pounds for each of the twenty-one Junker Ju52s and a total of 1,322.7 pounds for each of the three SM.79s (or one-third of their load capacity). If we consider a cargo average of 3,306 pounds for each of the twenty-one Ju52s and 4,409 pounds for each of the three SM.79s, we have a total amount of 90,389.5 pounds of bombs, or 41 tons.

In Richthofen's report *Effect of the Bombing of Spanish Cities*, he stated that the Condor Legion dropped 31 tons of bombs on Gernika, which I previously estimated was the minimum amount of bombs released over Gernika.[4] However, Richthofen lies in his report and tries to reduce the deadly effect of the raids. For instance, he says in the report that the number of people killed by the bombing of Durango was no more than 50, but we know today that the death toll was closer to 360 (it was public notice in May 1937 that the bombings of Durango had caused more than 190 deaths). Also, Richthofen fails to make any reference to the dropping of 55.1-pound (25-kilogram) boxes of incendiary bombs from the doors of the Junker Ju52s (in addition to the bombs dropped from the ESAC-250 cartridges). As a consequence, I think that the true amount of bombs dropped on Gernika was closer to 41 tons.

Maier also estimated that the maximum load of the Junker Ju52s (six 551-pound bombs) and the Heinkel He111s (eight 551-pound bombs) in late April 1937 was about 4.5 tons or 162 551-pound bombs (in kilograms: twenty-three Junkers × 1,500 = 34,500 plus three He111s × 2,000 = 6,000; total = 40,500 kilos). Indeed, the official table of performance indicated that the Junker Ju52s could transport between 1,000 and 1,200 kilos (and up to 1,500 kilos in optimal conditions by reducing the flight range) and that the Heinkel He111s could carry up to 1,500 kilos, although depending on the disposition of the bombs they could carry up to 2,000 kilos.[5]

The larger the proportion of incendiary bombs, the lower the weight of the total cargo of bombs since the incendiary shells were very light (2.2 pounds each). Although Richthofen mentions in his war diary that only a third of the bombs dropped were incendiaries, this is hard to believe in light of the data available on the number and nature of the bombs dropped during the month of April in the Basque Country and from reports of the intensity of the fires resulting from the bombing of Gernika.

According to the data given in *Gernika bonbardaketa/El bombardeo*, only 19.38 percent of the bomb loads consisted of incendiary shells (5.47 tons of incendiary bombs in a total of 28.22 tons of bombs: 39 shells of 250 kilograms, 260 shells of 50 kilograms, and 5,472 1-kilogram incendiary bombs).[6] The archival data I have points out that incendiary shells constituted more than 75 percent of the bombs dropped on Gernika on April 26, 1937. Moreover, as mentioned above, since German bombers equipped with ESAC-250 cartridges had a limited capacity, boxes of incendiary bombs were dropped from the door of the planes over Gernika.

# Notes

## Preface

1. Claude G. Bowers, *My Mission to Spain: Watching the Rehearsal for World War II* (New York: Simon and Schuster, 1954), 353–54.

## Introduction

1. Ancient Law of Bizkaia of 1452. Gregorio Monreal Zia, *The Old Law of Bizkaia (1452)* (Reno: Center for Basque Studies, University of Nevada, Reno, 2005), 166.

2. The states of Araba, Bizkaia, Gipuzkoa, Lapurdi, and Zuberoa were republics, and the two Navarrese states were kingdoms.

## 1 ■ The Coup d'État of July 18, 1936

1. Most historians use the term *Spanish Civil War* to describe the conflict. However, Narcissus Bassols and Isidro Fabela, representatives of the Mexican government at the League of Nations, criticized the categorization of the war as a "civil" conflict. US ambassador Claude G. Bowers stated that the war was neither Spanish nor civil but a prologue to World War II, and Congressman Jerry J. O'Connell offered a similar critique by saying that the bombing of Gernika was the work of German planes, German bombs, and German pilots. O'Connell asked Secretary of State Cordell Hull "to take official notice of what is common knowledge, namely, that Germany and Italy are in fact belligerents in the war of invasion now going on in Spain." *Congressional Record: Appendix of the First Session of the 75th Congress of the U.S.A.*, vol. 81, pt. 9, January 5–May 19, 1937 (Washington, DC: US Government Printing Office, 1937), 1131.

2. *Decreto número 138, nombrando Jefe del Gobierno del Estado Español al Excelentísimo Sr. General de División Don Francisco Franco Bahamonde, quien asumirá todos los Poderes del nuevo Estado*, Boletín Oficial de la Junta de Defensa Nacional de España no. 32, Burgos, September 30, 1936.

3. Carlism was a Catholic, traditionalist, and legitimist political movement seeking the restitution or devolution of the ancient laws in the Basque states. In the Basque Country, the Carlist Party was especially strong in the South—that is, in the territories of Araba and Navarre.

4. Isidro Gomá, *El caso de España: Instrucción a sus diocesanos y respuesta a unas consultas sobre la guerra actual* (Iruñea-Pamplona: Bescansa, 1936).

5. Ibid.

6. Julián Cassanova, *La Iglesia de Franco* (Madrid: Temas de Hoy, 2001), 41.

7. Antonio Montero, *Historia de la persecución religiosa en España* (Madrid: Biblioteca de Autores Cristianos, 1961), 704.

8. Ibid., 62, 96, 110–11, 207.

9. *Carta colectiva de los obispos españoles a los obispos de todo el mundo con motivo de la guerra en España* (Iruñea-Pamplona: Gráficas Descansa, 1937).

10. Mateo Múgica, *Imperativos de mi conciencia: Carta abierta al Presbítero D. José Miguel de Barandiaran* (Cambo: n.p., 1945).

11. Sermon of Advent, February 14, 1937, in Gunther Levy, *Die katholische Kirche und das Dritte Reich* (Munich: n.p., 1965), 108.

12. Montero, *Historia de la persecución religiosa en España*, 741.

13. William F. Montavon, *Insurrection in Spain* (Washington, DC: National Catholic Welfare Conference, 1937).

14. Ricardo de la Cierva, *La historia se confiesa: España, 1930–1976* (Barcelona: Planeta, 1976), 243.

15. Paul Preston, *The Spanish Civil War: Reaction, Revolution, and Revenge* (London: Harper Perennial, 2006), 120–21.

16. *News Chronicle* (London), July 29, 1936. See also Andrés Rueda, *Franco, el ascenso al poder de un dictador* (Madrid: Nowtilus, 2013), 186.

17. Juan Iturralde (pseudonym of Juan Jose Usabiaga Irazustabarrena), *El catolicismo y la cruzada de Franco* (Vienna: EGI Indarra, 1960), 2:88. See also José María Maldonado, *El frente de Aragón: La Guerra Civil en Aragón (1936–1938)* (Zaragoza: Mira Editores, 2007), 28.

18. Alberto Reig Tapia, *Ideología e historia: Sobre la represión franquista y la guerra civil* (Madrid: Akal, 1986), 146.

19. Jesús Salas Larrazabal, *Air War over Spain* (London: Allan, 1974).

20. An exhaustive list of the fifty-seven people killed that day was completed by Jon Irazabal. Jon Irazabal, *Otxandio en la Guerra Civil: Otxandio Gerra Zibilean (1936/37)* (Durango: Gerediaga Elkartea, 2003), 32–38. Further investigations have raised the death toll to sixty-one. See "Otxandio: El primer Gernika," *Deia*, April 22, 2013.

21. Gabriel M. Otalora, "30 de julio de 1936," *Gara*, August 8, 2004.

22. Irazabal, *Otxandio en la Guerra Civil*, 27.

23. Ibid.

24. *La Gaceta del Norte* (Bilbao), August 16, 1936.

25. *La Lucha de Clases* 52, no. 1965 (1937).

26. Florentino Bastarretxea was one of the people mobilized to bring logs that could be used to cover the shelters. "Más relatos impresionantes sobre la saña y la crueldad con que procedieron los rebeldes españoles en Guernica," *El Sol*, May 27, 1937, 2.

27. Castor Uriarte, *Bombas y mentiras sobre Guernica: Acusa su arquitecto municipal cuando la guerra* (Bilbao: Gráficas Ellacuria, 1976), 163–64.

28. Testimony of Castor Uriarte, in William Smallwood, "The Day Gernika Was Bombed" (manuscript in author's possession, 1972), 6.

29. Testimony by Jose Labauria in La Roseraie, April 2, 1938, in *La guerra civil en Euzkadi: 136 testimonios inéditos recogidos por Jose Miguel de Barandiaran*, edited by José María Gamboa and Jean-Claude Larronde (Milafranga: Bidasoa, 2005), 604. Joxe Iturria, a twenty-two-year-old man in 1937 who was in Gernika during the bombing, told me that in the Andra Mari refuge, 450 to 500 people lost their lives. Interview with Joxe Iturria, Lesaka, Navarre, May 17 and May 21, 2013.

30. Gamboa and Larronde, *La guerra civil en Euzkadi*, 604. Today, one of these refuges is used as a public urinal.

31. Ibid.

32. Ibid., 603.

33. William Smallwood interview with Irautza Asla (pseudonym), 1972, WSA, File Gernika, E. Irautza Asla, 1972.

34. Paul Preston and Ann L. Mackenzie, *The Republic Besieged: Civil War in Spain, 1936–1939* (Edinburgh: Edinburgh University Press, 1996), 21–52.

35. Professor Ángel Viñas has kindly sent to me two chapters of a manuscript entitled "Las armas y el oro," which is to be published by Pasado & Presente. This book covers in depth the nature and scope of Italo-German military and financial aid to the coup. Detailed information on the four contracts mentioned here is found in his contribution to *Tras los mitos del 18 de julio*, a work edited by Francisco Sánchez Pérez, to be published by Crítica. On this topic, see also Morten Heiberg, *Emperadores del Mediterráneo: Franco, Mussolini y la Guerra Civil española* (Barcelona: Crítica, 2003).

36. Preston and Mackenzie, *Republic Besieged*, 21–52.

37. In 1937 US$1.00 was about 19.01 lire. See William D. Grampp, "The Italian Lira, 1938–45," *Journal of Political Economy* 54, no. 4 (1946): 316–18. Also in 1937 US$1.00 was approximately 2.487 Reichmarks, 24.716 French francs, and 0.2023 British pounds.

38. Sánchez Pérez, *Tras los mitos del 18 de julio.*

39. Stanley G. Payne, "Fascist Italy Against Republican Spain," in *Spain and the Mediterranean Since 1898*, edited by Raanan Rein (London: Routledge, 1999), 99–127.

40. Bolín and Luca de Tena carried a letter of introduction from Alfonso XIII de Borbón, former king of Spain deposed by the Republic in 1931. Richard J. B. Bosworth, *Mussolini* (New York: Oxford University Press, 2002), 326.

41. Ibid., 326.

42. Preston and Mackenzie, *Republic Besieged*, 21–52.

43. Roberto Cantalupo, *Embajada en España* (Barcelona: Luis de Caralt, 1951), 37.

44. Report of a conversation between Il Duce and Minister Frank (Resoconto del Colloquio tra il Duce e il Ministro Frank), Palazzo Venezia, Rome, September 23, 1936, RG 242, Foreign Records Seized Collection, Papers of Count Ciano (Lisbon Papers), Received from the Department of State, Microfilm Publication T816, R. 1, 115-114.

45. Paul Preston, *La República asediada: Hostilidad internacional y conflictos internos durante la Guerra Civil* (Barcelona: Península, 1999), 60.

46. Preston and Mackenzie, *Republic Besieged*, 41–42.

47. Preston, *Spanish Civil War*, 102–18.

48. Interview of Count Ciano with the führer, Berchtesgaden, October 24, 1936, RG 242, Foreign Records Seized Collection, Papers of Count Ciano (Lisbon Papers), Received from the Department of State, Microfilm Publication T816, R. 1, 132–42.

49. Hispanicus, *Foreign Intervention in Spain: Documents Collected and Edited by "Hispanicus"* (New York: United Editorial, [1937]), 296, in the National Archives in Kew, England, Boxes 15–23.

50. Interview with German ambassador Ulrich von Hassell, Rome, October 3, 1936, RG 242, Foreign Records Seized Collection, Papers of Count Ciano (Lisbon Papers), Received from the Department of State, Microfilm Publication T816, R. 1, 117–20.

51. Hispanicus, *Foreign Intervention in Spain*, 296.

52. Interview with German foreign minister Konstantin von Neurath (Colloquio con il Ministro Neurath), Berlin, October 21, 1936, RG 242, Foreign Records Seized Collection, Papers of Count Ciano (Lisbon Papers), Received from the Department of State, Microfilm Publication T816, R. 1, 124–31.

53. Major C. S. Napier, War Office, to Mr. Roberts, War Office, January 11, 1937, in *Documents on British Foreign Policy (1919–1939)*, 2nd ser., vol. 18, *European Affairs* (January 2–June 30, 1937), edited by W. N. Medlicott and Dakin Douglas (London: Her Majesty's Stationery Office, 1980), 70.

54. Memorandum by G. A. Fisher on the departure of Italian volunteers, in ibid., 70.

55. Dispatch by William C. Bullitt, Ambassador to the French Republic, to Secretary of State Hull, Paris, February 22, 1937, in *Foreign Relations of the United States: Diplomatic Papers, 1937*, Vol. 1, *General* (Washington, DC: US Government Printing Office, 1954), 46.

56. Report by Horace H. Fuller to Cordell Hull, Paris, February 23, 1937, in ibid., 247. It is clear that he was exaggerating the number of German troops.

57. See Bowers, *My Mission to Spain* (see preface, n. 1).

58. "Italian Troops and Supplies in Spain," memorandum by the Office of Arms and Munitions Control of the US State Department, March 20, 1937, NARA, US Ambassador Claude G. Bowers Files (Files 852.222/ . . .), Document 852.222/375.

59. Bowers, *My Mission to Spain*, 325. Bowers makes reference only to the British case.

60. Since the Italian government had accepted in theory the Non-Intervention Agreement, members of the Italian military could not officially participate in the Spanish war. For this reason, many of these individuals adopted pseudonyms while serving in Spain.

61. Olao Conforti, *Guadalajara: La primera derrota del fascism* (Barcelona: Oikos-Tau, 1977).

62. According to the report by General Pietro Pinna of January 14, 1937, there were 204 pilots and 319 technicians. Pietro Pinna, *Dati concernenti il persone della*

*Regia Aeronautica inviato in Spagna: Situazione al giorno 14 Gennaio 1937*, Ministero dell'Aeronautica, Gabineto del Ministro, Busta 80, 12 Sepr., ADCGPM.

63. Vittorio Velani was Vincenzo Velardi's *nome di battaglia*, or pseudonym. Both Klaus Maier and Gordon Thomas quoted "Velani" and José Estornés Lasa "Vellani." Coverdale calls him "Velardi."

64. "Italian Troops and Supplies in Spain."

65. Four of them were being assembled on April 10. Designed by Antonio Parano and Giuseppe Panzeri, the Breda Ba.65 dive-bomber was conceived as a fighter, but it was afterward used also as a ground-attack and reconnaissance aircraft.

66. Twenty of them were being assembled. Each Fiat CR.32 cost approximately 664,000 lire.

67. Industrie Meccaniche e Aeronautiche Meridionali (Southern Mechanic and Aeronautic Industry) was a satellite company of Breda (Breda Meccanica Bresciana), a light-armament industry founded in 1925.

68. There was a Savoia-Marchetti S.55 flying boat in Spain in January 1937, and there is evidence of later shipments of Fiat BR.20 *Cicogna* (stork) bombers, Breda Caproni AP.1 fighters, Breda Ba.64 fighters, Breda Ba.88 ground-attack and long-range reconnaissance aircraft, Caproni-Bergamaschi Ca.310 Libeccio strategic reconnaissance aircraft, CANT Z.506 Airone strategic reconnaissance seaplanes, and Breda Ba.28 trainer biplanes.

69. Pietro Pinna, *Relazioni del General Pinna*, Salamanca, April 17, 1937, 9, Archivio Ufficio Storico, Aeronautica Militare, Busta 104, Fascicolo 8, ADCGPM. In virtue of the report by General Pinna mentioned earlier, *Dati concernenti il persone della Regia Aeronautica*, there were 158 Italian planes in the Iberian Peninsula in January 1937, among them 30 bombers and 92 fighters. According to the data provided by the different embassies, about 418 aircraft were sent to the war through September 1937, 376 under direct Italian command within the Aviazione Legionaria and 42 under Spanish air force command.

70. Telegram from Ulrich von Hassell to the Foreign Ministry of the Reich, Rome, March 25, 1937, in *Documents on German Foreign Policy (1918–1945)*, Ser. D (1937–45), vol. 3, *Germany and the Spanish Civil War (1936–1939)* (Washington, DC: Department of State, US Government Printing Office, 1950), 259.

71. However, General Ettore Bastico would be replaced by Lieutenant General Berti in October 1937, due to the fact that Franco, ignoring Batisco's promise of safe transit abroad to the Basque troops who had surrendered to the Italians, ordered their detention in Laredo and the execution of several of them. Franco's actions troubled both generals, resulting in Bastico's being relieved of his post.

72. Pinna, *Dati concernenti il persone della Regia Aeronautica*. According to the data provided by Coverdale, in total there were 13 Italian generals and 2,536 officers at war. John F. Coverdale, *Italian Intervention in the Spanish Civil War* (Princeton, NJ: Princeton University Press, 1975), 276.

73. Pinna, *Relazioni del General Pinna*, Salamanca, April 17, 1937, 9.

74. Pinna, *Dati concernenti il persone della Regia Aeronautica*.

75. According to General Pinna, Mussolini had accepted the shipment of forty

new Fiat CR.32 fighters and eight Breda 65s. Pietro Pinna, *Promemoria per S. E. General Bastico*, Salamanca, April 15, 1937, 1.

76. Admiral Canaris later became war minister of the Third Reich, and in 1935 he was named head of the Abwehr, the German military intelligence service.

77. George L. Steer, *The Tree of Gernika: A Field Study of Modern War* (London: Hodder and Stoughton, 1938), chap. 8.

78. Robert H. Whealey, *Hitler and Spain: The Nazi Role in the Spanish Civil War, 1936–1939* (Lexington: University Press of Kentucky, 2005), 7–8. See also Preston, *Spanish Civil War*, 118; and Michael Klepsch, *Picasso und der Nationalsozialismus* (Düsseldorf: Patmos, 2007), 84.

79. Wesley F. Craven and James L. Cate, eds., *Army Air Forces in World War II* (Washington, DC: Office of Air Force History, 1948), 75.

80. Treaty of Peace Between the Allied and Associated Powers and Germany, the Protocol Annexed thereto, the Agreement Respecting the Military Occupation of the Territories of the Rhine, and the Treaty Between France and Great Britain Respecting Assistance to France in the Event of Unprovoked Aggression by Germany, Signed in Versailles, June 28th, 1919, in *The Treaties of Peace, 1919–1923*, vol. 1, *Containing the Treaty of Versailles, the Treaty of St. German-en-Laye and the Treaty of Trianon* (Clark, NJ: Lawbook Exchange, 2007), 111–12.

81. Ian Kershaw, *Hitler, 1936–1945: Nemesis* (London: W. W. Norton, 2001), 13–16.

82. "Babies, Bombs & Battleships," *Time*, May 10, 1937.

83. On the geopolitical and economic reasoning, see Resoconto del Colloquio tra il Duce e il Ministro Frank, Palazzo Venezia, Roma, September 23, 1936, NARA, RG 242, Foreign Records Seized Collection, Papers of Count Ciano (Lisbon Papers), Received from the Department of State, Microfilm Publication T816, R. 1, 115-114.

84. Günter Schmitt, *Hugo Junkers and His Aircraft* (Berlin: Transpress VEB Verlag für Verkehrswesen, 1988).

85. *The Trial of German Major War Criminals: Proceedings of the International Military Tribunal Sitting at Nuremberg, Germany, Published Under the Authority of H. M. Attorney-General* (London: H. M. Stationery Office, 1948), pt. 18, July 2–15, 1946, 344–49.

86. Hispanicus, *Foreign Intervention in Spain*, 43.

87. Richard J. Overy, *Göring: The "Iron Man"* (London and Boston: Routledge & Kegan Paul, 1984), 44–46.

88. Amos E. Simpson, "The Struggle for Control of the German Economy, 1936–37," *Journal of Modern History* 31, no. 1 (1959): 37–45.

89. For further information on ROWAK, see Ángel Viñas et al., *Política comercial exterior en España, 1931–1975* (Madrid: Banco Exterior de España, Servicio de Estudios Económicos, 1979), 147–49, 166–70.

90. Hermann Wilhelm Goering, *Proceedings at the Nuremberg Trials*, Dr. Stahmer, March 14, 1946.

91. Hispanicus, *Foreign Intervention in Spain*, 15.

92. Overy, *Göring: The "Iron Man,"* 37–38.

93. Permanenza en Italia di S. E. Göring, Roma, January 30, 1937, NARA, RG 242, Foreign Records Seized Collection, Collection of Italian Military Records, 1935–1943, Microfilm Publication T821, R. 214, 4.

94. Promemoria per S. E. Il Capo di Stato Maiore Generale, Roma, February 1, 1937, NARA, RG 242, Foreign Records Seized Collection, Collection of Italian Military Records, 1935–1943, Microfilm Publication T821, R. 214, 3–5.

95. Ibid.

96. Ibid. In 1937 US$1.00 was 2.487 Reichsmark, in 1938 2.49 Reichsmark, in 1939 2.496 Reichsmark, and in 1940 2.499 Reichsmark.

97. On August 13, pilots Alfred Henke, Graf Hoyos, and Rudolf Moreau hit the Republican ship *Jaime I* with two 250-kg bombs dropped from five hundred meters. A report by Major Norman E. Fiske, military attaché at the US Embassy, indicated that the battleship had been seriously damaged, especially the "strike equipment." The *Jaime I* was taken to Cartagena on May 27 to be repaired, but on June 17 the ship sank after an explosion that killed many sailors. Memorandum by Major Norman E. Fiske to the Chief of Staff, December 9, 1936, NARA, RG 165, Records of the Military Intelligence Division Relating to Conditions in Spain (1918–1941), Microfilm Publication MI.1445, R. 7. Later, the sinking of the battleship *España* on April 30, when it was four miles off the coast of Santander by the action of two Bréguet 19s that got four direct hits with 70- to 100-kg bombs, demonstrated the vulnerability of ships during an aerial attack. In Report 6546 of Captain Townsend Griffiss and Colonel Stephen O. Fuqua, NARA, RG 242, Foreign Records Seized Collection, Papers of Count Ciano (Lisbon Papers), Received from the Department of State, Microfilm Publication T816, R. 1, 173–97.

98. James S. Corum, *Wolfram von Richthofen: Master of the German Air War* (Lawrence: University Press of Kansas, 2008), 140. See also Karl Drum, "Die deutsche Luftwaffe im spanischen Bürgerkrieg," Freiburg MFA/LW I, 221–26.

99. Notizie di carattere militare, February 1, 1937, NARA, Foreign Records Seized Collection, Collection of Italian Military Records, 1935–1943, Microfilm Publication T821, R. 214, 7.

100. Promemoria per S. E. Il Capo di Stato Maiore Generale, Roma, February 1, 1937, NARA, RG 242, Foreign Records Seized Collection, Collection of Italian Military Records, 1935–1943, Microfilm Publication T821, R. 214, 3–5.

101. Neurath, Blomberg, commander of the ground troops Werner von Fritsch, and chief of staff Ludwig Beck showed no enthusiasm for Hitler's war plans. In fact, Beck later became involved in a plot to assassinate Hitler, and, after failing, he committed suicide in 1944.

102. Erna Gruhn's mother had owned a brothel in Berlin and introduced her daughter to prostitution. Gruhn had also posed in pornographic photographs, several of which were acquired from police records by Reinhard Heydrich and reached Hitler's hands through the Gestapo. See Kirstin A. Schäfer, *Werner von Blomberg, Hitlers erster Feldmarschall: Eine Biographie* (Paderborn: Schöningh, 2006).

103. Blomberg had regulated certain aspects of German soldiers' marriages. By a decree of April 1, 1936, Blomberg had stipulated that the girlfriend of a German soldier had to be of Aryan blood. This was confirmed by Hitler's decree dated May 13, 1936, which expressly prohibited the union of any German soldier with people who were not of Aryan origin.

104. Overy, *Göring: The "Iron Man,"* 69.

105. "Babies, Bombs & Battleships." See also "Air Attack on Guernica Attributed to Göring," *New York Times*, April 30, 1937, 1.

106. Overy, *Göring: The "Iron Man,"* 71.

107. Proposals and requests brought by Admiral Canaris on August 28 in the name of the German government. Coverdale, *Italian Intervention in the Spanish Civil War*, 103.

108. Paul Preston, *Franco: A Biography* (New York: Basic Books / HarperCollins, 1994), 161.

109. Enclosure to the dispatch from German Foreign Minister Konstantin von Neurath to Ulrich von Hassell, German Ambassador in Italy, Berlin, October 30, 1936, in *Documents on German Foreign Policy*, 123–25.

110. "88" meant "HH," or "Heil Hitler," since *H* is the eighth letter of the alphabet.

111. Pinna, *Relazioni del General Pinna*, Salamanca, April 17, 1937, 30.

112. Ibid., 9.

113. Import of Aeronautical Products, Report 6495 by Captain Townsend Griffiss and Colonel Stephen O. Fuqua, Military Attaché to the US State Department, March 16, 1937, NARA, Bowers Files (Files 852.24/ . . .), Document 852.24/384, 2.

114. Pinna, *Relazioni del General Pinna*, Salamanca, April 17, 1937, 9.

115. "Italian Troops and Supplies in Spain."

116. Report by Alexander Kirk, Attaché of the US Embassy in Rome, to the Secretary of State, Rome, May 14, 1937, NARA, US Department of State Files, 1930–1939 (Files 852.00/ . . . , Box 6400), Document 852.00/5518.

117. *Euzko Deya* (Paris) 1, no. 4 (1936).

118. Hispanicus, *Foreign Intervention in Spain*, 143.

119. Report by Ambassador Bowers to the Secretary of State, Donibane Lohitzune, October 17, 1937, in *Foreign Relations of the United States: Diplomatic Papers, 1937*, 424.

120. "Possible Effect on England of the Application of Neutrality Laws to Germany and Italy," memorandum of the Division of European Affairs of the US State Department, Washington, DC, July 7, 1937, NARA, US Department of State Files, 1930–1939 (Files 852.00/ . . . , Box 6401), Document 852.00/5967.

121. *Les temps* (Paris), July 25, 1936.

122. Dispatch by Johannes Welczeck to German Foreign Minister Constantin Neurath, Paris, August 2, 1936, in *Documents on German Foreign Policy*, 22.

123. Welczeck was referring to the election by the Spanish Liberal Party of a new king, an event that gave rise to the Franco-Prussian War of 1871.

124. "Possible Effect on England of the Application of Neutrality Laws to Ger-

many and Italy," memorandum of the Division of European Affairs of the US State Department, Washington, DC, July 7, 1937, NARA, US Department of State Files, 1930–1939 (Files 852.00/ . . . , Box 6401), Document 852.00/5967.

125. Minutes of the meeting between Mussolini and Göring. Foreign minister Count Ciano and German counselor Schmidt were also present at the meeting (Colloquio del Duce col Presidente Goering, presenti S. E. Il Ministro degli affari esteri, Conte Ciano, e il Consigliere di legazione Schmidt). Palazzo Venezia, Rome, January 23, 1937, NARA, RG 242, Foreign Records Seized Collection, Papers of Count Ciano (Lisbon Papers), Received from the Department of State, Microfilm Publication T816, R. 1, 173–97.

126. This does not mean that the British prime minister did not pursue peace as his primary goal. But Britain's increasingly aggressive rearmament policy in the 1930s unmistakably shows that both Baldwin and Chamberlain were well aware of the risk of a war.

127. Letter from Sir Eric C. E. Phipps, British Ambassador to Berlin, to Anthony Eden, Foreign Secretary, Berlin, April 13, 1937, in *Documents on British Foreign Policy (1919–1939)*, edited by Medlicott and Douglas, 611.

128. Report by Ambassador Bowers to the Secretary of State, Donibane Lohitzune, October 17, 1937, in *Foreign Relations of the United States: Diplomatic Papers, 1937*, 424.

129. Konstantin F. von Neurath was foreign minister of the German government from June 2, 1932, to February 4, 1938.

130. Norman J. Padelford, *International Law and Diplomacy in the Spanish Civil Strife* (New York: Macmillan, 1939), 206–7.

131. Aide Memoire, Rome, January 6, 1937, NARA, RG 242, Foreign Records Seized Collection, Papers of Count Ciano (Lisbon Papers), Received from the Department of State, Microfilm Publication T816, R. 1, 167–69.

132. *Manchester Guardian*, September 28, 1936.

133. Augustus G. Stapleton, *Intervention and Non-Intervention* (London: Murray, 1866), 18.

134. *Time Magazine* (London), October 19, 1937.

135. Bowers, *My Mission to Spain*, 325.

136. Ibid.

137. Memorandum of Charles W. Yost, Office of Arms and Munitions Control of the US State Department, to Secretary of State Hull, Washington, DC, March 20, 1937, NARA, US Department of State Files, 1930–1939 (Files 852.20/82– . . . , Box 6429), Document 852.2221/375.

138. Report by Colonel Stephen O. Fuqua, Military Attaché of the US Embassy in Donibane Lohitzune, to Secretary of State Hull, Donibane Lohitzune, May 20, 1937, NARA, US Department of State Files, 1930–1939 (Files 852.20/82– . . . , Box 6429), Document 852.2221/413.

139. Ibid., Box 6400, Document 852.00/5500.

140. Ibid., July 2, 1937, Box 6401, Document 852.00/6028.

141. Report by Samuel Reber, Second Secretary of the US Embassy in Rome, to Secretary of State Hull, Rome, August 27, 1937, NARA, US Department of State Files, 1930–1939 (Files 852.20/82– . . . , Box 6404), Document 852.00/6383.

142. Report by Bowers to Secretary of State Hull, Donibane Lohitzune, August 30, 1937, NARA, US Department of State Files, 1930–1939 (Files 852.00/ . . . , Box 6404), Document 852.00/6444.

143. "To the Editor of the New York Times," *New York Times*, December 7, 1936.

144. "Minute by Sargent on Soviet Policy with Regard to the Spanish State," Foreign Office, January 8, 1937, in *Documents on British Foreign Policy (1919–1939)*, edited by Medlicott and Douglas, 280.

145. "Foreign Volunteers Serving with Spanish Government Forces," Report by Colonel Stephen O. Fuqua to the US State Department, Madrid, May 1937, NARA, Bowers Files (Files 852.222/ . . .), Document 852.222/413.

146. Klaus A. Maier, *Guernica: La intervención alemana en España y el "caso Guernica"* (Madrid: Sedmay, 1976).

## 2 ■ Terror Bombing at the Basque Front

1. In Basque, Euzko Alderdi Jeltzalea (EAJ); in Spanish, Partido Nacionalista Vasco (PNV).

2. Report on Basque Autonomy no. 1223, Report by Ambassador Bowers to the Secretary of State, Donibane Lohitzune, October 12, 1936, NARA, Bowers Files (Files 852.00/ . . . , Boxes 3687–3701), Document 852.00/3553, 1–2.

3. Dispatch by Johannes Welczeck to German Foreign Minister Constantin Neurath, in *Documents on German Foreign Policy*, 40 (see chap. 1, n. 70).

4. Memorandum by Colonel F. H. Lincoln for the US Chief of Staff, September 25, 1936, NARA, RG 165, Records of the Military Intelligence Division Relating to Conditions in Spain (1918–1941), Microfilm Publication MI.1445, R. 7.

5. Report by Ambassador Bowers to the Secretary of State, Donibane Lohitzune, April 12, 1937, NARA, Bowers Files (Files 852.00/ . . . , Boxes 3687–3701), Document 852.00/5238, 9–10.

6. Operazioni Fronte Nord, Informe del General Doria (Bastico) al conde Galeazzo Ciano, May 3, 1937, AMAE, Gabinetto del Ministro (1923–1943), Busta 1 (Uffizio Spagna no. 1244), 1–10.

7. By August 1937, the reduction of Italian troops forced the creation of mixed Italo-Spanish divisions of *Flechas Negras* (Black Arrows).

8. Interview with von Thoma, in Liddell Hart and Henry Basil, *The Other Side of the Hill* (London: Cassell, 1973).

9. Rear Admiral Carls Rolf was commander of the German fleet on the Spanish and Basque coasts from 1936.

10. Velardi was one of the officers in command of the atrocious raid on Barcelona on March 16, 1937.

11. Report by Consul William E. Chapman, Bilbao, to Secretary of State Hull,

Bilbao, March 31, 1937, NARA, US Department of State Files 1930–1939 (Files 852.00/ . . . , Boxes 6386 to 6407), Document 852.00/5149.

12. Pinna, *Relazioni del General Pinna*, Salamanca, April 17, 1937, 17 (see chap. 1, n. 69).

13. Karl L. Oertzen, *Grundsätze der Wehrpolitik* (Hamburg: Hanseatische Verlagsanstalt, 1933).

14. *Militär-Wochenblatt*, May 1937, in "Los bombardeos de las ciudades abiertas: Monstruosa doctrina militar de los nazis," *La Vanguardia* (Barcelona), May 11, 1937, 9.

15. Spanish Information Bureau, Spanish News Service, New York, May 19, 1937, NARA, RG 165, Records of the Military Intelligence Division Relating to Conditions in Spain (1918–1941), Microfilm Publication MI.1445, R. 7.

16. Telegram from Ulrich von Hassell to the Foreign Ministry of the Reich, Rome, March 25, 1937, in *Documents on German Foreign Policy*, 258–59.

17. Helen Graham, *The Spanish Civil War: A Very Short Introduction* (Oxford: Oxford University Press, 2005), 73. See also Preston, *Spanish Civil War*, 306 (see chap. 1, n. 15).

18. Preston, *Spanish Civil War*, 306.

19. Several copies of the leaflet are preserved in the Archive of Basque Nationalism in Bilbao.

20. *Daily Herald* (London), on April 29, 1937.

21. Richthofen, war diary, April 2, 1937. A copy of the war diary is preserved in the ADCGPM.

22. Steer, *Tree of Gernika*, chap. 12 (see chap. 1, n. 77).

23. Pinna, *Relazioni del General Pinna*, Salamanca, April 17, 1937, 9.

24. Ibid., 30; Maier, *Guernica: La intervención alemana en España*, 138 (see chap. 1, n. 146).

25. Report by Consul Chapman, Bilbao, to Secretary of State Hull, Bilbao, March 31, 1937, NARA, US Department of State Files 1930–1939 (Files 852.00/ . . . , Boxes 6386 to 6407), Document 852.00/5149.

26. Steer, *Tree of Gernika*, chap. 12.

27. Ibid.

28. Memorandum for Ambassador Bowers from Consul Chapman, Donibane Lohitzune, May 21, 1937, NARA, Bilbao Consulate General Records (1936–1946), Box 6, 1937, 1–2.

29. Steer, *Tree of Gernika*, chap. 12.

30. The flight register of Escadrille 25 (Sorta S.81 su Durango) shows indeed nine SM.81 bombers departing at 7:55 A.M. on March 31. Five of them returned at 9:05 A.M. after a seventy-minute flight and the other six at 9:10 A.M. after a seventy-five-minute flight. The dispatch mentions the names of the pilots involved in the attack: Martori, Mariani, Bianchedi, Recchi, Tranca, Corona, Alessi, Guglielmotti, and Milello. D.S. Spagna, vol. 8, C.S. 3/2, 25 Squadriglia C.T., ADCGPM.

We know the real names of most of the Italian pilots involved in the attacks against Durango, thanks to the document entitled "Elenco Nominativo del Personalle dell'Aviazione Legionaria," 1937, Ministerio dell'Aeronautica, C.75/C, ADCGPM.

| *Real name* | *Nome di battaglia, or pseudonym* |
|---|---|
| Stefano Castellani | Eraldo Di Domenico |
| Elio Re | Vito Paladini |
| Armando Francois | Arturo Martori |
| Corrado Ricci | Corrado Rocca |
| Enrico Puppi | Giorgio Del Frate |
| Luigi Capuzzo | Ottavio Guidi |
| Belfino Frattini | Constantino D'Angelo |
| Raoul Galli | Ricardo Rebecchi |
| Alfiero Vezzetti | Ottavio Mariani |
| Giovanni Beretta | Romualdo Bianchedi |
| Bruno Sartori | Giovanni Corona |
| Giuseppe Alessandri | Giuseppe Alessi |
| Adamo Guglietti | Ugo Guglielmotti |
| Giulio Cesare | Angelo Tranca |
| Luigi Mariotti | Alfredo Pascucci |
| Franco De Micheli | Francesco Costanzi |

31. The flight register of Escadrille 25 (Sorta S.81 su Verriz e Durango) shows seven SM.81 bombers operating in the afternoon of March 31. Six of them departed at 16:05 and returned at 17:10 after a sixty-five-minute flight. The other aircraft departed at 15:05 and returned at 16:10 after a sixty-five-minute flight. The dispatch mentions the names of the pilots involved in the afternoon attack: Martori, Pascucci, Boldetti, Costanzi, Garfini, D'Angelo, and Ricci. D.S. Spagna, vol. 8, C.S. 3/2, 25 Squadriglia C.T., ADCGPM.

32. "Resumen de las operaciones del día 31 de marzo y 2 de abril de 1937," in *1937 martxoak 31, Durango, 31 de marzo de 1937: Estudio sobre el bombardeo aéreo realizado contra la Villa de Durango el 31 de marzo de 1937*, by Jon Irazabal (Durango: Geirediaga Elkartea, 2001), 185–88.

33. Orden de colaboración de apoyo de las fuerzas aéreas con las Brigadas de Navarra, March 31, 1937.

34. Data taken from Steer, who wrote: "By then 127 corpses, not counting unexplained pieces, had been dug out in dangerous conditions, for roofs were continually shedding more beams and stones. Many unrecognised, and many of these women and children. Thus in the police list one reads, 'Male, approximate age four years,' 'Male, approximate age six years,' and 'Girl of two or three years,' among the unidentified bodies." Steer, *Tree of Gernika*, chap. 13.

35. Data provided by Manuel Irujo, Minister of Justice of the Republic, and Joseba Elosegi, Basque soldier, in their descriptions of the bombing. Manuel Irujo, *Un vasco en el Ministerio de Justicia: Memorias* (Buenos Aires: Ekin, 1979), vol. 2, pt. 1, 134; Joseba Elosegi, *Quiero morir por algo* (Barcelona: Plaza and Janés, 1977), 59.

36. Steer, *Tree of Gernika*, chap. 13.

37. Ibid.

38. Elosegi, *Quiero morir por algo*, 59–60.

39. Richthofen, war diary, April 30, 1937, ADCGPM.

40. Steer, *Tree of Gernika*, chap. 13.

41. The flight register of Escadrille 25 (Sorta s.81 su Durango e Elorri) shows six SM.81 bombers operating on the afternoon of April 2. All of them departed at 17:40 and returned at 18:35 after a fifty-five-minute flight. The dispatch mentions the names of the pilots of the bombers involved in the afternoon attack: Mariani, Pascucci, Recchi, Guidi, Del Frate, and Rebecchi. D.S. Spagna, vol. 8, C.S. 3/2, 25 Squadriglia C.T., ADCGPM.

42. Irazabal, *1937 martxoak 31, Durango, 31 de marzo de 1937*, 57, 105.

43. Report 6.514 by Captain Townsend Griffiss and Colonel Stephen O. Fuqua, Valencia, April 7, 1937, NARA, RG 165, Records of the Military Intelligence Division Relating to Conditions in Spain (1918–1941), Microfilm Publication MI.1445, R. 7.

44. Report 6.531 by Colonel Stephen O. Fuqua, Valencia, April 26, 1937, NARA, RG 165, Records of the Military Intelligence Division Relating to Conditions in Spain (1918–1941), Microfilm Publication MI.1445, R. 7.

45. *Durango ville martyre: Ce que furent les bombardements de la ville de Durango par les avions allemands* (Paris: Comité franco-espagnol, [1937]), microfilm copy, Library of Congress, Washington, DC.

46. The news was mainly reproduced in Europe but also in America. For instance, *Life* dedicated a rather long article to the bombing: "The Basques Become World Heroes: Shrine at Durango Bombed by the Rebels," *Life*, May 10, 1937, 60.

47. *Euzko Deya* (Paris), April 2, 1937. British consul Ralph C. Stevenson was not among the signatories.

48. As reported by the US consul at Bilbao, William E. Chapman, the rebels tried to kill Stevenson and bombed and burned his house in Areeta, near Bilbao, in retaliation for the British navy's escort of food-supply ships despite Franco's effort to blockade the Basque port. During the offensive against the Basques that started on March 31, Stevenson had supervised, under instructions from the Foreign Office, the evacuation of close to thirty thousand noncombatants in July 1937. The rebels had spies in Bilbao who passed, through the Austrian delegation or by other means, information to the German air force regarding targets to bomb in the city and their exact location. "The Conquest of Bilbao," second and final part of the report under the same title for Ambassador Bowers by Consul Chapman, Donibane Lohitzune, July 6, 1937, NARA, Bilbao Consulate General Records (1936–1946), Box 6, 1937, 12.

49. Report by Ambassador Bowers to the Secretary of State, Donibane Lohitzune, April 12, 1937, NARA, Bowers Files (Files 852.00/ . . . , Boxes 3687–3701), Document 852.00/5238, 10.

50. Second and final part of the report under the same title for Ambassador Bowers by Consul Chapman, Donibane Lohitzune, July 6, 1937, NARA, Bilbao Consulate General Records (1936–1946), Box 6, 1937, 6.

51. Alfred Lent, *Wir kämpften für Spanien: Erlebnisse eines deutschen Freiwilligen im spanischen Bürgerkrieg* (Oldenburg: G. Stalling, 1939).

52. Irazabal, *1937 martxoak 31, Durango, 31 de marzo de 1937*, 128.

53. Bowers, *My Mission to Spain*, 343 (see preface, n. 1).

54. Second and final part of the report under the same title for Ambassador Bowers by Consul Chapman, Donibane Lohitzune, July 6, 1937, NARA, Bilbao Consulate General Records (1936–1946), Box 6, 1937, 6–7.

55. Richthofen, war diary, March 31, 1937, ADCGPM.

56. The attacks over the Intxorta Mountains were described by one of the defense-line Basque commanders, Pablo Beldarrain, in his book *Intxorta mendiko burrukaldiak (1936–1937)* (Bilbao: GEU, 1980).

57. Telegram by Ulrich von Hassell to the German Foreign Ministry, Rome, April 9, 1937, in *Documents on German Foreign Policy*, 266.

58. Dispatch by Lieutenant General Wilhelm Faupel to the German Foreign Ministry, Salamanca, May 1, 1937, in ibid., 274–75.

59. The British also doubted the possibility of Bilbao being captured. As Ambassador Bowers reported to the secretary of state: "In Saint Jean de Luz are a number of British businessmen who are skeptical about the possibility of taking Bilbao from the land. It is the common belief here that the insurgents have concluded that Bilbao must be starved into submission. With this in view General Franco has declared a blockade, which has not, however, prevented ships from entering and leaving the harbor." Report by Ambassador Bowers to the Secretary of State, Donibane Lohitzune, April 19, 1937, NARA, Bowers Files (Files 852.00/ . . . , Boxes 3687–3701), Document 852.00/5296, 7.

60. Dispatch by Lieutenant General Wilhelm Faupel to the German Foreign Ministry, Salamanca, April 21, 1937, in *Documents on German Foreign Policy*, 274–75.

61. Steer, *Tree of Gernika*, chap. 14.

62. "Babies, Bombs & Battleships," *Time*, May 10, 1937.

63. Maier, *Guernica: La intervención alemana en España*, 138.

64. Pinna, *Relazioni del General Pinna*, Salamanca, April 17, 1937, 9.

65. "Los aviones que bombardearon Guernica y que actúan en el frente vasco son alemanes, conducidos por pilotos de la misma nacionalidad," *Ahora*, May 30, 1937, 8; "El bombardeo de Guernica: Informe de la Comisión de Expertos," ABC, May 30, 1937, 7.

66. *Foreign Wings over the Basque Country* (London: Friends of Spain, 1937), 18.

67. This conclusion is consistent with the report made by Colonel Fuqua who, along with Colonel Aureliano Álvarez Coque, visited the prison on the outskirts of Valencia where large numbers of Italian prisoners were taken after the Battle of Guadalajara. Most of them were not professional soldiers. Report 6510 by Colonel Stephen O. Fuqua, Valencia, April 4, 1937, NARA, RG 165, Records of the Military Intelligence Division Relating to Conditions in Spain (1918–1941), Microfilm Publication MI.1445, R. 7.

68. See note 59.

69. Report by Lieutenant General Wilhelm Faupel to the German Ministry of the Exterior, Salamanca, April 21, 1937, in *Documents on German Foreign Policy*, 274–75.

70. Ibid.; minutes of the meeting of April 2, 1937, between the Italian ambassador in Berlin, Bernardo Attolico, and General Göring, AMAE, Affari Politici (Spagna, 1931–1945), Busta 20 (1937), 49–56.

71. Ibid.

72. Vincenzo Velardi, Promemoria per S. E. Il Sottosecretario de Stato, Gasteiz, April 27, 1937, 1, USAM, Busta 70, Fascicolo 11.

73. Telegram from Ambassador to Rome William Phillips to Secretary of State Hull, Rome, April 23, 1937, NARA, US Department of State Files 1930–1939 (Files 852.00/ . . . , Boxes 6386 to 6407), Document 852.00/5311.

74. Pinna, *Relazioni del General Pinna*, Salamanca, April 17, 1937, 5.

75. "All Out for *Der Fuehrer*," *Lowell (MA) Sun*, April 27, 1937, 3.

76. Ricardo de la Cierva, "La polémica y la verdad sobre Guernica," in *La Historia se confiesa: España, 1930–1936*, facsimile no. 45 (Barcelona: Planeta, 1976), 283; Vicente Talón, *El holocausto de Guernica* (Barcelona: Plaza & Janés, 1987), 83–84. See also Jesús Salas Larrazábal, *Guernica* (Madrid: Rialp, 1987), 187.

77. Corum, *Wolfram von Richthofen*, 123–24 (see chap. 1, n. 98).

78. Maier, *Guernica: La intervención alemana en España*, 93–94. The Documentation Center on the Bombing of Gernika of the Gernika Peace Museum Foundation also has a partial copy of Richthofen's original war diary from the Bundesarchiv-Militärarchiv [Military Archives in Freiburg, Germany].

79. Literally, "in stretto e diretto accordo con il Comando dell' Esercito del Nord." Velardi, Promemoria per S. E. Il Sottosecretario de Stato, Gasteiz, May 6, 1937, 2, USAM, Busta 76, Fascicolo 14.

80. Telegram of General Doria (Ettore Bastico) to Count Galeazzo Ciano, June 24, 1937, AMAE, Gabinetto del Ministro (1923–1943), Busta 7 (Uffizio Spagna Leg. 44, no. 1250).

81. Statto maggiore italo-tedesco presso generale Franco, Berlin, February 10, 1937, AMAE, Gabinetto del Ministro (1923–1943), Busta 7 (Uffizio Spagna Leg. 44, no. 1250).

82. Imanol Villa, *Gernika bonbardaketa/El bombardeo* (Bilbao: Idem 4 / EITB, 2008), 91.

83. Maier, *Guernica: La intervención alemana en España*, 143.

84. Operazioni di Bilbao, Telegrama del general Carlo Bossi, Salamanca, April 27, 1937, AMAE, Gabinetto del Ministro (1923–1943), Busta 7 (Uffizio Spagna Leg. 44, no. 1250).

85. "Mola, el testaferro de Hitler en las Vascongadas, dice que arrasará Bilbao, 'porque es preciso destruir la capital de un pueblo pervertido, que se atreve a hacer frente a los nacionalistas'" [Mola, representative of Hitler in the Basque Country, says that he will sweep Bilbao, "for it is necessary to destroy the capital of a perverted people who dare to face the Nationalists"]. *Adelante*, May 5, 1937, 4. See also "Menace du general Mola," *Le Populaire*, April 29, 1937, 1.

86. *Llano* means "flat" in Spanish. Interview by William Smallwood with Natividad Apraiz, Gernika, 1972, WSA, File Gernika, E. Natividad Apraiz, 1972; interview

by Smallwood with Juan Zabala, Gernika, 1972, WSA, File Gernika, E. Juan Zabala, 1972.

87. Hilari Raguer, *La pólvora y el incienso* (Barcelona: Ediciones Península, 2001), 293.

88. Data provided by José Ángel Echániz and Vicente del Palacio, based on municipal records of July 20, 1936 (5,630 residents—2,504 men and 3,126 women). José Ángel Echániz and Vicente del Palacio, "Los muertos del bombardeo," *El Correo*, April 25, 2004. Humberto Unzueta mentions 5,729 residents, adding the residents of the neighborhood of Ajangiz (Errenteria) to the ones of Gernika. Unzueta, *Gernikako bonbaketa: Hildakoak, 1937-4-26* (Gernika: n.p., 1992), 9.

89. Five hundred residents in 1644, 4,500 in 1920, and 6,000 in 1936. Gonzalo Cárdenas Rodríguez, *Datos para la reconstrucción del pueblo adoptado de Guernica [Texto taquigráfico de la conferencia pronunciada por el arquitecto de la Dirección General de Regiones Devastadas, Gonzalo de Cárdenas Rodríguez, en el salón de actos de la exposición de la reconstrucción de España, el día 3 de julio de 1940]* (Madrid: Dirección General de Regiones Devastadas y Reparaciones, 1940), 21, Fundación Sancho el Sabio (FSS), ATV 20864. See also Gonzalo Cárdenas Rodríguez, "La reconstrucción de Guernica," *Boletín de la Real Sociedad Vascongada de Amigos del País* (Donostia) 2, no. 2 (1946): 16.

90. Ministerio de Gobernación, Dirección General de Regiones Devastadas, Comisión de Vizcaya, *Reconstrucción de la villa de Guernica: Memoria* (Madrid: n.p., 1940), 3, GBDZ, Regiones devastadas, Caja 1, Carp. 2 bis.

91. Testimony of Jose Labauria, La Roseraie, April 2, 1938, in *La guerra civil en Euzkadi*, edited by Gamboa and Larronde, 602 (see chap. 1, n. 29).

92. Ibid.

93. "L'atroce bombardement de Guernica," *L'Humanité*, April 28, 1937, 3. See also "La destruction de Guernica per des avions allemands," *La Croix*, April 29, 1937, 5; and "Les avions rebelles détruisent Guernica," *Le Populaire*, April 28, 1937, 1–2, Bibliothèque Nationale de France (Paris).

94. Noel Monks, "Priest Blesses City as Bombs Fall," *Daily Express* (London), April 28, 1937, 1, 3; "L'effroyable destruction de Guernica vue par les correspondants étrangers," *Euzko Deya*, April 30, 1937, 3.

95. "Les massacres des populations, des femmes et d'enfants dans les ruines de Gernica," *Ce Soir* (París), May 1, 1937, 3.

96. Report by Ralph C. Stevenson, British Consul at Bilbao, to British Ambassador Sir Henry Chilton, Bilbao, April 28, 1937, in *Documents on British Foreign Policy (1919–1939)*, edited by Medlicott and Douglas, 696–98 (see chap. 1, n. 53).

97. Jean Tarragó [Victor Montserrat], *Le drame d'un peuple incompris: La guerre au Pays Basque* (Paris: H. G. Peyre, 1937), 75.

98. "The Massacre of Guernica: Four Nurses' Evidence," *Manchester Guardian*, May 28, 1937. See also testimony by Guadalupe Urkiola, Jatsu, December 3, 1937, in *La guerra civil en Euzkadi*, edited by Gamboa and Larronde, 317.

99. "Des témoins du bombardement," *La Croix*, May 1, 1937, 2. See also "Le massacre de Guernica soulève l'indignation générale," *Le Petit Journal*, April 30, 1937,

3; and "Los aviones ametrallaban a las mujeres y niños que huían del incendio, dice la testigo presencial Maria Goitia," *Adelante,* May 5, 1937, 4.

100. Talón, *El holocausto de Guernica,* 40.

101. Xabier Irujo, *El Gernika de Richthofen: Un ensayo de bombardeo de terror* (Gernika: Gernikako Bakearen Museoa Fundazioa, Gernika-Lumoko Udala, 2012), 263–65.

102. Uriarte, *Bombas y mentiras sobre Guernica,* 64 (see chap. 1, n. 27).

103. Minutes of the meeting of the District Mayors of Gernika, Gernika, February 24, 1937, BFA, Busturia 0056/030.

104. Memorandum of the creation of the Permanent Commission of the District of Gernika and Bases under which is to be governed for the supply of the towns, February 15, 1937, BFA, Busturia 0056/030.

105. Joxe Iturria, who was a twenty-two-year-old soldier in April 1937, was one of the eyewitnesses who saw the market going on in Gernika on April 26. He also saw dead animals and parts of animals lying in the streets after the bombing in the market square, together with human bodies and parts of human bodies. Interview with Joxe Iturria in his house in Lesaka, Navarre, May 17 and May 21, 2013.

106. Imanol Agirre was one of the Gernika children who were evacuated to England on board the SS *Habana.* He wrote this letter at the Stoneham Camp (East Sussex) in July 1937. Most probably he was not even ten years old. See Yvonne Cloud (née Yvonne Kapp) and Richard Ellis, *The Basque Children in England: An Account of Their Life at North Stoneham Camp* (London: Victor Gollancz, 1937), 56–57. A Spanish translation of this beautiful description can be found in Bernardo Atxaga, *De Gernika a Guernica* (Barcelona: Ediciones de la Central, 2007).

107. Lee Kennett, *The First Air War, 1914–1918* (New York: Free Press, 1991), 138.

108. *Soldier* in Basque. The word is used both in Basque and in Spanish to make reference to the Basque soldiers.

109. Smallwood interview with Faustino Pastor, Paris, July 14, 1972, in Smallwood, "The Day Gernika Was Bombed" (manuscript in the author's possession, 1972), 38.

110. Ministerio de Gobernación, Dirección General de Regiones Devastadas, Comisión de Vizcaya, *Reconstrucción de la villa de Guernica,* 4.

111. Steer, *Tree of Gernika,* chap. 20.

112. Maurer Maurer, *The U.S. Air Service in World War I* (Washington, DC: Office of Air Force History, 1979), 4:502.

113. George Steer, "Guernica," *Times* (London), April 27, 1937.

## 3 ■ The Market Day Massacre

1. Apart from being difficult to believe, it would have been extremely dangerous for Colonel Juan Vigón to pass such an order without consultation with his superiors, and there is no reference to any official or unofficial admonition or reprimand to Vigón concerning what happened. See Irujo, *El Gernika de Richthofen,* 81–93 (see chap. 2, n. 101).

2. As Richthofen wrote in his war diary, the German command could not operate without the Spanish chief of staff's permission. This was a key part of their coordination. Richthofen, war diary, March 24 and 26, 1937, ADCGPM.

3. Ibid., April 25, 1937.

4. Gonzalo Cárdenas, *Datos para la reconstrucción del pueblo adoptado de Guernica*, 8 (see chap. 2, n. 89).

5. Kössinger, in an interview by Marc Bassets for the Catalan newspaper *La Vanguardia*, April 24, 2008.

6. Mathieu Corman, correspondent for *Ce Soir* (París), mentioned seven planes machine-gunning Gerrikaitz at noon. Enrique Goitiandia and Jose Mari Gerrikabeitia, of Munitibar, have confirmed to me that the attack against Munitibar affected Uloste and the areas near downtown, the road crossing Munitibar from Gerrikaitz, and the church. According to their testimony, for years after the bombing the bomb holes were perfectly identifiable.

7. The attack was concentrated against Gerrikaitz, but Munitibar was bombed as well, as Enrique Goitiandia and Jose Mari Gerrikabeitia, local residents who saw the holes caused by bombs, told me. As a result of the attack, several houses were damaged, including the church.

8. Alberto Onaindia, *Hombre de paz en la guerra* (Buenos Aires: Ekin, 1973), 240.

9. Relación de víctimas causadas por la aviación facciosa en sus incursiones del mes de abril de 1937, Eusko Jaurlaritzaren Artxibo eta Dokumentu Ondarearen Zerbitzua, Doc. GE-0037-03.

10. Steer, *Tree of Gernika*, chap. 20 (see chap. 1, n. 77).

11. Ibid.

12. The exact number of planes is still debated, but by using data provided by Richthofen and Steer, it is possible to make a estimate. As Steer stated, "beginning to talk and to try to understand their experience, the Basques asked each other how many planes had attacked their town. Some said eighty, others one hundred, others two hundred, others more. They could not tell; but those who were outside Gernika the whole afternoon say that between forty and fifty German planes attacked her, including ten fighters. The bombers reappeared again and again with fresh loads." Ibid.

13. George Steer said that because the bombers and fighters "reappeared again and again with fresh loads," it was difficult to calculate an exact number of planes. Ibid. Stevenson actually calculated fifty bombers over Gernika. Report by Consul Stevenson, Bilbao, to Ambassador Chilton, Bilbao, April 28, 1937, in Medlicott and Dakin, *Documents on British Foreign Policy (1919–1939)*, 696–98 (see chap. 1, n. 53). Zigor Mendiola, *gudari* of the Loiola Battalion, estimated that at least forty-five bombers grouped into five squadrons of nine aircraft each and eighteen fighters grouped into two squadrons took part in the attack. Interview by Smallwood with Zigor Mendiola, Gernika, 1972, WSA, File Gernika, E. Zigor Mendiola, 1972.

14. A complete list of the crews of the German K/88 bomber and J/88 fighter squads is in Maier, *Guernica: La intervención alemana en España*, 133–37 (see chap. 1, n. 146).

15. Commander of the Experimental Bomber Squadron VB/88, composed of three Heinkel He111s, three Junker Ju86s, and three Dornier Do17s in April 1937. According to Karl von Knauer, the squad led by Moreau did not fly that day over Gernika, but we know from Richthofen's diary that they did. Maier, *Guernica: La intervención alemana en España*, 121, 195.

16. According to Klaus Maier, there were three Junker Ju52 squads in Burgos, totaling twenty-six bombers. The data I have, based on the records of General Pinna, mention only twenty-three Ju52s in Burgos on April 17. However, we know that the German air command sent two Heinkel He111s and a Dornier Do17 under Rudolf von Moreau to Burgos between April 17 and April 25 to take part in the bombing of Gernika on April 26. So it is possible that the German command decided to send three more Junker Ju52s from the air base in Seville, together with the experimental unit under Moreau to take part in the attack.

The First Junker Ju52 Bomber Squad, led by Knauer, was composed of nine planes. Ibid., 135.

17. The Second Junker Ju52 Bomber Squad, led by von Beust, was composed of nine planes. Ibid., 136.

18. The Third Junker Ju52 Bomber Squad, led by Captain Ehrhart Krafft von Dellmensingen, was composed of eight planes. Ibid., 137.

19. Lützow was a former student of theology. During World War II he became a flying ace who died five days before the Germans surrendered in Italy. Kurt Braatz, *Gott oder ein Flugzeug: Leben und Sterben des Jagdfliegers Günther Lützow* (Moosburg: NeunundzwanzigSechs Verlag, 2005), 150, 159, 162.

20. According to Karl von Knauer, Major Fuchs's immediate superior, Fuchs flew in his own plane over Gernika; according to Thomas and Morgan-Witts, Major Fuchs was in Burgos. Maier, *Guernica: La intervención alemana en España*, 195.

21. "German Youth Doomed to Die by Loyalists," *Nevada State Journal* (Reno), May 26, 1937, 2. The documents that we currently have show that the mentioned squadrons took part in the bombing. However, this fact does not exclude the participation of more bombers or fighters. New documents may indicate that other pilots or flight commanders took part in the bombing. This is the case of Laschinski, a Junker Ju52 pilot who flew over Gernika on April 26, according to the new documentation published by Walter Waiss. Mentioned by Maier, his flight diary was missing. See Walter Waiss, *Legion Condor: Zweiter Band* (Aachen: Helios Verlag, 2014), 76–77.

22. Corrado Ricci wrote that, as a pilot of one of the Fiat CR.32s that patrolled the front that day, he escorted a Heinkel He111 to Gernika. Apparently, that plane was not bombing but taking photographs of the area being bombed. Ricci's statement suggests that the Germans were indeed documenting their warfare experiment. Corrado Ricci, *Vita di Pilota* (Milan: Mursia, 1976), 61–65.

23. Francesco Biondi (pseudonym Francesco Belforte), *La guerra civile in Spagna* (Milan: Istituto per gli Studi di Politica Internazionale, 1938–39), 3:147–50.

24. Ferdinando Pedriali, *Guerra di Spagna e aviazione italiana* (Pinerolo: Società Storica Pinerolese, 1989). See also Talón, *El holocausto de Guernica*, 148 (see chap. 2, n. 76).

25. Salas Larrazabal, *Guernica*, 133 (see chap. 2, n. 76). Captain Mario Viola's pseudonym was Mario Viotti. Elenco nominativo del personale dell'Aviazione Legionaria del continente, 15, Ministero dell'Aeronautica, Gabineto del Ministro, Busta 88, Fasc. 7.

26. Preston maintains that as many as fifteen Italian aircraft took part in the attack. Preston, *Franco: A Biography*, 243 (see chap. 1, n. 108). However, Pedriali does not admit to more than three bombers and some fighters from the Aviazione Legionaria taking part in the attack. Pedriali, *Guerra di Spagna e aviazione italiana*.

27. According to the Diario Storico of April 26, 1937, Captain Stefano Castellani piloted aircraft number 2, together with Lieutenant Gallina, Rubertini, Canollotti, Piazza, and Pecoraro; aircraft number 4 was piloted by Lieutenant Porro, with Cisterni, Nicola(naco), Lo Re (Elio Re), Accorsi, and Scotton; aircraft number 11 was piloted by Lieutenant Roberto Fracaso, with Cirmi, Todini, Benigni, Casoni, and Crosio. Archivio Ufficio Storico, Aeronautica Militare, Busta 68, Fascicolo 98. According to Talón, Giovanni de Prato piloted one of the planes, but the diary of war does not mention him.

28. Three Savoia-Marchetti SM.79s took part in the attack, as recorded in the dispatch signed by Vincenzo Velardi on April 26, 1937. The document lists a five-hour flight, in contradiction with the Diario Storico of Captain Castellani, which registered a one-and-a-half-hour flight. Diario Storico, Archivio Ufficio Storico, Aeronautica Militare, Busta 68, Fascicolo 98. Velardi's dispatch also mentions the activity of fifty-seven Fiat CR.32 fighters over both the Basque and the Aragonese fronts that day, a total of eighty-two flight hours, but it does not indicate how many acted on each front. There were thirty-five Fiat CR.32 pursuit planes in the airfields near the Basque front, so twenty-two fighters were transferred from Seville, probably those that were shipped and assembled in mid-April. Velardi mentions that five Fiat CR.32s were flying in the Basque Country for seven hours and fifty-five minutes; ten flew for nine hours and forty-five minutes, escorting the Junker Ju52s that bombed Gernika; two groups of ten pursuit planes each flew in the Basque Country for twelve hours and five minutes; and a single fighter flew from Gasteiz to Logroño in fifty-five minutes. In total, there were thirty-six Fiat CR.32s, in addition to the ten CR.32s that we have already mentioned under Captain Viola and Lieutenant Ricci. Archivio Ufficio Storico, Aeronautica Militare, Busta 71, Fascicolo 9.

29. See appendix 1, "The Number of Planes Involved in the Attack on Gernika."

30. Salas mentions thirty-nine aircraft: three Savoia-Marchetti SM.79s, two Heinkel He111s, one Dornier Do17, and five Fiat CR.32s during the first phase of the attack, and then nineteen Junker Ju52s, five Fiat CR.32s, and four Messerschmitt Bf.109s. Salas does not include the twelve aircraft of the first Heinkel He51 fighter squadron led by Harder, arguing that they did not attack Gernika itself but assaulted the suburbs (twelve aircraft). With the same reasoning, he did not include the five Fiat CR.32s led by Corrado Ricci that flew over the Durango front, less than a one-minute flight from Gernika. However, when Salas describes the bombing, he includes all these units in his description. Salas Larrazabal, *Guernica*, 150–54.

The fact that these fighters did not machine-gun the city center of Gernika (even though some eyewitnesses mention these planes flying over the city center) is not proof that these squads did not participate in the bombing. On the contrary, these pilots strafed the suburbs as an essential part of the attack, because their mission was to keep people confined inside the perimeter of fire within the town. In addition, smoke from the explosions did not allow the fighters to maneuver easily within the perimeter of the city, and people fleeing the center to the suburbs offered a much better target for aerial strafing.

31. The average crew of a Savoia-Marchetti SM.79 was six, and the fighters were operated by a single pilot. As noted, at least sixteen Fiat CR.32 fighters participated in the attack. However, we know that Fiat CR.32 fighter pilots Rocca (pseudonym of Corrado Ricci), Pongiluppi, and Constantini made two flights that afternoon. See also note 27 above.

32. The average crew of a Dornier Do17 was four men, the Heinkel He111 by a crew of five people, and the Junker Ju52 by three men. All fighters were flown by a single person. As for the crew of the bombers, Lieutenant Colonel Karl von Knauer (who flew with Major Robert Fuchs in the same plane) led the first squadron of Junker Ju52s from Burgos, Colonel Hans Henning von Beust led the second squad, and Captain von Krafft Ehrhart Dellmensingen the third. The experimental group was led by Rudolf von Moreau. The names of the complete crews of the bombers is in Maier, *Guernica: La intervención alemana en España*, 135–37.

We do not have a complete list of the German J/88 fighter pilots at Gasteiz who participated in the bombing, but among them we can mention the following. In the first He51 squadron led by Harro Harder: Hermann Beurer, Heinz Braunschweiger, Fritz Hillmann, Guido Höness, Hans Kolbow, Helmut Kühle, Karl Wilfert, Hans Joachim Wandel, and [?] Droste. Among the pilots of the second Bf.109 squadron led by Günther Lützow, of whom at least seven participated in the attack, we can name Peter Boddem, Adolf Buhl, Norbert Flegel, Franz Heilmayer, Rolf Pingel, Günther Radusch, and Urban Schlaffer. As for the third squadron led by Douglas Pitcairn—and we are not certain they participated in the attack—we can mention Walter Ehle, Karl-Heinz Greisert, Walter Leyerer, Ignaz Prestele, Leo Sigmund, Walter Fenske, and [?] Riedinger. Salas Larrazabal, *Guernica*, 248; *Militärische Operationen—Legion Condor*, http://www.Panzer-Archiv.de.

33. Captain Carlo Romagnoli (pilot) and Captain Filippo Mancuso (observer) flew on one observation plane from Logroño to Gasteiz between 8:00 and 8:30 A.M., and departed again at 5:30 P.M., landing in Logroño at 6:00 P.M. The two reconnaissance planes led by Lieutenant Giacinto Sibilla (pilot) and Agostino Medori (observer), and Saverio Garcea (pilot) and Armando Ochis (observer), returned to Logroño at the same time. 128 Squadrigli, USAM, Serie 10, Registri volo, vol. 20).

34. Velardi, Promemoria per S. E. Il Sottosecretario de Stato, Gasteiz, April 27, 1937, 3, USAM, Busta 76, Fascicolo 11.

35. As Colonel Ferdinando Raffaelli established in a report on bombing technics in 1937, the standard height for daylight bombing was between 1,200 and 1,800

meters (3,900 to 5,900 feet). Ferdinando Raffaelli, *Bombardamento: Quistionario*, Ufficio di Stato Maggiore della Regia Aeronautica, Aviazione Legionaria 21° Stormo B. T., 1.

36. "Effect of the Bombing of Spanish Cities," report by Wolfram von Richthofen, May 28, 1937. The document was at the Bundes-Archiv Zwischenarchiv Berlin-Hoppegarten, German Federal Archives at Berlin-Hoppegarten, but was transferred to the Freiburg Military Archive (Bundesarchiv-Militärarchiv). Professor Ángel Viñas provided me with a copy of the document, which was discovered by Stefanie Schüler-Springorum. The document is partially reproduced in Stefanie Schüler-Springorum, *Krieg und Fliegen: Die Legion Condor im Spanischen Bürgerkrieg* (Paderborn: Ferdinand Schöning Verlag, 2010), 186.

37. Thanks to Margarita Martín, director of the Meteorological Institute of Donostia-San Sebastián, we now have the reports of the Meteorological Observatory on Mount Igeldo, which show that on April 26, 1937, at 12:00 P.M. the north wind was blowing in the area of Gernika and that there was a bank of stratocumulus clouds at about 600 meters of altitude—high enough to bomb a population without air defenses. GBDZ, Boletín del Oberservatorio de Igueldo de la diputación de Guipúzcoa del 26 de abril de 1937 (Report of the Meteorological Observatory of Mount Igeldo of April 26, 1937).

38. Many witnesses mentioned seeing fighters strafe at low altitude. Alberto Onaindia mentioned pursuit planes flying as low as 200 meters (656 feet). Onaindia, *Hombre de paz en la guerra*, 238.

39. The schedule for the attack is well described by several authors. George L. Steer described the attack in *The Tree of Guernica*, chap. 20. Joseba Elosegi, in *Quiero Morir por algo* (see chap. 2, n. 35), and Canon Alberto Onaindia, eyewitnesses to the attack, wrote of their experiences and observations in their books and several articles or speeches. Elosegi told me his own description of the bombing. We also have the descriptions of Jose Labauria, mayor of Gernika, and Father Eusebio Arronategi, published under the title *Guernica: To Civilized Mankind* (Bilbao: Basque Government, May 1937). An excellent reproduction of this booklet can be found in Atxaga, *De Gernika a Guernica* (see chap. 2, n. 106). Colonel Richthofen briefly described the attack in his war diary, and there is archival evidence, such as the reports of the Italian and German air forces for April 26, many of them already published by Klaus Maier or Jesús Salas. Maier, *Guernica: La intervención alemana en España;* Salas Larrazabal, *Guernica*. Cava, Silvestre, and Arranz interviewed several eyewitnesses, who stated that the bombing began after 4:00 P.M., approximately at 4:20. It cannot be determined whether other planes passed through the town before von Moreau's flight. There is more agreement among witnesses in giving a final hour for the bombing, around 7:40 P.M. María Jesús Cava Mesa, María Silvestre, and Javier Arranz, *Memoria colectiva del bombardeo de Gernika* (Gernika-Lumo: Gernika Gogoratuz, 1996), 103–19.

40. Mathieu Corman, correspondent for *Ce Soir* (Paris), who was attacked by a Heinkel He52 while he was with George Steer in Gerrikaitz, mentioned seven aircraft strafing that village at noon.

41. Canon Alberto Onaindia passed through Munitibar that afternoon and described the effect of the attack that had taken place in the morning. Onaindia, *Hombre de paz en la guerra*, 240.

42. Testimony of Jose Ramon Urtiaga, in Smallwood, "The Day Gernika Was Bombed," 33–34 (manuscript in the author's possession, 1972).

43. Testimonies of Pedro Gezuraga, Aurelio Artetxe, Iñaki Rezabal, and Faustino Pastor, in ibid., 33–36, 40–41.

44. According to Jesús Salas Larrazabal, the two Heinkel He111s attacked at different times. In accordance with this scheme, at about 6:00 P.M. a Heinkel He111, escorted by five Fiat CR.32s led by Corrado Ricci, bombed the city. However, it is difficult to explain why the three Italian SM.79 bombers and the first two bombers of Moreau's squad would fly without an escort and why a single Heinkel He111 was shepherded by five Italian fighters.

45. A Dornier Do17 could carry up to 1,000 kg of bombs, that is, twenty 50-kg shells. Some of the most accurate statements by the eyewitnesses register the first bombing by the Heinkel He52 at 4:20 P.M., so the experimental squadron led by Moreau arrived some minutes later, at about 4:30. (Some eyewitnesses mention 3:20 P.M., probably because they had not adjusted their clocks forward one hour to daylight saving time.) According to witnesses, the first bombs were dropped on San Juan Church and the surrounding areas, such as the train station, where most of the people were concentrated, a strategy that led to many casualties. Cava Mesa, Silvestre, and Arranz, *Memoria colectiva del bombardeo de Gernika*, 115.

46. Steer mentions a Heinkel He111, though some authors state that this first plane was a Dornier Do17 that bombed the city from west to east.

47. According to Steer, a Heinkel He111 flew over the town and dropped six medium bombs, probably fifty-pounders, near the railroad station, along with a shower of grenades. A few minutes later, another Heinkel He111 arrived to bomb the same area, but closer to the center of town, then it machine-gunned the town at random and turned homeward. Steer, *Tree of Gernika*, chap. 20.

48. According to many witnesses, this bombing was carried out by two Heinkel He111s and a sole Dornier Do17 separately, one after another, not in a three-abreast formation, as the Junker Ju52s did subsequently.

49. Stefano Castellani's *nome di battaglia* (battle name or pseudonym) was Eraldo Di Domenico. The report signed by the commander of the Italian air base at Soria, Lieutenant Colonel Pilota, mentions the Savoia-Marchetti SM.79 bombers but makes no reference to the Fiat CR.32 pursuit planes.

50. Indeed, Captain Castellani wrote that when they were ready to bomb, they saw a lone German plane—one of von Moreau's planes—leaving Gernika.

51. The successive waves of German bombers took off from Burgos only after the Italians had landed at Soria. Consequently, the Italians were not eyewitnesses to the bombing with high-explosive and incendiary shells. The flight report by Lieutenant Acorsi, one of the Italian pilots, mentions the landing of the SM.79 at Soria at 17:05.

52. Colonel Richthofen wrote in his war diary that "the experimental bomber squadron attacked first with three planes," and Captain Castellani, leading Italian

fighter Squadron 280, wrote in his logbook that he saw an unidentified lone German bomber returning from Gernika after having bombed the city for the first time. Ricci, *Vita di Pilota*, 61–65.

Captain Joseba Elosegi, who was in Gernika during the bombing, described the attack of the experimental squadron led by Moreau:

> We immediately sighted a German bomber, Heinkel He111, which launched a few bombs on the people, then flew away. Dense columns of smoke rose from the village. The bombs had made impact in scattered areas; right in front of our headquarters, in the palace of the Counts of Arana, a bomb had been dropped, causing major damage and a serious fire. We ran to the center [of town] to rescue the victims, who no doubt had to be numerous. We thought the danger had passed and that the enemy was satisfied with the damage inflicted, since the surprise was complete and most of the inhabitants had been surprised by the bombing in their own homes. We started to remove dead bodies and rescue wounded people; we were trying to organize relief and to do the necessary to transport the injured to the few medical facilities in the village. Until then, there was no great material loss to mourn. Gernika was still standing, and most of its houses still intact. There was no uncontrollable fire because the existing fires seemed to be easy to locate and to extinguish. (Elosegi, *Quiero morir por algo*, 128)

53. Elosegi, *Quiero morir por algo*, 128.

54. Testimony of Maria Abaskal, in Smallwood, "The Day Gernika Was Bombed," 61.

55. Steer, *Tree of Guernica*.

56. There were twenty-one Heinkel He52s stationed at Gasteiz airfield. The Heinkel He52s were mainly used in the Gernika attack to experiment with ground-attack techniques.

57. There were seven Messerschmitt Bf.109 monoplanes in the Gasteiz airfield. Several eyewitnesses described these monoplane pursuit planes machine-gunning the population in Gernika.

58. Obviously, there were no survivors to machine-gun in the city center, which was already in flames, but there were people in the outer parts of the city and in nearby areas hiding in the forests, fields, huts, and any other kind of shelter. As a consequence, the fighters concentrated their attacks around the city and in areas up to 12.5 miles from Gernika. The objective of this phase of the bombing was to keep people within the perimeter of fire in the town. This is precisely what Mari Carmen Egurrola, who witnessed the bombing, told me. Interview with Mari Carmen Egurrola, Boise, Idaho, November 11, 2007.

Joseba Elosegi described this phase of the bombing:

> Numerous Heinkel He51 pursuit planes started acting and, where the lack of smoke permitted them certain visibility, they machine-gunned every living human being. About an hour had passed since the bombing started, when I arrived in the square where the market had taken place, in the heart of

> Gernika. The town had suffered terribly and fire was raging. Many houses were burnt down and many others had been torn from the roof to the street, keeping up only the main walls. However, some houses still remained intact, miraculously still standing, like the result of a tragic lottery, despite the huge shocks they had suffered. The square where the market had taken place featured a stunning look of death and desolation. (Elosegi, *Quiero morir por algo*, 131)

59. Steer, *Tree of Gernika*, chap. 20.

60. Ibid. See also, "1,280 Are Reported Killed Along Two Spanish Fronts," *Charleston (SC) Gazette*, April 28, 1937, 1, 9.

61. Steer, *Tree of Gernika*, chap. 20.

62. General Pietro Pinna stated in his report on April 17 that the German bombers took this extremely close flight formation (*strettamente serrati in un grappolo*) on several occasions, especially when they lacked the support of pursuit planes. Pinna, *Relazioni del General Pinna*, Salamanca, April 17, 1937, 20 (see chap. 1, n. 69).

63. Testimony of Aurelio Artetxe, in Smallwood, "The Day Gernika Was Bombed," 57. Artetxe was not the only person who recorded numerous passes by the German bombers over Gernika. Among those *gudaris* who shot at these bombers and witnessed how they veered to make a second pass over the town, we can mention the following: Faustino Pastor, Iñaki "Patxolo" Rezabal, Jose Ramon Segues, and Pedro Gezuraga. Ibid., 41, 44, 54, 57. Apart from these testimonies, Jose Ramon Urtiaga, Angeles Atxabal, Santiago Ondarru (pseudonym), and Juanita Barrutia also saw the German bombers veer and make new passes over the town. Ibid., 34, 35, 37.

64. Steer, *Tree of Gernika*, chap. 20.

65. The incendiary bombs were not heavy enough to penetrate the houses by themselves, in order to start fires in the interior. Therefore, it was necessary to previously fracture the ceilings so the flames could expand easily.

66. David Clay Large, *Between Two Fires: Europe's Path in the 1930s* (New York: W. W. Norton, 1990), 256. Hans Henning von Beust, one of the German pilots in command of one of the convoys, General Hugo Sperrle and Richthofen stated that, during the approach on Gernika, the pilots could not see anything from the city, only the smoke. Maier, *Guernica: La intervención alemana en España*, 143, 189, 192.

67. Corum, *Wolfram von Richthofen*, 133 (see chap. 1, n. 98).

68. Adolf Galland, *The First and the Last: The Rise and Fall of the German Fighter Forces, 1938–1945* (New York: Holt, 1954), 16.

69. Steer, *Tree of Gernika*, chap. 20.

70. Steer, "Guernica," *Times* (London), April 27, 1937.

71. Some of the eyewitnesses described the glasses worn by the pilots.

72. Joseba Elosegi described this phase of the bombing as follows:

> After each pass and dropping of bombs, those damn Junkers seemed to be definitely leaving, but unfortunately, the new wave of planes was not far to relieve the first one. In one of those pauses [between bombings] I tried to

organize aid and sent instructions with my assistant to headquarters. I never saw him again; he disappeared among the bombs. In Barrenkale I met our chaplain, Don Andres [Untzain], who together with the parish priest of Gernika, Father Arronategui, helped the dying people. I met Andres and he was desperate and pale as death. He said to me, "Get out of here, they will kill us all." People fled to the outskirts of the town seeking protection in the forests. We barely got to rescue some people badly injured from a shelter that had collapsed, and we put them in a row against a wall, waiting for their evacuation on stretchers that I had ordered to be brought from the barrack. Many others were calling for help [from underneath the debris], but we could not help them all because to dig out those mountains of rubble and logs would have required days of work. People kept like crazy looking for their relatives and begging for help. Then, a new wave [of bombers] came to the distress of everyone. This time, heavy explosive bombs fell, along with incendiary bombs that burst into flames when exploding. (Elosegi, *Quiero morir por algo*, 129–30)

73. *Expediente-Informe del ayuntamiento de Guernica solicitando a la Dirección General de Regiones Devastadas de Madrid la elaboración de un proyecto para la reconstrucción de la villa. Anexo: Relación de daños en edificios públicos* (Gernika, November 3, 1939).

74. Alberto Onaindia, "A Priest's Account," *Times* (London), May 3, 1937.

75. This is an incorrect translation of the Spanish original, which literally states, "La criminal aviación facciosa bombardeó a unas poblaciones de la retaguardia, actuando especialmente sobre Guernica." Bulletin received by the US State Department from Madrid Radio, April 27, 1937, NARA, Bowers Files (Files 852.00/ . . . , Boxes 3687–3701), Document 852.00/5262.

76. Ibid. Bulletin received by the US State Department from Madrid Radio, April 27, 1937, NARA, Bowers Files (Files 852.00/ . . . , Boxes 3687–3701), Document 852.00/5262.

77. In Cloud and Ellis, *Basque Children in England*, 56–57 (see chap. 2, n. 106).

78. It should say "out in the streets." The lapse is intentional.

79. Lieutenant Colonel Karl von Knauer also wrote in his war diary that a sortie carried out against the bridge of Errenteria in Gernika had had a "good effect." Large, *Between Two Fires*, 256.

80. Another member of the Condor Legion general staff, Erwin Jaenecke, considered the bombing a triumph: "Guernica was a total success of the German air force. The only way for the withdrawal of the entire red coast was cut in full by the fire and a pile of rubble of two meters on the roads." Report by Erwin Jaenecke in the curse of a visit to Gernika, May 18, 1937. Maier, *Guernica: La intervención alemana en España*, 180.

81. Richthofen's war diary, quoted in Large, *Between Two Fires*, 256.

82. *Daily Herald* (London), April 29, 1937.

83. Bulletin received by the US State Department from Madrid Radio, May 1, 1937, NARA, Bowers Files (Files 852.00/ . . . , Boxes 3687–3701), Document 852.00/5284.

## 4 ■ An Analysis of the Attack

1. Pinna, *Relazioni del General Pinna*, Salamanca, April 17, 1937, 9 (see chap. 1, n. 69).

2. Pietro Pinna, *Dati concernenti il persone della Regia Aeronautica*, 2 (see chap. 1, n. 62).

3. In total, the report, written on April 15, indicates that there were eighty-two Italian fighters (instead of seventy-nine), twenty-six bombers (instead of twenty-eight), and twenty-seven reconnaissance planes (instead of twenty-three, possibly including the three seaplanes in this section). The planes that are missing from the list of April 17 could have been destroyed. Pinna, *Promemoria per S. E. General Bastico*, Salamanca, April 15, 1937, 1.

4. Import of Aeronautical Products, Report 6495 by Captain Townsend Griffiss and Colonel Stephen O. Fuqua, Military Attaché to the US State Department, March 16, 1937, NARA, Bowers Files (Files 852.24/ . . .), Document 852.24/384, 2.

5. "Italian Troops and Supplies in Spain" (see chap. 1, n. 58).

6. Memorandum by G. A. Fisher on the departure of Italian volunteers, in *Documents on British Foreign Policy (1919–1939)*, edited by Medlicott and Douglas, 70 (see chap. 1, n. 53).

7. Pinna, *Relazioni del General Pinna*, Salamanca, April 17, 1937, 9.

8. As I have explained, however, there is strong evidence that the total number of planes involved in the attack could be greater.

9. Three Savoia-Marchetti SM.79s, thirteen Savoia-Marchetti SM.81s, twenty-three Junker Ju52s, three Junker Ju86s, and four Henschel Hs123s. We may add to these forty-six bombers, two Heinkel He111s, and one Dornier Do17 that participated in the bombing.

10. Ten Italian Fiat CR.32 fighters, twenty-seven German Heinkel He51 fighters, and seven Messerschmitt Bf.109s.

11. There were four Henschel Hs123 bombers in Gasteiz.

12. From a total of thirty-three planes, operative or not, twenty-four were used (as mentioned, I include the two Heinkel He111s and the one Dornier Do17).

13. Including nonoperative planes.

14. Ten Fiat CR.32s, twenty-seven Heinkel He51s, and seven Messerschmitt Bf.109s.

15. No report mentions fighter planes in Soria in April 1937.

16. Pinna, *Dati concernenti il persone della Regia Aeronautica*, 6.

17. "Effect of the Bombing of Spanish Cities," report by Wolfram von Richthofen, May 28, 1937. The document was at the Bundes-Archiv Zwischenarchiv Berlin-Hoppegarten, German Federal Archives at Berlin-Hoppegarten, but was transferred to the Freiburg Military Archive (Bundesarchiv-Militärarchiv). See appendix 2, "The Quantity and Type of Bombs Dropped on Gernika."

18. See appendix 2.

19. Esplosivo lanciato durante il mese di aprile sul fronte di Bilbao, Diario Storico, Archivio Ufficio Storico, Aeronautica Militare, Busta 82, Fascicolo 5.

20. A. Porreta, Bombe lanciate, Diario Storico, Archivio Ufficio Storico, Aeronautica Militare, Busta 82, Fascicolo 5.

21. Ibid.

22. Only a few days after the destruction of Gernika, the *Frankfort Zeitung* published an article on modern warfare, describing with precision the use of planes and incendiary bombs made at Gernika. Obviously, the article does not mention the bridge as a target of the incendiaries. Report by Ambassador Bowers to Secretary of State Hull, Donibane Lohitzune, May 5, 1937, NARA, Bowers Files (Files 852.00/ . . . , Boxes 3687–3701), Document 852.00/5427, 3–5.

23. *Guernica: Being the Official Report of a Commission Appointed by the National Government to Investigate the Causes of the Destruction of Guernica on April 26–28, 1937* (a.k.a. Herrán Report) (London: Eyre & Spottiswoode, 1938), 14, 16. See also Herbert R. Southworth, *Guernica, Guernica: A Study of Journalism, Diplomacy, Propaganda and History* (Berkeley: University of California Press, 1977), 356.

24. This commission was made up of Estanislao Herrán, civil engineer and member of the Commission for Public Works and Communications, as president, and the following members: José Usera, magistrate of the Court of Justice of Pamplona; Tomás Pereda, magistrate of the Court of Justice of Gasteiz; and Joaquín García, chief engineer of the Public Works of Bizkaia. *Guernica: Being the Official Report*, 1.

25. Cárdenas Rodríguez, *Datos para la reconstrucción del pueblo adoptado de Guernica*, 29–30 (see chap. 2, n. 89). See also Cárdenas Rodríguez, "La reconstrucción de Guernica" 163 (see chap. 2, n. 89); *Guernica* [booklet], 233, in FSS, ATV 6452. See also Southworth, *Guernica, Guernica*, 356; and Ministerio de Gobernación, Dirección General de Regiones Devastadas, Comisión de Vizcaya, *Reconstrucción de la villa de Guernica*, 5 (see chap. 2, n. 90).

26. *Aprobación por parte del ayuntamiento de Guernica del proyecto de la oficina técnica de la comisión de Vizcaya de Regiones Devastadas*, Gernika, February 12, 1941, 1, GBDZ, Regiones devastadas, Caja 1, Carp. 1.

27. There are 318 buildings in the town of Gernika to which the Division of Devastated Regions makes reference, represented in their plans, reports, and other materials. According to the division, 271 buildings were completely destroyed "in town," and not in the whole valley of Urdaibai.

Jesús Salas Larrazabal, based on the census of Bizkaia of 1930, included in the computation of the buildings of Gernika-Lumo (314 according to the census) the buildings in the surrounding neighborhoods, Arana, San Pedro, Zallo, and Errenteria, which represented a total of 492 buildings. Given that 271 buildings were destroyed, the author follows that 55 percent of the buildings in the "urban cluster of Guernica" were completely destroyed. Salas Larrazabal, *Guernica*, 163 (see chap. 2, n. 76). However, it should be noted that the Division of Devastated Regions made explicit reference in their project to a total of 318 buildings in Gernika. As a consequence, it is incorrect to include the buildings in the neighborhoods and surrounding areas and valleys in order to reduce the percentage of buildings completely destroyed in Gernika. As regards the neighborhood of Ajangiz of Errenteria, the Division of Devastated Regions' project for the reconstruction of Gernika is very explicit when pointing out that this neighborhood was not incorporated into Gernika until 1941, after the preparation of the reconstruction project, so it was left out of the analysis of the damage caused by the bombing.

28. Report by Consul Stevenson, Bilbao, to Ambassador Chilton, Bilbao, April 28, 1937, in *Documents on British Foreign Policy (1919–1939)*, edited by Medlicott and Douglas, 696–98.

29. As indicated, Salas increased the buildings in Gernika-Lumo to 492, and he further adds those in the neighborhood of Errenteria, then concludes that between 55 to 63.9 percent of the buildings were completely destroyed. However, Salas makes reference to 71 percent of the buildings as completely destroyed, in line with the Herrán Report of 1938. Salas Larrazabal, *Guernica*, 163.

30. Cárdenas Rodríguez, *Datos para la reconstrucción del pueblo adoptado de Guernica*, 29–30 (see chap. 2, n. 89).

31. The document refers to 11,940.791 pesetas (12,000). Southworth guessed, as I do, that this is a mistake and that it should say 11,940,791 pesetas (12 million), which coincides with the number that Gonzalo Cardenas himself gave in 1940. In 1941 11,940,791 pesetas amounted to approximately US$1 million. Dirección General de Regiones Devastadas y Reparaciones, Comisión de Vizcaya, *Ayuntamiento adoptado de Guernica: Relación de edificios de carácter público destruidos por acción de guerra, formulada en cumplimiento de la orden de 7 de octubre de 1939, año de la victoria* (Gernika and Bilbao: n.p., November 1939), 30.

32. Letter from Wolfram von Richthofen to Kindelán, Burgos, August 9 1937, at the Archive of the Documentation Center of the Gernika Peace Museum. A copy of part of the report was also reproduced in Villa, *Gernika bonbardaketa/El bombardeo*, 93 (see chap. 2, n. 82).

33. Salas Larrazábal, *Guernica*, 189 and annex 30.

34. Ibid., 158.

35. Statement by von Beust in 1955, in Maier, *Guernica: La intervención alemana en España*, 191 (see chap. 1, n. 146).

36. Steer, *Tree of Gernika*, chap. 20 (see chap. 1, n. 77).

37. Luis M. Jiménez de Aberasturi and Juan C. Jiménez de Aberasturi, *La guerra en Euskadi* (Donostia: Txertoa, 2007), 68. See also Talón, *El holocausto de Guernica*, 40 (see chap. 2, n. 76).

38. Castor Uriarte dissents. He writes that the Loiola Battalion was at the Mercedarias' Convent in Errenteria (Axangiz). Uriarte, *Bombas y mentiras sobre Guernica*, 170 (see chap. 1, n. 27).

39. Uriarte gives the names of the doctors, assistants, and nurses working at the war hospital in the Carmelitas' convent. Ibid., 160.

40. For the exact location of the battalions and hospitals, I have consulted José M. Aguirre et al., *Historia General de la Guerra Civil en Euskadi* (Bilbao: Naroki SA and Luis Haranburu, 1979), 165–215.

41. Richthofen, war diary, April 26, 1937, ADCGPM. See also Maier, *Guernica: La intervención alemana en España*, 121.

42. The distance between Arta and Gernika is about fourteen miles.

43. Richthofen, war diary, April 26, 1937, ADCGPM. See also Maier, *Guernica: La intervención alemana en España*, 121.

44. Reports by von Richthofen, Jaenecke, Meise, and Knauer, and statements by von Beust and von Knauer, in Maier, *Guernica: La intervención alemana en España*, 179–95.

45. Report by Henning von Beust, March 16, 1973, in ibid., 191.

46. Interview with Pete C. Cenarrusa, Boise, Idaho, Monday, April 18, 2010. The Condor Legion had Henschel 123s and Junker Ju87s known as Stukas (an abbreviation of *Sturzkampfflugzeug—dive-bomber* in German).

47. Pinna, *Relazioni del General Pinna*, Salamanca, April 17, 1937, 30, annex 1.

48. Mando Truppe Volontaire N. 327, May 1, 1937, Archivio Ufficio Storico, Aeronautica Militare, Busta 76, Fascicolo 14.

49. For instance, on May 22, 1940, near Cambrai, a unit of He123s attacked with great success a company of forty French tanks in motion, making direct hits on several of them and forcing the withdrawal of the company.

50. Interviews with Cenarrusa, April 18 and November 11, 2010.

51. The three interviews took place in Boise, Idaho, on November 8, 9, and 10, 2010.

52. Xabier Irujo, *On Basque Politics: Conversations with Pete Cenarrusa* (Brussels: EURI, 2011), 138.

53. Interview with Cenarrusa, April 18, 2010. Cenarrusa, head of the education department of the training squadron, served in Corpus Christi, Texas, as a flying instructor during World War II and later became a member of a US Marine dive-bomber squadron stationed at Cherry Point, North Carolina.

54. Ibid., April 18 and November 11, 2010.

55. By the 1960s, Francoist historiography recognized the reality of the bombing, although it stressed that General Franco had no direct involvement in the events and made the Condor Legion accountable for the attack, claims that later gave rise to lively debate.

56. Kössinger, interviewed by Marc Bassets for the Catalan newspaper *La Vanguardia*, also said that the pilots knew what they were doing, that the information was restricted, and that they were deceived by their government. *La Vanguardia*, April 24, 2008. As stated in the diary of Sergeant Romeo, the Italian command ordered the pilots of reconnaissance planes to photograph Gernika in the days following the attack, in this case April 29, the day the rebel troops took the town (Diario Storico 3 2 Squadra, Romeo Archivio Ufficio Storico, Aeronautica Militare, Busta 62, Fascicolo s/n, Archive of the Documentation Center of the Gernika Peace Museum). Specifically, as is clear from the record of squadron Flight 25, they flew on April 29 on two separate sorties to Gernika. Ro.37 captain Arthur Martori (commander of the 5th Fighter Squadron), along with M. D. Recchi and Angelo Ricci, took off at 1:30, Martori and Recchi landing ninety minutes later, at 3:00, and Ricci ten minutes later, after a hundred minutes of flight. Similarly, on May 5, six Ro.37s piloted by Mariani, Costanzi, Trance, Del Frate, D'Angelo, and Panizzutti came with

orders to photograph Gernika and Bermeo at 8:55, returning at 10:35, after one hundred minutes of flight (D.S. Spagna, vol. 8, C.S. 3/2, 25 Squadriglia C.T.).

57. *La Vanguardia*, April 24, 2008. Kössinger was also interviewed by the History Channel.

58. Letter written by Hans Henning von Beust, March 16, 1973, in Maier, *Guernica: La intervención alemana en España*, 156.

59. Salas Larrazábal, *Guernica*, 158.

60. Villa, *Gernika bonbardaketa/El bombardeo*, 94.

61. Robert Jackson, *Aerial Combat: The World's Great Air Battles* (London: Weidenfeld and Nicolson, 1976), 54.

62. Velardi, Promemoria per S. E. Il Sottosecretario de Stato, Gasteiz-Vitoria, April 27, 1937, 5, Archivio Ufficio Storico, Aeronautica Militare, Busta 76, Fascicolo 11.

63. *Ibaizabal* means "wide river" in Basque. The river occupies an area of approximately 416 square kilometers along 43 miles before its confluence with the river Nervión and has an average flow of 3,430 cubic feet per second. By contrast, the Oka River, a beautiful watercourse that is part of the Urdaibai Biosphere Reserve, is 10.5 miles long and has a flow of 127 feet per second.

64. Pinna, *Relazioni del General Pinna*, Salamanca, April 17, 1937, 16.

65. Maier, *Guernica: La intervención alemana en España*, 132.

66. Velardi, Promemoria per S. E. Il Sottosecretario de Stato, Gasteiz-Vitoria, May 6, 1937, 2, Archivio Ufficio Storico, Aeronautica Militare, Busta 76, Fascicolo 14.

67. Velardi, Promemoria per S. E. Il Sottosegretario di Stato, Gasteiz-Vitoria, April 23, 1937, 5, Ministero dell'Aeronautica, Prot. M.2325.

68. Pinna, *Relazioni del General Pinna*, Salamanca, April 17, 1937, 18.

69. "Dopo aver affermato che la pressa di Bilbao si presentava difficile e durissima salvo che non si fosse prodotto il collasso morale delle troppe." *Oggetto: Offensiva su Bilbao*, Ministero dell'Aeronautica, Leg. 97.

70. Velardi, Promemoria per S. E. Il Sottosegretario di Stato, 6, Ministero dell'Aeronautica, Prot. M.2325.

71. Raffaelli, *Bombardamento: Quistionario*, 3 (see chap. 3, n. 35).

72. Ibid., 7.

73. Maurer, *U.S. Air Service in World War I*, 4:420 (see chap. 2, n. 112). See also the debate in the House of Commons of March 29, 1923, on this concrete point, HC Deb, March 20, 1923, vol. 161, cc2399–471.

74. Corrado Corradino, *Bombardamento: Quistionario*, 5.

75. Ibid.

76. Pinna, *Relazioni del General Pinna*, Salamanca, April 17, 1937, 5.

77. Ibid., 6.

78. Ibid., 16.

79. Ibid., 10–11.

80. Ibid., 17.

81. Report by Consul Chapman, Bilbao, to Secretary of State Hull, Bilbao, March

31, 1937, NARA, US Department of State Files 1930–1939 (Files 852.00/ . . . , Boxes 6386 to 6407), Document 852.00/5149.

82. Operazioni Fronte Nord: Informe del General Doria (Bastico) al conde Galeazzo Ciano, May 3, 1937, AMAE, Gabinetto del Ministro (1923–1943), Busta 1 (Uffizio Spagna no. 1244), 1–10.

83. Report by Consul Chapman, Bilbao, to Secretary of State Hull, Bilbao, March 31, 1937, NARA, US Department of State Files 1930–1939 (Files 852.00/ . . . , Boxes 6386 to 6407), Document 852.00/5149.

84. *Comunicato* (Rome), April 26, 1937, USSME, F. 18.

85. *Proposte per la resa di Bilbao*, Report by General Doria (Bastico) to Count Galeazzo Ciano, April 27, 1937, AMAE, Gabinetto del Ministro (1923–1943), Busta 7 (Uffizio Spagna Leg. 44, no. 1250).

86. Telegram from Ambassador Bullitt, Paris, to Secretary of State Hull, Paris, April 30, 1937, NARA, US Department of State Files 1930–1939 (Files 852.00/ . . . , Boxes 6386 to 6407), Document 852.00/5280.

87. "General Mola Takes Two Cities on Drive to Bilbao," *Circleville (Ohio) Herald*, April 26, 1937, 7.

88. Telegram from Ambassador Bowers to Secretary of State Hull, Donibane Lohitzune, April 30, 1937, NARA, US Department of State Files 1930–1939 (Files 852.00/ . . . , Boxes 6386 to 6407), Document 852.00/5276. On a radio broadcast, General Franco urged the Basque government to surrender in order to save the rich industrial area of Bizkaia from destruction. Report 6.531 by Colonel Stephen O. Fuqua, Valencia, April 26, 1937, NARA, RG 165, Records of the Military Intelligence Division Relating to Conditions in Spain (1918–1941), Microfilm Publication MI.1445, R. 7.

89. Report from Ambassador Bowers, Donibane Lohitzune, to Secretary of State Hull, Donibane Lohitzune, May 5, 1937, NARA, US Department of State Files 1930–1939 (Files 852.00/ . . . , Boxes 6386 to 6407), Document 852.00/5427. The day after the bombing of Gernika, Mola announced the destruction of Bilbao if the Basque troops did not surrender. "Le général Mola annonce la destruction de Bilbao," *Ce Soir* (París), April 29, 1937, 23. This was not the first time Mola had threatened destruction. His ultimatum demanding the unconditional surrender of Basque troops before midnight on September 25, 1936, with the threat of an attack by land, sea, and air, was never answered by the Basque government. Memorandum by Colonel F. H. Lincoln to the chief of staff, September 25, 1936, NARA, RG 165, Records of the Military Intelligence Division Relating to Conditions in Spain (1918–1941), Microfilm Publication MI.1445, R. 7. See also "Mola, el testaferro de Hitler en las Vascongadas, dice que arrasará Bilbao, porque es preciso destruir la capital de un pueblo pervertido, que se atreve a hacer frente a los nacionalistas," *Adelante*, Wednesday, May 5, 1937, 4; and "Menace du general Mola," *Populaire*, Thursday, April 29, 1937, 1 ("Nous raseront Bilbao et son emplacement un et désolé ôtera l'envie aux anglais de soutenir contre notre volonté les bolcheviks basques").

90. Report from Colonel Stephen O. Fuqua, Military Attaché of the US Embassy in Donibane Lohitzune, to Secretary of State Hull, Donibane Lohitzune, April 28,

1937, NARA, US Department of State Files 1930–1939 (Files 852.00/ . . . , Boxes 6386 to 6407), Document 852.00/5325.

91. Letter from Cardinal Isidro Gomá to Alberto Onaindia, May 5, 1937; Paul Preston, *El holocausto español* (n.p.: Random House Mondadori, 2011); Paul Preston, *La muerte de Guernica* (n.p.: Random House Mondadori, 2011), 573. See also José Andrés-Gallego and Antonio M. Pazos, eds., *Documentos de la guerra civil. 5: Abril–Mayo de 1937* (Madrid: CESIC, 2003), 357. As stated by Peter Elstrob, Adolf Galland was lying when he said on July 10, 1970, during a reception with the Royal Air Force that the adventure of the Legion Condor produced no valid strategic experience; he failed to mention the strategy of intensive bombing of defenseless cities to achieve the demand of submission, at any price. Peter Elstrob, *Condor Legion* (New York: Ballantine Books, 1973), 153.

92. Report 6.547 by Captain Townsend Griffiss and Colonel Stephen O. Fuqua, Valencia, May 11, 1937, RG 165, Records of the Military Intelligence Division Relating to Conditions in Spain (1918–1941), NARA, Microfilm Publication MI.1445, R. 7.

93. The complete title of the report is *Guernica: Being the Official Report of a Commission Appointed by the National Government to Investigate the Causes of the Destruction of Guernica on April 26–28, 1937.*

94. Address by the vice president of the Basque government and minister of justice and culture, Jesus Maria Leizaola, Radio Euzkadi, Bilbao, May 4, 1937.

95. *Registry of the Victims of the Rebel Aviation in the Raids of April 1937 in the Basque Country*, Euskadiko Dokumentu Ondarearen Zentroa Centro de Patrimonio Documental de Euskadi, Doc. GE-0037-03.

96. Telesforo Monzon and his wife, Maria Josefa, Francisco Arregui, and Anton Irala arrived in Gernika at about 10:20 P.M. on April 26, about three hours after the bombing ended (Jose Labauria, La Roseraie, April 2, 1938, in *La guerra civil en Euzkadi*, edited by Gamboa and Larronde, 604 (see chap. 1, n. 29).

97. "The Massacre of Guernica: Four Nurses' Evidence," *Manchester Guardian*, May 28, 1937. See also *Euzko Deya* (Paris), May 27, 1937, 2; Southworth, *Guernica, Guernica*, 359; and Gamboa and Larronde, *La guerra civil en Euzkadi*, 319.

98. Gamboa and Larronde, *La guerra civil en Euzkadi*, 319.

99. Pedro Basaldúa, *En defensa de la verdad* (Buenos Aires: Ekin, 1956), 114.

100. "Pope to Hear Guernica Story," *Daily Herald* (London), April 30, 1937, 2. See also "Appeal to the Pope," *Daily Express* (London), April 30, 1937, 2. Txomin Onaindia, Alberto's brother, also declared to Smallwood in 1972 that he calculated the death toll to be between eight hundred and one thousand. Smallwood interview with Alberto Onaindia, Paris, 1972, WSA, File Gernika, E. Txomin & Alberto Onaindia, 1972.

101. Report by Ambassador Bowers to Secretary of State Hull, Donibane Lohitzune, May 5, 1937, NARA, Bowers Files (Files 852.00/ . . . , Boxes 3687–3701), Document 852.00/5427, 5–6.

102. According to his testimony on April 2, 1938, Labauria stayed in Gernika until April 29, the morning when Gernika was occupied by the rebels. Gamboa and Larronde, *La guerra civil en Euzkadi*, 604.

103. Message by Jose Labauria and Eusebio Arronategi, Radio Euzkadi, Bilbao, May 4, 1937, in *Guernica: To Civilized Mankind* (see chap. 3, n. 39). See also Atxaga, *De Gernika a Guernica* (see chap. 2, n. 106).

104. Testimony at La Roseraie Hospital, April 2, 1938, in *La guerra civil en Euzkadi*, edited by Gamboa and Larronde, 604.

105. "Heroísmo y Dolor de Euzkadi," *Ayuda*, May 16, 1937, 4–5.

106. George Steer, "The Tragedy of Guernica: Town Destroyed in Air Attack," *Times* (London), April 28, 1937, 17; "Historic Basque Town Wiped Out: Rebel Fliers Machine-Gun Civilians," *New York Times*, April 28, 1937, 1.

107. "German Airmen Atrocity Shocks World," *Daily Herald* (London), April 28, 1937, 1–2.

108. "800 Victimes a Quirnica," *Ce Soir* (París), April 27, 1937, 1, 5; Mathieu Corman, *Ce Soir*, April 28, 1937; Mathieu Corman, "Dans les ruines de Guernica," *Ce Soir*, April 29, 1937, 1, 3; "A travers les ruines de Guernica," *Ce Soir*, April 30, 1937, 1, 3.

109. "Dans Guernica en flammes: Le récit d'un témoin oculaire," *Ce Soir* (París), May 1, 1937, 3.

110. "El 'Yo Acuso' de un periodista inglés: Puedo jurar que los aviadores alemanes de Franco bombardearon Guernica; yo digo al mundo lo que vi," *Tierra Vasca*, May 18, 1937, 1; "Puedo jurar que los aviadores alemanes de Franco bombardearon Guernica: Yo digo al mundo lo que vi," *La Tarde*, May 18, 1937, 3.

111. "I Saw the German Planes Bomb Guernica," *Daily Express* (London), May 1, 1937, 10. See also *Foreign Wings over the Basque Country*, 41 (see chap. 2, n. 66).

112. Keith S. Watson, "They Murdered Hundreds in Guernica," *Daily Worker*, April 28, 1937, 1. See also "La mayor atrocidad del siglo," *El Liberal*, April 30, 1937, last page.

113. "Les massacres des populations, des femmes et d'enfants dans les ruines de Gernica," *Ce Soir* (París), April 30, 1937, 3.

114. Published by the *Times* (London) on June 11. See also *Foreign Wings over the Basque Country*, 51; and *El clero vasco, fiel al Gobierno de la República, se dirige al Sumo Pontífice, para hacer constar que la vandálica destrucción de Durango y Guernica se debió exclusivamente a la acción de los aviones alemanes* (Madrid and Valencia: Ediciones Españolas, May 11, 1937).

115. As mentioned by Joxe Migel Barandiaran, who interviewed Mentxaka, Pedro Mentxaka and Agustín Isusi were received in Rome thanks to Bishop Mateo Mugica under two conditions—that it was not known that they were being received and that they did not discuss the bombing.

116. I have already included the testimony of Father Arronategi, who testified on Radio Euzkadi on May 4, 1937, so I need include in this group only the nine remaining witnesses of the bombing. The letter was signed by the following priests: Vicar General Ramon Galbarriatu, Pedro Mentxaka, Augustín Isusi, Enrique Ledesma, José María Markoartu, Jose Elordi, Fortunato Unzeta, Felipe Gastañatorre, Getulio Aranzabal, Alejandro Etxebarria, Jesus Orbe, Manuel Madariaga, coadjutor of Gernika Eusebio Arronategi, archpriest of Durango Francisco Abaitua, Pedro Atutxa, coadjutor of Murelaga Dionisio Oararteta, coadjutor of Abarzegi Parca-

sio Etxezarraga, coadjutor of Gerrikaitz Eugenio Aranaz, coadjutor of Berriatua Matias Uribe, coadjutor of Santa Ana Juan Mendibe, coadjutor of Larrauri Jose Maria Oararteta, coadjutor of Markina Jose Antonio Oararteta (the last ten were eyewitnesses of the bombing).

117. Testimony reproduced by Hilari Raguer from the unpublished memoirs of Aita Patxi, "En Euzkadi: Mi odisea pasionista," 223, in *Aita Patxi: Prisionero con los gudaris*, by Hilari Raguer (Barcelona: Claret, 2006), 117. See also José Ignacio Lopategui, *Aita Patxi: Testimonio. 1a parte: En la guerra (1937–1939)* (Bilbao: n.p., 1978), 63.

118. Report by Consul Stevenson, Bilbao, to Ambassador Chilton, Bilbao, April 28, 1937, in *Documents on British Foreign Policy (1919–1939)*, edited by Medlicott and Douglas, 696–98.

119. "They Murdered Hundreds in Guernica," *Daily Worker*, April 28, 1937, 1; "Fascist Airmen Had Planned in Detail the Murder of the Innocents in Tragic Guernica," *Daily Worker*, April 28, 1937, 3; "He Was 'over Guernica': Nazi Pilot Proves German Intervention," *Daily Worker*, May 14, 1937, 1.

120. "Emocionante relato de un testigo," ABC, May 13, 1937, 9. See also "Des témoins du bombardement," *La Croix*, May 1, 1937, 2; "Le massacre de Guernica soulève l'indignation générale," *Le Petit Journal*, April 30, 1937, 3; and "Los aviones ametrallaban a las mujeres y niños que huían del incendio, dice la testigo presencial Maria Goitia," *Adelante*, May 5, 1937, 4.

121. "Los aviones ametrallaban,"4.

122. Gamboa and Larronde, *La guerra civil en Euzkadi*, 174.

123. "Le marty de Guernika," *Journal des Nations*, November 26, 1937. This article was also published in *Diario de Madrid* on November 11, 1937.

124. Stefanie Schüler-Springorum, "El mito de Guernica: Proyección, propaganda, política," *Historia del presente* 14 (2009): 133.

125. Maier, *Guernica: La intervención alemana en España*, 139. Francoists were considered to be the white pilots and their opponents the reds, or communists.

126. "El consejero de educación, Don Alfredo Espinosa, pronuncia una vibrante alocución," *El Liberal*, April 30, 1937, last page.

127. "Guernica, ville cobaye," *L'Humanité*, May 12, 1937, 1; "Experiencia bárbara del estado mayor alemán," *El Diario Montañés*, May 14, 1937, 1.

128. "Guernica, ville cobaye," 1.

129. Smallwood interview with Kaxtor Amunarriz, 1972, WSA, File Gernika, E. Kaxtor Amunarriz, 1972. See also Smallwood interview with Xabier Alkorta, 1972, WSA, File Gernika, E. Xabier Alkorta, 1972.

130. Smallwood interview with Jose Ramon Urtiaga, 1972, WSA, File Gernika, E. Jose Ramon Urtiaga, 1972. Urtiaga, who lived in Gernika until he was nine, when he was sent to the college of the Augustinians of the village to learn Spanish, testified that he saw between twenty and thirty bodies in the river, between Arteaga and Forua, most of them women and children.

131. Smallwood interview with Maria Fe Ormaetxea, 1972, WSA, File Gernika, E. Maria Fe Ormaetxea, 1972.

132. Smallwood interview with Julio Gorria (pseudonym), 1972, WSA, File Gernika, E. Julio Gorria, 1972.

133. Elosegi, *Quiero morir por algo*, 137 (see chap. 2, n. 35).

134. Smallwood interview with Jose Arrieta (pseudonym), París 1972, WSA, File Gernika, E. Jose Arrieta, 1972.

135. Gamboa and Larronde, *La guerra civil en Euzkadi*, 558.

136. Such is the case, among others, of Sebastian Uria, Federico Iraeta, Francisca Arriaga, Carmen Zabaljauregi, Andresa Idoiaga, Andresa Zumeta, Uxua Makazaga, Maria Angeles Basabe, Antonio Uriguen, and many eyewitnesses of the events, such as Miren Begoña Urrutikoetxea, Mari Carmen Egurrola, and Kontxi Martija, whom I have interviewed.

137. "J'ai vu brûler Guernica," *Ce Soir* (París), May 7, 1937, 3.

138. Cloud and Ellis, *Basque Children in England*, 56–57 (see chap. 2, n. 106). In regards to Imanol A.'s identity, see ASV, no. 975, Fasc. 3, Listado de niños refugiados en Inglaterra—Reclamaciones, GBDZ, 0009/001/46, ARC-00346.

139. Jean Armengaud, "Les Leçons de la Guerre d'Espagne," *Revue des Deux Mondes*, August 15, 1937, 767.

140. "Pour le peuple basque," *L'Aube*, May 8, 1937, 1. The article was signed by François Mauriac, André Belliver, Charles Du Bos, Stanislas Fumel, Francisque Gay, Georges Bidault, Hélène Iswolski, Georges Hoog, Olivier Lacombe, Maurice Lacroix, Jacques Madaule, Gabriel Marcel, Jacques Maritain, Emmanuel Mounier, Jean de Pange, Domenico Russo, Schoezer Boris, Pierre van der Meer of Walcheren, Maurice Merleau-Ponty, Martin Moré, Claude Bourdet, Claude Leblond, Paul Vignaux, and a group of twenty-eight students at the Ecole Normale Supérieure.

141. *Foreign Wings over the Basque Country*, 43.

142. "Una carta sobre la destrucción de Guernica," *La Vanguardia*, May 16, 1937, 8.

143. Southworth, *Guernica, Guernica*, 19.

144. Smallwood with Andresa Zumeta, 1972, WSA, File Gernika, E. Andresa Zumeta, 1972. See also testimony of Andresa Zumeta, in Smallwood, "The Day Gernika Was Bombed," 124 (manuscript in the author's possession, 1972); testimony of Andresa Idoiaga, in ibid., 123; Francisco M. Vargas Alonso, "El Partido Nacionalista Vasco en Guerra: Euzko Gudarostea (1936–1937)," *Vasconia* 31 (2001): 307; Archivo Histórico Nacional–Sección Guerra Civil de Salamanca (AHN-SGC), PS (Político-Social) Bilbao, Leg. 122, Expte. 8.

145. Entrevista de William Smallwood a Margarita Lauzirika, 1972, WSA, File Gernika, E. Margarita Lauzirika, 1972.

146. Smallwood interview with Manuela Garai, 1972, WSA, File Gernika, E. Manuela Garai, 1972.

147. Ministerio de Gobernación, Dirección General de Regiones Devastadas, Comisión de Vizcaya, *Desescombro de Guernica*, Bilbao, December 24, 1941, 1, GBDZ, Regiones devastadas, Caja 3, Carp. 1. Ver asimismo, Ángel B. Puente, *Reconstrucción de Guernica, Munguía, Maruri, Gatica, Bilbao* (1941), 19, FSS, ATV 6453.

148. Interview with Joxe Iturria, Lesaka, Navarre, May 17 and 21, 2013.

149. *Guernica: Being the Official Report*, iv–v.

150. Adolf Galland, *The First and the Last: The German Fighter Force in World War II* (London: Methuen, 1955), 26.

151. "El mito de Guernica, donde no murieron ni siquiera una docena," in Pedro Pascual, "La Guerra del 36, su historia y su circunstancia," *Arriba* (Madrid), January 31, 1970. See also Southworth, *Guernica, Guernica*, 363. Elsewhere, de la Cierva stated that "the number of deaths might have been high, about one hundred, but it did not reached the fantastic propaganda figures that mention thousands." Ricardo de la Cierva, "La polémica y la verdad sobre Guernica," *España, 1930–1936: La historia se confiesa* (Barcelona), no. 45 (December 1976): 297. See also Ricardo de la Cierva, "Guernica: Los documentos contra el mit," in *Nueva y definitiva historia de la guerra civil* (Madrid: DINPE, 1986); Ricardo de la Cierva, "La polémica y la verdad sobre Guernica," 281–99.

152. Crozier would repeat that figure thirteen years later in the Spanish version of his work. Brian Crozier, *Franco: Crepúsculo de un hombre* (Barcelona: Planeta, 1980), 172.

153. Uriarte, *Bombas y mentiras sobre Guernica*, 82, 138.

154. Smallwood interview with Castor Uriarte at his house in Labastida, June 6, 1972, WSA, File Gernika, E. Castor Uriarte, 1972.

155. Salas Larrazábal, *Guernica*, 166. See also 36–37, 163–67, 308–12. But this is not the only time Salas calculated a low death toll. He claimed 80 deaths during the bombing of Durango, in *Guernica: El bombardeo* (Madrid: Galland, 1981). In the 1987 edition, this figure was increased to 99. Salas Larrazábal, *Guernica*, 206–8. Today, the number of victims of the bombing of Durango is estimated at 336 people, 276 identified and 60 unidentified. Jon Irazabal, *1937 martxoak 31, Durango, 31 de marzo de 1937: Estudio sobre el bombardeo aéreo realizado contra la Villa de Durango el 31 de marzo de 1937* (Durango: Geredíaga Elkartea, 2001), 97–102.

156. He described the Errenteria as a railroad bridge. Rolf-Dieter Müller, *La muerte caída del cielo: Historia de los bombardeos durante la Segunda Guerra Mundial* (Barcelona: Destino, 2008), 50–55. The original German edition was published in 2004.

157. Ibid., 54.

158. Corum, *Wolfram von Richthofen*, 21 (see chap. 1, n. 98).

159. Unzueta, *Gernikako bonbaketa: Hildakoak, 1937-4-26*, 1–64 (see chap. 2, n. 88).

160. Smallwood, "The Day Gernika Was Bombed," 124; testimony of Andresa Idoiaga, in ibid., 66.

161. Vargas Alonso, "El Partido Nacionalista Vasco en Guerra."

162. Unzueta, *Gernikako bonbaketa, Hildakoak, 1937-4-26*.

163. Smallwood interview with Sabin Apraiz, 1972, WSA, File Gernika, E. Sabin Apraiz, 1972. Andresa Zumeta also saw the corpses of the Garteiz sisters and the bodies of Juanita Beotegi and Leandro Ormaetxebarria's wife among the people lying in rows near the cemetery. Smallwood interview with Andresa Zumeta, 1972, WSA, File Gernika, E. Andresa Zumeta, 1972.

164. Smallwood interview with Zumeta. See also testimony of Andresa Zumeta, in Smallwood, "The Day Gernika Was Bombed," 124; and testimony of Andresa Idoiaga in ibid., 123. There is a precedent for these mass graves, the bombing of Durango. As noted in the registry of fatalities of the Basque government entitled *Durango, 1937*, the Basque authorities recorded that 84 of the first 127 corpses recovered were buried in the Santa Cruz Cemetery in town, in two mass graves. The remaining 43 bodies were buried in the graves and tombs of their relatives, since they were identified. The reason for burying the victims so quickly was essentially epidemic control.

165. Address by Minister of Justice and Culture of the Basque Government Jesús María Leizaola, Radio Euzkadi, Bilbao, May 4, 1937.

166. Declaration of Hans H. von Beust, March 16, 1973, in *Guernica: La intervención alemana en España*, by Maier, 192.

167. Interview of Marc Bassets for *La Vanguardia* and the History Channel, in Marc Bassets, "Maldigo las guerras," *La Vanguardia*, April 26, 2007, 20.

168. Ibid.

169. Testimony of Pedro Agirre, in Smallwood, "The Day Gernika Was Bombed," 124.

170. Testimony of Andresa Zumeta, in ibid., 124; testimony of Andresa Idoiaga, in ibid., 123.

171. *Expediente de reparación del camión regadora* BI-2883 (Bilbao: n.p., 1938), Bizkaiko Foru Aldundiko Ondare Historikoaren Foru Agiritegia / Archivo Histórico de la Diputación Foral de Bizkaia (Bilbao, Basque Country), Administrativo J-02416/011, 3.

172. There is not to this day an official record, beyond the list of 3 victims at Basurto mentioned by Salas. Salas Larrazábal, *Guernica*, 165–66.

173. Unzueta, *Gernikako bonbaketa, Hildakoak, 1937-4-26*, 22.

174. Ibid.

175. José Ángel Echániz and Vicente del Palacio, "Los muertos del bombardeo," *El Correo*, April 25, 2004. Gonzalo Cárdenas estimated that Gernika had 6,000 inhabitants in 1937, and the memory for the reconstruction of Gernika stated that Gernika had 5,075 inhabitants in 1930 and 6,234 in 1936. Cárdenas Rodríguez, *Datos para la reconstrucción del pueblo adoptado de Guernica*, 21 (see chap. 2, n. 89). See also Cárdenas Rodríguez, "La reconstrucción de Guernica," 16; Ministerio de Gobernación, Dirección General de Regiones Devastadas, Comisión de Vizcaya, *Reconstrucción de la villa de Guernica*, 3.

176. Unzueta, *Gernikako bonbaketa, Hildakoak, 1937-4-26*, 10.

177. Dirección General de Regiones Devastadas y Reparaciones, Comisión de Vizcaya, *Ayuntamiento adoptado de Guernica*, 28.

178. Unzueta, *Gernikako bonbaketa, Hildakoak, 1937-4-26*, 10.

179. Major Pacinotti reported at 6:30 P.M. to the Italian High Command that Gernika had been occupied at exactly 12:30 P.M. *Giorno 29 aprile 1937*, USSME, F. 7, Diario Storico, CTV Ufficio Generale Mancini dal 27 aprile al 20 maggio 1937.

180. *Guernica: Being the Official Report*, 24. Testimony reproduced in Salas Larrazábal, *Guernica*, 196.

181. Salas did not translate properly the English version of the Herrán Report into Spanish and quoted "en un refugio sin terminar se encontraron 45 muertos" (Salas Larrazabal, *Guernica*, 196). In other words, the author translated "unnamed" as "unfinished." The fact is that the Andra Mari refuge is the main and biggest unfinished refuge in Gernika, and many authors, following Salas, have concluded from this translation that 45 people died in that refuge. The number has thereafter been repeated by several authors.

182. According to the Herrán Report, Andra Mari Street was 12 feet wide, that is, 3.65 meters. *Guernica: Being the Official Report*, 6. This figure, which I have taken as good with reservations, is not very credible if we consider that the new street of Andra Mari projected in 1941 had a width of 6 meters, that is, 24 feet. Ministerio de Gobernación, Dirección General de Regiones Devastadas, Comisión de Vizcaya, *Reconstrucción de la villa de Guernica*, 13.

183. Testimony of Castor Uriarte, in Smallwood, "The Day Gernika Was Bombed," 6.

184. Testimony of Sebastián Uria, in ibid., 55.

185. Smallwood interview with Juan Ibai, 1972, WSA, File Gernika, E. Juan Ibai, 1972.

186. Smallwood interview with Uxua Makazaga, 1972, WSA, File Gernika, E. Uxua Makazaga, 1972.

187. Jose Labauria, La Roseraie, April 2, 1938, in *La guerra civil en Euzkadi*, edited by Gamboa and Larronde, 604.

188. According to Unzueta, Miguel Gutiérrez was also identified by Juanito Arrien as one of the victims in the Andra Mari Street shelter. See Unzueta, *Gernikako bonbaketa, Hildakoak, 1937-4-26*, 52. The Herrán Report mentions 22 bodies being recovered from the Andra Mari shelter after April 26 (although we know that Felipe Bastarretxea, included in this list, did not die in the shelter). Discounting Bastarretxea, only 4 of those bodies were identified. *Guernica: Being the Official Report*, 51–54.

- May 4: Felipe Bastarrechea Albizua (he also figures in the defunct book of Andra Mari Church); Lázaro Lejarza Guezuraga ("Legarrea," natural son of "Corterubé" [Kortezubi], according to the report); and 4 unidentified corpses. However, the report explicitly states that only 4 among these 7 were found in the Andra Mari shelter on May 4.
- May 5: 7 unidentified corpses.
- May 6: Eustaquio Ubillos ("Eustaquio Lovillos," according to the report), Pantaleón Zuñiga Gomera, and 2 unidentified corpses.
- May 7: 3 unidentified corpses.
- May 8: Aurelio Learreta Bilbao (he also figures in the defunct book of Andra Mari Church), and 1 unidentified corpse.
- May 29: 1 unidentified corpse.

Total: 22 corpses (4 of them identified, without counting Bastarretxea).

Juanito Arrien testified that Miguel Gutiérrrez died in the shelter (this could be one of the unidentified bodies registered by the Herrán Report). Besides these, Salas included in the list of those killed in the shelter of Andra Mari 20 other people, "with no justification for this figure" (Salas Larrazábal, *Guernica*, 166).

189. The impact of two 551-pound bombs on both sides of the shelter was registered by Labauria, and the Herrán Report also mentioned the impact and the subsequent collapse of the facades of the adjacent buildings on top of the refuge. Salas Larrazábal, *Guernica*, 148, 159.

190. Smallwood interview with Jose Ramon Urtiaga, 1972, WSA, File Gernika, E. Jose Ramon Urtiaga, 1972. See also Entrevista de William Smallwood a Kaxtor Amunarriz, 1972, WSA, File Gernika, E. Kaxtor Amunarriz, 1972.

191. Smallwood to interview with Francisca Arriaga, 1972, WSA, File Gernika, E. Francisca Arriaga, 1972.

192. Testimony no. 50, in Smallwood, "The Day Gernika Was Bombed," 123.

193. Maria Medinabeitia, Baiona, August 30, 1937, in *La guerra civil en Euzkadi*, edited by Gamboa and Larronde, 173. Two of Maria Medinabeitia's sisters worked as nurses at the Karmele Deuna Hospital in Gernika.

194. Certainly, Sebastian Uria was one of the few wounded people whom Castor Uriarte helped rescue from the shelter. Uriarte, *Bombas y mentiras sobre Guernica*, 80.

195. Unzueta, *Gernikako bonbaketa, Hildakoak, 1937-4-26*, 35–53.

196. Southworth, *Guernica, Guernica*, 353–70.

197. Gregory H. Stanton, "Eight Stages of Genocide," http://www.genocidewatch.org/.

198. Noel Monks, "I Saw the German Planes Bomb Guernica," *Daily Express* (London), May 1, 1937, 10. See also *Foreign Wings over the Basque Country*, 41.

199. Noel Monks, *Eyewitness* (London: Frederick Muller, 1955), 92–99.

200. Monks, "I Saw the German Planes Bomb Guernica." See also *Foreign Wings over the Basque Country*, 41; and "El yo acuso de un periodista inglés," *Tierra Vasca*, May 18, 1937, 1.

201. Noel Monks, "Guernica Destroyed by German Planes, 26 April 1937," in *Eyewitness to History*, edited by John Carey (Cambridge, MA: Harvard University Press, 1987), 519–21.

202. Southworth, *Guernica, Guernica*, 353–70.

203. Hugh Thomas, *The Spanish Civil War* (London: Penguin Books, 2003), 607.

204. Preston, *Spanish Civil War*, 267–71 (see chap. 1, n. 15).

205. Michael Alpert, *A New International History of the Spanish Civil War* (New York: Palgrave Macmillan, 1998), 125–26, 129.

206. Phillip Knightley, *The First Casualty: The War Correspondent as Hero and Myth-Maker from the Crimea to Kosovo* (London: Prion Books, 2000), 220.

207. Helen Graham, *The Spanish Republic at War, 1936–1939* (Cambridge: Cambridge University Press, 2002), 308. See also Francisco J. Romero Salvadó, *The Spanish Civil War: Origins, Course and Outcomes* (New York: Palgrave Macmillan, 2005), 148.

208. Ian Patterson, *Guernica and Total War* (Cambridge, MA: Harvard University Press, 2007), 29–30.

209. *Daily Express* (London), April 29, 1937.

## 5 ■ The Aftermath of the Bombing

1. Monks, "Guernica Destroyed by German Planes, 26 April 1937," 519–21 (see chap. 4, n. 205).

2. Operazioni di Bilbao, Telegrama del general Carlo Bossi, Salamanca, April 27, 1937, AMAE, Gabinetto del Ministro (1923–1943), Busta 7 (Uffizio Spagna Leg. 44, no. 1250).

3. *Euzkadi* or *Euskadi* in modern Basque is the Basque Country.

4. The areas of Spain controlled by the National Movement.

5. Radio Salamanca, April 27, 1937.

6. Report from Consul Charles A. Bay, Seville, to the Secretary of State, Seville, May 3, 1937, NARA, Bowers Files (Files 852.00/ . . . , Boxes 3687–3701), Document 852.00/5410, 1–4.

7. Telegram from Lieutenant General Wilhelm Faupel, German Ambassador to the Spanish regime, to State Secretary Hans Georg von Mackensen, Salamanca, May 5, 1937, in *Documents on German Foreign Policy*, 281 (see chap. 1, n. 70).

8. Robert H. Whealey, "Nazi Propagandist Joseph Goebbels Looks at the Spanish Civil War," *Historian* 61, no. 2 (1999): 350.

9. Report by Joaquín Miláns del Bosch and Vicente Machimbarrena, Gasteiz, May 1, 1937, in Talón, *El holocausto de Guernica*, 299 (see chap. 2, n. 76).

10. As mentioned, Queipo de Llano had previously denied that any planes had flown that day due to the rain.

11. Dispatch no. 1267 from Ambassador to the Portuguese Regime Robert G. Caldwell to US State Department, Lisbon, May 6, 1937, NARA, Bowers Files (Files 852.00/ . . . , Boxes 3687–3701), Document 852.00/5481, 2.

12. *Guernica: Being the Official Report*, 15–16 (see chap. 4, n. 27).

13. Knightley, *First Casualty*, 224 (see chap. 4, n. 210).

14. Monks, "I Saw the German Planes Bomb Guernica" (see chap. 4, n. 202).

15. Paul Preston, *Idealistas bajo las balas: Corresponsales extranjeros en la Guerra de España* (Barcelona: Debols!llo, 2011), 19. See also the original English edition of this work: Paul Preston, *We Saw Spain Die: Foreign Correspondents in the Spanish Civil War* (London: Constable and Robinson, 2008).

16. Knightley, *First Casualty*, 225.

17. *Die Zeit*, March 22, 1991.

18. Dispatch no. 1267 from US Minister to the Portuguese Regime Robert G. Caldwell to the US State Department, Lisbon, May 6, 1937, NARA, Bowers Files (Files 852.00/ . . . , Boxes 3687–3701), Document 852.00/5481, 1.

19. Communication on Radio Euzkadi, Bilbao, April, 1937, Boise State University Library, MSS 260 Box 1 F. 5.

20. Friends of Spain, *Help Us to Defeat Fascism!* (London: n.p., n.d.), 10.

21. Telegram from Lluis Companys, president of the Catalan government, to the president of the United States, Franklin D. Roosevelt, Barcelona, April 29, 1937, NARA, Bowers Files (Files 852.00/ . . . , Boxes 3687–3701), Document 852.00/5274.

22. Report from Ambassador Bowers to Secretary of State Hull, Donibane Lohitzune, April 30, 1937, NARA, Bowers Files (Files 852.00/ . . . , Boxes 3687–3701), Document 852.00/5276.

23. Report from Ambassador Bowers to Secretary of State Hull, Donibane Lohitzune, May 5, 1937, NARA, Bowers Files (Files 852.00/ . . . , Boxes 3687–3701), Document 852.00/5427, 3–5.

24. Letter from Florencio Laucirica, president of the Basque American Benevolent Association, Inc., to Secretary of State Hull, New York, April 29, 1937, NARA, Bowers Files (Files 852.00/ . . . , Boxes 3687–3701), Document 5266.

25. Telegram from Ambassador Bullitt to US State Department, Paris, April 30, 1937, NARA, Bowers Files (Files 852.00/ . . . , Boxes 3687–3701), Document 852.00/5280.

26. Application by Dean Dryscoll to the Secretary of State, Boise, Idaho, December 18, 1937, NARA, Bowers Files (Files 852.48/ . . .), Document 852.48/Relief-Regis, Basque Sheepherders' Overall Dance Association/1.

27. The Basque spelling of this name would be John Atxabal.

28. Subtracting expenses for the transfer of the funds ($262), the Red Cross received a total of $1,104 for the relief of Basque refugee children.

29. Letter from the Committee for the Aid of the Basque Refugee Children in France to the US State Department, Washington, DC, November 1, 1937, NARA, Bowers Files (Files 852.48/ . . .), Document 852.48/Relief-Regis, Committee for the Aid of the Basque Refugee Children in France/1.

30. For the American press, see Xabier Irujo, "The Impact of the Bombing of Gernika in the North American Press," in *War, Exile, Justice, and Everyday Life, 1936–1946*, edited by Sandra Ott (Reno: Center for Basque Studies, University of Nevada, 2011), 33–57.

31. Christopher Holme's chronicle of the event for Reuters was printed in the *News Chronicle*, the *Evening News*, and the *Evening Standard*. The *Star* also printed the article but said that Holme was in Gernika at the time of the attack, which was not accurate.

32. *Foreign Wings over the Basque Country* 12 (see chap. 2, n. 66); NARA, Bowers Files (Files 852.48/ . . .), Document 852.6552.

33. Ibid.

34. Chronicles by George L. Steer.

35. Chronicle by Watson.

36. Chronicles by Noel Monks.

37. Chronicle by Elizabeth Wilkinson.

38. Articles in the *News Chronicle*, the *Evening News*, and the *Evening Standard* were written by Christopher Holme (Reuters). Holme was having dinner with George L. Steer and other international correspondents when Anton Irala, a member of the Basque government, told them of the event.

39. The *Daily Herald* headlined its article "German Airmen Atrocity Shocks World."

40. The *Morning Post* and the *Daily Mail*, which both tacitly supported the military uprising, did not deny that the bombing was executed by General Emilio Mola's air force.

41. *La Croix* was the main daily of the Catholic Church in France.

42. "1,280 Are Reported Killed Along Two Spanish Fronts," *Charleston (SC) Gazette*, April 28, 1937, 1, 9.

43. Irujo, "Impact of the Bombing of Gernika," 33–57. The survey was done by using newspaper databases such as Access Newspaper Archive, Times Digital Archive, ProQuest Historical Newspapers, LexisNexis Congressional, and other secondary files.

44. This article was written by George L. Steer.

45. The list is too long to reproduce, but it includes most of the well-known newspapers, such as the *Washington Post* and the *New York Herald Tribune*.

46. The Canadian press also reported the event, and newspapers such as the *Montreal Daily Star*, the *Toronto Daily Star*, and *La Presse* emphasized that Mola's air force was responsible for the attack.

47. Cloud and Ellis, *Basque Children in England*, 58 (see chap. 2, n. 106).

48. Telegram from Sir George Ogilvie-Forbes, Counselor at the British Embassy in Berlin, to Foreign Secretary Anthony Eden, April 29, 1937, in *Documents on British Foreign Policy (1919–1939)*, edited by Medlicott and Douglas, 688 (see chap. 1, n. 53).

49. Ibid.

50. Report from Ambassador Bowers to Secretary of State Hull, Donibane Lohitzune, April 30, 1937, NARA, Bowers Files (Files 852.00/ . . . , Boxes 3687–3701), Document 852.00/5276.

51. Note from Ray Atherton (1883–1960), Counselor of the US Embassy at London, to the US State Department, London, May 5, 1937, NARA, Bowers Files (Files 852.00/ . . . , Boxes 3687–3701), Document 852.00/5602, 8.

52. The next meeting of the committee would be held on May 26.

53. Southworth, *Guernica, Guernica*, 199 (see chap. 4, n. 27).

54. Note from Ray Atherton (1883–1960), Counselor of the US Embassy in London, to the US State Department, London, May 5, 1937, NARA, Bowers Files (Files 852.00/ . . . , Boxes 3687–3701), Document 852.00/5602, 7–8.

55. *Daily Telegraph*, May 5, 1937.

56. Southworth, *Guernica, Guernica*, 204.

57. Telegram from State Secretary Hans Georg von Mackensen to Ulrich F. W. Joachim von Ribbentrop, German Ambassador to Great Britain, Berlin, May 5, 1937, in *Documents on German Foreign Policy*, 280.

58. Ibid.

59. Dispatch from Foreign Secretary Eden to Neville Henderson, British Ambassador to Berlin (1937–39), Foreign Office, May 7, 1937, in *Documents on British Foreign Policy (1919–1939)*, edited by Medlicott and Douglas, 717.

60. Note from Atherton, Counselor at the US Embassy in London, to the US State

Department, London, May 5, 1937, NARA, Bowers Files (Files 852.00/ . . . , Boxes 3687–3701), Document 852.00/5602, 8.

61. Report from Consul Stevenson, Bilbao, to Ambassador Chilton, Bilbao, April 28, 1937, in *Documents on British Foreign Policy (1919–1939)*, edited by Medlicott and Douglas, 696–98.

62. Telegram from von Ribbentrop, German Ambassador to Great Britain, to German Foreign Minister Constantin Neurath, London, May 6, 1937, in *Documents on German Foreign Policy*, 283.

63. Ibid., 283–84.

64. Southworth, *Guernica, Guernica*, 205.

65. Ibid., 214.

66. Conclusions of the fiftieth meeting of the Chairman's Subcommittee of the Non-Intervention Committee, Foreign Office, May 7, 1937, in *Documents on British Foreign Policy (1919–1939)*, edited by Medlicott and Douglas, 715.

67. Ibid., 716.

68. To the General in Command of the Black Feathers in Deba, Operation Instructions, Gasteiz, April 28, 1937, USSME, F. 18.

69. Marc Bassets, "Maldigo las guerras," *La Vanguardia*, April 26, 2007, 20.

70. Report by Joaquín Miláns del Bosch and Vicente Machimbarrena, Gasteiz, May 1, 1937, in Talón, *El holocausto de Guernica*, 299.

71. "Franco ha risposto al generale Sanders, che lo aveva interpellato per conto del governo di Berlino, un no secco," Promemoria, Mayo 8, 1937, AMAE, Gabinetto del Ministro (1923–1943), Busta 1 (Uffizio Spagna no. 1244), 1–3.

72. Five months later, in his famous Chicago speech of October 5, 1937, President Roosevelt proposed a "quarantine of aggressor nations" as an alternative to the system of neutrality and nonintervention. Spanish prime minister Juan Negrin applauded Roosevelt's words, but American public opinion was against intervention. Informe 6.895 del coronel Stephen O. Fuqua, Valencia, October 18, 1937, NARA, RG 165, Records of the Military Intelligence Division Relating to Conditions in Spain (1918–1941), Microfilm Publication MI.1445, R. 12.

73. Unofficial dispatch from the British Embassy, Washington, DC, to US State Department, Washington, DC, May 15, 1937, NARA, Bowers Files (Files 852.00/ . . . , Boxes 3687–3701), Document 852.00/5478.

74. Memorandum of conversation with Mr. Broadmead, First Secretary of the British Embassy, Washington, DC, May 20, 1937, NARA, Bowers Files (Files 852.00/ . . . , Boxes 3687–3701), Document 852.00/5521, 1–2.

75. Ibid.

76. Telegram from Prentiss Gilbert (1883–1939), Ambassador to the League of Nations, to the Secretary of State, Geneva, May 25, 1937, NARA, Bowers Files (Files 852.00/ . . . , Boxes 3687–3701), Document 852.00/5522, 2.

77. Southworth, *Guernica, Guernica*, 222.

78. A copy was communicated to His Majesty's Government by the Spanish ambassador on April 30, and His Majesty's Government subsequently informed

the principal European powers and invited their observations on the suggestion for an inquiry, adding that if, in their view, such an international inquiry could usefully be made, it could, if thought desirable, be extended to cover other incidents of a similar nature and that His Majesty's Government for their part would be ready to cooperate in such an inquiry whatever its scope. Report under no name, May 26, 1937, NARA, Bowers Files (Files 852.00/ . . . , Boxes 3687–3701), Document with no number, between 852.00/5795 and 852.00/5831, 1–2.

79. Note from Hiram (Harry) Bingham IV (1903–88), at the US Consulate in London, to the Secretary of State, London, June 1, 1937, NARA, Bowers Files (Files 852.00/ . . . , Boxes 3687–3701), Document 852.00/5570. Bingham was later distinguished for his "constructive dissent." While serving during World War II as a vice consul at the US consulate in Marseilles, Bingham issued visas to refugees escaping from the Gestapo and the Vichy police. His attitude, which was soon emulated by other diplomats, saved the lives of more than two thousand Jews and other refugees, among them one of this author's grandparents, who boarded the liner *Alsina* in Marseille on the way to exile in America in January 1941.

80. Report from Consul Walter C. Thurston, Valencia, to the Secretary of State, Valencia, May 31, 1937, NARA, Bowers Files (Files 852.00/ . . . , Boxes 3687–3701), Document 852.00/5555.

81. Telegram from the USS *Kane* to the US State Department, USS *Kane*, June 1, 1937, NARA, Bowers Files (Files 852.00/ . . . , Boxes 3687–3701), Document 852.00/5601.

82. Message from Vice Admiral to Admiralty, Gibraltar, May 30, 1937, in *Documents on British Foreign Policy (1919–1939)*, edited by Medlicott and Douglas, 825.

83. Telegram from Ambassador to Italy William Phillips to Secretary of State Hull, Rome, May 31, 1937, NARA, Bowers Files (Files 852.00/ . . . , Boxes 3687–3701), Document 852.00/5560.

84. Padelford, *International Law and Diplomacy*, 95 (see chap. 1, n. 130). See also *La Lucha de Clases* 62, no. 1.965 (1937). Also reproduced in Southworth, *Guernica, Guernica*, 225–26.

85. Note by Mr. Hemming of action agreed at the Non-Intervention Committee, London, May 26, 1937, in *Documents on British Foreign Policy (1919–1939)*, edited by Medlicott and Douglas, 809. In 1937 US$1.00 was about 0.2023 British pounds; £1.5 million roughly amounted US$7.4 million.

86. "The Mockery of Control." Report by Ambassador Bowers to Secretary of State Hull, Donibane Lohitzune, May 18, 1937, NARA, Bowers Files (Files 852.00/ . . . , Boxes 3687–3701), Document 852.00/5591.

87. *League of Nations Official Journal* (March–April 1937): 263–64.

88. Note from Julio Álvarez del Vayo to Foreign Secretary Eden, in *Documents on British Foreign Policy (1919–1939)*, edited by Medlicott and Douglas, 543.

89. *League of Nations Official Journal* (March–April 1937): 264.

90. Ibid., 572.

91. The booklet was published in three languages, Spanish, French, and

English. The original title in Spanish was *La agresión italiana: Documentos ocupados a las unidades italianas en la acción de Guadalajara.* A French version of the booklet was sent by Ambassador Bowers to the secretary of state: "The Spanish Situation," May 31, 1937, NARA, Bowers Files (Files 852.00/ . . . , Boxes 3687–3701), Document 852.00/5676, enclosure.

92. *League of Nations Official Journal* (March–April 1937): 263–64.

93. "The Spanish Situation," 5.

94. *League of Nations Official Journal* 18, nos. 5–6 (1937): 572.

95. Ibid., 333–34.

96. Extracts from the verbatim record of the Plenary Meetings of the Eighteenth Ordinary Session of the Assembly, Ninth Plenary Meeting, League of Nations, Official Journal, Sino-Japanese Conflict, Appeal by the Chinese Government, Special Supplement no. 177, Tuesday, September 28, 1937, 27.

97. Preamble to the Covenant of the League of Nations, January 10, 1920.

98. *The Parliamentary Debates,* 5th ser., vol. 323, House of Commons, Official Report, in the second session of the Thirty-Seventh Parliament of the United Kingdom of Great Britain and Northern Ireland, vol. 7 of Session 1936–1937 (London: His Majesty's Stationery Office, 1937), cols. 312–20.

99. Ibid.

100. Her book was entitled *Searchlight on Spain* (Harmondsworth: Penguin Books, 1938).

101. Some of her impressions were published by Manuel Irujo Ollo (1891–1981), minister of justice for the Republic, in Manuel Irujo, *Un vasco en el Ministerio de Justicia: Memorias* (Buenos Aires: Ekin, 1979), vol. 2, pt. 1, 127–30.

102. *The Parliamentary Debates,* House of Commons, col. 319.

103. Published in London on April 29, 1937.

104. Telegram from Foreign Secretary Eden to Ambassador Chilton, Hendaia, April 30, 1937, in *Documents on British Foreign Policy (1919–1939),* edited by Medlicott and Douglas, 690–91.

105. Because of the war, in 1936 the British Embassy to the Spanish Republic had been relocated in Hendaia, a small town in the northern part of the Basque Country, within France.

106. Dispatch from Ambassador Chilton, Hendaia, to Foreign Secretary Anthony Eden, April 28, 1937, in *Documents on British Foreign Policy (1919–1939),* edited by Medlicott and Douglas, 686–87.

107. Lord Cecil was president of the British League of Nations Union (1923–45) and chairman of the International Peace Campaign. Among his publications on peace and international affairs during this period were *The Way of Peace* (1928), *A Great Experiment* (1941), and *All the Way* (1949).

108. *The Parliamentary Debates,* 5th ser., vol. 115, House of Lords, Official Report, in the second session of the Thirty-Seventh Parliament of the United Kingdom of Great Britain and Northern Ireland, vol. 2 of Session 1936–1937 (London: His Majesty's Stationery Office, 1937), cols. 86–87.

109. Ibid., col. 88.

110. This was not true. That very day, April 29, Bilbao was bombed again, and British consul Stevenson was in the city. His house in Areeta, close to Bilbao, was later targeted by German and Spanish agents and bombed. One day later, on April 30, Hugh Dalton (1887–1962) asked Eden if he was aware of General Mola's declaration that he intended to raze Bilbao to the ground and whether the British government would consult with the principal parties on the Non-Intervention Committee to stop the general's plan. Eden was forced to admit that he had received such a report. Ibid., col. 683.

111. Ibid., cols. 91–92.

112. Ibid., cols. 767–68.

113. Dispatch from Consul Stevenson, Bilbao, to Foreign Secretary Eden, May 3, 1937, in *Documents on British Foreign Policy (1919–1939)*, edited by Medlicott and Douglas, 699.

114. Report from Consul Stevenson, Bilbao, to Ambassador Chilton, Bilbao, April 28, 1937, in ibid., 696–98.

115. Henderson wrote several books dealing with international peace and armament reductions: *Conference for the Reduction and Limitation of Armaments: Preliminary Report on the Work of the Conference* (Geneva: n.p., 1936), *Consolidating World Peace: The Burge Memorial Lecture for the Year 1931* (Oxford: Clarendon Press, 1931), *Labour's Way to Peace* (London: Methuen, 1935), and *Labour's Foreign Policy* (London: Labour Party, 1933).

116. *The Parliamentary Debates*, House of Commons, cols. 1131–32.

117. Memorandum by G. A. Fisher on the departure of Italian volunteers, in *Documents on British Foreign Policy (1919–1939)*, edited by Medlicott and Douglas, 70.

118. Moreover, when Henderson asked Undersecretary of State for Foreign Affairs Viscount Cranborne on May 6 whether he was aware of reports indicating that, during the last two weeks of April, large numbers of German bombers and Italian chasers had arrived in Spain, Cranborne answered that he had received "several reports of various kinds." As Henderson pointed out, the system of placing observers along Spanish borders was proving to be completely ineffective.

119. Germany sent one hundred more airplanes to Franco, April 27, 1937, NARA, Bowers Files (Files 852.24/ . . .), Document 852.24/393.

120. Naval Communication for the information of the US State Department, May 1, 1937, NARA, Bowers Files (Files 852.00/ . . . , Boxes 3687–3701), Document 852.00/5285.

121. *The Parliamentary Debates*, House of Commons, cols. 1133–34.

122. Ibid., cols. 1149–50.

123. Ibid., cols. 1343–45.

124. Southworth, *Guernica, Guernica*, 230.

125. Anthony Eden, *Facing the Dictators: The Memoirs of Anthony Eden, Earl of Avon* (London: Cassell, 1962), 499.

126. Southworth, *Guernica, Guernica*, 228.

127. Ibid., 234.

128. Geoffrey H. Thomson, *Front-Line Diplomat* (London: Hutchinson, 1959), 138.

129. Possible effect on England of the Application of Neutrality Laws to Germany and Italy, Memorandum of the Division of European Affairs of the US State Department, Washington, DC, July 7, 1937, NARA, US Department of State Files 1930–1939 (Files 852.00/ . . . , Box 6401), Document 852.00/5967.

130. Ibid.

131. *Congressional Record: Proceedings and Debates of the First Session of the 75th Congress of the U.S.A.*, pt. 3, 3316.

132. Report to the Secretary of State, May 18, 1937, NARA, Bowers Files (Files 852.00/ . . . , Boxes 3687–3701), no reference. Between Documents 852.00/5602 and 852.00/5641.

133. Report from the Ambassador of the Spanish Republic to the United States, Fernando de los Ríos, to the Secretary of State, June 4, 1937, NARA, Bowers Files (Files 852.00/ . . . , Boxes 3687–3701), Document 852.00/5735.

134. Letter from the Ambassador in Spain to Secretary of State Jean de Luz, January 12, 1937, in *Foreign Relations of the United States: Diplomatic Papers, 1937*, 255 (see chap. 1, n. 55).

135. *Congressional Record: Appendix*, 1131 (see chap. 1, n. 1).

136. Ibid.

137. Ibid., 3317.

138. The number of German troops was intentionally exaggerated. Report from Horace H. Fuller to Cordell Hull, Secretary of State, Paris, February 23, 1937, in *Foreign Relations of the United States: Diplomatic Papers, 1937*, 247.

139. "Italian Troops and Supplies in Spain" (see chap. 1, n. 58). Import of Aeronautical Products. See also Report 6495 of Captain Townsend Griffiss to Colonel Stephen O. Fuqua, March 16, 1937, NARA, Bowers Files (Files 852.24/ . . .), Document 852.24/384, 2.

140. William E. Chapman, US consul in Bilbao.

141. *Congressional Record: Proceedings and Debates*, pt. 3, 3317.

142. Ibid., 3319.

143. Ibid., pt. 4, 4237.

144. Senators Homer T. Bone of Washington, William E. Borah of Idaho, Arthur Carper of Kansas, Carter Glass of Virginia, Gerald E. Nye of North Dakota, Elmer Thomas of Oklahoma, and Robert Wagner of New York.

145. Ibid., pt. 9, 1225.

146. Ibid., 1131.

147. Ibid., pt. 4, 4270.

148. Letter 6, written by Manuel García, made reference of the capturing of Durango. Ibid., 4271.

149. Ibid., 4271–4304.

150. Ibid., 4624.

151. Ibid., pt. 9, 1172–73.

152. Letter from Bishop Francis McConnell to the Secretary of State, Washington,

DC, May 17, 1937, NARA, Bowers Files (Files 852.00/ . . . , Boxes 3687–3701), Document 852.00/5466.

153. Letter from the Women's International League for Peace and Freedom to the US President, Washington, DC, May 6, 1937, NARA, Bowers Files (Files 852.00/ . . . , Boxes 3687–3701), Document 852.00/5365.

154. Letter from the Women's International League for Peace and Freedom to the US President, Washington, DC, May 28, 1937, NARA, Bowers Files (Files 852.00/ . . . , Boxes 3687–3701), Document 852.00/5589.

155. Letter from Robert J. Bulkley to the Secretary of State, Washington, DC, June 3, 1937, NARA, Bowers Files (Files 852.00/ . . . , Boxes 3687–3701), Document 852.00/5641.

156. For instance, a day after the letter from McConnell, on May 18, R. E. Thomason, mayor of El Paso, Texas, received a telegram regarding rapes that had occurred in areas captured by the rebel forces: "The morning paper carries a very horrible picture of probable impeding fate for the young girls and women of Bilbao Spain if rebels enter that city stop is there not some way that our government can quietly communicate with the rebels and secure safety for these people stop let them know the eye of every Christian in America is upon them and very gravely concerned for their safety and treatment." Thomason sent the letter to the US State Department, Washington, DC, May 19, 1937, NARA, Bowers Files (Files 852.00/ . . . , Boxes 3687–3701), Document 852.00/5477.

157. Letter from Arthur A. Bolsterli to Senator Augustine Lonergan, Washington, DC, May 31, 1937, NARA, Bowers Files (Files 852.00/ . . . , Boxes 3687–3701), no numerical reference.

158. *Congressional Record: Proceedings and Debates*, pt. 5, 5236.

159. Representatives Jerry J. O'Connell, John T. Bernard, John M. Coffee, Robert G. Allen (1902–63), Henry G. Teigan (1881–1941), Gerald G. Boileau (1900–1981), and Dewey W. Johnson (1899–1941).

160. Letter from US Senator Jerry O'Connell to the Secretary of State, Washington, DC, June 2, 1937, NARA, Bowers Files (Files 852.00/ . . . , Boxes 3687–3701), Document 852.00/5629. The text of the resolution: Joint Resolution 390, 75th Cong., 1st sess., House of Representatives, June 1, 1937.

161. *Congressional Record: Appendix of the First Session of the 75th Congress of the U.S.A.*, vol. 81, pt. 10, May 19–August 21, 1937 (Washington, DC: US Government Printing Office, 1937), 1390.

162. Ibid.

163. Memorandum of the Office of Arms and Munitions Control of the US State Department, Washington, DC, June 28, 1937, NARA, US Department of State Files 1930–1939 (Files 852.00/ . . . , Box 6404), Document 852.00/6336.

164. Donald F. Crosby, "Boston's Catholic and the Spanish Civil War, 1936–1939," *New England Quarterly: A Historical Review of New England Life and Letters* (March 1971): 83.

165. "Lifters, Keepers," *Time*, January 23, 1939.

166. The report, "List of Casualties Provoked by the Rebel Air Raids During April

1937," is focused on the number of victims and not on the number of air raids, which certainly is much higher. "Relación de víctimas causadas por la aviación facciosa en sus incursiones del mes de abril de 1937," in Irargi archive, GE-0037-03.

167. The international press published news of the bombings in the Basque Country; for instance, in the United States, *Life* published a long article with photographs of the bombings in Bilbao during the Spring Offensive: "First Pictures of the Bombardment of Bilbao (March 31–June 19, 1937)," *Life*, May 31, 1937, 68.

168. "Significance of Bilbao." Report from Ambassador Bowers to the Secretary of State, Donibane Lohitzune, June 15, 1937, NARA, Bowers Files (Files 852.00/ . . . , Boxes 3687–3701), Document 852.00/5831.

169. Galeazzo Ciano, *Ciano's Hidden Diary, 1937–1938* (New York: E. P. Dutton, 1953).

170. A year before, on January 2, 1937, the Italian regime had signed a "gentlemen's agreement" with the British administration, according to which the two governments recognized the others' interests in the Mediterranean.

171. Edward Frederick Lindley Wood (1881–1959).

172. *Boletín Oficial del Estado* (Burgos), no. 349 (October 4, 1937): 397.

173. *Congressional Record: Appendix*, pt. 9, 1131.

174. Report to the Secretary of State, May 18, 1937, NARA, Bowers Files (Files 852.00/ . . . , Boxes 3687–3701), no reference. Between Documents 852.00/5602 and 852.00/5641.

175. *Congressional Record: Proceedings and Debates*, pt. 1, 74.

176. Ibid., pt. 3, 3316.

177. Joint Resolution 390, 75th Cong., 1st sess., House of Representatives, June 1, 1937.

178. Bowers, *My Mission to Spain*, 354 (see preface, n. 1).

179. Eden, *Facing the Dictators*, 499.

180. *Times* (London), April 29, 1937.

## 6 ■ Rebuilding Gernika

1. Giorno 29 aprile 1937, USSME, F. 7, Diario Storico, CTV Ufficio Generale Mancini (dal 27 aprile al 20 maggio 1937).

2. Smallwood interview with Margarita Lauzirika, 1972, WSA, File Gernika, E. Margarita Lauzirika, 1972.

3. María Jesús Cava Mesa et al., *Memoria colectiva del bombardeo de Gernika* (Gernika-Lumo: Gernika Gogoratuz, 1996), 242–44.

4. Gamboa and Larronde, *La guerra civil en Euzkadi*, 605 (see chap. 1, n. 29).

5. Alberto Onaindia wrote to Cardinal Goma about this shooting, referring to Lauxeta as a "first-class Basque poet, laureate with the highest honors, a spiritually fine boy, arrested in Gernika when accompanying a foreign journalist." Gomá showed no compassion. Letter from Alberto Onaindia to Isidro Cardinal Gomá, Donibane Lohitzune, July 2, 1937, Archivio Storico Diplomatico del Ministero degli Affari Esteri (Rome), II Semestre 1937, Repporti Politici, Spagna 1, 1931–1945, Busta 14.

6. Hugh Thomas, "Heinkels over Guernica," *Times Literary Supplement*, April 11, 1975.

7. Gernika-Lumoko Udala, Libro de Registro de los enterramientos en los Cementerios Municipales, Caja 620/1.

8. Ibid.

9. Interview with Mari Carmen Egurrola, Boise, Idaho, November 11, 2007. Mari Carmen's family lost everything, as did most of the rest of the citizens of old Gernika.

10. Telegram from Ambassador Bowers to Secretary of State Hull, Donibane Lohitzune, May 4, 1937, NARA, US Department of State Files 1930–1939 (Files 852.00/ . . . , Boxes 6386 to 6407), Document 852.00/5317.

11. Memorandum for Ambassador Bowers from Consul Chapman, in regard to the proposed evacuation of women and children from Bilbao, Donibane Lohitzune, May 21, 1937, NARA, Bilbao Consulate General Records (1936–1946), Box 6, 1937, 7. The *New York Times* numbered in 205,000 the refugees in Bilbao at the beginning of May. "The News of the Week in Review: Besieged Bilbao, War from the Air," *New York Times*, May 2, 1937, E1.

12. Ibid.

13. Notificación de la Orden del Presidente de la Audiencia Provincial de Bilbao de 6 de julio de 1937, Gernika, July 6, 1937, Bizkaiko Foru Aldundiko Ondare Historikoaren Foru Agiritegia, Ereño Juzgado 0001/002.

14. Expediente de Depuración abierto al medico de Inspección de Cadáveres, Bilbao, July 20, 1937, Bizkaiko Foru Aldundiko Ondare Historikoaren Foru Agiritegia, Bilbao Decimosexta 0022/1555.

15. Ibid.

16. Cava Mesa et al., *Memoria colectiva del bombardeo de Gernika*, 242–44.

17. Testimony of Pedro Agirre, in Smallwood, "The Day Gernika Was Bombed," 124 (manuscript in the author's possession, 1972).

18. Smallwood interview with Alisa Jaio, 1972, WSA, File Gernika, E. Alisa Jaio, 1972.

19. Interview with Mari Carmen Egurrola, Boise, Idaho, November 11, 2007.

20. Vicente del Palacio, "El exilio gerniqués," *Aldaba Gernika-Lumoko Aldizkaria*, no. 110 (March–April 2001): 37–50.

21. Al general jefe Flechas Negras en Deba, Instrucciones sobre Operaciones, Gasteiz, April 28, 1937, USSME, F. 18.

22. Talleres Guernica SA and Fábrica de armas Unceta y Cía. Rufino Unceta, owner at that time of the Unceta y Cía factory, was in communication with the combined forces to work for them after the city was captured. This factory closed in 1998.

23. Interview with Alfons Kössinger, in Marc Bassets, "Maldigo las guerras," *La Vanguardia*, April 26, 2007, 20.

24. Pilar Mur, "La reconstrucción de Guernica," *Arbola* (Bizkaiko Foru Aldundia), no. 8 (1987).

25. Cárdenas Rodríguez, *Datos para la reconstrucción del pueblo adoptado de*

*Guernica*, 29–30 (see chap. 2, n. 89). See also Cárdenas Rodríguez, "La reconstrucción de Guernica," 163 (see chap. 2, n. 89); *Guernica* [booklet], 233, FSS, ATV 6452; Ministerio de Gobernación, Dirección General de Regiones Devastadas, Comisión de Vizcaya, *Reconstrucción de la villa de Guernica*, 5 (see chap. 2, n. 90); Southworth, *Guernica, Guernica*, 356 (see chap. 4, n. 27).

26. Cárdenas Rodríguez, *Datos para la reconstrucción del pueblo adoptado de Guernica*, 29–30.

27. Angel Angoso, "Projet de Reconstruction et Urbanization de la Ville de Guernica," *La Construction Moderne* 53 (June 1938): 452–54.

28. Antonio Iturmendi, *El régimen municipal en los pueblos adoptados* (Madrid: Dirección General de Regiones Devastadas y Reparaciones, 1940), 12–14.

29. José Ángel Echániz Ortúñez and Vicente del Palacio, "Presos políticos: Mano de obra barata . . ."

30. Edurne Beaumont and Fernando Mendiola, "Vinieron un montón de prisioneros: Los batallones de soldados trabajadores vistos y recordados por la población de la montaña Navarra," *Els camps de concentració durant la guerra civil i el franquismo*, http://www.cefid.uab.es/files/C%C3%B2pia%20comuniII-1.pdf.

31. A philosophy similar to *Arbeit Macht Frei* (Work will set you free) at the Nazi concentration camps in Auschwitz, Dachau, and Sachsenhausen.

32. Echániz Ortúñez and del Palacio, "Presos políticos."

33. Cárdenas Rodríguez, *Datos para la reconstrucción del pueblo adoptado de Guernica*, 32–39.

34. Ibid., 31.

35. However, POWs continued performing labor in this region until the 1950s. In 1950 it was POWs who finished the reconstruction at the Port of Bermeo and on the extension of the railroad from Pedernales to Bermeo.

36. "Una protesta del Gobierno Vasco ante la UNESCO," *Euzko Izpar Banatzea* (Paris), no. 1 (November 16, 1954): 3.

## 7 ■ Gernika in the Courts of Justice

1. Steer, *Tree of Gernika*, chap. 7 (see chap. 1, n. 77).

2. Hispanicus, *Foreign Intervention in Spain*, 168–69 (see chap. 1, n. 49).

3. Whealey, *Hitler and Spain*, 144–47 (see chap. 1, n. 78).

4. Hispanicus, *Foreign Intervention in Spain*, 172–73.

5. Ibid., 187–88.

6. Steer, *Tree of Gernika*, chap. 7.

7. Among them, Karl Gustav Schmidt, Walter Kienzle, Günther Schulze-Blank, Paul Freese, Adalberto Butz, and Hans Joachim Wandel.

8. *Guernica: To Civilized Mankind* (see chap. 3, n. 39). A reproduction of this booklet can be found in Atxaga, *De Gernika a Guernica* (see chap. 2, n. 106).

9. *Times* (London), May 15, 1937.

10. "Captured German Flier Is Said to Have Admitted Taking Part in Guernica Bombing; Flier Admits Guernica Raid," *New York Times*, May 14, 1937, 7.

11. *Times* (London), May 22, 1937.

12. *Foreign Wings over the Basque Country*, 25–27 (see chap. 2, n. 66).

13. George Steer, "Rebel Planes Strafe Roads Inside Bilbao Fortifications," *New York Times*, May 22, 1937, 1, 3.

14. *Foreign Wings over the Basque Country*, 25–27.

15. Ibid.

16. "Captured German Flier Is Said to Have Admitted Taking Part," 7. See also "German Pilot Captured," *Joplin (MO) Globe*, May 14, 1937, 1.

17. "German Pilot Is Shot Down," *Reno (NV) Evening Gazette*, May 13, 1937, 1.

18. "German Youth Doomed to Die by Loyalists," *Nevada State Journal* (Reno), May 26, 1937, 2.

19. *Foreign Wings over the Basque Country*, 17–20.

20. "Basques Doom German Flier," *Findlay (OH) Republican Courier*, May 26, 1937, 1.

21. "German Youth Doomed to Die by Loyalists," 2.

22. "German Airmen Reprieved," *Sydney Morning Herald*, May 25, 1937, 11.

23. "Execution of Three Postponed," *Joplin (MO) Globe*, May 27, 1937, 15. See also "Respite to Nazi Pilots," *Daily Capital News* (Jefferson City, MO), May 27, 1937, 4.

24. "Rebels Open Fierce Drive for Bilbao," *Syracuse (NY) Herald*, May 27, 1937, 1, 55.

25. "To Be Released," *Joplin (MO) Globe*, May 30, 1937, 31.

26. "Berlin Gratified by Basque Action," *New York Times*, May 27, 1937, 12.

27. German Iñurrategi, *Al servicio de la justicia en tiempo de Guerra* (Gasteiz: Eusko Jaurlaritzaren Argitalpen Zerbitzu Orokorra, 2005), 88.

28. Bowers, *My Mission to Spain*, 348 (see preface, n. 1).

29. *Draft Hague Rules of Aerial Warfare;* Adam Roberts and Richard Guelff, *Documents on the Laws of War* (Oxford: Clarendon Press, 1982). See also Natalio Ronzitti, *The Law of Naval Warfare: A Collection of Agreements and Documents with Commentaries* (Boston: Martinus Nijhoff, 1988).

30. *League of Nations Official Journal* (May–June 1937): 333–34.

31. Note from Atherton, counselor at the US Embassy in London, to the US State Department, London, May 5, 1937, NARA, Bowers Files (Files 852.00/ . . . , Boxes 3687–3701), Document 852.00/5602, 8.

32. Roberts and Guelff, *Documents on the Laws of War*, 121–35.

33. *Congressional Record: Appendix*, pt. 9, 1225 (see chap. 1, n. 1).

34. "An Appeal to the Conscience of the World," letter from Senator Francis McConnell to the Secretary of State, Washington, DC, May 17, 1937, NARA, Bowers Files (Files 852.00/ . . . , Boxes 3687–3701), Document 852.00/5466.

35. Unofficial dispatch from the British Embassy in Washington, DC, to US State Department, Washington, DC, May 15, 1937, NARA, Bowers Files (Files 852.00/ . . . , Boxes 3687–3701), Document 852.00/5478.

36. Memorandum of conversation with Mr. Broadmead, First Secretary of the British Embassy, Washington, DC, May 20, 1937, NARA, Bowers Files (Files 852.00/ . . . , Boxes 3687–3701), Document 852.00/5521, 1–2.

37. Note from the US Embassy in London to the Secretary of State Hull, London, September 30, 1938, NARA, US Department of State Files 1930–1939 (Files 752.00114/51- . . . , Box 4274), Document 752.00116/110.

38. See also the debate in the House of Commons of June 21. HC Deb, June 21, 1938, vol. 337, cc919–1045.

39. Dietrich Schindler and Jiøí Toman, *The Laws of Armed Conflicts: A Collection of Conventions, Resolutions, and Other Documents* (The Hague: BRILL, 1988), 223–24.

40. José Doria et al., *The Legal Regime of the International Criminal Court: Essays in Honour of Professor Igor Blishchenko* (The Hague: BRILL, 2009), 110. See also *Department of State Bulletin* 1, nos. 1–27 (1939): 181; Ministry of Foreign Affairs of the Republic of Poland, *Official Documents Concerning Polish-German and Polish-Soviet Relations (1933–1939)* (London and Melbourne: Hutchinson, 1940), 128.

41. Doria et al., *Legal Regime of the International Criminal Court*, 110.

42. Irujo, *El Gernika de Richthofen*, 371–87 (see chap. 2, n. 101).

43. Xabier Irujo and Pete Cenarrusa, *On Basque Politics: Conversations with Pete Cenarrusa* (Brussels: EURI, 2012), 198.

44. Jose Antonio Aguirre, *Escape via Berlin: Eluding Franco in Hitler's Europe* (Reno: University of Nevada Press, 1991).

45. Xabier Irujo, *Expelled from the Motherland: The Government of President Jose Antonio Agirre in Exile (1937–1960)* (Reno: Center for Basque Studies, University of Nevada, Reno), 123.

46. Iñaki Goiogana, ed., *José Antonio Agirre Lekube: Diario, 1941–1942* (Bilbao: Fundación Sabino Arana/Sabino Arana Kultur Elkargoa, 2010), 161–64.

47. Irujo, *Expelled from the Motherland*, 121–49.

48. *El problema de España ante el mundo internacional: Resolución aprobada por la 1ª Asamblea General de Naciones Unidas; Texto y discusión de la misma* (London: Spanish Republic, Ministry of State, 1946), 13.

49. Statement released by the US State Department, March 4, 1946.

50. A phrase used by von Richthofen in his war diary on April 30, 1937.

51. From 1937 to 1939, the raids of the Italian and German air forces against the capital city of Catalonia did not stop, but Barcelona was heavily bombed for the first time on March 16, 1938, an attack that lasted two days. See Irujo, *El Gernika de Richthofen*, 335–46. See also "Franco Bombs Barcelona as a Loud Prelude to His Invasion of Catalonia," *Life*, April 11, 1938, 25–28; "Barcelona: A City at War; Between Bombing Raids, the People Try to Live," *Life*, November 28, 1938, 16–17.

52. Rotterdam was bombed on Göring's orders on May 14, 1940. Irujo, *El Gernika de Richthofen*, 363–67.

53. Starting on September 24, 1939, for two long days, hundreds of bombing sorties were flown against Warsaw in an attempt to terrorize the populace. As in Gernika, the city was bombed with heavy explosives and incendiary bombs.

54. On the discrepancy found between the originals of Article 6, paragraph (e), of the charter in Russian, on the one hand, and the originals in English and French, on the other.

55. Southworth, *Guernica, Guernica*, 242 (see chap. 4, n. 27).

56. On the contrary, after the war, Second Lieutenant Hans W. Asmus rose in the German Federal Air Force to major general.

## 8 ▪ Gernika as an Icon of Terror Bombing

1. Talón, *El holocausto de Guernica*, 198, 214 (see chap. 2, n. 76).

2. "Spain's Picasso Paints Bombing of Guernica for Paris Exposition (Bombed by Rebels April 27)," *Life*, July 26, 1937, 64.

3. Dore Ashton, *Picasso on Art: A Selection of Views* (New York: Da Capo Press, 1988), 149.

4. *American Scientist* (March 1849). See also "Bombardment by Means of Balloons," *Weekly Wisconsin*, April 10, 1849, 1.

5. Haile Selassie, *Appeal to the League of Nations* (Geneva, June 30, 1936).

6. Address by Hugh R. Wilson Before the Bureau of the Disarmament Conference at Geneva, May 31, 1937, in *Foreign Relations of the United States: Diplomatic Papers, 1937*, 20–21 (see chap. 1, n. 55).

7. Ibid., 24–25.

8. Pinna, *Relazioni del General Pinna*, Salamanca, April 17, 1937, 10–11 (see chap. 1, n. 69).

9. Report by Erwin Jaenecke in the course of a visit to Gernika, May 18, 1937, in Maier, *Guernica: La intervención alemana en España*, 180 (see chap. 1, n. 146).

10. In the words of Stuka pilot Hans U. Rudel, "Verloren ist nur, wer sich selbst aufgibt" (Only those who give up are lost). Hans U. Rudel, *Mein Leben in Krieg und Frieden* (Rosenheim: Deutsche Verlagsgesellschaft, 1994, 120). See also Günther Just and Hans U. Rudel, *Hans-Ulrich Rudel: Adler der Ostfront* (Hannover: National-Verlag, 1971).

11. *Die Zeit*, March 22, 1991.

12. According to other estimates, up to thirty-eight Zeppelins were brought down, thirty of them being authenticated: five in 1914, seventeen in 1915, and sixteen in 1916. Francis J. Reynolds et al., *The Story of the Great War* (New York: P. F. Collier and Son, 1917), 191–92.

13. Ibid., 623.

14. Galland, *Rise and Fall of the German Fighter Forces*, 16 (see chap. 3, n. 68).

15. The intervals between waves were intended to follow the pattern A-A, A being one-hour intervals. It is possible (because, as Richthofen recorded in his war diary, this had happened on prior occasions during the campaign in the Basque Country) that the first wave of Italian bombers arrived late to the target and that consequently the initial diagram A-A did not work as planned, resulting something like A-B-A, B being the Italian out-of-order intervention.

16. Corum, *Wolfram von Richthofen*, 133 (see chap. 1, n. 98).

17. Alberto Onaindia, "A Priest's Account," *Times* (London), May 3, 1937.

18. And thereafter many of the cities bombed during World War II. However,

the relative amounts of incendiary shells would be increased, up to 66 percent of the total, during the bombing campaign of the Royal Air Force over German cities in 1943–45.

19. Galland, *Rise and Fall of the German Fighter Forces*, 16.

20. House of Commons debate online in HC Deb, March 7, 1929, vol. 226, cc675–709.

21. In addition, the twenty-one German Junker Ju-52s, the Dornier Do17, the two Heinkel He111s, and the three Savoia-Marchetti SM.79s that bombed Gernika had a substantively larger capacity than the bombers used in prior wars. The new German and Italian bombers were designed with the intent of attaining a much larger cargo capacity and had an internal bomb bay that made it possible to mount several bombs on a single deposit, whereas older aircraft had carried bombs externally. However, just as the invention of dynamite and nitroglycerin had perfected the bombs of the nineteenth century, considerably amplifying their destructive capability and thus revolutionizing the concept of bombing and bombers, aerial bombing techniques would not significantly evolve until bomb-guidance systems were invented. In 1937 combatants had only unguided gravity bombs—that is, bombs dropped from aircraft followed a ballistic trajectory. The method of dropping shells varied according to the goal pursued by the bomber. Thus, dive-bombing and area or saturation bombing are different methods of bomb delivery.

22. "Basque Town Destroyed: Mass Slaughter by German Planes; Civilians Shot in Flight," *Morning Post* (London), April 28, 1937.

23. Ibid.

24. Noel Monks, "Here an Eye-witness Tells His Story," *Daily Express* (London), April 29, 1937.

25. Noel Monks, "Priest Blesses City as Bombs Fall," *Daily Express* (London), April 28, 1937.

26. "Basque Town Destroyed: Mass Slaughter by German Planes."

27. Anna R. Mask, "The Bombing of Guernica," *New York Times*, May 3, 1937, 18; Irujo, "Impact of the Bombing of Gernika," 33–57 (see chap. 5, n. 30).

28. Onaindia, "A Priest's Account."

29. "Basque Message to the Pope," *Times* (London), June 11, 1937. The letter was signed by Father Ramon Galbarriatu, vicar general of the diocese; Father Pedro Mentxaka, a canon and chancellor of the diocese; ten parish priests from Bilbao; the coadjutor of Gernika; the coadjutor of the Church of Santa Maria in Durango; the parish priest of Abadiño; and the Coadjutors of Murelaga, Arbazegi, Gerrikaitz, Berriatua, and Markina, the last nine being eyewitnesses of the events described.

30. *Hammond (IN) Times*, April 27, 1937, 8.

31. D. W. Brogan, "No Longer an Isle: Britain Moves Uncertainly," *New York Times*, July 4, 1937, 75.

32. *Foreign Wings over the Basque Country* (see chap. 2, n. 66).

33. "The News of the Week in Review: Besieged Bilbao; War from the Air," *New York Times*, May 2, 1937, E1.

## 9 ■ Gernika in Modern Memory

1. Joseph Eiguren, *Kashpar* (Boise, ID: Joseph Eiguren, 1988), 109.

2. Directive Commission of Centro Euskaro Español, Act no. 824, July 9, 1943, Irujo-Ametzaga archive.

3. *El País* (Montevideo), September 11, 1944, Irujo-Ametzaga archive.

4. *Lealtad* (Montevideo), April 29, 1944, Irujo-Ametzaga archive.

5. Municipal Board of Soriano, Act, September 17, 1943, Irujo-Ametzaga archive.

6. "Al Intendente municipal," *Euskal Erria* (Montevideo), 33, no. 897 (1944): 114; "Respuesta del Intendente municipal," ibid.

7. Letter from Bingen Ametzaga to President José Antonio Agirre, Montevideo, May 22, 1944, Irujo-Ametzaga archive.

8. "Homenaje al árbol de Guernica," *Euzko Deya* (Paris) 10, no. 208 (1945): 10.

9. Ibid.

10. *El País*, September 11, 1944.

11. José Azcona et al., *Historia de la emigración vasca al Uruguay en el siglo XX* (Montevideo: Ministerio de Educación y Cultura de Uruguay, 1996), 240–41.

12. *Euzko Deya* (Paris) 12, no. 261 (1947).

13. *El Plata* (Montevideo), April 26, 1948. Arantzazu Ametzaga, a writer, is the author's mother.

14. "Homenaje vasco a la Guernica inmortal," *Acción* (Montevideo), April 26, 1953; "Homenaje a Guernica," *El Diario* (Montevideo), April 26, 1953.

15. Apart from the public names of streets and squares, there is a Gernika tavern in New York City (25 Avenue B); a Guernica Tavern in Sausalito, California (2009 Bridgeway); and the well-known Gernika Basque Pub and Eatery in Boise, Idaho (202 South Capitol Boulevard). In fact, there are hundreds of such businesses around the United States, such as Guernica Condominiums, Inc. (142 Southwest Eighteenth Avenue, Miami, Florida); Guernica Realty and Investments (Key West, Florida); Guernica & González (7200 Northwest Nineteenth Street, no. 301, Miami, Florida); and Guernica Eneida B (219 Saint Croix Place, Key Largo, Florida).

16. Ordinance no. 14332, Expedient HCD 1807-U-2001; Register no. O-8573, City Council of Mar del Plata, November 9, 2001.

17. Discourse by Miguel Asqueta, Diario de Sesiones de la Cámara de Representantes, Tercer Período Ordinario de la 46 Legislatura, 14ª sesión. Montevideo, April 27, 2007.

18. "Spain's Picasso Paints Bombing of Guernica," 64 (see chap. 8, n. 2).

19. Charles Harrison and Paul Wood, *Art in Theory, 1900–2000: An Anthology of Changing Ideas* (Malden, MA: Blackwell, 2003), 649.

20. "Picasso Tapestry from U.N. to London," *Washington Times*, February 16, 2009. After being exposed in Paris, Picasso's *Guernica* was exposed in Great Britain as part of a fund-raising campaign that started on September 30, 1938, in aid of the National Joint Committee for Spanish Relief. It was first displayed at the New Burlington Galleries in London's West End. Later, Picasso's *Guernica* was exhibited at

the Whitechapel Art Gallery in the East End of London in January 1939. Clement Attlee opened the Whitechapel exhibition. This explains why in 2009 Rockefeller's canvas was moved to Whitechapel, where it still remains.

21. Pío Cabanillas (1977–79), Manuel Clavero (1979–80), Ricardo de la Cierva (1980), Íñigo Cavero (1980–81), Soledad Becerril (1981–82), Javier Solana (1982–88), Jorge Semprún (1988–91), Jordi Solé Tura (1991–93), Carmen Alborch (1993–96), Esperanza Aguirre (1996–99), Mariano Rajoy (1999–2000), Pilar del Castillo (2000–2004), and Carmen Calvo (2004–7).

22. http://www.guggenheim.org/guggenheim-foundation/foundation-press/3115-preliminary-studies-urdaibai.

## Epilogue

1. *Official Gazette of the Basque Country*, November 11, 1983.

2. *Boletín Oficial del Parlamento Vasco*, III Legislatura, Serie B, IV Proposiciones no de Ley, número 6–7 (d), Gasteiz, April 23, 1987.

3. http://www.gernikagogoratuz.org.

4. Juan Gutiérrez has been awarded the German Cross of Merit (1999) and the first Gernika Prize for Peace and Reconciliation (2005).

5. Gernika has already developed close cultural ties with Dresden and Pforzheim, two German cities leveled by Allied bombing during World War II.

6. Roman Herzog was president of Germany from 1994 to 1999.

7. Roman Herzog, "Message to the Citizens of Gernika," Bonn, March 27, 1997. The message is framed and hanged on one of the walls of the city council of Gernika. The Documentation Center of the Peace Museum Foundation has a copy of the document.

8. http://www.peacemuseumguernica.org/en/information/historyinfo.html.

9. Ibid.

10. Tadatoshi Akiba, mayor of Hiroshima, is also president of the Mayors for Peace association, joining 539 large cities all over the world.

## Appendix 1

1. Testimony of Colonel von Beust, 1955, with an additional script of March 16, 1973, in *Guernica: La intervención alemana en España*, by Maier, 191 (see chap. 1, n. 146).

2. Ibid., 66.

3. Exposición de la Sección Científica de Guerra del Arma Aérea, in ibid., 189.

4. Maier, *Guernica: La intervención alemana en España*, 195.

5. Ibid., 121.

6. Lopategui, *Aita Patxi*, 65 (see chap. 4, n. 121).

7. Salas Larrazabal, *Guernica*, 143 (see chap. 2, n. 76).

8. George Steer, "Rebel Planes Strafe Roads: Inside Bilbao Fortifications," *New York Times*, May 22, 1937, 3.

9. "At Vitoria, to which he flew the day after, he found at least two squadrons of

German fighters, consisting of 12 aeroplanes each." *Foreign Wings over the Basque Country*, 19 (see chap. 2, n. 66).

10. Patrick Laureau, *Condor: The Luftwaffe in Spain, 1936–39* (Mechanicsburg, PA: Stackpole Books, 2010), 111.

11. "Los aviones que bombardearon Guernica y que actúan en el frente vasco son alemanes, conducidos por pilotos de la misma nacionalidad," *Ahora*, May 30, 1937, 8; "El bombardeo de Guernica: Informe de la Comisión de Expertos," ABC, May 30, 1937, 7; O. D. Gallaguer, "Death Sentence on Third Nazi Pilot," *Daily Express* (London), May 26, 1937, 1.

12. Maier, *Guernica: La intervención alemana en España*, 121.

13. *Foreign Wings over the Basque Country*, 19.

14. Salas Larrazabal, *Guernica*, 153.

15. Laureau, *Condor*, 120.

16. Attività Giornalera dell'Aviazione Legionaria dal Dicembre 1936–Luglio 1937, vol. 1, USAM, Busta 70, Fascicolo 7.

17. Diario Storico, USAM, Busta 68, Fascicolo 98.

18. Aviazione, AMAE, Gabinetto Minister, Busta 1236, 1–10.

19. Bollettini dell'Attività Aerea dell'Aviazione Legionaria trasmessi a Montecelio dal 12 marzo al 31 diciembre 1937, USAM, Busta 71, Fascicolo 9.

20. Attivitá Giornalera dell'Aviazione Legionaria del Continente dal Luglio 1936 al Dicembre 1937, vol. 1, USAM, Busta 70, Fascicolo 7.

21. Registro dell'Attivitá di Volo, 3er Stormo aeroplani di cacica XVI Gruppo 26 Squadrigli, USAM, Serie 10, Registri volo, vol. 9.

22. Attivitta di volo svolta dai reparti dell'Aviazione Legionaria nel giorno 26 aprile 1937, USSME, Fondo 6, Legajo 50.

23. Pinna, *Relazioni del General Pinna*, Salamanca, April 17, 1937, 9.

## Appendix 2

1. Maier, *Guernica: La intervención alemana en España*, 183–87 (see chap. 1, n. 146).

2. Attivitá Giornalera dell'Aviazione Legionaria del Continente dal Luglio 1936 al Dicembre 1937, vol. 1, Ufficio Storico dell'Aeronautica Militare (Rome), Busta 70, Fascicolo 7.

3. The document was at the Bundes-Archiv Zwischenarchiv Berlin-Hoppegarten, German Federal Archives at Berlin-Hoppegarten, but it was transferred to the Freiburg Military Archive (Bundesarchiv-Militärarchiv). The document was recently discovered there by Stefanie Schüler-Springorum. Professor Ángel Viñas provided me with a copy of the document. The document is partially reproduced in Stephanie Schüler-Springorum, *Krieg und Fliegen: Die Legion Condor im Spanischen Bürgerkrieg* (Paderborn: Ferdinand Schöning Verlag, 2010), 186.

4. Irujo, *El Gernika de Richthofen*, 143, 151 (see chap. 2, n. 101).

5. Maier, *Guernica: La intervención alemana en España*, 70.

6. Villa, *Gernika bonbardaketa/El bombardeo*, 27 (see chap. 2, n. 82).

# Notes on Sources

This book is in the main based on primary sources, archival documentation, and printed collections of documents or written testimonies. I have compiled and cataloged more than twelve thousand documents from more than twenty archives in Germany, Spain, the United States, the Basque Country, Catalonia, France, Italy, Switzerland, the United Kingdom, Uruguay, and the Vatican. This work has been possible thanks to the excellent work of the Documentation Centre of the Bombing of Gernika, headed by Ana Teresa Núñez, which holds the largest existing collection of documents on this historical event.

In addition, I have interviewed several witnesses of the attack, former soldiers, refugee children who had suffered the raids of the German bombers, and pilots. Thanks to Pete T. Cenarrusa, I have had access to an unpublished manuscript (1972) by William Smallwood (Egurtxiki) containing 129 interviews with eyewitnesses of the bombing and dozens of original photographs, the majority of which we now know were taken by Faustino "Basurde" Pastor. The manuscript was published in 2011 by the Gernika Peace Museum Foundation under the title *The Day Guernica Was Bombed*.

The following lists of sources are divided into three main sections:

- primary sources: archival documentation and printed collections of documents; these are contemporary documents written by people involved in the events that took place at that time, most of them registered as diplomatic or political files
- interviews: testimonies and unpublished written or recorded accounts of the massacre and its consequences
- secondary sources

## Primary Sources

### *List of Archives*

| | |
|---|---|
| ADCGPM | Archive of the Documentation Center of the Gernika Peace Museum |
| AGA | Archivo General de la Administración de Alcalá de Henares (Spain) |
| AGMA | Archivo General Militar de Ávila (Spain) |
| AGMS | Archivo General Militar de Segovia (Spain) |
| AHEA | Archivo Histórico del Ejército del Aire de Villaviciosa de Odón (Spain) |
| AMAE | Archivio Storico Diplomatico del Ministero degli Affari Esteri (Rome) |

| | |
|---|---|
| AMT | Arxiu Montserrat Tarradellas i Macià—Monestir de Poblet, Poblet (Cayalunya) |
| ASV | Archivio Segreto Vaticano, Nunziatura di Madrid (Vatican City) |
| BFA | Bizkaiko Foru Aldundiko Ondare Historikoaren Foru Agiritegia / Archivo Histórico de la Diputación Foral de Bizkaia (Bilbao, Basque Country) |
| BL | British Library (London) |
| BM | Bundesarchiv-Militärarchiv (Department Military Archives in Freiburg) |
| BNCR | Biblioteca Nazionale Centrale di Roma (Italy) |
| BNF | Bibliothèque Nationale de France (Paris) |
| CA | Cenarrusa Archive (Boise, Idaho) |
| CDMH | Centro Documental de la Memoria Histórica (Salamanca, Spain) |
| EAA | Sabino Arana Fundazioko Euskal Abertzaletasunaren Agiritegia (Bilbao, Basque Country) |
| FSS | Fundación Sancho el Sabio (Gasteiz, Basque Country) |
| GBDZ | Gernikako Bonbardaketari buruzko Dokumentazio Zentruko Agiritegia / Archivo del Centro de Documentación del Bombardeo de Gernika (Gernika, Basque Country) |
| HC Deb | Debates Parlamentarios de la Cámara de los Comunes (online) |
| HMM | Hemeroteca Municipal de Madrid (Spain) |
| IAA | Irujo Ametzaga Agiritegia (Altzuza, Basque Country) |
| ICRC | International Committee of the Red Cross Archives (Geneva, Switzerland, and Salamanca, Spain) |
| IRARGI | Eusko Jaurlaritzaren Artxibo eta Dokumentu Ondarearen Zerbitzua / Servicio de Archivos y Patrimonio Documental del Gobierno Vasco (Bilbao, Basque Country) |
| ISHS | Idaho State Historical Society (Boise, Idaho) |
| NAK | National Archives in Kew (United Kingdom) |
| NARA | National Archives and Records Administration (College Park, Maryland) |
| PAAA | Politisches Archiv des Auswärtiges Amt (Diplomatic Archive of the German Ministry for Foreign Affairs, Berlin) |
| UABSU | University Archives—Boise State University (Idaho) |
| UNRBA | Basque Archive of the University of Nevada, Reno (Nevada) |
| USAM | Ufficio Storico dell'Aeronautica Militare (Rome) |
| USSME | Ufficio Storico del Stato Maggiore dell'Essercito (Rome) |
| WSA | William Smallwood Archive (Arizona) |

The Gernikako Bake Museoa (Gernika Peace Museum) is a member of the International Peace Museum Network, and its documentation center has two separate collections, both of which are open to researchers. The first one is composed of nonoriginal documentation digitized from Basque, Spanish, French, Italian, German, British, and US archives and libraries. The second is a collection of books, booklets, pamphlets, leaflets, photographs, and other printed or video-recorded material on the bombing or on topics related to it. A complete description of the collections and other information of interest may be consulted at its website in four languages (http://www.peacemuseumguernica.org).

Most of the documentation on the bombing of Gernika that I have studied in Italian, German, and French archives is deposited at the documentation center of the Gernika Peace Museum, and I have direct access to it in Gernika.

The Euskal Abertzaletasunaren Agiritegia (Archive of Basque Nationalism) is part of the Sabino Arana Foundation, and it is the main source of archival documentation on the war of 1936 and the subsequent Basque exile (1936–75). The Archive of Basque Nationalism houses nearly 30,000 monographs on Basque topics. The archive also contains more than 5,000 periodical publications—over 130,000 copies—and more than 1 million documents on the history of Basque nationalism from the archives of the Basque Nationalist Party (1894–2008). It has more than 1,200 private donations (documents, photographs, and various objects). Apart from the abundant archival documentation (letters, governmental administrative documentation, photographs, and the like), the archive has a rich library containing hundreds of pamphlets, magazines, books, and other printed or video-recorded documents and a museum. The categories of classification and the inventories—Microsoft Word or .pdf format—of the documentation available in the archive are fully described on the web page of the Sabino Arana Foundation (http://www.sabinoarana.org).

For American researchers, the National Archives and Record Administration in College Park, Maryland, offers an essential source of archival documentation. The files at the National Archives are organized according to the nature of the collections housed there. Information regarding the war in the Basque Country (1936–37) is almost entirely covered by collections from the US Department of State, deposited in the headquarters of the National Archives in College Park. The College Park National Archive is the largest archive in the world, and apart from files in paper and digital or audiovisual format, it contains photographs, posters, maps, drawings, and other graphic material of interest. The National Archives holds very significant documentation of the US Embassy to the Spanish Republic generated by the US ambassador Claude G. Bowers and the US consul in Bilbao William E. Chapman. The documentation may be sought as follows:

For the US embassy: Bowers's documentation

Register Number 59/Stack Area 250/Row 29/Compartment 34/Shelves 02–03

Central decimal File 1930–1939, 852.00/Boxes 3687–3701 (also 852.001/, 852.01/, 852.222/, 852.24/, 852.48/ . . .)

For the US Consulate at Bilbao: Chapman's documentation

Register Number 84/Stack Area 350/Row 67/Compartment 35/Shelves 02–07

Spain v.c. Bilbao Consulate General Records {1936–1946}

All of this documentation is microfilmed and easily accessible. For a complete description of the funds regarding the war in the Basque Country, see Xabier Irujo, "National Archives and Records Administration of the United States (NARA)," in *Guía de Fuentes documentales de la Guerra Civil en Euskadi*, edited by José Luis De la Granja and Santiago De Pablo (Donostia: Eusko Ikaskuntza, 2011), 247–71.

The Center for Basque Studies' Archive and Library at the University of Nevada, Reno, is the largest library on Basque issues outside the Basque Country. The Basque Library has a vast archive with documents going back to the eighteenth century and houses a good collection of documents related to the 1936 war, as well as other files donated by Basques from all over the Americas, especially from the United States. Further information may be found on the web page of the Basque Library (http://knowledgecenter.unr.edu/basquelibrary/Default.aspx).

The Irujo-Ametzaga Archive in Altzuza (Basque Country) is a private collection of documents generated by both the Irujo and the Ametzaga families in exile (1936–75). The archive houses about five thousand documents of diverse nature, among them letters, political documents, manuscripts, reports, and photographs. All the holdings are being progressively published. The first part of the funds to be published was an anthology of the press articles by Bingen Ametzaga written in exile: Arantzazu Amezaga, ed., *Nostalgia/Herrimina* (Donostia: Eusko Jaurlaritzako Kultura Saila, 1993). The poems in Basque by Bingen Ametzaga were also published: Xabier Irujo, ed., *Itsaso aurrean* (Zarautz: Susa, 2006). The letters on cultural issues by Bingen Ametzaga in America (1940–69) have been compiled by Xabier Irujo in various volumes published by Utrusque Vasconiae: *Bingen Ametzaga Aresti: Gutunak I (1941–1968)* (Donostia and San Sebastián: Utriusque Vasconiae, 2009) and *Bingen Ametzaga Arestiri egindako gutunak II (1939–1969)* (Donostia and San Sebastián: Utriusque Vasconiae, 2009).

Apart from the collections of documents in Basque, Spanish, Italian, German, and French included in the general bibliography, there exists a large collection of documents originally written in English or translated into English related to the bombing of Gernika and the nonintervention policy. The documentation housed at the National Archives in College Park, Maryland, that pertains to the war in the Basque Country is much larger than what was compiled and published in the collections entitled *Foreign Relations of the United States*, but certainly this document collection contains the most essential files. The documentation was published and compiled in chronological order, so that the volumes containing the years 1936 and 1937 have sections devoted to the war and, within them, abundant references to the war in Euskadi and to the bombings.

The bibliographic references of this collection as related to the war in the Basque Country are as follows:

*Foreign Relations of the United States: Diplomatic Papers, 1936*. Vol. 2, *Europe*, 437–795. Washington, DC: US Government Printing Office, 1954.

*Foreign Relations of the United States: Diplomatic Papers, 1937.* Vol. 1, *General,* 215–604. Washington, DC: US Government Printing Office, 1954.

All these documents are in the Bowers and Chapman files at the National Archives. I have to emphasize that, when cited, if a document has been printed, I have quoted from the edited version from the US Government Printing Office so the researcher has easier access to the source.

Apart from these anthologies of documents, there is interesting documentation in English on the bombings in the printed collections of records, proceedings, and debates in the US Congress and in both British Houses (Commons and Lords).

*US Congress*

*Congressional Record: Proceedings and Debates of the First Session of the 75th Congress of the U.S.A.* Vol. 81, pt. 1, January 5–February 12, 1937. Washington, DC: US Government Printing Office, 1937.

*Congressional Record: Proceedings and Debates of the First Session of the 75th Congress of the U.S.A.* Vol. 81, pt. 3, March 18–April 16, 1937. Washington, DC: US Government Printing Office, 1937.

*Congressional Record: Proceedings and Debates of the First Session of the 75th Congress of the U.S.A.* Vol. 81, pt. 4, April 19–May 18, 1937. Washington, DC: US Government Printing Office, 1937.

*Congressional Record: Proceedings and Debates of the First Session of the 75th Congress of the U.S.A.* Vol. 81, pt. 5, May 19–June 17, 1937. Washington, DC: US Government Printing Office, 1937.

*Congressional Record: Appendix of the First Session of the 75th Congress of the U.S.A.* Vol. 81, pt. 9, January 5–May 19, 1937. Washington, DC: US Government Printing Office, 1937.

*Congressional Record: Appendix of the First Session of the 75th Congress of the U.S.A.* Vol. 81, pt. 10, May 19–August 21, 1937. Washington, DC: US Government Printing Office, 1937.

*House of Commons*

*The Parliamentary Debates.* 5th ser., vol. 323, House of Commons, Official Report, in the second session of the Thirty-Seventh Parliament of the United Kingdom of Great Britain and Northern Ireland, 7th vol. of Session 1936–37. London: His Majesty's Stationery Office, 1937.

*House of Lords*

*The Parliamentary Debates.* 5th ser., vol. 115, House of Lords, Official Report, in the second session of the Thirty-Seventh Parliament of the United Kingdom of Great Britain and Northern Ireland, 2nd vol. of Session 1936–37. London: His Majesty's Stationery Office, 1937.

The anthology of papers of the British Foreign Office also provides interesting documents:

Medlicott, W. N., and Dakin Douglas, eds. *Documents on British Foreign Policy (1919–1939)*. 2nd ser., vol. 18, *European Affairs* (January 2–June 30, 1937). London: Her Majesty's Stationery Office, 1980.

Finally, the German foreign policy documents for the period 1918–45 are published by the US State Department:

*Documents on German Foreign Policy (1918–1945)*. Ser. D (1937–45), vol. 3, *Germany and the Spanish Civil War (1936–1939)*. Washington, DC: Department of State, US Government Printing Office, 1950.

## Interviews

I have interviewed fighter pilots, *gudaris*, and eyewitnesses of the events that took place in the Basque Country in 1937. I am grateful for the information they have provided and also for their time and for their patience.

**Agirre, Maria Teresa** (1909–2003). Algorta, Bizkaia, October 7, 2000. I interviewed Maria Teresa Agirre, sister of President José Antonio Agirre, at her home in Algorta, facing the bay where, on April 20, 1937, William H. Roberts, captain of the *Seven Seas Spray*, introduced thirty-six hundred tons of salt, oil, flour, green beans, ham, honey, peas, beans, and wine for the starving refugee population of Bilbao. Maria Teresa was an exceptional witness to the political and military events that took place in the Basque Country between 1931 and 1937. She was an eyewitness to some of the bombings that took place in the Bilbao area in the spring of 1937.

**Atxabal, Julian** (1936–2011). Boise, Idaho, February 26, 2006. I interviewed Julian Atxabal and also invited him to lecture at Boise State University in 2006. He recounted his experiences as a soldier. According to his testimony, when he joined the US Army during the Second World War, he had in mind what the Germans had done in Gernika. He was one of the founding members of Euzkaldunak, Inc., the Boise Basque Center.

**Cenarrusa, Pete T.** (1917–2013). Boise, Idaho, April 18 and November 11, 2010. I interviewed Pete T. Cenarrusa at his home in Boise, Idaho, several times between 2007 and 2013. Cenarrusa was a Republican politician who served the state of Idaho for fifty-two years, nine terms in the state house of representatives (1950–67), in 1963, 1965, and 1967 as Speaker of the house, and nine terms as secretary of state (1967–2002). Cenarrusa became a naval aviator specializing in dive-bombing as a F4U Corsair pilot. Son of Ramona Gardoki, from Gernika, Cenarrusa promoted and led the delegation of Idaho during the twinning process of Gernika and Boise in 1993. The information provided by Cenarrusa regarding the bombing of Gernika was very relevant because he was familiar with bombing techniques and knew the main characteristics of the airplanes of that era. In addition, he had been to Gernika several times and had studied the city and the events of April 26, 1937.

**Egurrola, Mari Carmen** (b. 1930). Boise, Idaho, November 11, 2007. I have interviewed Mari Carmen Egurrola several times since November 2007. Mari Carmen is one of several witnesses to the bombing who currently lives in the United States. She was six years old in 1937. Her family lost all of their belongings, their home, and the print shop that they had in Gernika. It was a long night for her and her mother, who did not know whether her husband, Antonio Egurrola, had died during the attack. After the bombing, they were forced to live with various relatives outside Gernika. Later, she married and moved abroad, to Idaho, with her husband. Her testimony was substantially useful for understanding the impact of the bombing on the surviving families and the vicissitudes of the Basque immigrants in the context of the postwar depression.

**Elizalde, José** (1914–2006). Altzuza, Navarra, February 2, 2000. José Elizalde was a *gudari* who fought on the front of Biscay from July 1936 until June 1937. He and a companion shot down one of the few Heinkel He51s that the Basque army was able to gun down. As a frontline soldier, José suffered repeatedly during the bombing and strafing of German and Italian aircraft, and he was wounded on several occasions. After the capture of Bilbao on June 19, 1937, he fought in a Basque battalion on the Catalan front until 1939. He was imprisoned in the concentration camps of Argelès-sur-Mer and Gurs, France. During World War II, he served in the French Resistance and, captured by the Germans, was part of a labor battalion in charge of the building of the Atlantic Wall. He escaped from the Germans and fought in the Gernika Battalion under the command of Major Ordoki during the liberation of France in 1945. After the war, he was recruited as a volunteer in the US Army. He lived in exile in Venezuela and returned to die in the Basque Country. I interviewed him several times between August 25 and September 17, 2000. We met regularly after the attack on the Twin Towers in 2001, which visibly affected him. He wrote a manuscript on Gernika and gave it to me before he died. His testimony has been of great importance for the study of the effect of air attacks on the front line in the Basque Country in 1937.

**Elosegi, Joseba** (1915–90). Altzuza, 1987. Joseba Elosegi, captain of the Saseta Battalion, witnessed the attack on Guernica and was the author of the book *Quiero morir por algo* (I want to die for something). Elosegi is one of the main sources of information regarding the bombing of Gernika and Durango. To protest the bombing of Gernika in particular and the Spanish dictatorship in general, on September 19, 1970, he set fire to himself in front of General Franco during a Basque ball game in Donostia. In 1984 he took the *ikurriña* (Basque flag) of the Itxarkundia battalion that was exhibited in the Army Museum in Madrid with the dictum "Trophy captured to the enemy." During a visit to our house in Altzuza in 1987, Elosegi described to Arantzazu Ametzaga, Pello Irujo, and myself what happened in Guernica in April 1937.

**Iribarren, Mercedes** (1905–80). Mercedes Iribarren witnessed the bombings of Areeta, Algorta, Plentzia, and Bilbao. She recorded her biography in a collection of tapes in 1970. On May 26, 1937, a German aircraft bombed the house of her parents in Areeta and the hospital nearby, killing a nurse and wounding several children. During the war, Iribarren lost her own home in Plentzia, Bizkaia, damaged by a bomber, which also killed her neighbor's cattle. Her testimony is relevant for studying the effects of the bombing campaign on civilians.

**Iriondo, Luis** (b. 1922). Gernika, May 17, 2014. Born in Gernika, Luis Iriondo survived the bombing in one of the shelters of Pasealeku. After the bombing, his family lost everything, including their house near the train station, so they had to move to Bilbao. Shortly before the fall of the Basque capital, he was transported to Santander. Due to the avalanche of Basque refugees and the difficulty of receiving supplies, children were transported on a British ship that managed to get through the blockade to a colony for refugee children in Vernon Eure, Normandy, one thousand kilometers from Gernika. On his return to Euskadi, Luis realized that Franco's government had denied that Gernika had been bombed and accused the Basques of being the authors of the destruction of the city. In 1997, during the celebration of the sixtieth anniversary of the bombing, Iriondo received on behalf of the victims of the bombing the German ambassador, who read a message from President Roman Herzog in which he recognized that the legion had executed the bombing. Thereafter, Iriondo has participated in all meetings of the victims of the bombing of Gernika and, through Gernika Gogoratuz, has seen many journalists interested in the bombing.

**Iturria, Joxe** (1914–2014). Lesaka, May 17, 2013. Joxe Iturria lived through three of the most dramatic bombardments of the war in the Basque Country, the first bombing of Durango on September 25, 1936, and on March 31, 1937, as well as the bombing of Gernika on April 26. Joxe was in the barracks of the Loyola headquarters in Donostia when the insurrection broke out and lived through the events that led to the takeover of the fort by the Republican authorities. He was one of the few recruits with a driver's license for trucks, and consequently he became a truck driver of the Third Heavy Artillery Regiment of the Republican army. He was the victim of numerous attacks by rebel planes. Following the bombing of Durango of September 25, 1936, he was entrusted with the task of transporting the bodies of the dead from the city center to the cemetery. After the fall of Bilbao, he was captured and imprisoned in a concentration camp. Given his age and combat experience in 1937, Iturria's testimony is one of the most relevant for the reconstruction of the events that took place in Durango and in Gernika in 1937. I interviewed Joxe several times and published his memoirs in the Bombing of Gernika Series of the Peace Museum Foundation (2013), included below.

**Lasaga, Pello** (b. 1926). Lesaka, June 4 and July 30, 2013. The war broke out while Pello Lasaga was in his uncle's house in Lezo, an area controlled by the Basques. After the uprising, his hometown, Lesaka, was quickly occupied by the rebels, so he could not go home. With the advance of the rebel troops, he was transferred to Deba and to Bilbao. Because of the food shortages, Pello was moved along with other children to Kortezubi—a few miles from Gernika—by November 1936 and remained there for about six months. He saw the bombing of the city from a mountain nearby, close to some *gudaris* who were hiding there. No one in his family had any news on the whereabouts of Pello, and he did not know anything about his mother or sisters. Like many other Basque children, Pello was transported to school overseas until 1939, when he returned to Lesaka. For forty-five years he worked in the construction company run by his cousin Joxe Iturria. They never spoke of the bombing. I interviewed them separately.

**Martija, Kontxi** (b. 1925). Algorta, May 27, 2012. Kontxi Martija was twelve in 1937. She spent the bombardment in the basement of her home located on Asilo Calzada Street, not far from the weapons factory, which was not hit by the bombs. The basement had a little window to the street from which they could hear the rattle of the German machine guns and the explosions. After the bombardment, her family abandoned Gernika. Like many children, she went into exile on a ship from Cantabria. She was in one of the schools that the Basque government organized abroad. After the capture of the northern Basque Country by the Germans, her family moved back to Gernika, where it was forbidden to speak about the bombardment and one was harshly punished for doing so.

**Murua, Iñaki** (b. 1926). Zarautz, July 25, 2011. Iñaki Murua was one of the thousands of refugees who were in Gernika in April 1937. Son of Hilario Murua, *gudari* of the Itxarkundia battalion, he was a ten-year-old boy in 1937. Alongside his mother, Joxepa, and brother, Kepa, he suffered the bombing in the shelter of the city council. This shelter was blocked because the building of the city council collapsed under it. They were rescued several hours after the bombing when a group of *gudaris* opened a hole in the roof and rescued all the people trapped there. I have also had access to the interview conducted in 2009 by his nephew Imanol Murua, under the title "Iñaki Murua: Gerra zibileko oroitzapenez elkarrizketa."

**Robinson, F. Willard.** Boise, Idaho, November 8, 2010. Willard "Robbie" Robinson is the author of the book *Navy Winds of Gold*, narrating his experiences as a dive-bomber pilot during World War II. Robinson fought in the Pacific theater. He was shot down during the Battle of Midway, yet he continued to fight after that date. I interviewed Robinson for his skills as a pilot of a bomber of that era.

**Urrutikoetxea, Miren Begoña** (b. 1923). Donostia, June 16, 2012. Miren Begoña Urrutikoetxea was born in Bilbao. After her father's death on January 30, 1936, Urrutikoetxea lived in Abadiño, Mungia, and Bilbao. In March 1937, her family moved to a rented house on the edge of the road between Gernika and Kortezubi in order to escape from the constant bombings of Bilbao and the food shortages. The bombing shocked Miren Begoña. She was thirteen years old. She was near her home in a place known as the Bartolo iturri meadow. The fighters strafed the area constantly, chasing anyone who moved. She saw a young couple killed, gunned down. Miren Begoña remained lying over her two-year-old brother, Joseba, and kept repeating to him that they were having a party in Gernika and that they were setting off rockets. After the bombing, she stood up and saw the whole city in flames. At dusk she crossed the Errenteria bridge with her grandmother and felt the intense heat produced by the fire. She saw scenes of chaos, *gudaris* lying wounded or dead, near the bridge. She also remembered a woman screaming, looking for her son. They were transported in a truck to Bilbao, where they arrived the next morning, due to the heavy traffic. After the fall of Bilbao and the subsequent exile, her family faced a harsh postwar period. Her cousin was also in Gernika, but after seventy-seven years they have never spoken about what happened that day.

**Winder, Chuck.** Boise, Idaho, November 10, 2010. I interviewed Chuck Winder, senator of Idaho (District 14, Ada County) and former US Navy pilot during the Vietnam War, in Elmer, where members of the Association of Naval Aviation meet monthly. I interviewed Winder for his experience as a fighter pilot in relation to bombing from the air and air-to-ground strafing strategies.

**Zorrozua, Kontxi** (b. 1926). Gernika, May 17, 2014. Kontxi Zorrozua underwent the bombing while hidden in a ditch south of the city. She emigrated to America during the economic and political depression of the Franco dictatorship. She ran the Mint Restaurant in Haley, Idaho, frequented by Ernest Hemingway. After many years in Idaho, she sold her restaurant to Bruce Willis and returned with her family to Gernika. Zorrozua is currently the only living witness of the 129 interviewed by William Smallwood (Egurtxiki) in 1972.

## Secondary Sources

This section covers an abstract of the general bibliography consulted for writing the book. The general bibliography on the bombing of Gernika, Durango, and other Basque cities that I include in the following list is limited to the books directly related to the bombing. I have not included a general bibliography on the war in the Basque Country or manuscripts, books, or accounts somehow linked but not directly related to the bombing of Gernika. An excellent bibliographic approach on the bombing of Gernika may be read at Iratxe Momoitio, "La repercusión internacional del bombardeo de Guernica," Sancho el Sabio, no. 11 (1999), 217–49, available at dialnet.unirioja.es/servlet/fichero_articulo?codigo=157619&orden=68524. Iratxe Momoitio is the director of the Gernika Peace Museum. See also José Angel Etxaniz and Carmelo Landa, "Bibliografía sobre el Bombardeo de Guernica (1937–1997)," in *Herbert R. Southworth: Bizitza eta Lana, Vida y Obra* (Gernika-Lumo: Gernika-Lumoko Udala/Gernikako Bakearen Museoa, 2001), 255–75.

Aguirre, José Antonio. *Escape via Berlin: Eluding Franco in Hitler's Europe*. Introduction and annotations by Robert P. Clark. Reno: University of Nevada Press, 1991.

Aguirre Lekube, José Antonio. "Gernika's Message to America." In *Freedom Was Flesh and Blood*, 228–88. London: Gollancz, 1945.

Aiestaran, Ignazio. *Walter Benjaminen Aingerua Gernikako bonbardaketatik*. Donostia and San Sebastián: Elkar, 2010.

Ametzaga Aresti, Bingen. "Un árbol y un nombre son nuevo testimonio de Gernika." *Euzko Deya* (Buenos Aires), September 20, 1944.

Amilibia, Miguel de. "Arde Guernica: La tragedia de los separatistas vascos." *Crónica de la guerra española* (Buenos Aires), codex, no. 62 (1967).

Arnheim, Rudolf. *Picasso's "Guernica": The Genesis of a Painting.* London: Faber & Faber, 1962.
Ashton, Dore. *Picasso on Art: A Selection of Views.* Cambridge, MA: Da Capo Press, 1988.
Astigarraga Larrañaga, Andoni de (Astilarra). *Guernica en Elosegui.* Buenos Aires: FEVA, 1972.
Atxaga, Bernardo. *De Gernika a Guernica.* Barcelona: Ediciones de la Central, 2007.
Aznar, Yayo. *The Guernica.* [Madrid]: Edilupa, 2004.
Bacigalupe, Carlos, and Jose A. Etxaniz Ortuñez. *75 años en la historia de Guernica.* Bilbao: Leaders Editorial, 1992.
Bare, Alfred. *Symposium on Guernica.* New York: Museum of Modern Art, 1947.
Basaldua, Pedro. *En defensa de la verdad (Refutación a Mons. Francheschi).* Buenos Aires: Ekin, 1956.
*The Basque Country and the European Peace: An Analysis of German Domination of Euzkadi.* London: Government of Euzkadi, 1937.
Bastian, Gert, and Petra Kelly. *Guernica und die Deutschen: Dokumentation einer gescheiterten Wiedergutmachung.* Darmstadt: Luchterhand, 1992.
Beaumont, Edurne, and Fernando Mendiola. "Vinieron un montón de prisioneros: Los batallones de soldados trabajadores vistos y recordados por la población de la montaña Navarra." *Els camps de concentració durant la guerra civil i el franquismo.* http://www.cefid.uab.es/files/C%C3%B2pia%20comuniII-1.pdf.
Becraft, Melvin E. *Picasso's "Guernica": Images Within Images.* N.p.: M. E. Becraft, 1981.
Bell, Mikel. *The Tree of Gernika, for 2 Trumpets, 2 Horns, Trombone, Euphonium and Tuba.* Boise, ID: Lighthouse Music, 2007.
———. *Variations on the Gernikako Arbola, for Piano.* Boise, ID: n.p., 2007.
Biondi, Francesco [pseudonym Francesco Belforte]. *La guerra civile in Spagna.* 4 vols. Milan: Istituto per gli Studi di Politica Internazionale, 1938–39.
Blas, Juan Antonio de. *Hay árboles en Guernica?* Madrid: Júcar, 1987.
Blunt, Anthony. *Picasso's "Guernica."* Oxford: Oxford University Press, 1969.
*Bombardements et agressions en Espagne.* Paris: Comité Mondial contre la Guerre et le Fascisme, 1938.
Bowers, Claude G. *My Mission to Spain: Watching the Rehearsal for World War II.* New York: Simon and Schuster, 1954.
Bowles, Steve, ed. *La generación del Guernica.* Video recording. Barcelona: ETB, IDEM, in cooperation with Discovery Channel, Art Mood Entertainment, 2003.
Bravo Morata, Federico. *Guernica: El impulso soberano.* Madrid: Fenicia, 1978.
Brey, Gérard. "La destrucción de Guernica: Cuarenta años de polémica." *Tiempo de Historia,* no. 29 (April 1977): 4–12.
Brunner, Kathleen. *Picasso Rewriting Picasso.* London: Black Dog, 2004.
Cardenas, Gonzalo. *Datos para la reconstrucción del pueblo adoptado de Guernica.* Madrid: Dirección General de Regiones Devastadas y Reparaciones, 1940.
Castresana, Luis. *El otro árbol de Guernica.* Bilbao: El Arenal, 1967.

———. *El otro árbol de Guernica*. Barcelona: Ediciones Internacionales Universitarias, 1992.

———. *La verdad sobre "El otro arbol de Guernica."* Bilbao: La Gran Enciclopedia Vasca, 1972.

Cava Mesa, María Jesús, María Silvestre, and Javier Arranz. *Memoria colectiva del bombardeo de Gernika*. Gernika-Lumo: Gernika Gogoratuz, 1996.

Cazalis, Segundo, ed. *Los hijos de Gernika: La lucha del pueblo vasco por la libertad*. Caracas: EGI, 1968.

*Chillida at Gernika: Birth of a Monument, "Gure aitaren etxea," "Our Father's House."* La Jolla, CA: Tasende Gallery, 1988.

Chipp, Herschel B. *Picasso's "Guernica": History, Transformations, Meanings*. Berkeley: University of California Press, 1988.

Corum, James S. *Wolfram von Richthofen: Master of the German Air War*. Lawrence: University Press of Kansas, 2008.

Cox, Harvey. "Guernica to Vietnam: The Capacity for Horror." *Commonweal* 86, no. 6 (1967): 164–65.

*The Crime of Guernica*. New York: Spanish Information Bureau, 1937.

Crozier, Brian. *Franco: A Biographical History*. London: Eyre & Spottiswoode, 1967.

———. "Hoary Republican Myths." *Nacional Review*, August 31, 1973, 938.

Dallek, Robert. *Franklin D. Roosevelt and American Foreign Policy, 1932–1945*. Oxford: Oxford University Press, 1995.

De La Cierva, Ricardo. "Guernica: Los documentos contra el mito." In *Nueva y definitiva historia de la guerra civil*. Madrid: DINPE, 1986.

———. "La polémica y la verdad sobre Guernica." In *España, 1930–1977: La historia se confiesa*, 3:281–99. Barcelona: Planeta, 1978.

De Pauw, Valère. *Opdracht in Guernica*. Brecht: De Roerdomp, 1988.

*La destruction de Guernica*. Paris: Comité Franco-espagnol, 1937.

Dix, Otto. *Der Krieg = Gerra. Gernika-lumo bakearen hiria = La Guerra: Gernika-lumo ciudad de la paz*. Bilbao: Bizkaiko Foru Aldundia, 1997.

Doumanian, Alice. *Picasso's "Guernica" After Rubens's "Horrors of War": A Comparative Study in Three Parts, Iconographic and Compositional, Stylistic, and Psychoanalytic*. Philadelphia: Art Alliance Press, 1984.

*Durango, Ville martyre: Ce que furent les bombardements de la ville de Durango par les avions allemands*. Paris: Comité franco-espagnol, 1937.

Echegaray, Carmelo. *La Casa de Juntas de Guernica*. Bilbao: Imprenta Provincial de Vizcaya, 1936.

Eden, Anthony. *Facing the Dictators: The Memoirs of Anthony Eden, Earl of Avon*. London: Cassell, 1962.

Elosegi, Joseba. *Quiero morir por algo*. Barcelona: Plaza & Janés, 1977.

Elosegi, Joseba, and Ángel Viñas. "La destrucción de Guernica." *Historia* 16, no. 5 (1976): 131–37.

Ensunza Arrien, Maider. *Gernika: Azterketa historiko-artistikoa*. Bilbao: Bizkaiko Foru Aldundia, 2003.

Erikson, R. *Durango martyrstaden*. Stockholm: n.p., 1937.

Estornés Lasa, José. *Un gudari navarro en los frentes de Euzkadi, Asturias y Cataluña: Problematica Vasca*. Donostia: Auñamendi, 1979.

Etxaniz, José Ángel. "Los muertos de una guerra civil." *Aldaba Gernika-Lumoko Aldizkaria* 13, no. 152 (2008): 37–48.

Etxaniz, José Ángel, and Vicente del Palacio. "Los muertos del bombardeo." *El Correo*, April 25, 2004.

Etxaniz Ortúñez, José Angel, and Vicente del Palacio Sánchez. "Presos políticos: Mano de obra barata; El Hospital Penitenciario y el Batallón de Trabajadores durante la reconstrucción de Gernika-Lumo (1938–1945)." In *Els camps de concentració durant la guerra civil i el franquismo*. http://www.cefid.uab.es/files/C%C3%B2pia%20comuniI-1.pdf.

Ezkiaga, Patxi. *Gernika*. Donostia: Erein, 1987.

Fernández Granell, Eusebio. *Picasso's "Guernica": The End of a Spanish Era*. Ann Arbor, MI: UMI Research Press, 1981.

*Foreign Wings over the Basque Country*. London: Friends of Spain, 1937.

Fox, Hugh. *Guernica Cycle: The Year Franco Died—a Selection from the Spanish Journals*. Cherry Valley, NY: Cherry Valley Editions, 1986.

Gamboa, Jose Maria, and Jean-Claude Larronde, eds. *La Guerra Civil en Euzkadi: 136 testimonios inéditos recogidos por José Miguel de Barandarian*. Bidasoa: Milafranga, 2007.

García de Cortazar, Fernando. "Guernica, cincuenta años después." *Historia 16*, no. 133 (1987): 23–30.

García Volta, Gabriel. *Guernica*. Barcelona: Bruguera, 1975.

*Gernika bonbardaketa/El bombardeo*. 3 DVDs and 1 CD. EITB, 2007.

*Gernika eta zinea—Gernika y el cine*. Gernika: Gernika-Lumoko Udala, 2003.

Gernikazarra Historia Taldea. *El bombardeo de Gernika, Exposición*. Gernika-Lumo: Gernikazarra Historia Taldea, 1991.

———. *El bombardeo de Gernika: Memoria gráfica; Gernikako bonbardaketa: oroimen grafikoa*. Gernika-Lumo: Gernikazarra Historia Taldea, 2007.

———. *Gernika: Berreraiketaren argazkiak*. Gernika: Gernikazarra Historia Taldea, 1989.

Granados, Anastasio. *El Cardenal Gomá: Primado de España*. Madrid: Espasa-Calpe, 1969.

———. "El Cardenal Gomá y los vascos." *Historia y Vida*, no. 24 (March 1970): 36–55.

Granja, José Luis de la, and José Ángel Echániz, eds. *Gernika y la Guerra Civil: Symposium, 60 aniversario del bombardeo de Gernika*. Gernika: Gernikazarra Historia Taldea, 1998.

*Guernica*. Bilbao: Gobierno de Euzkadi, 1937.

*Guernica, 26 de abril de 1937: Sólo el árbol vasco quedó en pie*. Caracas: n.p., 1958.

*Guernica: Being the Official Report of a Commission Appointed by the National Government to Investigate the Causes of the Destruction of Guernica on April 26–28, 1937*. London: Eyre & Spottiswoode, 1938.

*Guernica: The Biography of a Twentieth-Century Icon*. New York: Bloomsbury, 2004.

*Guernica: La mainmise hitlérienne sur le Pays basque.* N.p.: Comité International du Coordination et d'Information pour l'Aide a l'Espagne Republicaine, 1937.

*Guernica: El terrible 26 de abril de 1937.* Caracas: n.p., 1958.

*Guernica: To Civilized Mankind.* Bilbao: Basque Government, May 1937.

*Guernica: Tres horas que conmovieron al mondo.* Video recording. Iowa City: Project for International Communication Studies, [1980?].

Hamill, Sam, et al. *Poets Against the War.* New York: Thunder's Mouth Press / Nation Books, 2003.

Haranburu Altuna, Luis. *Gernika.* Donostia: Kriselu, 1977.

Hart, Jeffrey. "The Great Guernica Fraud." *National Review,* January 5, 1973.

Heinrich-Bóll, ed. *Petra nelly, Gernika-berradiskidetzearen lehen urratsa.* Berlin: Heinrich-Bóll Stiftung, 1997.

*Herbert R. Southworth, vida y obra = Herbert R. Southworth, bizitza eta lana.* Gernika-Lumo: Gernika-Lumoko Udala / Gernikako Bake Museoa, 2001.

Huber, Maximilia, Hubert Hutfless, and Annemarie Moser. *Guernica: Ein Fanal.* Aktion Mitmensch Wiener Neustadt, no. 2, 2007.

Hughes, Robert. *The Portable Picasso.* New York: Universe, 2003.

Ibáñez-Angulo, Monia. "The Nation Within the State: Basque Nationalism and Everyday Life in Gernika." PhD thesis, University of Chicago, 1999.

*Incontrovertible Facts Regarding the Destruction of Guernica* [Speech by Mr. Leizaola, Minister of Justice of the Basque Government], North American Committee to Aid Spanish Democracy, n.d.

Irazabal, Jon. *1937 martxoak 31, Durango, 31 de marzo de 1937: Estudio sobre el bombardeo aéreo realizado contra la Villa de Durango el 31 de marzo de 1937.* Durango: Gerediaga Elkartea, 2001. http://www.gerediaga.com/proiektuak/argitalpenak/argitalpenak_publicaciones.

———. *Otxandio en la Guerra Civil: Otxandio Gerra Zibilean (1936/37).* Durango: Gerediaga Elkartea, 2003. http://www.gerediaga.com/proiektuak/argitalpenak/argitalpenak_publicaciones.

Iturria, Jose. *Memorias de Guerra.* Gernika-Lumo: Gernikako Bakearen Museoa Fundazioa, Gernika-Lumoko Udala, 2013.

Jiménez de Aberasturi, Luis M., and Juan Carlos Jiménez de Aberasturi. *La guerra en Euskadi.* Barcelona: Plaza & Janés, 1979.

Kasper, Michael. *Gernika y Alemania: Historia de una reconciliación.* Bilbao: Bakeaz, 1998.

———. *Gernika y Alemania: Historia de una reconciliación.* Gernika: Gernika Gogoratuz, 1998.

Kellerhoffs, Sven. *Rezension zu: Guernica, Warschau, Hamburg; Die Psychologie des Bombenkriegs.* Television documentary on the air raids in the Second World War. *Die Welt,* June 28, 2004.

Knightley, Phillip. "Commitment in Spain, 1936–1939." In *The First Casualty: The War Correspondent as Hero and Myth-Maker from the Crimea to Irak.* Baltimore: John Hopkins University Press, 2004.

Laboa, Mikel. "Gernika, 1972." In *Lekeitioak* [sound recording]. Donostia: Elkar, 2007.

———. *Gernika Zuzenenan 2* [sound recording]. Donostia: Elkar, 1999.

Labrun, Jeanne. *Mourir á Guernica*. Paris: Orban, 1975.

Lang, Franz. *Guernica: Ein Fanal des Faschismus*. Strasbourg: Editions Promeìtheìe, 1937.

Large, David Clay. *Between Two Fires: Europe's Path in the 1930s*. New York: W. W. Norton, 1990.

Larrea, Juan. *Guernica: Pablo Picasso*. New York: Curt Valentin, 1947.

Larronde, Jean-Claude. *El Batallón Gernika, Gernika Batallun Euskalduna: Los Combates de la Pointe-de-Grave (Abril de 1945)*. Baiona: Bidasoa, 1995.

Leguineche, Manuel. *Guernica, un horror experimental: Los Grandes Hechos del Siglo* XX. No. 1. Barcelona: Orbis, 1985.

Lucarelli, Carlo. *Guernica*. Barcelona: Edhasa, 2000.

Maier, Klaus A. "The Condor Legion: An Instrument of Total War?" In *The Shadows of Total War: Europe, East Asia and the United States, 1919–1939*, edited by Roger Chickering and Stig Förster, 285–94. Cambridge: Cambridge University Press, 2003.

———. "Guernica, Fakten und Mythen." *German Studies Review*, no. 18 (October 1995): 465–70.

———. *Guernica: La intervención alemana en España y el "caso Guernica."* Madrid: Sedmay, 1976.

———. *Guernica 26-4-1937: Die Deutsche Intervention in Spanien un der "Fall Guernica."* Freiburg: Rombach, 1975.

Mees, Ludger. "Guernica/Gernika como símbolo." *En Historia Contemporánea, la Guerra Civil en el País Vasco: Un balance histórico* 2, no. 35 (2007): 529–57.

Momoitio, Iratxe. "La repercusión internacional del bombardeo de Guernica." *Sancho el Sabio*, no. 11 (1999): 217–49.

Monks, Noel. *Eyewitness*. London: Frederick Muller, 1956.

Müller, Rolf-Dieter. *Der Bombenkrieg*. Berlin: Ch. Links, 2004.

———. *La muerte caída del cielo: Historia de los bombardeos durante la Segunda Guerra Mundial*. Barcelona: Destino, 2008.

Mur, Pilar. "La reconstrucción de Guernica." *Arbola*, no. 8 (1987).

Nash, Steven A., ed. *Picasso and the War Years, 1937–1945* [organized by the Fine Arts Museums of San Francisco, in collaboration with the Solomon R. Guggenheim Museum, New York]. New York: Thames and Hudson, 1998.

Nono, Luigi. *La Victoire de Guernica for Mixed Choir and Orchestra*. Faksimile-Studienpartitur, Ars Viva/H. Zurich: Scherchen, 1954.

Olmi, Massimo. *Cattolici scomodi: Storia della sinistra cattolica in Francia*. N.p.: Lucarini, 1987.

Onaindia, Alberto. *Hombre de paz en la guerra*. Buenos Aires: Ekin, 1973.

Onaindia, Santiago. *Gernika*. Larrea: Aita Onaindia, 1987.

Oriol, A. *Guernica al desnudo*. Barcelona: Ediciones Polígrafa, 1979.

Orkoya, Juan Pascual de. *La verdad sobre la destrucción de Gernika: Réplica a Mons. Gustavo J. Francheschi*. Buenos Aires: Sebastián de Amorrortu, 1937.

Padelford, Norman J. *International Law and Diplomacy in the Spanish Civil Strife*. New York: Macmillan, 1939.

Palacio, Vicente del. "El exilio guerniqués." *Aldaba Gernika-Lumoko Aldizkaria*, no. 110 (March–April 2001): 37–50.

Pariset, Dante. "Clamorose rivelazioni que frantumano un mito: Guernica fue distruta dai rossi e non dall'aviazione di Hitler." *Il Tempo*, February 5, 1973.

Patterson, Ian. *Guernica and Total War*. Cambridge, MA: Harvard University Press, 2007.

———. *Guernica y la guerra total*. Madrid: Turner, 2008.

Pedriali, Ferdinando. *Guerra di Spagna e Aviazione Italiana*. Pinerolo: Società Storica Pinerolese, 1989.

Peña y Goñi, Antonio, et al. *Iparraguirre y el árbol de Guernica*. Bilbao: Imprenta de la Biblioteca Bascongada, 1896.

Petacco, Arrigo. "Italiani a Guernica." *Il Resto del Carlino*, November 3, 1984.

———. "Italiani nel cielo di Guernica." *Corriere della Sera*, March 18, 1981.

———. "Volando su quella cittá in fiame." *Il Resto del Carlino*, October 9, 1984.

*Picasso-Gernika, 70. Urteurrena. 70 Aniversario. 70th Anniversary. 70éme Anniversaire*. Madrid: Gernika-Lumoko Udala, 2007.

Prieto, Indalecio. "Guernica, la mártir." *Siempre* (Mexico), March 16, 1955.

Raento, Paulina, and Cameron J. Watson. "Gernika, Guernica, *Guernica*? Contested Meanings of a Basque Place." *Political Geography*, no. 19 (2000): 707–36.

Ramírez, Juan Antonio. *Guernica: La historia y el mito, en proceso*. Madrid: Electa España, 1999.

Rankin, Nicholas. *Crónica desde Guernica: George Steer, corresponsal de guerra*. Madrid: Siglo XXI, 2005.

———. *Telegram from Guernica: The Extraordinary Life of George Steer, War Correspondent*. London: Faber & Faber, 2003.

Ricci, Corrado. *Vita di Pilota*. Milan: Mursia, 1976.

Rodríguez Fouz, Marta. *Los retos de la identidad: Jürgen Habermas y la memoria del "Guernica."* Madrid: Centro de Investigaciones Sociológicas, 2004.

Rojo, Alberto, et al. *Gernika: el bombardeo = Gernika: bonbardaketa*. Bilbao: EITB, 2007.

Russel, Martin. *Picasso's War: The Destruction of Guernica and the Masterpiece That Changed the World*. London: Dutton, 2002.

Russell, Martin. *Picasso's War: The Destruction of Guernica and the Masterpiece That Changed the World*. New York: Plume, 2003.

Rutledge, Harry C. *The Guernica Bull: Studies in the Classical Tradition in the Twentieth Century*. Athens: University of Georgia Press, 1989.

Salas Larrazabal, Jesús. *Air War over Spain*. London: Allan, 1974.

———. *Guernica*. Madrid: Rialp, 1987.

———. *Guernica: El bombardeo*. Madrid: Galland, 1981.

Saura, Antonio. *Contra el Guernica: Libelo*. Madrid: Turner, 1982.

Schüler-Springorum, Stefanie. "El mito de Guernica: Proyección, propaganda, política." *Historia del presente* 14 (2009): 123–36.

Smallwood, William. *The Day Guernica Was Bombed: A Story by Witnesses and Survivors*. Gernika-Lumo: Gernikako Bakearen Museoa Fundazioa, Gernika-Lumoko Udala, 2012.

———. *El día en que Gernika fue bombardeada: Un relato contado por testigos y supervivientes*. Gernika-Lumo: Gernikako Bakearen Museoa Fundazioa, Gernika-Lumoko Udala, 2013.

Southworth, Herbert R. *La destrucción de Guernica: Periodismo, diplomacia, propaganda e historia*. Barcelona-Valencia: Ruedo Ibérico, 1977.

———. *Guernica, Guernica: A Study of Journalism, Diplomacy, Propaganda and History*. Berkeley: University of California Press, 1977.

Stani, Gorka. *Les cavaliers de Guernica*. Paris: J. Martineau, 1970.

Steer, George L. *The Tree of Gernika: A Field Study of Modern War*. London: Hodder and Stoughton, 1938.

Stradling, Robert. *Your Children Will Be Next: Bombing and Propaganda in the Spanish Civil War, 1936–1939*. Cardiff: University of Wales Press, 2008.

Sturzo, Luigi. *Sritti inediti*. Vol. 2, *1924–1940*. Rome: F. Rizzi, 1976.

*Sustrai Erreak: Gernika, 1937*. Gernika: Gernikako Aldaba, 1987.

Talón, Vicente. *Arde Guernica*. Madrid: San Martín, 1970.

———. *El holocausto de Guernica*. Barcelona: Plaza & Janés, 1987.

Thadden, Adolf. *Guernica—Greuelpropaganda oder "kriegsverbrechen"? Ein Bombenschwindel*. Munich: Druffel-Verlag, 1982.

Thomas, Gordon, and Max Morgan-Witts. *El día que murió Guernica*. Barcelona: Plaza & Janés, 1976.

———. *Guernica: The Crucible of World War II*. New York: Ballantine Books, 1975.

Thomas, Hugh. "Heinkels over Guernica." *Times Literary Supplement*, April 11, 1975.

Thomson, Geoffrey H. *Front-Line Diplomat*. London: Hutchinson, 1959.

Tierney, Dominique. *FDR and the Spanish Civil War: Neutrality and Commitment in the Struggle That Divided America*. Durham, NC: Duke University Press, 2007.

Tuñón de Lara, Manuel, José Luis de la Granja, and Carmelo Granja, eds. *Gernika: 50 años después (1937–1987): Nacionalismo, República, Guerra Civil; VI Cursos de Verano en San Sebastián = VI. Udako Ikastaroak Donostian*. Lehioa: Servicio Editorial, Universidad del País Vasco, 1987.

Unzueta, Humberto. *Gernikako bonbaketa: Hildakoak, 1937-4-26*. Gernika: n.p., 1992.

Unzueta, Humberto. "Los muertos inoportunos." *Aldaba Gernika-Lumoko Aldizkaria* 2, no. 86 (1997).

Uriarte, Castor. *Bombas y mentiras sobre Guernica: Acusa su arquitecto municipal cuando la guerra*. Bilbao: Gráficas Ellacuria, 1976.

Van Hensbergen, Gijs. *Guernica: La historia de un icono del siglo XX*. Madrid: Debate, 2005.

Vidal, César. *La destrucción de Guernica*. Madrid: Espasa-Calpe, 1997.

Villa, Imanol. *Gernika bonbardaketa/El bombardeo*. Bilbao: Idem 4 / EITB, 2008.

Viñas, Ángel. "El bombardeo de Guernica: Aún faltan datos." *Historia 16*, no. 5 (1976): 135–37.

———. "Guernica, quién lo hizo?" In *Historia General de la Guerra Civil en Euskadi*, 165–215. Bilbao: Naroki SA & Luis Haranburu, 1979.

———. "Guernica: El último fraude?" *Historia 16*, no. 9 (1977): 135–40.

Vovard, Paul. *Le Martyre de Guernica*. Paris: Cahiers de la Démocratie, 1938.

Waqar, H. Zaidi. "Aviation Will Either Destroy or Save Our Civilization: Proposals for the International Control of Aviation, 1920–45." *Journal of Contemporary History* 46 (January 2011): 150–78.

Waiss, Walter. *Legion Condor: Zweiter Band*. Aachen: Helios Verlag, 2014.

Wilson, Arnold T. *Guernica: Being the Official Report of a Commission Appointed by the Spanish National Government to Investigate the Causes of the Destruction of Guernica on April 26–28, 1937*. London: Eyre & Spottiswoode, 1938.

Zabalgogeaskoa, Olga, and Vincent von Jauregi [pseudonym Vicente del Palacio]. "La reconstrucción de Gernika: Entrevista con las cuatro personas de aquella época, que viven actualmente en Gernika." *Aldaba Gernika-Lumoko Aldizkaria*, no. 13 (January–February 1985): 15–19.

Zia, Gregorio Monreal. *The Old Law of Bizkaia (1452)*. Reno: Center for Basque Studies, University of Nevada, 2005.

# Index